I baptize you with water;
but one who is more powerful than I is coming. . . .
He will baptize you with the Holy Spirit and fire.
LUKE 3:16 NRSV

I see no reason why we should not have
a greater Pentecost than Peter saw,
and a Reformation deeper in its foundations,
and truer in its upbuildings than all the reforms
which Luther or Calvin achieved.
CHARLES H. SPURGEON

The Pentecostal spring of the early Christian Church
stands in the strongest contrast
to the icily rigid Christianity
of our day.
EBERHARD ARNOLD

Holy Spirit, renew your wonders in our day
as by a new Pentecost.
POPE JOHN XXIII

· CHRISTIAN FOUNDATIONS ·

THE
HOLY
SPIRIT

WORKS & GIFTS

DONALD G. BLOESCH

INTERVARSITY PRESS
DOWNERS GROVE, ILLINOIS 60515

InterVarsity Press
P.O. Box 1400, Downers Grove, IL 60515
World Wide Web: www.ivpress.com
E-mail: mail@ivpress.com

InterVarsity Press® is the book-publishing division of InterVarsity Christian Fellowship/USA®, a student movement active on campus at hundreds of universities, colleges and schools of nursing in the United States of America, and a member movement of the International Fellowship of Evangelical Students. For information about local and regional activities, write Public Relations Dept., InterVarsity Christian Fellowship/USA, 6400 Schroeder Rd., P.O. Box 7895, Madison, WI 53707-7895.

Scripture quotations, unless otherwise noted, are from the Revised Standard Version of the Bible, copyright 1946, 1952, 1971 by the Division of Christian Education of the National Council of the Churches of Christ in the U.S.A., and are used by permission.

The lyrics by A. W. Tozer on page 139 are used by permission of Christian Publications. The lyrics by Frank Buchman on page 141 are used by permission of Helmers & Howard.

Cover illustration: Guy Wolek

ISBN 0-8308-1415-9

Printed in the United States of America ∞

Library of Congress Cataloging-in-Publication Data

Bloesch, Donald G., 1928-
The Holy Spirit: works & gifts/Donald G. Bloesch.
p. cm.— (Christian Foundations)
Includes bibliographical references.
ISBN 0-8308-1415-9 (cloth: alk. paper)
1. Holy Spirit. I. Title.
BT121.2.B57 2000
231'.3—dc21

00-057504

*Dedicated to the
memory of
John Wesley & George Whitefield*

Acknowledgments

I gratefully acknowledge the help I have received in preparing this volume from the following persons: my wife, Brenda, for her diligent copyediting and research; Debbie Lovett and Luann LeConte for their careful typing of this manuscript; Joel Samuels, Sharon Killian and Susan Reiter of the Dubuque Seminary library; John Weborg of North Park Seminary, Elmer Colyer and Mark Achtemeier, faculty colleagues at Dubuque Theological Seminary; Natalee Colyer, for giving me information on the Torchbearers; David MacLeod and John Rush of Emmaus Bible College; Ralph Quere, church historian at Wartburg Theological Seminary; Bryan Burton, Presbyterian pastor and scholar; Mike Thiel, Disciples of Christ pastor; James Dauer, recent graduate of Dubuque Seminary; and my nephew David Bloesch, who provided me with books on Pentecostalism. I am also grateful to the *Reformed Review* for granting permission for the republication of my essay "Evangelical Rationalism and Propositional Revelation," which first appeared in the spring 1998 issue of that magazine.

Abbreviations for Biblical Translations

KJV   King James Version

NKJ   New King James Version

NIV   New International Version

NRSV   New Revised Standard Version

NEB   New English Bible

REB   Revised English Bible

JB   Jerusalem Bible

NJB   New Jerusalem Bible

GNC   God's New Covenant

LB   Living Bible

NLT   New Living Translation

(Note: Bible references not otherwise indicated are from the Revised Standard Version)

Foreword

This is a book on spirituality and historical theology as well as on systematic theology. In order to grasp the mystery of the working of the Spirit as delineated in the Bible, one also needs to explore the manifestations of the Spirit in the history of the church. A comprehensive theology of the Spirit is formed not only out of the testimony of the prophets and apostles of biblical history but also out of the thoughts and deeds of the great saints in the various traditions of the church. With Karl Barth, I regard church tradition as a secondary, not a primary, witness to the faith once delivered to the saints; yet it is still a bona fide witness. It can even be viewed as normative when it is judged and corrected by holy Scripture.

On the basis of the witness of Scripture and church tradition, one can conclude that the two deadliest enemies of true faith are formalism and spiritualism. We cannot put the Spirit of God in a sacramental box, but the Spirit is nonetheless free to make use of outward signs in communicating to us the truth of the gospel. We must affirm both "the sovereign unpredictability of the Spirit" (David du Plessis) and the faithfulness of the Spirit to honor Jesus Christ by kindling the gift of faith in those who hear the church's proclamation of Christ.

Against the sacramentalist churches I am constrained to make the audacious statement that it is possible to be baptized, confirmed and even ordained to Christian ministry and still not to have received the Holy Spirit. At the same time, I maintain against Pentecostals and charismatics that it is possible to have hands laid upon one and to speak in other tongues and yet have no enduring relationship with the Spirit. It is even possible to be divinely healed of sickness and not have the Spirit as an indwelling principle of new life. Rites and sacraments can aid and strengthen us in our spiritual journey, but they do not guarantee that the Spirit is present—either in the outward ceremony or in the inner self.

If we have been baptized and have made a sincere profession of faith, we are not then obliged to seek a higher experience of the Spirit that would purify us from all sin and thereby render us worthy to receive the graces of God. Those who blithely urge believers to seek a baptism with fire that supersedes sacramental baptism with water should remember that the former is a baptism of judgment as well as of grace (Mk 10:38-40; Lk 12:50). At the same time, if we are only nominal Christians, if we have fallen away from our baptismal commitment, if we have only the faith of servants and not of sons and daughters, then it is not only permissible but laudable to seek baptism with the Spirit, for not until that event are we truly engrafted into the mystical body of Christ. We must also not close our eyes and minds to new works of the Spirit within us after we become Christians, to gifts that equip us for the ministry to which we are all called as sons and daughters of the most high God.

I fully agree with John Mackay, former president of Princeton Theological Seminary, that it is better to err on the side of enthusiasm than of formalism. A cold formalism is an insidious threat to Christian faith because it quenches the Spirit even while it preserves theological propriety. Yet we need to realize that Pentecostalism can become a new formalism, that words of prophecy and speaking in tongues can simply be outward acts that assure us of acceptance by our peers and be completely bereft of the sanctifying presence of the Spirit of God.

This book should be viewed as an effort to build bridges between the various traditions of Christian faith, particularly between Reformed theology and the Pentecostal movement. I basically speak out of the perspective of the Protestant Reformation, but I do not see the Reformation as encompassing the whole counsel of God, though it did indeed recover the essence of the gospel—justification by grace through faith alone. Where I fully concur with the Reformers is in their emphasis on the complementarity of Word and Spirit, the priority of grace over works, including works of faith and repentance, and the practice of Christian love as the cardinal sign and evidence of genuine faith. Where I agree with the Pentecostals is in their perception that the work of the Spirit involves empowering for witness as well as being sealed into the body of Christ for salvation. I also endorse their contention that the gifts of the Spirit continue in the church in every age, though unlike some Pentecostals I do not limit the gifts to the particular charisms enunciated in Paul's epistles. In addition, I acknowledge the truth of the mystical tradition of the church as we see it in Roman Catholicism and Eastern Orthodoxy, that the Spirit calls us to holiness of life as well as to a decision of faith. We are obliged to draw near to God through the disciplines of the spiritual life as well as to serve our neighbor in outgoing, sacrificial love.

I am firmly convinced that we must constantly be on guard against certain perilous delusions that incontrovertibly lead us away from the vision of an evangelical catholicity. One of these is that we are already regenerated at our baptism, even if this rite takes place in our infancy and real faith is not yet a viable possibility for us. A second is that the spectacular charismatic gifts belong to the past history of the church and that the mission of the church is simply to preach faith without also cultivating the gifts of the Spirit. A third deception is that we can attain the baptism of the Spirit through carefully defined methods or techniques, thereby making our conversion rest on human preparation rather than on divine grace. A fourth misapprehension is that salvation consists only in God coming to us, not also in our coming to God. If our message is exclusively *sola gratia* (salvation by grace alone), we then lose sight of the truth that we are justified not only *by* grace but also *for* holiness. Finally, we must resist the temptation to entertain a pathway to God that bypasses faith in his Son. In certain strands of Christian mysticism it is sometimes implied that we can come to the Father by an immediate work of the Spirit on us rather than by the necessary mediation of Jesus Christ.

In this whole discussion one should keep in mind that the new birth, the baptism with the Holy Spirit and fire, is not within the purview of any human being or agency, not even the church of Jesus Christ. The new birth must not be confounded with any particular experience or outward sign. Instead, it signifies the invisible and unexpected movement of God into the inner recesses of the human creature. The Spirit ordinarily works through outward signs, what we in the Reformed tradition call "means of grace," but he is not bound to these signs. Yet if we continue to stand on the promises and testimonies of God revealed in the Bible, we can then have solid grounds for hoping that we will receive the Spirit—not only at the beginning of our faith pilgrimage but throughout our sojourn here on earth. Luther was right in describing the new birth as in itself "impalpable" and "insensible," but it will have many visible manifestations. It does not arise out of human effort, but human decision and obedience arise out of the new birth. It may well be accompanied by what the mystics call spiritual consolations, but it cannot be reduced to any particular experience or affection. Our being in Christ is finally a matter of faith, not of visions and raptures. I agree with Martin Luther as well as some of the leading mystics (Meister Eckhart, John of the Cross, François Fénelon) that true spirituality does not involve aspiring after extraordinary experiences of God or the Spirit. At the same time, we should earnestly pray that the fruits of the Spirit might be manifested in our daily walk. If we serve Christ and our neighbor in love and diligently hold up the name of Christ before the world, we can then have assurance that we have indeed been baptized by the Spirit into the service of the kingdom of God. If we seek first the kingdom of God and his righteousness (Mt 6:33), even before our own happiness and security, we then have firm grounds for believing that we have indeed been born again from above, that the truth of the Spirit resides within us.

I wish to do justice to the Pentecostal experience, even while taking issue with certain aspects of Pentecostal doctrine and practice. I refuse to dismiss the Pentecostal revolution as belonging to the vagaries of a sectarian religious enthusiasm as do some of my Calvinist colleagues in academia, but I do wish to maintain the integrity of the faith of the holy catholic church. Faith must not be reduced to experience, but faith will entail experience—not only of God in his awesome holiness but also of God in his inexpressible joy and abounding love. Yet faith will always point us beyond our experiences; it will finally take us out of ourselves into the service of God in the darkness of the world. The evidence of our new birth by the Spirit of God lies in the depth of our devotion to the gospel of God in our daily lives.

A Dialogical Approach

Those who follow my work will discern that my method in all the volumes in this series is dialogical. In this volume I begin with holy Scripture and then proceed to dialogue with church tradition and finally with contemporary theology. I also offer a prolegomenon, highlighting the issues that divide the church in our time. Building on this interaction with sacred Scripture and sacred tradition, I then present my own position, continuing to draw on both the inspired biblical writers and the fathers and teachers of the historic church, especially of the Reformation church. In this endeavor I try to glean insights from classical and current philosophies as well.

What distinguishes this volume from its predecessors is that it gives much more attention to historical background and includes in the dialogue heterodoxical and marginal movements that stand in some cases at the outer perimeters of Christian thought and faith. Such groups often represent a direct appeal to the Spirit apart from the mediation of holy Scripture and therefore warrant a critical investigation so that the extent of their deviation can be ascertained. It is my contention that we can learn positively from these movements as well as negatively since the gifts of the Spirit abound in a significant number of them, though these gifts are invariably misunderstood. The search for signs and wonders can easily lead away from faith, rather than strengthen and confirm faith. At the same time, in the light of the cross of Christ we can discern a measure of light in enthusiastic and sectarian movements that frequently challenge the church to reexamine its claims and thereby move it to return to the wellsprings of faith—the original encounter with the Word of God in holy Scripture.

In dialoguing with Scripture and church tradition we must acknowledge that this is a dialogue not only with the Word of God but also under that Word. We must allow ourselves to be judged by the Word even in our attempts to explicate the Word and relate it to the contemporary situation. There will always be an infinite qualitative difference between our thoughts and God's thoughts (Is 55:8-9), even while we strive for a correspondence between them. We should be actively engaged in forging an ecumenical consensus that is in harmony with the deepest insights of holy Scripture; yet we must be alert to the fact that this ecumenical consensus is not itself the final word on the salient issues of the faith, and that the task of reformulation and purification must continue. An ecumenical consensus may in some cases stand in contradiction to the fullness of light in Jesus Christ and may have to be overturned before it can be deepened.

In my restatement of the faith in this volume, I wish to maintain continuity with what I have said about the Holy Spirit in previous volumes in this Christian Foundations series. Therefore I shall continue to explore the role of the Holy Spirit in revelation as well as in creation and salvation. This is why I have returned to questions of theological method and authority in the first chapter and its appendix.

I have also reopened the inquiry into the relation between the Bible and the church. In articulating this relation we need to remember that the Spirit is active in the church as well as in the Bible, though due to its unique inspiration and its proximity to original revelation, the Bible will always stand over the church. By the work of the Spirit the written Word will enable us to discern what is authentic and what is aberrant in church tradition. This volume, like the others, is in the service of a theology of Word and Spirit in which the written Word of God is basically at one with the living voice of the church, which can be rightly heard, however, only in the obedience of faith.

The focus of this book is on the work of the Spirit in renewing the church and shaping the Christian life rather than on his person—though I give some attention to the latter, for person and mission are finally inseparable. (See my discussion of the Trinity in volume three of this series.) Irenaeus trenchantly observed that where the Spirit of God is, there is the church. There can be no vital Christian fellowship unless the Spirit is animating this fellowship and directing its members to trust in Jesus Christ. The Spirit is the agent of Christ as well as a partner with Christ in the revival of the church and the renewal of the world. It is not only Christ but also the Spirit who bids us to drink of the water of life and thereby be empowered for service under the cross (Rev 22:17).

·ONE·

INTRODUCTION

The Supreme Judge . . . can be no other but the Holy
Spirit speaking in the Scripture.
WESTMINSTER CONFESSION 1:10

Do not think of the Holy Ghost as a genial light, but
as mighty power, almighty, creative power.
P. T. FORSYTH

The message of the Gospel is the awakening from death.
From the resurrection on, Christ is proving himself the
Son of God in the constantly renewed coming down of the Holy Spirit.
EBERHARD ARNOLD

The Spirit cannot give new revelation but through
the preaching of witnesses can cause everything that
Jesus said and did to be revealed in a new light.
HANS KÜNG

In the present theological milieu Word and Spirit are increasingly separated, and this cleavage runs through evangelicalism as well. On the one hand we find those who appeal to Holy Scripture or to the teaching magisterium of the church. The role of the Spirit is to assist the will to assent to Scripture or the teachings of the church. On the other hand are those who base their case on a universal experience of the Spirit or an all-encompassing Spiritual Presence that is discernible not only in all the world religions but also in the secular world—in politics, economics, the arts and so on.

A theology of Word and Spirit, which I espouse, challenges both rationalist and spiritualist theologies. It seeks for the unity of wisdom and spirit, *logos* and *pneuma*. It is both logocentric and pneumocentric in that it discerns the gospel as both a rational message and the power unto salvation (Rom 1:16). It does not denigrate the need for propositions in the communication of faith, but it gives propositions a subordinate role. Faith terminates not in propositions but in the reality of the self-revealing God. A theology of Word and Spirit will be christocentric but not christomonistic. The Trinity is not absorbed into Christ, but each person of the Trinity is involved in the manifestation and proclamation of Christ's redemption. Similarly, this kind of theology will not be biblicistic in the sense that it anchors all of its premises in the express testimony of Scripture. Instead, it will be evangelical in that its final criterion lies outside the textuality of Scripture in the living Christ whom Scripture attests and acclaims. At the same time, it will resist the temptation to divorce the transcendent reality of the gospel from the earthen vessel in which this comes to us—the scriptural witness and the church proclamation.

George Lindbeck's typology is helpful in this connection.[1] He discusses three separate approaches in theology: the *cognitive-propositional*, which reduces the message of faith to propositional declarations accessible to human reason; the *experiential-expressive*, which finds the ground of theology in a universal human experience; and the *cultural-linguistic*, which sees the task of theology as transmitting the language and symbols of the faith from one generation to another. Those who embrace this last approach are committed to the priority of language over experience. They shrink from making universal or ontological claims on the basis of Scripture and church tradition, but they invite all peoples to enter into the stories of Scripture and thereby find meaning and purpose in their existence. Their concern is to maintain the patterns of ritual, belief and conduct that shape a community, not to develop a worldview that can effectively challenge other worldviews (as in the first approach) or give conceptual expression to those primal experiences that stir the religious imagination (as in the second approach).

For Lindbeck the criterion for truth in theology is intrasystematic consistency rather than correspondence with ultimate or ontological reality. Every claim and rule that direct the life of the faith community must be shown to be consistent with the way the community has come to understand its role and mission. The theological task is both descriptive and regulative: "setting forth the particular story which the community lives by, and ensuring that what is said and done conforms to the shape of this story."[2] Lindbeck believes that the community is obliged to furnish rules and guiding principles for its own members, but it must not impose its claims on the general public or on other faith communities.[3] In place of an apologetic theology that seeks to reach the secular mind by appealing to a mutually acknowledged framework of meaning, Lindbeck proposes an intratextual theology of social embodiment designed to help believers draw on the spiritual resources available to them in their own faith tradition.

Lindbeck is to be commended for clarifying the ways theologies have diverged on some important questions. The problem with his typology is that it does not adequately cover a major strand in contemporary theology, including Karl Barth, Thomas Torrance, Kenneth Hamilton, Arthur Cochrane and Donald Bloesch. It also fails to do justice to a number of luminaries of the past, including Luther, Calvin and Peter T. Forsyth, all of whom appealed to Christian experience but not to a universal religious experience.

I propose another option in theology, which I prefer to call *revelational-pneumatic*. Here the appeal is not to a mystical experience or a universal human experience but to a divine revelation in a particular history, a revelation recorded and enshrined in the Bible. The focal point of attention is not stories and shared experiences of people of faith but the intervention of God in human history, particularly in the person of Jesus Christ. Priority is given neither to experience nor to language but to the divine-human encounter in the Jesus Christ of biblical history. A revelational-pneumatic theology allows for the critical work of the Holy Spirit not only in moving the will to accept the Word of God but in making known the meaning of this Word.

A revelational-pneumatic theology will make a respected place for propositions, yet it will see the essence of faith not in propositional declarations but in a personal relationship between the giver and the receiver of divine revelation. The Spirit communicates an objective revelation that cannot be captured in concepts and categories, but can be stated in propositions and affirmations. At the same time, there will always be a qualitative disjunction between the proposition and the reality to which it points. I concur with Karl Barth that there can never be an identity between human statements of faith and divine revelation, but there can be a correspondence through the illumination of the Spirit. Propositions play a decisive role but always a servant role. They are never exhaustive but always reformable and open-ended.

In a helpful book that is basically supportive of narrative or postliberal theology, *Beyond Liberalism and Fundamentalism*,[5] Nancey Murphy seeks to dialogue with my position and suggests that I am trying to unite aspects of the experiential-expressive and the cognitive-propositional approaches. She has much to say that is informative and challenging, but rationalists, among others, will be startled to find my position described as "an uncompromised propositionalism."[6] It is possible to affirm the propositional element in revelation without collapsing the content of revelation in propositions. A theology of Word and Spirit will subordinate propositional knowledge to the knowledge of acquaintance rooted in an I-Thou encounter. Revelation consists essentially not in the transmission of propositions but in personal address by the living God, which involves the communication of information, yet only in the context of mystical participation in the spiritual reality that the propositions seek to express.

A revelational-pneumatic theology assigns an important place to Christian experience—not as the source of faith but as the medium of faith, the catalyst that deepens faith. The source of faith is the Spirit of the living God who brings home to us the gospel of what God has done for us and for all humanity in the person and work of Jesus Christ. Yet no one can receive the Spirit without being convicted of sin and assured of God's forgiveness. Luther put it well: "No one can correctly understand God or His Word unless he has received such understanding immediately from the Holy Spirit. But no one can receive it from the Holy Spirit without experiencing, proving and feeling it."[7]

What I am advocating is a biblical theology of Word and Spirit in which the sanctifying work of the Spirit is tied to the redeeming work of Jesus Christ on the cross. We begin with the message of the biblical revelation and then endeavor to relate this to experiences of seekers of truth in all cultures and religions. At the same time, we must always be aware of the biblical fact that no one can rightly seek unless one is already grasped by the power and love of the Lord Jesus Christ. The seeking for God in the natural person is always mixed with a seeking to be God that makes our quest for God self-serving.

I find much I can agree with in the theology of Clark Pinnock and appreciate his willingness to recognize truth in Roman Catholicism and Orthodoxy as well as in Protestant traditions.[8] Yet I fear that he tends to begin with the Spirit's work in creation and then relate this to Christ's work in redemption. He sees the Spirit as the perfecter of the creation "of which Jesus is the highest expression."[9] By stressing the continuity between creation and redemption he ends up giving us a natural theology of the Spirit. In his view, natural knowledge of God is a steppingstone to the redeeming knowledge of God that we find in the Christ revelation. Pinnock is surely right in affirming the universal working of the Spirit, but I wish to stress that the knowledge of *Spiritus Creator* lies in *Spiritus Recreator*—the gift of regeneration through faith in Jesus Christ, who imparts the Spirit in his own way and time. The knowledge of God in creation is not a potentially saving knowledge but a condemning knowledge, for we are reminded of our perfidy and helplessness by meeting the God outside Jesus Christ. Creation does not lead to redemption because human sin has spoiled creation and converted our seeking for God into a seeking for our own security and happiness. Yet in the light of redemption we can discern signs of the perduring goodness of creation that is marred but not eradicated by sin. In the light of the Christ revelation we can perceive little lights and true words in other cultures and religions. Creation does not lead to redemption, but redemption secures and crowns creation. We do not come to Christ by exploring the traces of the work of the Spirit in creation, but we receive the Spirit when we hear the good news of what Christ has done for us as this is set forth in the biblical revelation.

I also have difficulty with Pinnock's recommendation that we as Christians should build "redemptive bridges to other traditions and inquire if God's word has been heard by their adherents."[10] This seems to substitute a global religion of the Spirit for the evangelical faith kept alive in the church through the power of the Spirit. I agree that it is possible to experience the work of the Spirit even in cultures and religions where Jesus is not named, but this experience accentuates our guilt and helplessness rather than assuring us that we are on the right path to salvation. We should, of course, always be open to people of other faiths, and I fully share Pinnock's aversion to dogmatism and religious triumphalism. Yet I believe we must distinguish between relating to persons and relating to belief systems. The biblical testimony affirms overwhelmingly that the truth of the Word of God judges and overthrows the human religious quest for ultimacy. The children of Israel were nowhere urged to combine their faith system with those of the Canaanites and other pagan tribes but were invariably commanded to eschew even the taint of syncretism. While it is true that God's electing grace reaches out to many people sometimes long before they come to a saving faith in Christ, it should not be forgotten that such individuals have already been exposed to the means of grace whether this be Scripture, the sermon, books of theology and devotion, and so on. In the case of Cornelius in Acts 10, one may conclude that he was assiduously seeking for the God of Jesus Christ on the basis of his encounter with the Hebrew Scriptures.[11]

The Collapse of Modernity

A growing number of prescient voices herald the collapse of modernity and the emergence of a thoroughgoing relativism and nihilism in which the quest for ultimacy in meaning is rendered fruitless and self-defeating. The hallmark of the Enlightenment was an unfailing trust in human cognitive faculties to unravel the meaning of the universe, to discover the foundational order that holds all things together. Already in the nineteenth century the perspicacious prophet of postmodernism, Friedrich Nietzsche, flatly denied that humans can ever gain access to ultimate reality. There is no ideal world but only a "perspectival appearance" that has its origins in our own creative imagination.[12] In the early- and mid-twentieth century, Martin Heidegger called into radical question the Enlightenment idea of truth as correspondence with external reality and instead reconceived truth as the disclosure of being. What we should aim for is not a comprehension of the whole of reality but "openness to mystery." In place of calculative thinking Heidegger advocated "meditative thinking." A potent critic of modernity in our time is Jacques Derrida, who has launched an assault on "logocentrism," the idea that language is a carrier of meaning, and the "metaphysics of presence," which presupposes that at the foundation of our language there is an essence or presence of being that can be apprehended by human reason. Another contemporary proponent of postmodernism is the American pragmatist Richard Rorty, who insists that the only guidelines that direct us on our life journey have their source in the communities in which we participate.

What is particularly striking on the current scene is the erosion of foundationalism and the emergence of post-foundationalism. Foundationalism is associated with René Descartes, who has aptly been called the father of the Enlightenment. Descartes held that all knowledge is based on innate ideas that furnish axiomatic certainty. As the Enlightenment unfolded this kind of rationalism was increasingly questioned. With the rise of historicism it is now generally believed that every idea and perception is conditioned by historical and cultural forces that impinge on the human consciousness. No idea or principle is exempt from historical conditioning, and therefore no idea can be regarded as incorrigible or irreformable (as in foundationalism). Rorty's contention that it is impermissible to set forth first principles or canons of rationality that provide foundations for truth is increasingly being taken seriously, even in evangelical circles.[13]

I share the growing discomfort with foundationalism not only on the basis of the new historical consciousness but even more on the basis of the witness of Holy Scripture, which holds the mysteries of faith to be unsearchable and inscrutable (Ps 139:6; Rom 11:33; 1 Cor 2:9; Eph 3:8). Yet instead of retreating into a cultural-linguistic fortress that preserves the ethos of the faith community, I propose that we move into the public domain with a gospel that is both rationally compelling and spiritually inviting. It is compelling, however, only to those whom the Spirit enlightens. Its affirmations carry the ring of certainty only for those who are grasped by the reality to which Scripture bears witness. Its claims cannot be established by logical demonstration or empirical validation, but they can be confirmed in moral obedience. I agree with the anti-foundationalists that we cannot rest our case on general first principles, but we can bear witness to the One who in himself constitutes the foundation for all rationality. Our trust is not in first principles but in the living Lord who never deceives.

As Christians we must avoid meeting the challenge of postmodernism and anti-foundationalism with a call to repristination—simply returning to past stances that predate the Kantian critique of the Enlightenment and also the Barthian critique of evangelical rationalism and neo-Protestant experientialism. To embrace a premodern perspective is to deny the working of the Holy Spirit in modernity. We should not forget that the Enlightenment helped the church discover the real humanity of the Bible as well as appreciate the fallibility and relativity of the church's creeds and confessions. Taking refuge in an earlier position will always be an option for those who refuse to face the challenges of any particular historical era, but this path invariably leads to an obscurantism and dogmatism that can only repel those inquisitive and venturesome spirits who wish to make sense of their faith. The restorationist mentality is apparent in Mother Angelica and the Eternal Word Network, as well as in the Chicago Council on Inerrancy and the Cambridge Declaration.[14]

Another pitfall we must sedulously strive to avoid is accommodationism, in which we compromise or dilute the message of faith in order to gain a hearing from the culture. The answer to postmodern philosophy is not postmodern theology but a critique of the postmodern consciousness grounded in a fresh exposition of Scripture. Postmodern theology often presents itself as "spirituality-based" rather than "creedal-based." Postmodern apologists for the faith are understandably attracted to narrative theology, which signals a retreat from ontology to spirituality. In a postmodern Christian perspective the locus of authority becomes the community of interpretation rather than a transcendent Word of God that judges both the community of faith and the self-consciousness of the culture.

I propose a transmodern theology that does not simply return to the past but draws on the past critically. It does not slavishly try to accommodate to the present but dialogues with the present in order to demonstrate the profound inadequacy of current philosophies to deal with the human condition. It is transmodern because its source lies in God's self-revelation in Jesus Christ, which does not arise out of culture but breaks into human culture and history from the transcendent beyond. It is not anti-modern, because it discerns that all of culture and history is directed by the providential hand of the living God and that this God speaks to us in the culture as well as in the church, though only those with the eyes and ears of faith can hear what the Spirit is saying to the people of our age. A theology centered in the Word and Spirit will not simply strive to expose the idolatrous pretensions of human culture and religion but will try to ascertain what is genuinely good and uplifting in cultural and religious enterprises. Christian revelation constitutes both the abolition and elevation of human religion.[15]

The theology of Word and Spirit that I propose must be sharply distinguished from a theology of Spirit that builds on the religious experiences of all peoples and cultures. A theology of Spirit will tend to be monistic or pantheistic, since it sees all reality as encompassed by Spirit. A theology of Word and Spirit, to the contrary, will be theistic in the biblical sense, since it views God as the creator of a reality outside himself. It will also be personalistic, for it sees revelation involving dialogue between the living God and the human subject.

Modernism is in crisis, but it has not yet folded. Even the most radical postmoderns still reveal an affinity to the impulse of modernity, such as the idea of progress.[16] I see modernism continuing in the guise of inclusivism, which aspires to bring all world religions into the service of an emerging global religious consciousness. Postmodernism by contrast is inclined to embrace pluralism, which denies any substantial commonality among the religions. Inclusivism and pluralism tend to reinforce each other: they both manifest a willingness to view positively all variations of religious expression so long as they proceed from a sincere heart.

Reactionary Christianity sounds the call to an uncompromising exclusivism that raises the Bible or the church above the ebb and flow of human history. Such an approach invariably ends in some kind of idolatry, since it is prone to confound the finite and the infinite, the relative and the absolute. In the evangelical theology I uphold, we must be both inclusive and exclusive. The call of the gospel goes out to the whole human creation, but it is a call for an exclusive commitment to Jesus Christ as the way, the truth and the life. The role of the Spirit is not to lead us to a direct experience of God in the religions in which we find ourselves, but to direct us away from our own religious biases and commitments to the Word of God, which was incarnate in human garb at only one time and place in history.

It is my earnest conviction that the Spirit must not be separated from the Word, nor should the Word ever be divorced from the Spirit. There is no pathway to God that is direct and unmediated. We come to

God through his revelation in Christ, which is communicated by the Spirit. The Son seeks to save all the lost through the power of the Spirit. While Christ was revealed fully and decisively at only one point in history, this position does not deny that Christ manifests his presence through the Spirit outside the parameters of Christian faith and community. I can affirm a hidden Christ, but it is only people of faith who rightly perceive the Spirit of Christ at work in secular or non-Christian religious culture. I have more difficulty with Paul Tillich's conception of a latent church, for this implies that a church is waiting to be born in the religious imaginings of seekers for truth in every culture and religion.[17] The church does not arise out of human experience but is created by the Spirit in the midst of human culture and experience, but always against the grain of what people want to believe—about God and about themselves.

A Theology of the Christian Life

A theology of Word and Spirit will be at the same time a theology of the Christian life, since the Spirit not only illumines the criterion of the Word but also empowers people of faith to follow the Word in costly discipleship. One must, of course, guard against both ethical moralism and rigorism in articulating such a theology. Our source of authority is neither general moral principles nor the universal human awareness of God, but God's self-revelation in Jesus Christ as attested in Holy Scripture.

It is not difficult to discern an affinity between the approach delineated here and that of John Calvin, who has been rightly acclaimed as "a theologian of the Holy Spirit." The theme of Calvin's *Institutes of the Christian Religion* was neither predestination nor extrinsic justification, but regeneration understood as the lifelong sanctifying process worked within us by the Holy Spirit. In his later works Calvin's emphasis shifted to predestination,[18] and in certain strands of Reformed orthodoxy the call to live the Christian life was regrettably subordinated to an emphasis on the eternal decrees of God.

I also acknowledge areas of agreement with the Pietists and Puritans, who focused on the practical implications of Christ's work of
redemption. While they were adamant that we are justified by grace
alone and faith alone, they nevertheless stressed that the verification
of faith lies in its ethical achievements.[19] The inclination of these spiritual renewalists was to find the source of our certainty in the faith
experience rather than in God's promises in holy Scripture (as with
Luther and Calvin). I would rather say that certainty is found in God's
promises, yet not as they exist objectively in Scripture but as they are
sealed within us by the Spirit. Both the Reformers and the Pietists
might find this way of stating the matter acceptable. A more serious
problem with Pietism was its synergistic theology in which we cooperate with prevenient or preparatory grace in coming to a saving knowledge of God in Christ.[20] In my theology we are moved by prevenient
grace to seek for salvation, but we are not drawn into the kingdom of
God except through the transforming work of the Spirit of God within
us. We do not cooperate with grace in facilitating the new birth, but we
respond to grace in bearing witness to the new birth.

Karl Barth, too, gave special attention to the Christian life, despite
his emphasis on the objectivity and all-sufficiency of Christ's work of
atonement.[21] His point was not that the Christian life could merit or
secure our salvation but that it could proclaim and demonstrate
Christ's salvation to others. His theology was essentially a theology of
the Word of God, whereas mine is a theology of Word and Spirit. Yet
the Holy Spirit played an ever more significant role as his theology
unfolded, so that there are points of convergence between our systems. The major difference in emphasis lies in Barth's contention that
the decision of faith follows the event of redemption, whereas I am
inclined to say that the moment of decision is the culmination rather
than the aftereffect of the work of redemption.[22]

I am more Reformed than Lutheran in embracing not simply faith
but faith and obedience, not simply the gospel but the gospel and the
law. Against neo-Lutherans like Gustav Aulén and Anders Nygren I

uphold not an agape spirituality but a spirituality of gospel and law. In contrast to the Pietists, I wish to give prominence not only to the fellowship of love (the koinonia) but also to the church and the sacraments.

As a churchman in the Calvinist tradition I try to maintain a respect for the law of God even while affirming that salvation comes by faith in the gospel. I want to do justice to the legal dimension of Christian salvation without falling into legalism in which good works become a condition for grace. I see the cross of Christ primarily as an expression of God's forgiveness rather than a payment that makes it possible for God to forgive (as in the legalistic understanding).[23] God's love does not cancel the demands of the law, but it goes beyond these demands. The satisfaction of the law is not the condition for God's forgiveness but the means by which this forgiveness is communicated to us.

While recognizing the pivotal place for ritual in faith and worship, I decry the aberration of ritualism in which the free movement of the Spirit is blocked by an almost idolatrous trust in the efficacy of ritual performance. I acknowledge the critical role of the sacraments in Christian life and devotion, but I have profound reservations concerning sacramentalism in which the sacramental rite is believed to have automatic efficacy. Against the symbolists I contend that God really does communicate to us through outward signs. Yet while the outward sign has an important role in confirming and deepening our faith, it must never be confounded with the thing signified (the gift of the Spirit). The sign is not extraneous to the reality that it represents, but it is always distinct from this reality. This is why, in my opinion, the Catholic doctrine of transubstantiation irremediably breaks the dialectic between the visible sign and the invisible grace. In the Reformed view the elements of holy Communion do not change into the body and blood of Christ, but they become vehicles of the Spirit who communicates to us the real presence of Christ so long as we have faith in his work of redemption.[24]

In this theological perspective, pneumatology becomes spirituality.

The person of the Spirit is integrally related to his mission: to seal the fruits of Christ's atoning death and glorious resurrection in the hearts of all those chosen to believe. The Spirit's role is not only to enlighten the mind but also to empower the will to live out our faith in daily repentance and obedience. A spirituality that is both catholic and evangelical will be a spirituality of the cross since it is through Christ's atoning sacrifice that we are equipped to live a life of self-giving love. When I say that our religion is founded on the cross, I have in mind not simply Christ dying on the cross but Christ reigning from the cross. The crucifix and the *Christus Rex* (Christ the King) must be held together in creative tension. In Reformed theology the most potent symbol of Christian faith is the empty cross, for here we are reminded that Christ is risen, that his work of redemption is complete. At the same time, while his redeeming work is complete on one level, on another it is incomplete, since we need to appropriate and receive what he has won for us through faith and repentance. The work of the cross must be supplemented by the work of the Holy Spirit, who seals the fruits of Christ's redemption within us and empowers us to live a life of victory over the powers of sin, death and the devil.

Appendix A: Evangelical Rationalism & Propositional Revelation

In any in-depth reflection on the ground of certainty in Christian thought, particularly as this bears on the intermeshing of Word and Spirit, it is fitting to explore the rationalist legacy within evangelicalism. I have often observed that one of the banes of modern evangelicalism is rationalism, although it is always necessary to point out that this is a believing rationalism. In such a perspective reason prepares the way for faith and confirms faith, but it does not procure faith. Rationalists in both Catholic and Reformation traditions have acknowledged the role of the Spirit in assisting the will to embrace what reason plainly shows to be true. In the deism and latitudinarianism of the seventeenth and eighteenth centuries the Spirit was largely eclipsed by an emphasis on the universal logos and the omnicompetence of reason to discover and establish truth.

Rationalism takes the form of either the logic of deduced conclusions (as in most idealistic philosophy) or the logic of evidential confirmations (as in empiricist philosophy).[25] By contrast, the focus of biblical Christianity is on particular events in salvation history whose meaning is drawn out by faithful exposition under the illumination of the Spirit. We can perhaps speak of this as the logic of adduced meanings inasmuch as it deals with unique events and persons. In the first kind of logic the test for truth is rational coherence; in the second, empirical verification. The test for truth in a more authentically biblical religion is fidelity to divine revelation. Biblical faith is free to employ both deduction and induction, but it will see these exercises of reason in terms of drawing out the implications of the truth of the gospel rather than arriving at this truth independently of the supernatural bestowal of grace.

A legacy reexamined. In this period of theological history we are witnessing a profound reaction against rationalistic methodology and a renewed appreciation of the mythic or narrational dimensions of Christian revelation. This reaction is clearly perceptible in evangelical circles. Many of these descendants of the Protestant Reformation wish to remain true to their theological heritage but still be conversant with contemporary themes in the academy. Some of these scholars call themselves postconservative evangelicals and seek to forge an alliance or at least some kind of working relationship with postliberals (like George Lindbeck and Hans Frei).[26] At the same time a growing number of young evangelicals distrust the foray into narrative theology and sedulously strive to retain the rationalist agenda of an earlier period. They are intent on reclaiming a logocentric theology—one that is centered in the logos or reason of God as opposed to a spirit theology that aspires to get beyond rational concepts to communion with a transformative reality that impinges on the whole of both history and nature.[27]

One of the pressing questions in this debate is whether the Reformers themselves held to a propositional model of revelation. Theologians of a neo-orthodox persuasion have generally, though not always convincingly, contended that the magisterial Reformers basically subscribed to an existential understanding of revelation, but this side of their theology was obscured by the readiness of their followers to draw on Hellenistic (especially Aristotelian) wisdom to make the faith rationally credible and viable for their time.[28]

A rational thrust can be discerned in Protestant orthodoxy from the very beginning, but very few of its luminaries ever became full-blown rationalists. Even those defenders of Reformation faith in the late seventeenth and eighteenth centuries were still prone to make a place for mystery in faith, though they were not immune to the spell of the Enlightenment. The emphasis shifted increasingly from an open-ended declaration of faith to a comprehensive systematic statement. Revealed truths came to be championed over symbolic expressions. Dogmatic affirmations took precedence over dramatic unfoldings. Revelation was reduced to verbal concepts as opposed to personal encounter. The Bible as a book was increasingly identified with divine revelation rather than seen as a conduit of revelation (as with the Reformers). A theology of synthesis with cultural wisdom took the place of a theology of Word and Spirit. A preoccupation with timeless truth muted the notion of historical truth. Faith was no longer childlike trust in God's mercy but rational assent to revealed truth. In rationalism there is an identity between human thoughts and God's thoughts. In the biblical understanding, our thoughts never coincide with God's thoughts (cf. Ps 139:6; Job 42:3; Is 55:8; Rom 11:33-34), but they can reflect God's thoughts. In modern fundamentalism the Spirit merely aids the will to acknowledge what can be shown to be historically probable.

Rationalism tends toward a univocal predication of God over equivocity and analogy. It is assumed that our language about God communicates directly who God really is and what he demands of us. While the older Protestant theologians recognized that human reason could not fully grasp the mysteries of faith, they nevertheless exuded a profound confidence in the capacity of human language to give an adequate portrayal of these mysteries. William Placher sees in Reformed, Lutheran and neo-Catholic scholasticism a "'shift to univocity'—the growing confidence that our language about God makes roughly the same sort of sense as our language about creatures."[29] The seventeenth-century philosophers and theologians did not believe that God is "utterly different from us. God's omniscience, omnipotence, and infinite goodness are the same sorts of qualities we have, differing only in degree."[30] Univocity with regard to our language about God is especially evident in the writings of such evangelical stalwarts in our time as Carl Henry, Edward John Carnell, Gordon Clark and Ronald Nash.[31]

Thomas Torrance is helpful in his explication of what he calls "the Latin heresy," which identifies the deposit of faith with a fixed formula (the *regula fidei*) that can be handed down from one generation to another.[32] This rule of faith is a compendium of "irreformable truths" that is "formulated in definitive statements regarded as identical with the truths which they were meant to express."[33] Sacred Scripture is treated like Aristotelian first principles from which we derive theological doctrines. "Thus through processes of reasoning from first principles to conclusions, [Latin theology] sifted out the ideas deduced from the Scriptures and built them into a logico-deductive system of propositional truths and definitive articles of belief."[34] Torrance sees this development beginning with Tertullian and culminating in modern fundamentalism, which he contends "cuts off God's revelation in the Bible from the living, dynamic being of God himself and his continual self-giving through Christ and in the Spirit."[35] The Bible is treated as "a fixed corpus of revealed propositional truths which can be arranged logically into rigid systems of belief."[36]

The rationalism that Torrance warns against is exemplified in Carl Henry, who finds the unity of Scripture in a "logical system of shared beliefs."[37] While acknowledging that the logos of God cannot be restricted to words, he insists that it is now veritably embodied in

Scripture by virtue of divine inspiration. In this theology divine revelation becomes identical with the "logically interconnected content" of Scripture.[38] George Hunsinger makes a potent case that Henry's position stands in palpable contrast to both Abraham Kuyper, who saw the role of Scripture as bringing the *esse* of Christ to our consciousness, and Herman Bavinck, who viewed the scriptural narratives not as precise history but as prophecy.[39]

Propositional versus narrational theology.[40] One can discern on the contemporary scene the emergence of a new language paradigm that heralds a decisive break with what Lindbeck calls the cognitive-propositional model of truth in the direction of an experiential-expressive model on the one hand and a cultural-linguistic model on the other.[41] The emphasis on the Bible as narrative rather than doctrine is especially noticeable in the last model, where truth becomes a matter of transmitting the symbols that bind a community together, but narration is also associated with the projection of inner experiences on the plane of history.

The new emphasis on narrational over propositional content is striking in Geiko Müller-Fahrenholz, who makes a distinction between "rational, purposive discourse" and "symbolic-mythic communication."[42] "Such communication does not have to do with information about the objects, processes and circumstances that fill our everyday life. Instead, it seeks assurance about what ultimately maintains and concerns us."[43] "Encounters with the divine *pneuma* are beyond analysis and categorization. They are testified to, narrated, announced and disclosed."[44] Concrete, tangible language is vastly superior in this domain to abstract, theoretical language.

Similarly Jürgen Moltmann seeks to unite a theology of hope and a narrative concept of truth in which the truth of Christian doctrine is a reference "not to a state of being, but to a history."[45] The truth of doctrine, he says, "can only be told through the narrative of a community whose own existence, fellowship and activity springs from the biblical story of liberation . . . a 'story-telling fellowship.'"[46] The human speech that conforms most closely to divine reality is narrational rather than propositional in form. "The foundations of orthodoxy . . . are to be found in narrative differentiation. At the center of Christian theology stands the eternal history which the triune God experiences in himself."[47] While distrusted by evangelical rationalists, Moltmann appeals to Pietists and Spiritualists—those who are prone to base their case on the immediate guidance of the Spirit.

In this postmodern climate mythos takes priority over logos, pneumatology over christology, henotheism over monotheism, pluralism over both exclusivism and inclusivism.[48] The content of the Bible is no longer irreformable truth but narrative history. In many circles theologians refer no longer to a meta-story that gives unity to the Bible but now simply to a plurality of stories that are held together by the consensual memory of the people of God.[49] The language of poetry takes precedence over the language of being in delineating the new theology. Here we see the influence of Martin Heidegger and other scholars of a neo-gnostic bent such as Carl Jung and Joseph Campbell, and the erosion of the authority of the philosophers of the Age of Reason— Descartes, Leibniz and John Locke.[50] The gnosis that is sought in this new spirituality is not conceptual or propositional knowledge but mystical communion with ineffable reality.[51]

Revelation is reconceived as narrational rather than propositional. A proposition in this context is a truth that is expressed in declarative statements that clearly affirm or deny what is at issue. A narration is a truth that is expressed through the telling of a story and may take the form of poetry as well as prose. Its truth is gleaned through an existential participation in the drama being depicted, so it is more experiential than strictly logical. A propositional truth is immediately accessible to reason whereas a narrational truth can be grasped only by a heightened imagination. Propositional revelation entails the communication of clear and distinct ideas (à la Descartes). Narrational revelation is the conveyance of insights that can be assimilated only through the obedience of faith. Propositional revelation carries the implication that reve-

.lation is exhaustively rational. Narrational revelation presupposes that revelation is polydimensional—appealing to the will and the affections as well as to reason and logic. Propositional revelation imparts notional knowledge; narrational revelation imparts affectional knowledge.

God's self-revelation in Jesus Christ cannot be reduced either to propositions or to narrations, but it enlists various linguistic and literary forms in order to reach the hardened hearts of sinners and give guidance to the open hearts of saints. It more readily takes symbolic than theoretical form, since it has to do with mysteries beyond the pale of human perception and conception.[52] At the same time, it can be elucidated by concepts and propositions, since its subject matter is intelligible and, through the intervention of the Spirit, apprehensible. Revelation can be expressed in semi-conceptual as well as mythopoetic or narrational language, but in both cases the language is incomplete and awaits further illumination from the Spirit. In conceptualization we are further removed from the original content of revelation than in narration and poetry, and this is why systematic theology must always be open-ended, subject to further amplification and even correction.

As it is used in contemporary theology, propositional revelation rests on a long philosophical tradition including Aristotle, Thomas Aquinas, Descartes, Leibniz, John Locke and Thomas Reid. Narrational revelation finds more affinity with the Platonic and Neoplatonic traditions, though there is a strong rationalistic thrust in Plato as well as in Aristotle.[53] From the vantage point of biblical evangelical theology it is more appropriate to speak of a dynamic personal revelation than of either propositional or narrational revelation. The narratives themselves are not revealed, but they are the earthen vessels that carry truth that is both suprarational and suprahistorical.

Those who defend narrational revelation can appeal to the Bible itself, since the Bible is composed largely of narratives that are related to the unfolding of sacred history. But the Bible is not wholly narrational, for it also contains ongoing reflection on the narratives of biblical history. In my opinion we need to steer clear of both the rationalistic theology of neo-scholasticism and the narrative theology of current symbolism. Both have a partial grasp of the meaning of biblical revelation.

The narrative theology associated with the Yale school (Frei, Lindbeck, Placher, Garrett Green) stresses the need to examine the world through the lens of the scriptural text. In the older liberal theology the world absorbed the text. In the evangelical theology I espouse both world and text are critiqued in the light of God's self-revelation in Jesus Christ. The infallible norm is not the text as such nor the narrative history in which the text is set but the transcendent meaning of the gospel, the product of the creative speech of God, that is imparted through the text to the world by the Spirit of the living God.

Toward a theology of Word and Spirit. The theology I propose is not to be confounded with either narrational or propositional theology, though it acknowledges that the Bible contains both realistic narrative and propositional truth. A theology of Word and Spirit seeks to transcend the cleavage between dogmatism and mysticism, logos and mythos. It perceives the unity of logos and mythos in the dramatic unfolding of the salvation history mirrored in the Bible. With both Thomas Aquinas and Karl Barth it propounds a middle way between equivocity and univocity—the way of analogy. We do not attribute qualities in the creature to the Creator (the *analogia entis*), but we see the glory of the Creator reflected in the creature (the *analogia fidei*).

While sensing an affinity with the proponents of narrative theology, I contend that the Bible presents truth claims as well as stories, that it yields infallible information concerning God and his revelatory action as well as poetic elaboration of God's mighty deeds. Against certain strands in narrative theology, I hold that the gospel is more than an inspiring story. It constitutes a metaphysical criterion that enables us to distinguish between what is true and what is false. We find truth not in the story itself but in God's intervention in our reading or telling of the story. The truth of divine revelation is not self-evident in the Bible, nor is it immediately apprehensible (as in propositional or rationalistic theology). Neither is it inherent in the narrations of the Bible waiting to be discovered (as in some kinds of narrative theology). Truth is an event of the speech of God rather than insightful cognition on the one hand or propositional consistency on the other.

This position is not really innovative, though it may appear so in the light of the theological options available on the current scene. It was anticipated in a number of the church fathers, including Augustine, in the mainstream Reformers Luther and Calvin, in Peter T. Forsyth and in Karl Barth. Augustine's distinction between the sign and the thing signified reflects the Platonic polarity between the material copy and the original, but it also mirrors the biblical truth that God condescends to meet us in visible signs or acts. Luther's contention that the whole Bible testifies to Christ reveals his commitment to the role of the Spirit in leading us beyond the natural meaning of the text to the transcendent reality of the gospel. Calvin's distinction between the human intention of the author of the text and the divine intention attests his adherence to the Pauline emphasis on spirit over letter. The pivotal role of the Spirit in bringing illumination to the Word is set forth in the Westminster Confession, which speaks of the Spirit as being the final judge in theological authority.[54] For Barth the Bible and church proclamation constitute the objective pole of divine revelation and the interior illumination of the Spirit the subjective pole. Both are necessary to hear and know the real Word of God.

Thomas Aquinas is often treated as the exemplar of propositional revelation, but he too anticipates a theology of Word and Spirit. Without discounting the rationalizing proclivity in his theology, we would do well to remember that Thomas did not equate revelation immediately with sacred Scripture but held that Scripture is grounded in an antecedent divine revelation.[55] While perceiving that propositions can elucidate the truth of faith, he was convinced that the full-fledged knowledge of God "cannot be a merely propositional matter. It must come embodied . . . in a human soul."[56] Natural cognition cannot prepare the way for a life of faith apart from grace. Eugene Rogers makes a persuasive case that Thomas denied that nature in and of itself is open to grace. Nature must be vitalized by grace, reason must be perfected by faith. Faith moreover "is a perfection precisely because it is not merely an extension . . . of the natural powers of the intellect."[57] Thomas held that unbelievers cannot be convinced of the God of revelation by demonstrative arguments. Moreover, what God primarily reveals is Jesus Christ himself, not propositional information. This excursus on Thomas is important because many conservative evangelicals appeal to Thomas as their model in theological method.[58]

A more convincing example of evangelical rationalism is Wolfhart Pannenberg, who despite his christocentric thrust allows the world to become another criterion for faith besides the God of the Bible.[59] Because he believes that Anselm begins with rational argument alone, he refuses to hold that truth is decided in advance. Pannenberg adopts Augustine's view that the affirmation of God's truthfulness "rests on perception of the coherence and unity of all that is true."[60] Paul Molnar trenchantly discerns that a subtle shift in logic has taken place. "Theology shifts away from God (and the need for faith) to our perceptions and then discovers God as the locus of this presupposed unity."[61] Pannenberg is adamant that theology should understand the unity of reality only in the light of the Christ event. Yet "since his method is dictated by his belief that the question about the whole of reality 'is not first envisaged from the side of Jesus Christ, but is always posed priorly . . . as the question of philosophy,' his philosophical question about the whole of reality actually sets the ground rules for theology."[62] For him, it seems, revelational theology is based on natural theology, since he identifies the trinitarian God with the "field of the infinite to which the human mind is open from its origin."[63] Against Barthianism Pannenberg holds that the events of the historical saga of Israel's faith pilgrimage carry their own meaning, and meaning is inherent in words. Pannenberg makes an important place for myth in theological exposition, but at the same time he betrays a proclivity to resolve myth into propositional truth.

While open to the concerns of narrative theology, I agree with Colin Gunton that the time has come to reclaim the propositional dimension of revelation as well.[64] Although truth is not a property of a proposition, propositions can attest truth. The truth of being takes precedence over the truth of statement, but the latter can transmit the former through the power of the Spirit. Propositions are not themselves sentences but declarations embodied in sentences. Propositions can be gleaned from revelation, but they always point beyond themselves to mysteries that can be only dimly grasped by the enlightened human mind. I affirm both the necessity and the inadequacy of propositions in communicating revelatory truth. Propositions can serve truth but not exhaust truth. They can elucidate the truth of the gospel but not secure this truth. Faith terminates not in propositions but in the reality to which they point.[65]

Jacob Neusner is helpful in his contention that narrative as well as strict logic can serve propositional truth.[66] He draws an important distinction between "the logic of propositional cogency" and the logic of "teleological or narrative cogency."[67] In the first kind of logic we "offer a proposition, lay out the axioms, present the proofs, and test the proposition against contrary argument."[68] The second way to demonstrate propositional truth is to tell a story, which may be historical, fictional or parabolic. "Narrative conveys a proposition through the setting forth of happenings in a framework of inevitability, in a sequence that makes a point, that is, establishes not merely the facts of what happens, but the teleology that explains those facts."[69] Neusner also discusses the logic that rests on sharing in a community of faith. Here we do not gain cogency through declarative affirmations, for "the cogency derives from a source other than shared propositions."[70]

I see four options today for the church and theology. The first is a rationalistic orthodoxy that views the Bible as a compendium of propositions or a storehouse of facts inviting systematic analysis.[71] Second is a process ontology that may appeal to Whitehead, Hegel or Teilhard de Chardin. Here the Bible is treated as a mythical vision containing abiding insights into the human condition. The symbols of biblical discourse need to be translated into ontological concepts if they are to be made relevant to the modern situation. Third is a narrative theology that cultivates shared memories of a common tradition of faith, rather than proposing a worldview or ontology that stands in competition with other ontologies. Finally, there is a theology of Word and Spirit, which I also call a theology of divine-human encounter or a theology of crisis in that its focus is on the divine judgment over human history.[72] It does not claim to set forth a revealed metaphysic, but at the same time it does not shrink from engaging in metaphysical speculation, for the revelation in Scripture has profound metaphysical implications. In this theology the Bible is not fundamentally a narrative history, though it assuredly contains narrative. Neither is it a handbook of revealed propositions or irreformable truths. Instead it is the mirror of God's self-condescension in Jesus Christ. Narrative is the preponderant form of revelation but not the content. The content is the gospel and the law, a transcendent structure of meaning that is revealed by the Spirit through an encounter with the apostolic proclamation in Scripture and the church.

Because my position has striking affinity with the hermeneutics of many of the church fathers it could be called an ecumenical orthodoxy. Yet its orthodoxy consists not in simply returning to past formulations but in open dialogue with other traditions within the Christian orbit in order to express the age-old truth of God's saving act in Jesus Christ in a fresh and relevant way. Its orientation is not simply about the past but also about the future, for the full uncovering of the mystery of faith is not realizable until the eschaton, when faith shall be supplanted by sight (2 Cor 5:7).

A theology of Word and Spirit will give proper recognition to rationality in faith, but it will resist rationalism—the tendency to dissolve mystery into logic. It will not hesitate to employ propositions in demonstrating the cogency of faith, but it will refuse to reduce revelation or faith to propositions. It will see faith as both *credentia* (intellectual assent) and *fiducia* (trust in God's mercy). It will be fully cognizant of the narrational language in Scripture without turning church proclamation into narration or storytelling. Its aim will not be to transmute divine revelation into "clear and distinct ideas" (as in Descartes); at the same time, it will not affirm with Langdon Gilkey that "when a word becomes important, it becomes imprecise."[73] Its ultimate criterion is neither religious experience nor the biblical record but God's self-revelation in Jesus Christ, which comes to us through various means, especially Scripture and the preaching of the gospel.

Such a theology recognizes with the Anglican divine Jeremy Taylor (d. 1667) that the Scriptures are "written within and without," that besides the light that shines on the face of the Scriptures there must be a light shining in our hearts if we are to hear and know the real Word of God. According to Taylor a purely rational theology understands "by reason," a spiritual theology understands "by love." In the latter case the interpreter "does not only understand the sermons of the Spirit, and perceives their meaning: but he pierces deeper, and knows the meaning of that meaning; that is, the secret of the Spirit, that which is spiritually discerned, that which gives life to the proposition, and activity to the soul."[74]

Under the impact of the later Enlightenment evangelical rationalism has assumed an empiricist rather than idealistic hue. Showing its indebtedness to Scottish Common Sense realism, its apologetic often takes the form of evidentialism in which external evidences shore up Christian affirmations. Yet the role of deductive logic is not negated by evangelicals in this tradition, as can be seen in the manner they develop their doctrine.[75] Evangelical rationalism in its current state tends toward factual accuracy and precision. It thereby feeds into biblical literalism. By contrast, narrational symbolism tends toward the imaginative reconstruction of the text in question. Biblical personalism, which I uphold, tends toward the faithful reproduction of the message that resounds in the salvific events and in the scriptural text. This message, however, does not inhere in the words, but must be always spoken anew by the Spirit of God as he reaches out to both struggling saints and lost sinners with the Word of life.

When we seek evidences for faith we end by placing our faith in such things. Faith is not "a resting of the soul in the sufficiency of the evidence"[76] but trusting in the faithfulness of Jesus Christ to speak his Word to all who hunger and thirst for righteousness. The self-disclosure of the living Christ does not negate or bypass the written word of Holy Scripture but leads us more deeply into this word through the illumination of the Spirit. Our assurance of God's favor toward us lies in our being known by God (1 Cor 8:3; Gal 4:9), not in the certainty of human perception and logic. Evangelical rationalism needs to be superseded by a biblical evangelicalism that respects mystery in faith, yet is adamant that meaning shines through mystery. God really speaks and acts, but only those with the eyes and ears of faith can hear and know.

·TWO·

THE

C͟ONTEMP͟ORARY

DEBATE

There can be Pentecostal phenomena . . .
that are not from God,
that are not part of the mystery of his will in Christ.
SIMON TUGWELL

The Spirit is not the last thing to be said about God, but the first:
He is the outward-reaching freedom in love of the Father and the Son.
PHILIP ROSATO

External rites are not to be identified or confused with internal realities;
external rites are futile and invalid, even though given by God,
unless there is a correspondingly internal reality.
JAMES DUNN

The Spirit indwells and empowers the church to be a vanguard,
a visible sign of God's coming reign of reconciliation and communion.
AMY PLANTINGA PAUW

Whereas in the first part of the twentieth century the Holy Spirit seemed to be the missing person of the Trinity, this is now more true of the Father. Within the past several decades a plethora of books on the Holy Spirit has appeared, and innumerable conferences on the Spirit and on spirituality have taken place. The mid and latter parts of the century have also witnessed the unprecedented growth of Pentecostal and charismatic fellowships and denominations not only in America but even more in the Third World—Latin America, Africa and Asia. The Joachim vision may be being realized: It seems that we are passing from the Age of the Son to the Age of the Spirit.[1]

The burgeoning interest in pneumatology and spirituality is nowhere more manifest than in the Roman Catholic and Orthodox churches. For Pope John XXIII and Cardinal Suenens of Belgium the key to spiritual renewal in our time lay in a new Pentecost.[2] This same sentiment was echoed by Metropolitan Ignatius of Latakia addressing the Assembly of the World Council of Churches in Uppsala (1968): "Without the Holy Spirit God is far away. Christ stays in the past, the Gospel is simply an organization, authority a matter of propaganda."[3]

While the contemporary church shares a common interest in the nature and role of the Holy Spirit, it is hampered at the same time by the absence of a common vision. With the crisis of modernity and the rise of postmodernism the Spirit is being reconceived as a vital energy in the world or as a field of force (Michael Welker, Peter Hodgson, Wolfhart Pannenberg) rather than a supernatural person. Schleiermacher's legacy is becoming more pronounced, with the Spirit envisaged as "the spiritual determination of human consciousness."[4] Many theologians today encourage us to seek a doctrine of the Spirit "from below"—beginning with the impact of the Spirit in human life—rather than one "from above," in which we begin with the doctrine of the immanent Trinity.[5] In some avant garde circles the Spirit is not so much the catalyst for church growth as the inspirer of the universal quest for unity with "the Real." Amy Plantinga Pauw laments the contemporary focus on the Spirit as a creative force within nature or as "a generic term for human religiosity."[6] "Christian references to the Spirit need to retain their roots in the community's texts and traditions, in a confession that continues the Old Testament witness to the Spirit of God and that has developed within the framework of trinitarian theology."[7]

Besides the divide between traditionalists and modernists or liberals, we also need to consider what separates mainline Protestants and evangelicals. The mainline is prone to stress faith and nurture over a crisis experience of conversion.[8] The role of the Spirit is to lead us into greater spiritual maturity and higher planes of virtue. By contrast, evangelicals see the Spirit as God decisively reaching out and turning us toward Christ in faith and repentance. It is the difference, as William James trenchantly observed, between the once born and the twice born.[9]

Another division in the church is that between Catholics and Orthodox on the one hand and evangelical pietists on the other. While the former adhere strongly to baptismal regeneration, the latter insist that we are not regenerated until we personally appropriate what Christ offers in religious experience. This barrier is not insuperable, since many of the Catholic and Orthodox mystics (such as Symeon the New Theologian) have also emphasized the need for personal decision and faith.

Traditionalist evangelicals are also at loggerheads with Pentecostals and charismatics, who teach the need for a second work of the Spirit after conversion in which we are empowered for ministry. Here one can discern a remarkable convergence of Pentecostalism with mainstream Catholic spirituality, which contends that the sacrament of baptism must be supplemented and fulfilled in the sacrament of confirmation, one that allegedly strengthens us for kingdom service.

Finally, it is important to consider the intratrinitarian relation that binds the Spirit to the Son and the Father. A controversy that has separated the Eastern and Western churches is whether the Spirit proceeds from the Father alone or from the Father *and* the Son (the *filioque*). I deal with this more directly in the following section.

The Person of the Spirit
Not only the work of the Spirit but also the person of the Spirit has been a subject of controversy in the church. Is the Spirit a separate per-

son (*hypostasis*) in the Trinity or simply the action and power of God in Christ? Is the Spirit subordinate to both Father and Son, or is the Spirit equal to the other members of the Trinity? Does the Spirit proceed not simply from the Father but also from the Son, or does the Spirit merely receive from the Son? Is the Spirit a "person" in the modern sense of the word, or is he better described as "the common Spirit of the Christian society" (Schleiermacher), "the principle of evolution" (Moltmann) or "serendipitous creativity" (Clark Pinnock)?[10]

The relation of the Spirit to the other persons in the Trinity has precipitated an ongoing debate between Eastern and Western churches. Ever since Metropolitan Photius (c. 810-895), the Eastern church has been adamant that the Spirit proceeds only from the Father. Just as the Son is generated by the Father, so the Spirit is breathed out by the Father. The Western church has inserted into the Nicene Creed the *filioque*—the Spirit proceeds from the Father *and* the Son. Those who would try to mediate between these positions sometimes depict the Spirit as proceeding from the Father and sent by the Son. Eastern Christianity fears an erosion of the monarchy of the Father if the Son is envisaged as an ontological source of the Spirit.

Sometimes the Spirit is portrayed as the catalyst for community between Father and Son (Augustine, Karl Barth, Paul Evdokimov). The Spirit then becomes the bond of unity in the Trinity, though the question arises whether the Spirit is then an ontological subject in the Trinity. The Eastern Orthodox theologian Paul Evdokimov suggests that the Holy Spirit "is in the middle of the Father and the Son. He is the one who brings about the communion between the two. He is the communion, the love between the Father and the Son."[11] It appears that the Spirit is no longer an ontological subject but only a force that relates Father and Son.

Those who emphasize the unity of the Trinity are reluctant to speak of three different persons in a relationship of ongoing love. The noted Baptist theologian H. Wheeler Robinson (d. 1945) contends that the Trinity connotes an evolving self-consciousness rather than three distinct centers of consciousness.[12] For Karl Barth the Trinity does not imply three interacting persons but three modes of being united in one intelligence and one will. Hendrikus Berkhof envisages the Trinity not as a community of persons but as an extension of activities.[13] Like Tillich, Robinson and many others, Berkhof conceives of the Spirit as the all-inclusive dimension of the Trinity; the Father and Son become modes of the Spirit's activity.

How the Spirit is related to Christian experience is another intriguing question. For Robinson the Trinity is "an explanation of Christian experience" rather than a revealed doctrine. In classical church tradition the Spirit is the generator of Christian experience but is not dependent on such experience for its reality. The mission of the Spirit is to penetrate the world with the life-giving power of Jesus Christ. In accomplishing this mission the Spirit draws from the Father as well as from the Son. Modern theology is inclined to focus on the work of the Spirit in creation and redemption rather than on the person of the Spirit within the ontological Trinity. Theologians like Philip Rosato propose a pneumatology "from below," in which we begin with the Spirit's action in human history, rather than "from above," in which we begin with the procession of the Spirit from the Father.[14]

Baptism and Conversion

Another critical issue that continues to divide Christian theology is the relationship between baptism and conversion. While sacramentalists are inclined to see the gift of the Spirit imparted through the sacramental sign of baptism, pietists and ethicists insist that the only absolute condition for receiving the Spirit is repentance and faith. This latter view is reflected in J. H. E. Hull: "Nowhere is it claimed in Acts that baptism of itself, or the laying on of hands as such, or even a combination of them both, confers or can confer the Spirit. If there is any *sine qua non,* and indeed there is, that is to be found in repentance and faith (trust) in Christ. For these two factors there is no substitute at all."[15] By contrast, the Catholic and Orthodox traditions, which see the Spirit working sacramentally, contend that the ritual of baptism itself communicates the Spirit, though this does not imply that the Spirit is fully appropriated at the time of baptism. Contemporary Protestant theologians who affirm the sacramental power of baptism include G. W. H. Lampe, Dale Bruner, Richard Jensen, Michael Green and Clark Pinnock.[16] The Catholic ecumenist Yves Congar refers to "two supernatural causes" in our regeneration: water baptism and the gift of the Spirit.[17]

Is it theologically proper to speak of two baptisms in the New Testament—by the Spirit and by water—or of one baptism—by the Spirit through water? Karl Barth and his son Markus were adamant that these two baptisms not be confounded.[18] For these scholars baptism is an act of obedience, not a mystery or sacrament. Baptism should ideally follow the gift of conversion rather than precede it. James Dunn, who is close to the Barthian position, sees baptism as a vehicle of faith rather than the vehicle of the Spirit.[19] The Pentecostal theologian David Pawson takes a mediating position: "The two baptisms [water and Spirit] are never so closely identified in the New Testament that either 'mediates' the other. Though they often happen very close together, there is no recorded case of them happening simultaneously."[20]

While Catholicism and Eastern Orthodoxy stress the objective efficacy of the sacrament of baptism, these traditions also contain voices that underscore the need for a personal act of faith and conversion. Catherine of Siena taught that it is possible to have the form of holy baptism but none of its light, for we can be deprived of God's light "by a cloud of sin."[21] Symeon the New Theologian contended that we do not enter the full dispensation of grace except through repentance and faith.[22] In our time, the Catholic charismatic movement has emphasized the need for experiential appropriation of the fruits of Christ's sacrifice made available to us in the sacrament of baptism in particular.

Baptism and Confirmation

Once we allow for a distinction between the sacrament of baptism and the gift of the Spirit, the door is open to seeing baptism as only a preparation for the Spirit and to the need for a second rite that actualizes the Spirit's coming. In the early church, theologians like Origen and Tertullian held to a post-baptismal imposition of hands, which supposedly mediated the gift of the Spirit. Augustine strongly endorsed baptismal regeneration but at the same time made a place for a post-baptismal anointing that conveys the unction of the Spirit. Cyril of Jerusalem (c. 315-386) taught that the Spirit baptizes in the moment of immersion but also in a "mystical chrism" that completes baptism. In the Middle Ages confirmation became a full-blown sacrament believed to impart the sevenfold gift of the Spirit for service in the name of Christ. In another development the sacrament of penance filled the need for restoration to the favor of God after post-baptismal sin. The seal of the Spirit is indeed given in baptism, but it can be lost through deliberate sin. This idea was already expressed in the *Shepherd of Hermas* (second century).

In modern theology a palpable cleft exists between those who affirm the completion of baptism in a rite of confirmation (Dewar, Mason, Dix, Thornton) and those who see the gift of the Spirit as fully communicated in the sacrament of baptism (Lampe, Bruner, Jensen, Neunheuser). The principal question is whether the ancient practice of laying on of hands was part of the baptismal rite or a sacrament in its own right. Similarly, is the anointing with oil a supplemental adornment of baptism or the visible sign of a new invisible grace that imparts power for mission?

The Catholic charismatic movement allows for a Pentecostal experience that is supplementary to the rites of the church but by no means renders these rites superfluous. In the words of Kevin and Dorothy Ranaghan: " 'Baptism in the Holy Spirit' is not something replacing baptism and confirmation. Rather it may be seen as an adult re-affirmation and renewal of these sacraments, an opening of ourselves to all their sacramental graces."[23]

The Holiness movement coming out of Wesleyanism posits a second blessing beyond baptism, one that imparts the fullness of the Spirit or the gift of entire sanctification. It is not an outward rite but an inner experience that signifies the unction of the Spirit, which conforms us to the image of Christ.

Pentecostalism goes a step further and insists that the gift of the Spirit after baptism imparts not perfection in character but power for witnessing. The visible sign of this spiritual endowment is speaking in other tongues (glossolalia). The affinities between Pentecostalism and the Catholic tradition are obvious, for both see the need for an infusion of grace after baptism that completes the intention of baptism.

Assurance and Evidence

Because the gift of the Spirit is invisible and intangible (at least for Reformed Christians), the question inevitably arises whether one can attain certainty concerning this gift. Are there external evidences that can assure one that the Spirit has indeed been imparted? This was an issue in the early church, and it continues to be one today.

In the Eastern church, evidences for the Spirit were highly valued. Ammonas of Egypt (late fourth century) contended that the highest of them all is effective service. The East Syrian mystic 'Abdīsho' Hazzāya held that the first sign of the Spirit's operation is "the love of God" that "burns in the heart of a person like fire."[24] Other signs that he mentioned were humility, perfect love and inner illumination. Symeon the New Theologian emphasized the sign of *penthos,* "an abiding sorrow for sin."[25]

In Reformation theology we do not need to look for evidences of our standing in the sight of God, for faith itself brings us the assurance that we are loved by God and forgiven through the sacrifice of Christ. John Wesley and also many of the Puritans made a distinction between faith and the full assurance of faith, which was seen as a gift given only to some. For Jonathan Edwards Christian practice is the cardinal sign that we have been endowed with the Spirit. Protestant orthodoxy was inclined to make adherence to a creedal formula the badge of belonging to the body of Christ.

The signs of the manifestation of the Spirit play a prominent role in charismatic spirituality, but many theologians in this movement warn against seeking after signs or putting our trust in signs. Simon Tugwell declares, "There is a mysticism, and there are miracles, which are worldly and serve the 'Prince of this world.'"[26] Some of the so-called signs are "signs precisely of the recalcitrance of our nature under the operation of grace."[27] While the gospel assuredly brings power, "this power is made perfect in weakness, and if we would be powerful for the Lord, and not just for success in the world, we must take our stand on the weakness of the cross, and on that poverty of spirit which the Lord himself declared to be blessed."[28] By contrast, in mainstream Pentecostal theology Christians are encouraged to expect signs of the movement of the Spirit, which make us certain of being in the Spirit.[29]

Aspects of Salvation

The salvific role of the Holy Spirit is still another issue that has split the church—in the past and in the present. Does the Spirit impart to the believer the assurance of a salvation already procured by Christ through his sacrifice on the cross, or does the Spirit infuse us with the life-giving energy of Jesus Christ, which conforms us more and more to his image? Is grace an infusion of the righteousness of Christ or the imputation of Christ's righteousness to those who remain sinners but who are now free to combat sin and subdue it? Is grace the elevation of human nature (the emphasis in Roman Catholicism and Orthodoxy), or basically the forgiveness of sins (the emphasis of the Reformers)? In a theologian like Augustine we find both motifs, though he sees justification primarily as *gratia infusa* rather than forensic imputation (Luther's position).[30]

The mystical tradition in the church, which encompasses Orthodoxy, Roman Catholicism and a segment of Protestantism, has conceived of the work of the Spirit in terms of deification by which we are made not only more godly but more godlike. Dionysius the Pseudo-Areopagite (c. 500) envisaged deification as including the whole process of sanctification. In both Eastern and Western Christianity deification is conceived as both a divine gift and an act of the human will. It is by means of synergy or human cooperation with grace that we proceed to make the ascent to union with God. For Gregory Palamas deification entails our participation in God's energies; we thereby become deified "in a literal and absolute sense—we become God and therefore we become, by grace, uncreated."[31] Protestants in the Reformation tradition emphasize that grace restores our true humanity but does not make us superhuman.

The doctrine of justification is pivotal in this whole discussion. The Reformers conceived of justification in terms of the imputation of righteousness and sanctification in terms of the infusion of righteousness, but the former is given priority. God justifies us while we are still in our sins and sanctifies us through daily purification and renewal. Some theologians like Regin Prenter and Arthur Crabtree regard justification and sanctification as referring to the one work of grace from different perspectives.[32] Others like R. C. Sproul see justification as basically a change in status rather than a change of being, but the latter follows the former.[33] Does God justify us while we are still in our sins, or does God's justifying work actually make us righteous? Moreover, is God's gift of justification contingent on our becoming righteous with the aid of prevenient grace? Here we discern a major divergence between Catholics, who tend to absorb justification into sanctification, and Reformation Protestants, who view justification as the ground of sanctification.[34]

Word and Spirit

Some theologians have erred by subordinating the Spirit to the Word; others by elevating the Spirit over the Word. If we mean by the latter the living Word, Jesus Christ, then we must view him as equal to the Spirit, though he has a certain priority in the economy of salvation. If we are thinking of the written Word, however, the Spirit clearly has precedence, since the Bible was produced by the inspiration of the

Spirit, and the Spirit uses the Bible to bring sinners to the knowledge of Jesus Christ.

Scholastic theology tends to elevate the Word unduly, whereas spiritualistic theology is prone to make the Word ancillary to the Spirit. Symeon the New Theologian saw water baptism as only a symbol and the only saving baptism as that of the Spirit. For Symeon the sacrament is empty without the Spirit, just as is the office of the priest. In spiritualism the inner baptism of the Spirit is valued over the outer baptism, the sacramental rite. By contrast, the Reformers were adamant that Word and Spirit belong together and that authority rests in the paradoxical unity of Word and Spirit.

To view the Spirit as both the primary author and the interpreter of the Bible means that the Bible has a spiritual as well as a natural or literal meaning. Orthodox and Catholic theologies have stressed the spiritual sense of Scripture but often at the price of severing the spiritual from the natural sense. Many theologians in these traditions, however, have recognized the value of beginning with the natural sense and then proceeding to the spiritual sense—the christological meaning of the text.[35] Paul Quay has rightly discerned that when we lose the spiritual sense altogether we can no longer regard the Old Testament as a Christian book.[36]

The Reformers were adamant that the natural sense of the scriptural passage is normative, but they too perceived the need to rise above this plain meaning in order to ascertain how the passage is related to the center of Scripture—God's self-revelation in Jesus Christ. They had deep reservations regarding mystical forays into higher truths, but they did acknowledge the rightful place for typological exposition, seeing in Old Testament events and characters anticipations of the fullness of divine revelation in Jesus Christ.

Today there is a movement away from propositional theology to narrational theology, from logos to mythos. A christocentric theology is being overshadowed by a pneumatocentric theology in which the living voice of the Spirit is viewed as a higher authority than the written Word of God. The appeal is no longer to what Scripture says but to the sanctified imagination of the reader. The new light that breaks forth from God's holy Word supersedes the old light contained in sacred Scripture of the past.

John Calvin is sometimes acclaimed as a propositional theologian and at other times as an existential theologian.[37] The truth of the matter is that neither of these designations does justice to Calvin's theological contribution. He cannot be reduced to a propositional theologian because his appeal was not to Scripture alone but to Scripture illumined by the Spirit.[38] But neither was he an illuminist or existentialist, for the Spirit's illumination must always be tested by the product of the Spirit's inspiration—the written Word of God. Like Augustine and Luther, Calvin is best described as a theologian of the Word and Spirit, one whose appeal rests on the dialectical interplay between the present work of the Spirit and his past revelation. Theology today needs an alternative to both scholasticism and spiritualism or illuminism, and we find this alternative in many of the church fathers as well as in the Protestant Reformers. It can also be discerned in P. T. Forsyth, Karl Barth and Emil Brunner.

Spiritual Gifts

One of the salient fruits of the Pentecostal revival has been the rediscovery of the gifts of the Holy Spirit, including healing, prophecy, tongues, discerning of spirits and miracles. The apostle Paul devoted much attention to these gifts (Rom 12:3-8; 1 Cor 12, 14), and they are also referred to in the Gospels (see esp. Mk 16:17-18). Whereas the emphasis in the apostolic church was on miraculous phenomena of the Spirit, the patristic church emphasized such gifts as virginity, readiness for martyrdom and voluntary poverty. The gift of tears was particularly evident in the Eastern church in such theologians as Ammonas of Egypt (late fourth century) and Symeon the New Theologian. By contrast, John Chrysostom had profound misgivings over the search for signs and wonders and emphasized character over charismata.

Thomas Aquinas subordinated the gifts to the practice of the virtues, holding that the gifts enable us to do virtuous deeds perfectly.

In our day the Toronto Blessing movement and the Vineyard Fellowship have called attention to such bizarre manifestations of the Spirit as being slain in the Spirit, barking and holy laughter. The mainstream charismatic movement has sought to downplay these so-called extraordinary charisms and has focused attention on the gifts that edify and build up the body of Christ.[39]

Since the Second Vatican Council the Roman Catholic Church has been remarkably open to the gifts of the Spirit in theology and in devotion. Pope Paul VI declared: "How wonderful it would be if the Lord would again pour out the charisms in increased abundance, in order to make the Church fruitful, beautiful and marvelous, and to enable it to win the attention and astonishment of the profane and secularized world."[40] Cardinal Suenens of Belgium called for a Holy Spirit revival in the Catholic Church.[41]

Several theological issues emerge with the manifestations of the Spirit. One question is whether these gifts belong properly to the apostolic era and therefore cannot be replicated. The mainstream of the Reformed tradition tends to downplay these gifts,[42] whereas Pentecostals and many Catholics contend that the gifts are not only relevant but also necessary for an effective Christian ministry. Another question is whether the tongues-speaking that appeared at the first Pentecost constituted foreign languages or simply ecstatic utterance, as was found in the Corinthian church. Again, do these gifts signify the maturation of human potentialities or supernatural operations of the Spirit? Finally, are these gifts infallible signs of the Spirit's presence or only clues that direct us to a mystery surpassing human understanding?

Gender of the Spirit

With the rise of feminist theology the whole idea of gender in God is being reappraised. Church tradition is emphatic that the God of the Bible transcends gender and that references to God as Father and Son do not imply that God is male. Yet it is also generally recognized that God encompasses gender within himself, for he created both male and female in his image. God in his relationship to his creation is overwhelmingly but not exclusively depicted in the masculine mode. In the wisdom literature, the feminine Sophia (wisdom) is sometimes associated with the Word and then again with the Spirit. Several Christian Gnostic texts refer to the Spirit as "the Divine Mother." *The Odes of Solomon,* a product of the Syrian church (second century), contains references to the Spirit as feminine.[43] The Christian mystics occasionally described the divine in feminine terms, as did also the Lutheran and Reformed Pietists.[44] For Count Zinzendorf the Holy Spirit was the Christians' "actual and true Mother."[45]

Contemporary theologians are increasingly divided over this vexatious question. Elizabeth Johnson sees the feminine side of God in both the Son and the Spirit.[46] Moltmann contends that in the experience of God in regeneration the Spirit becomes "the Mother of Life."[47] Geiko Müller-Fahrenholz identifies *ruah* (spirit) with *sophia* (wisdom) and *shekinah* (glory), both of which are feminine. He calls *ruah* "the motherly-and-fatherly energy which inspires all creation with expectation, power and fertility."[48] The process of creation is interpreted as a process of gestation, as a coming out of the mother's womb. Edward Schillebeeckx calls the Holy Spirit the "mother of the church."[49] Donald Gelpi refers to the Spirit as "the Divine Mother."[50]

On the other side of the ledger more traditionalist theologians argue that although God is like a mother and a sister in some respects, his name is Father, Son and Holy Spirit.[51] A name is not a simile but a title that God gives himself in his revelation. To refer to the Spirit or the Son as feminine and the Father as masculine creates a bifurcation in the Trinity so that we are pushed into binitarianism: a God partly male and partly female. Orthodox theologian Thomas Hopko argues that we are not at liberty to emend the trinitarian names for God because this "'nameless God' has personally revealed himself . . . as Father through the person of Jesus Christ the Son, by the person of the Holy Spirit."[52]

Yves Congar cautions us not to abandon traditional terminology simply because *ruah* in Hebrew and Syriac happens to be feminine. He reminds us that in many instances *ruah* is used in both languages to denote the masculine.[53]

Outreach of the Spirit

With the rise of the theology of religions another issue has come to the fore: the outreach of the Spirit. Does the Spirit restrict his work to the community of believers, or does the Spirit also work in the wider world—in political movements, in humanitarian enterprises, in other religions and ethical systems? This question is not new in the church, for the apologists of the early church were quite emphatic that the Spirit prepares people in non-Christian cultures for the message of redemption in Jesus Christ. The early church theologian Ambrosiaster was quite willing to acknowledge the Holy Spirit as the source of truth in all philosophies and religions: "All truth, no matter where it comes from, is from the Holy Spirit."[54] The Lutheran Pietist Count Zinzendorf held that the Spirit went ahead of the missionaries preparing people in other lands to receive the Word of God. In our time the Korean theologian Chung Hyun-Kyung created an uproar at the 1991 Canberra Assembly of the World Council of Churches when she claimed to discern "icons of the Holy Spirit" in the suffering of her people.[55] Amy Plantinga Pauw advances the view that "if the Holy Spirit is free and universal, the church must expect surprising manifestations of it in all peoples and cultures."[56] She warns, however, that "this edge of the Spirit's work is blunted by attempts to construct a 'universal' theory of religious experience, in which the Holy Spirit masquerades as a generic term for human religiosity or world process."[57]

A pivotal question is whether the Spirit is sent from the Father only or from the Father and the Son. Both Eastern and Western churches have held that in the mission of the Spirit to the world both the Son and the Father are active in this salvific movement. This means that the purpose of the Spirit is to bring people not simply to the Father but to the Son as well. *Spiritus Creator* must not be separated from *Spiritus Redemptor.* Common grace is in the service of redeeming grace. The mission of the Spirit is not something other than the mission of the Son. Congar expresses well my own sentiments: "We simply do not know the frontiers of the Spirit's activity in this world, nor the ways in which he acts. We can only be sure that they are related to Christ, whose spiritual body is formed with men by the Spirit."[58]

Karl Barth conceived of a third circle of witnesses: prophetic voices outside the community of faith, who testify to the work of the Spirit in the world at large.[59] The first circle refers to the biblical prophets and apostles and the second to the fathers and doctors of the church through the ages. Unlike the prophets in biblical and ecclesiastical history the witnesses in the world outside the church naturally comprehend neither the source of their illumination nor their goal or *telos.*

I have no problem in speaking with Reinhold Niebuhr of a "hidden Christ" who works secretly in the non-Christian world pointing people to the One whom they only dimly recognize or may not recognize at all as the divine Savior of humanity. I do have reservations regarding Karl Rahner's concept of the "anonymous Christian," one who serves Christ and even believes in Christ without being conscious of Christ's true identity. Faith is not something implicit or unconscious but indicates a conscious decision for Christ, one that includes the assurance of being chosen by Christ. The Spirit is indeed working everywhere in human history, and his purpose is not merely to restrain the forces of evil but to prepare the way for faith in the living Christ as he is attested in the Bible. Prevenient grace is simply the first stage in redeeming grace. But against Pelagianism and semi-Pelagianism I affirm that prevenient grace is not dependent on human cooperation but instead gives rise to human seeking, a seeking that hopefully will eventuate in saving faith, though not necessarily. The Spirit is not only the source of believing in Christ but also the source of seeking for Christ. In addition he enables us to remain in Christ in the life of costly discipleship.

·THREE·

THE DESCENT
OF THE SPIRIT IN
BIBLICAL
UNDERSTANDING

Then you send your Spirit, and new life is born to
replenish all the living of the earth.

PSALM 104:30 LB

In him you also, when you had heard the word of truth,
the gospel of your salvation, and had believed in him, were
marked with the seal of the promised Holy Spirit.

EPHESIANS 1:13 NRSV

The storm of the Spirit is stronger than any other
wind. The life of the Spirit alone stands firm when all
other life is doomed to destruction.

EBERHARD ARNOLD

The Spirit is not bound to his means. He is completely
free in his mastery of the means.

REGIN PRENTER

We find in the Bible a progressive development of the idea
of Spirit, beginning with the primitive conception of Spirit
as personal power or quasi-personal invasive energy to
Spirit as a divine agency or as the living God himself in action. Spirit in

the sense of *ruah* can mean breath, water, wind, power, soul and life. It is also closely linked to fire (connoting judgment and purification)[1] and to oil or unction (signifying health and strength). In the Old Testament *ruah* is differentiated from *nephesh,* which means the life or soul of a human being. *Ruah* is supernatural and belongs to God. It can enter the human psyche but always remains something alien to human being. In the New Testament *pneuma* is what we receive from God and what becomes part of us. *Nous* on the other hand denotes that side of the human being that is open to the divine. In Isaiah 44:3-4 and Ezekiel 36:24-38 the image of water is used to describe the outpouring of the Spirit. In Ezekiel 37:9-10 the metaphors of wind and life are applied to the activity of the Spirit. Wind is a salient metaphor in John 3:8 and Acts 2:2. In Genesis 1:2 the Spirit is portrayed as hovering like a bird or sweeping like a wind. The Spirit is the source of kingly power (David), prophecy (Saul) and extraordinary strength (Samson). In the Old Testament the Spirit manifests itself primarily as mystery and power. In the New Testament the Spirit is an extension of the personal presence of God, although this idea was anticipated in the Old Testament, especially among the canonical prophets.

Divergent Views

A careful reading of the canonical books reveals three different views of the Spirit. First is the animistic, associated with primitive religion, in which the Spirit is thought of as a self-contained subject who takes possession of humans, endowing them with leadership gifts or prophetic powers.[2] This way of understanding reflects the ancient culture of which the people of Israel were a part.[3] Then there is the dynamistic view, which portrays the Spirit as an immanent vivifying force or substance. This mode of interpretation was dominant in Hellenistic culture, though in rabbinic or ritualistic Judaism the idea of Spirit as an energizing force was also very marked. The Hellenistic view gained ascendancy in the intertestamental period and constituted the background of some New Testament passages. The position that prevailed among the major prophets of Israel and continued into the New Testament depicted the Spirit as the personal presence of the living God and sometimes as a mode of God's being and action. Here the Spirit is not simply power but the power of vicarious love. He is not simply energy but the arm of Yahweh. He is not simply mystery but the God who reveals himself as master, Lord and friend. In the early strands of Old Testament history *ruah* was pictured as a distinct power, but then was gradually subordinated to Yahweh, becoming a dimension of the divine subject.[4]

Although *ruah* was originally thought of as a spirit power that falls upon people and subsequently controls their personality at least for a time, eventually it was impressed on the prophets of Israel that all spirit manifestations are under the direction and control of Yahweh. Even evil spirits were believed to be sent from God and therefore carrying out the purposes of God (cf. Judg 9:23; 1 Sam 16:23; 19:9; 1 Kings 22:23). Alasdair Heron observes that a supernatural *ruah* was only gradually drawn into Israelite religion, "subordinated to Yahweh, and consequently also refined."[5]

One can say that in Israelite history the Spirit was originally either a spirit-like being or a nonmoral invasive energy;[6] then it became an extension of the personal presence of God. Finally it began to be thought of as a person or mode of being in the Trinity. This last note is only implied even in the New Testament, but it signified the fruit of faithful reflection on biblical themes by the apostolic church.

In animistic religion the idea of Spirit represents a fusion of naturistic and personalistic motifs.[7] Conscious life is ascribed to natural objects or phenomena. In ritualistic religion Spirit is equated with a supernatural power or substance that is communicated through external rites and ceremonies. In biblical prophetic religion, which overcame both animism and ritualism, Spirit is elevated to signify the living God himself who encounters the human subject as a divine Thou. In this last view Spirit is Lord of both nature and church and cannot be manipulated or controlled by the leaders and clerics of the church.[8]

In biblical parlance the Spirit is sometimes referred to as the "Spirit of the Lord" and at other times as the "hand of the Lord," the "angel of the Lord" and the "word of the Lord" (though these terms are not always congruous with one another). All of these signify God as a personal subject who bestows power as well as communicates meaning. The Spirit definitely has a personal demeanor in 1 Kings 22:24, Ezekiel 37:9 and Isaiah 48:16. In John 14-16 the Spirit is referred to by male personal pronouns, though *pneuma* is neuter in gender. Sometimes the Spirit is spoken of as being grieved by sin (Is 63:10; Eph 4:30), which indicates the Spirit as a personal subject. Then again the Spirit can testify against the sinner (Neh 9:30), which expresses much the same view. John 4:24 states that "God is spirit," though scholars have debated whether this refers to Spirit in the generic sense or as a personal being. Bultmann is helpful in his comments on this passage: "It is not . . . an attempt to define the mode of being proper to God as he is in himself, by referring to it as the mode of being of a phenomenon from the observable world, i.e., the *pneuma*. It does, however, 'define' the *idea* of God, by saying what God *means,* viz. that for man God is the miraculous being who deals wonderfully with him."[9]

Among the charismatic prophets of the Old Testament the Spirit was often depicted as an invasive energy sometimes with quasi-personal attributes which takes possession of a human being and gains control of his or her personality. The Spirit could come mightily on a person (1 Sam 16:13; Ezek 11:5; Acts 11:15) and clothe that person with power (Judg 6:34; 14:6; cf. Lk 24:49). As biblical religion developed, the Spirit was depicted more and more as respecting the personal integrity of humans and dialoguing with rather than overwhelming them. Yet the ideas of power and possession must not be dismissed, since these belong to the person and work of the Spirit throughout biblical history. J. E. Fison observes wisely:

> This uprush of the primitive, the elemental and the unconscious, this "possession" by the Spirit, is not the be-all and end-all of the biblical evidence for the doctrine of the Holy Spirit. But it is the start-

ing point of that doctrine, and only if we are prepared to start where the Bible starts are we likely to know in experience anything of the higher reaches of the Spirit's work. We cannot jump the queue.[10]

A closely related issue is whether the Spirit is masculine or feminine. Once the Spirit is identified as personal or as a personal subject, the gender question at once becomes paramount. While *ruah* is feminine, one must keep in mind that Hebrew has no neuter gender and that neuter meanings are therefore conveyed through both feminine and masculine words. According to some scholars, the *chaos* in Genesis 1:2 has underlying it the idea of a cosmic egg hatched by a brooding spirit, though this notion is foreign to the narrative as a whole.[11] The story of the wind animating the dry bones of Ezekiel (Ezek 37:1-14) could suggest a motherly activity, though this is by no means certain. One can speculate that when Spirit means "wind" or "breath" it may have a feminine connotation, but one must not press this point unduly, since these words are basically neuter in meaning. When Spirit is used in the context of "Spirit of the Lord," it is consistently thought of as masculine. The association of the feminine *sophia* (wisdom) and *pneuma* is very evident in the apocryphal Wisdom of Solomon. While this note is also discernible in the canonical Scriptures and significantly in the New Testament,[12] in the latter Jesus Christ himself is seen as the seat of wisdom. It is he who is made our wisdom and sanctification (cf. 1 Cor 1:24, 30; Col 2:3; Eph 3:10). Texts that portray the Spirit as an almost impersonal force emanating from God are Genesis 1:2; Psalm 33:6; and Ezekiel 37:1-10. Here the Spirit is an agent in creation.

In the New Testament the Spirit increasingly takes the form of the masculine, especially in relation to the human subject (see Jn 14—16).[13] As the Spirit became identified more and more with the third person of the Trinity in the early church, the Spirit was conceived of as predominantly masculine, though the feminine dimension of the Spirit as well as of the Son was never eradicated. The Spirit was both the arm of Yahweh reaching out to a lost humanity and the counselor and comforter who accompanied the children of Yahweh on their sojourn in this world. From my perspective when the Spirit connotes the divine being taking the initiative in creation and redemption, bringing people into the kingdom, calling people to be sons and daughters of the most high God, it is appropriately designated as masculine. When the Spirit connotes a force or energy going out from God to the creation, it is probably best to describe it as neuter.

One must resist the temptation to use feminine pronouns for the Spirit, since such a practice prepares the way for a picture of God as partly male and partly female, indicating a diminishing of his triunity in favor of binitarian understanding. Yet there is a biblical basis for describing God by similes and metaphors that reveal a feminine side or dimension of his activities. We can certainly say that God or Wisdom or the Spirit of God is "like a mother" in relationship to his children. It is quite another matter to invoke God as Mother or Sister in services of public worship, since this is in effect replacing the trinitarian name for God—Father, Son and Spirit—with images that serve the cause of goddess spirituality.[14]

Transmission of the Spirit

It is God who communicates his Spirit to humanity, but the Bible makes clear that God uses various means to accomplish this end. Sometimes the Spirit is portrayed as being transmitted directly by dreams or visions. Jacob saw God face to face at Peniel, an encounter that left him limping (Gen 32:22-32).[15] Isaiah had a vision of the most high God and was cleansed by the angel of the Lord (Is 6). Peter received a direct command from the Spirit to confront Cornelius with the gospel (Acts 10:19-20). The Spirit urged Philip to go and meet the chariot (Acts 8:29), and he later snatched Philip away so that the eunuch saw him no longer (Acts 8:39).

At other times the Spirit is imparted by the laying on of hands. Moses laid his hands on Joshua, and thereby Joshua received the Spirit of wisdom (Num 27:23; Deut 34:9). In Acts 8 the Spirit was transmitted to the Samaritans when the apostles laid hands on them even though they had already been baptized (Acts 8:4-24; cf. 19:6).[16] Paul received the Spirit through the laying on of hands by Ananias (Acts 9:17).

Water is another key element in the Spirit's transmission, and often water and Spirit are used interchangeably. Ezekiel 36:24-26 points to the integral relation between water and Spirit baptism that will take place in the last days: "I will sprinkle clean water upon you, and you shall be clean from all your uncleannesses, and from all your idols I will cleanse you" (36:25). Jesus said that in order to see God we must be born of water and the Spirit (Jn 3:5). Albert Schweitzer believed that the baptism with water was given in the footwashing ceremony and the baptism with the Spirit after the resurrection (Jn 20:21-22).[17] The epistle to the Hebrews admonishes us to "draw near with a true heart in full assurance of faith, with our hearts sprinkled clean from an evil conscience and our bodies washed with pure water" (Heb 10:22). In Titus 3:5 we are told that "he saved us, not because of deeds done by us in righteousness, but in virtue of his own mercy, by the washing of regeneration and renewal in the Holy Spirit." I explore the enigmatic relationship between the Spirit and the external rite of baptism later in this book, but the New Testament makes clear that one can receive the Spirit without baptism and one can be baptized without receiving the Spirit. Apollos in Acts 18:24–25 was in the Spirit, but he had had only the baptism of John.[18] The Samaritans in Acts 8 had been baptized, but they had not yet received the Spirit. The Spirit is free to use or not use external rites and means to reveal the presence and message of Christ, but ordinarily it seems that he relates himself to us through designated means.

Oil or unction is still another means by which the Spirit communicates the life-giving energy of the Son of God or the Word of God. In the Old Testament elevation to kingship was signified by the anointing with oil (2 Kings 9:6; Ps 89:20). In 1 Samuel 10 Saul is anointed by Samuel and soon afterward receives the Spirit (vv. 1-6). In 1 Samuel 16:13 Samuel takes the horn of oil and anoints David in the midst of his brothers, and "the Spirit of the Lord came mightily upon David from that day forward." Moses is directed by God to ordain Aaron and his sons as priests by the anointing with oil (Ex 30:30-31). Prophets too were sometimes anointed with oil as a sign of being commissioned by the Spirit (Is 61:1). We read that Jesus himself was anointed with the oil of gladness (Heb 1:9), though this refers not so much to his official inauguration as Messiah when he was baptized with the Holy Spirit for power and mission as to "the joy with which God has blessed Him in acknowledgment of His vindication of divine justice."[19] In the apostolic church oil was generally a metaphor for the infusion of the Spirit rather than a special rite that guaranteed the presence of the Spirit. It was the Gnostics rather than the mainstream Christians who emphasized the importance of oil in relaying the Spirit.[20]

The proclamation of the Word of God is indeed another means or sign by which the Spirit is imparted. The Fourth Gospel testifies that the one who "utters the words of God" also "gives the Spirit" (Jn 3:34). In Acts we read that the Holy Spirit "fell on all who heard the word" (Acts 10:44). Similarly in Ephesians, all who "heard the word of truth" and believed in him "were sealed with the promised Holy Spirit" (1:13). Paul resolutely insists that the power of the Holy Spirit accompanies the witness that he as an apostle makes by both word and deed (Rom 15:18-19).

A credible case can be made that the gift of the Spirit was interpreted in different ways by the inspired witnesses of God. In some the mystical element is predominant as the Spirit is given immediately apart from rites and even words. Other passages indicate a sacramental dimension in the Spirit's outpouring—through water or unction. Nevertheless, the emphasis of the canonical prophets was on the inseparable relation of Spirit and word. Mystical phenomena were not excluded, but they were generally underplayed (with some exceptions, such as Ezekiel). The tradition of Christian mysticism was inclined to relativize the role of the sacraments and even of the word, since the goal of the Christian pilgrimage was to get beyond material signs and conceptual images to the vision of God—a direct or immediate encounter with God that is face to face. Ritualistic religion in the church has relegated the preaching of the Word to the background and has sought to contain mysticism by pressing the need for ritual observance. Primitive religion gives special emphasis to the ecstatic and paranormal in religious life, and this note is discernible in both Old and New Testaments. In biblical history the primitive and the ecstatic always loom in the background, and when they appear they are subordinated to the prophetic call to repentance and obedience.

I cannot emphasize too strongly that in the highest phase of biblical religion the Spirit is free both to impart himself and to withdraw himself. He is not a supernatural fluid that depends on external channels to reach its destination. He descends into external rites and signs by his free decision, and he relates himself to seekers after truth at his discretion. The Spirit in the fuller biblical understanding is neither an impersonal vivifying force (*dynamis*) that is transmitted by external agency, nor a personlike subject who seeks to gain possession of human agencies in order to demonstrate its power. Charisma cannot be passed on or inherited. It is a gift of the Spirit, who may work through external means but who acts freely though mysteriously in his relationship to humanity. God can withdraw his Spirit from flesh and thereby produce death (Gen 6:3). Or he can bestow his Spirit on flesh in order to produce life, even life eternal (Ezek 37:1-14). G. R. Beasley-Murray describes accurately the salient thrust in New Testament religion: "The grace offered in baptism, as in the eucharist, is no impersonal influence, injected through material substances, but *the gracious action of God Himself.*"[21]

While the Spirit can enter into human personality and direct the human will, the prophets and apostles agreed that the Spirit would not rest or abide permanently until the coming of the Messiah. An old rabbinic saying was that "the Holy Spirit that abides on the prophets does not abide except by measure." But God imparts his Spirit on his beloved Son not by measure, for Christ is permanently filled with the

Spirit and thereby lives in inseparable union with the Father (cf. Jn 3:34-36).

Dimensions of the Spirit's Activity

The Spirit of God has various roles, and it is a mistake to magnify one of these over all the others. The Spirit is active in creation, as is also the Word or Logos. He is at work in revelation, opening our eyes to the significance of what God has accomplished for us in Jesus Christ. He is the principal agent in our regeneration by which we are born anew into a life of service and freedom (cf. Ezek 36:25-27; Jn 3:1-15; 2 Cor 3:17). He preserves the people of God and indeed all of humanity from the destroying powers of sin, death and hell. He convicts people of their sins and drives them to Christ for mercy and consolation. He empowers the people of God to bear witness to Christ and triumph over the principalities of the world. Together with the other members of the Trinity the Spirit is responsible for the incarnation of God in Jesus Christ. In addition he plays a unique role in the inspiration or supervision of the writing that bears testimony to God's saving act in Christ, the writing that now forms the canon of Holy Scripture (2 Tim 3:16-17; 2 Pet 1:20-21).

The Spirit is also the source of the gifts that equip Christians for their holy vocation to be witnesses and ambassadors of the Lord Jesus Christ (cf. Is 11:2; 1 Cor 12, 14; Heb 2:4). Among these is the gift of prophecy, which includes prediction of the future. We see this in Joseph, who was enabled by the Spirit to interpret Pharaoh's dream (Gen 41:38). It is also evident in Micaiah, who foresaw the utter defeat of King Ahab's army (1 Kings 22:13-28). We find it again in Jeremiah, Isaiah, Micah, Amos, Second Isaiah and the other canonical prophets, all of whom called Israel to repentance in order to mitigate and possibly avert the impending outpouring of God's wrath.

Other spiritual gifts that spring from the working of the Spirit are healing, miracles, discerning of spirits, tongues, the interpretation of tongues, wisdom, preaching, teaching and leadership. Paul even describes lowly service as a gift of the Spirit (Rom 12 :7; 1 Cor 12:28). In the Old Testament craftsmanship was regarded as a spiritual gift (Ex 31:3-4; 35:31; 1 Chron 29:5). Kingship too was valued as a charism of the Spirit, at least in the cases of Saul and David. Miracles were associated with the ministries of Elijah and Elisha as well as Jesus, Peter, Paul and other apostles in the New Testament.

The emphasis in the canonical prophets was more on the gifts that relate directly to a righteous and holy life as opposed to spectacular gifts or so-called mystical phenomena—tongues, healings, levitations, mystical rapture, preternatural dreams, dancing in the Spirit, the reading of minds and so on—which were generally associated with the schools of the prophets. This does not mean that the mystical dimension ceased among the higher prophets, but they did attach much more importance to ethical behavior than to an altered state of consciousness. One should bear in mind that the canonical prophets regarded most charismatic or ecstatic prophets with considerable reserve because it seemed that their concern was with extraordinary feats of supernatural power rather than with obedience to the will of God.[22] Quite a number of these lesser prophets were condemned for basing their message on "false and deceptive visions" (Lam 2:14; cf. Is 3:12; 9:15-16; Jer 23:13-15; Ezek 13:8-16).

The Spirit pours out the blessings of almighty God on individuals and on large numbers of peoples, even nations. In Numbers we read that the Lord came down to Moses in the cloud and "spoke to him, and took some of the spirit that was upon him and put it upon the seventy elders; and when the spirit rested upon them, they prophesied" (Num 11:25). Joel predicts that the Spirit will be poured out on all flesh, meaning all the people of God, and all will be moved to prophesy (Joel 2:28-29).

Eschatological Significance
In both Old and New Testaments the gift of the Spirit is associated with the eschaton—the consummation of God's salvific purposes in the

coming of the kingdom. Isaiah declares:

> The palace will be forsaken, the populous city deserted; the hill and the watchtower will become dens for ever, a joy of wild asses, a pasture of flocks; until the Spirit is poured upon us from on high, and the wilderness becomes a fruitful field, and the fruitful field is deemed a forest. Then justice will dwell in the wilderness, and righteousness abide in the fruitful field. (32:14-16)

Zechariah foretells that living waters will flow out from Jerusalem enabling the Lord to become king over all the earth (Zech 14:8-9). The Holy Spirit will also play a pivotal role in the last days preceding the establishment of the eternal kingdom of God (Joel 2:28-32). His task will be to sustain the church amid persecution: "When they bring you to trial and deliver you up, do not be anxious beforehand what you are to say; but say whatever is given you in that hour, for it is not you who speak, but the Holy Spirit" (Mk 13:11). We are already living in the age of the Spirit, since the Spirit has been poured out on Pentecost, and the signs and wonders that he works point to eschatological fulfillment in Christ's second coming (cf. 2 Cor 3:7-18).

In rabbinic thought in the first century before Christ and also following Christ the Holy Spirit was linked to the age to come. Indeed, the new age was sometimes described as the age of the Spirit. Eminent rabbis were declared to be "worthy of the Holy Spirit," but not to possess the Holy Spirit.[23] The New Testament's depiction of the Spirit is even more strongly eschatological. R. P. C. Hanson argues cogently that "this eschatological presentation of the Holy Spirit means that the Spirit in the New Testament is not a vague influence associated with Jesus Christ but the form in which, or in whom, God appears to reign over his people at the Last Time."[24]

In his *Church Dogmatics* Karl Barth associated the work of Christ with reconciliation (Christ *for* us) and the work of the Spirit with redemption, where the focus is on Christ *in* us and in the whole of creation. Yet Barth was also convinced that God's redeeming activity is included in his reconciling work, just as redemption signifies the fulfillment or completion of reconciliation. As people of faith we are already reconciled through Christ, but we look forward to the day of redemption when the Spirit of God shall have distributed the graces of Christ to the whole of humanity.

Complementary Emphases

While the New Testament is our final norm for assessing the person and work of the Holy Spirit, we must recognize that in that corpus various traditions and interpretations exist in tension. They do not finally contradict one another, but it is sometimes difficult to discern their complementarity and unity.

The Gospel writers and apostles were definitely not saying the same thing in the same way, but they were saying something similar in different ways. In the Markan and Lukan writings the Holy Spirit is power; in Matthew the Spirit is primarily presence. In John the Spirit is both power and an indwelling spiritual principle. The emphasis in Matthew and Mark is on the purifying work of the Spirit, whereas Luke and John see the principal work of the Spirit as empowering for mission. Luke's distinctive emphasis is on the charismata, whereas Paul's preeminent concern is with salvation. For Luke the charismata are given for missionary empowering; in Paul they are imparted for the upbuilding of the church. In the Synoptic Gospels Jesus is the receiver and bearer of the Spirit; in John and Paul, Jesus is the sender of the Spirit. Hendrikus Berkhof reminds us that these two themes are not contradictory. Before Jesus could send the Spirit he had to receive the Spirit.[25] Whereas Luke stresses the consequences of the Spirit's action, Paul searches for a criterion for judging the work of the Spirit. Luke regards the baptism of the Holy Spirit as an empowering for service and mission; Paul views Spirit baptism as incorporation into the body of Christ. In Luke-Acts the charismata are perceived as ecstatic, outside human control; in Paul the faithful have them under control (1 Cor 14:32). While Luke associates the gift of tongues with empowering for service, Paul sees its significance in personal edification. Mark finds the reason for Christian baptism in the baptism of Jesus, which points forward to

Jesus' baptism into death. Luke relates Christian baptism to the descent of the Spirit at Pentecost. For Paul Christian baptism gives tangible form to the fellowship of believers.[26] In John the Spirit is imparted at the resurrection of Christ; in Acts the gift of the Spirit is bestowed at Pentecost; in Paul the gift of the Spirit is concomitant with faith.

Here again we are reminded that Scripture does not yield a systematic delineation of revealed truth; instead it constitutes a compendium of narrative and faithful reflection that together form a variegated though consistent witness to God's salvific action in the history of a particular people—the Jews—and in the life history of Jesus of Nazareth. From this variation in witness and emphasis we can derive a clear picture of God's plan of salvation as this is implemented by the Spirit in the creaturely world. This picture is trustworthy and reliable, but it is also incomplete and open-ended. In this earthly pilgrimage we will never be able to construct a finalized system of truth, as in propositional theology,[27] but we can arrive at affirmations of truth that are compelling and convincing to all who seek for deeper understanding of the gospel through the power of the Holy Spirit.

·FOUR·
FATHERS,
ENTHUSIASTS &
MYSTICS

The coming of Christ was the fulfilling of the Law,
the coming of the Holy Ghost is the fulfilling of the Gospel.
TERTULLIAN

If you have faith you will not only receive remission of your sins,
you will also do things beyond human power.
CYRIL OF JERUSALEM

All visions, revelations and impressions of heaven,
however much the spiritual man may esteem them,
are not equal in worth to the least act of humility.
JOHN OF THE CROSS

The Spirit became more and more confined to "the Church,"
until in all but name "the Church" stood above the Spirit.
JAMES D. G. DUNN

While the Bible was taken as the supreme authority for faith
and morals in the early and medieval church, this was not
sufficient to guarantee a universal consensus on the person and work of the Holy Spirit. It was generally agreed that the Holy
Spirit is equal to the other persons in the Trinity, but a subordinationist
strand persisted, reducing the role of the Spirit to carrying out the dictates of the Father and the Son. In the apostolic church the gifts or

charisms of the Spirit were prominent in the practice of ministry and worship, but by the fourth and fifth centuries the extraordinary gifts were deemphasized and the Spirit came to be thought of as increasingly under the control of the clerics of the church. A sacerdotalism replaced the priesthood of believers, and a sacramentalism came to bind the Spirit to the rituals of the church.[1]

The Church Fathers

The term *church fathers* refers to those witnesses to the truth of the gospel in the four centuries following the apostles, when the ecumenical creeds took form. Because the Eastern and Western churches were formally united in this period, the church fathers have a certain normative status throughout Christendom, though their testimony must always be subordinate to that of the apostles in the New Testament.

In the second century one can detect a growing tendency in the church to tie the impartation of the Spirit to ritual performance. Baptism itself came to be regarded as the seal of the Spirit. Confirmation was administered by the imposition of hands, often immediately following baptism, supposedly adding a special endowment of grace for the service of God. It was baptism, however, that conferred the eschatological seal of the Spirit for the day of redemption. Only in the Gnostic sects was the sealing administered with a rite of unction. Except among the Gnostics no distinction was drawn between a rite of water baptism and another of Spirit baptism.[2] In the *Shepherd of Hermas* we find the conception of penance as a restoration of the seal of the Spirit, lost by post-baptismal sin. Penance later came to be regarded as a second baptism in which sins are forgiven and the Spirit is sealed anew in the hearts of those who believe.

Origen (d. 254) was familiar with the use of chrism (consecrated oil) in the rite of initiation into the Christian community. Yet he did not attach the bestowal of the Spirit to this rite. He regarded it as a ceremony that denotes either faith in the anointed or the inward unction of the Spirit conferred in baptism. He avoided, however, the suggestion that Christian initiation consists in two parts, a negative cleansing and a positive sealing. While associating the forgiveness of sins as closely as possible with visible baptism, he was adamant that visible baptism has meaning and efficacy only when related to spiritual baptism. Origen also referred to a baptism by blood (martyrdom), which washes away our sins and allows us to take our place under the heavenly altar.

Irenaeus (second century) regarded the Word and the Spirit as the two hands of God: both are necessary for the realization of salvation in the lives of the people of God.[3] He sometimes referred to the Holy Spirit as the ladder by which we ascend to God. Irenaeus was open to the spiritual gifts and believed that those who possess prophetic gifts and speak in other tongues truly declare the mysteries of God. Such persons who engage in a charismatic ministry have become truly spiritual. By contrast, those who disdain the spiritual gifts remain imperfect or carnal Christians. They possess the image of God but have not yet received the fullness of the Spirit.

Tertullian (c. 160-c. 225) was a strong believer in the sacrament of baptism, but he also saw the need for personal conversion and response to what God has done for us in Jesus Christ. "Not that in the waters we receive the Holy Spirit, but cleansed in water, and under the angel, we are prepared for the Spirit."[4] While he sometimes spoke of a postbaptismal anointing (chrismation), he seems not to have regarded this as a sacramental sign of the gift of the Spirit. He also advanced the view that the medium of the descent of the Spirit is not the "seal" given in baptism but the laying on of hands. Tertullian was not always consistent, but his refusal to tie the Spirit absolutely to any external rite and his reservations concerning infant baptism reveal his commitment to the biblical principle that baptism, repentance and faith belong together. Tertullian exhorted the newly baptized as they emerged from the font of baptism to pray for a "distribution of the charisms."[5]

Clement of Alexandria (c. 150-c. 215) appears to have held a similar view, for he regarded the baptized convert as not yet being in possession of "the perfect gift." Yet he did not view baptism as deficient and in need of being fulfilled in a special rite of confirmation. The spiritual gifts are conveyed through baptism itself, not in a rite of unction or a laying on of hands after baptism.[6] The "perfect gift" must signify the final state of perfection foreshadowed in baptism.

Cyprian (d. 258) was the first writer who directly associated the seal of the Spirit with the laying on of hands. Yet baptism was still regarded as fundamental for initiation into the family of God, though as a purely outward rite it cannot stand by itself. Those who are baptized must be presented to the bishops, by whose prayers and imposition of hands "they receive the Holy Ghost and are perfected with the seal of the Lord."[7] For "water alone is not able to cleanse away sins, and to sanctify a man, unless he also has the Holy Spirit."[8] Cyprian found infant baptism prefigured in Jewish circumcision.

For Cyril of Jerusalem (c. 315-386) what saves is not the rite itself but baptism joined with repentance, faith and piety. "Upon you also, if you possess sincere piety, the Holy Spirit will descend."[9] The water may confer on the seeking person the blessing of the church but not the Spirit. Cyril acknowledged a "second kind of faith," a "special gift" that enables us to do things beyond human power.[10] He sometimes saw the rite of baptism climaxing in an anointing with chrism. In his view martyrs do not need baptism by water, since they experience a baptism of blood. Cyril added to the list of spiritual gifts chastity, virginity, readiness for martyrdom and voluntary poverty.

Basil of Caesarea (c. 330-379) likewise underscored the integral relation between baptism and personal faith. While faith receives its completion in baptism, baptism is founded in faith. "The profession of faith leads us to salvation, and then baptism follows, sealing our affirmation."[11] Even so, Basil sometimes gave the impression that salvation rests wholly on the rite of baptism: "How will you enter Paradise without having been sealed by Baptism? The flaming sword turns its back upon the faithful, but presents its edge to the unsealed."[12]

Few theologians have emphasized the efficacy of the sacramental rites of the church more than Augustine. He believed that in baptism we are stamped with a *character indelibilis*.[13] At the same time he was convinced that the outward rite has little power without personal conversion and commitment. "Faith and conversion of heart can fill up what is lacking in baptism."[14] Even in his anti-Pelagian period he did not believe the sign has actual power to effect grace.[15] Now and again he alluded to a rite of chrismation that assumed the status of a *sacramentum* distinct from baptism.

The church fathers generally agreed that while the outward seal is baptism, the inward seal is the Holy Spirit. Lampe wisely observes:

> It is sometimes dangerously easy to become so fully preoccupied with detailed problems of the manner of the seal's bestowal—Baptism, consignation, the imposition of hands—and to become so far confused by the patristic tendency to apply the term "seal" to external rites, that one forgets that orthodox doctrine does not really lose sight of the essential truth that the seal which is impressed upon the faithful is in the last resort no outward sign but the activity and presence of the Holy Spirit.[16]

Later Development in Catholicism

While the original baptismal rite included the laying on of hands and also sometimes an anointing with chrism, little by little baptism with water became separated from the other parts of Christian initiation. Finally a second rite or sacrament resulted, called at first consignation, then confirmation. Already toward the end of the fourth century Pacianus, bishop of Barcelona, could say: "In baptism our sins are cleansed, in confirmation the Spirit is poured upon us."[17] Pope Leo the Great (fifth century) contended that heretics returning to the church should have hands laid on them, for they had only received the form of baptism without the virtue of sanctification. At the end of the fifth century John the Deacon held that the gift of the Spirit is given proleptically at baptism but not realized in its fullness until confirmation.

In addition to chrism and the laying on of hands, the sign of the cross was eventually added to the baptismal ceremony of initiation. It was so powerful a symbol that it came to be identified with the Pauline seal of the Spirit and was regarded as the completion of baptism. Whereas in the East chrism was seen as the seal of the Spirit, in the West this seal was sometimes identified with the laying on of hands after baptism or the sign of the cross, sometimes performed with oil.

In the West confirmation developed into a sacrament of the empowering of the Spirit. Its peculiar role was to equip Christians for spiritual warfare. It served not so much the forgiveness of sins as the increase and defense of righteousness. Whereas baptism was the sacrament of the new birth, confirmation came to be considered the sacrament of growth and spiritual maturity.

For Thomas Aquinas (c. 1225-1274) confirmation is not the sealing of the Spirit, but the sign of the cross conferred at confirmation is the outward badge or sign of the Christian soldier. At confirmation we are granted the sevenfold gifts of the Spirit. Confirmation is thus a strengthening rite. It perfects baptism and penance and therefore confers a fuller remission of sins. Yet its primary purpose is to strengthen us for righteousness. Thomas considered chrism as absolutely essential for the sacrament of confirmation, but he did not mention the laying on of hands. Interestingly Thomas used the phrase "baptism of the Holy Spirit" to refer to the inner baptism assured to one who earnestly desires to be born again but is unable for any reason to be baptized. Catherine of Siena employed the term "baptism of fire" in the same sense.[18]

In both East and West Christian initiation came to be regarded as incomplete apart from confirmation. One was not a perfect Christian unless one was anointed by the bishop with holy oil. In the West the laying on of hands was included in the initiatory rite, but chrism was seen as the essential element. The indwelling of the Spirit begins in baptism; the seven gifts of the Spirit (based on Is 11:1-3) are bestowed at confirmation. It is in confirmation that we receive the fullness of the Spirit.

In popular devotion the baptism with the Spirit and fire was regarded as subsequent to water baptism. Spirit baptism was often linked to the rite of confirmation, at other times to a special infusion of love or upsurge of power. This desire for a higher gift of the Spirit beyond baptism is reflected in this Latin hymn of the ninth century:

Come, Holy Ghost, our souls inspire

And lighten with celestial fire;

Thou the anointing Spirit art,

Who dost thy sevenfold gifts impart.[19]

In the modern Catholic liturgical rite for confirmation the bishop's prayer is: "Almighty and eternal God, who in your kindness gave to these your servants a new birth through water and the Holy Spirit, and granted to them remission of all their sins; send forth from heaven upon them your sevenfold Spirit, the Holy Consoler."[20] The words in the confirming rite itself are: "I sign you with the sign of the cross and I confirm you with the Chrism of salvation."[21] In September of 1971 Pope Paul VI announced a new rite of confirmation. The new words revert to a fourth-century Byzantine formula, still used by most Eastern Catholic and Orthodox churches: "Receive the seal of the gift of the Holy Spirit," or something similar.[22]

It is well to note that the developing monastic spirituality also postulated a twofold blessing of the Spirit. In baptism we receive the remission of sins; in monastic dedication we receive the fullness of the Holy Spirit. The latter was often envisaged as a second conversion or a second Pentecost. For the desert monks a commitment to the monastic vocation "was rewarded by a living awareness of the Holy Spirit, and a life open to the charismatic and the miraculous."[23] The commissioning to life in a monastic religious order was viewed not as the seal of the Spirit but as a new empowering of the Spirit for vocation. Conversion then meant a retiring from the world and a commitment to the religious life. Bernard of Clairvaux (1090-1153) called the monastic life a "second baptism," a "second regeneration" that "restores the divine image in the human soul and makes us Christlike."[24] Similarly Thomas Aquinas described the taking of the monastic cowl as "a second baptism," restoring the sinner to the state of innocence that he or she enjoyed when first baptized.

Although the charismatic gifts of the Spirit continued among many of the mystics of the church, they were increasingly questioned by clerics and theologians who regarded spiritual security as dependent on right order and right theology. John Chrysostom (c. 347-407) contended that the evidence of the Spirit is character, not the display of charismatic powers. The extraordinary gifts of the Spirit played a positive role in the apostolic church, but now the challenge was to live a holy life through faith working by love. In the fifth century Theodore of Mopsuestia stated that "without a doubt" the miraculous gifts of the Spirit "accompanied the effusion of the Spirit in the Apostolic age, but they have ceased long ago to find a place among us."[25] As the gifts were more and more relegated to the background by the theologians and ruling authorities of the church, they began to crop up in the new movements of religious enthusiasm that sought to fill a growing spiritual vacuum.

Religious Enthusiasm

While mainstream Catholic theology became increasingly sacramental, movements arose in and outside the church that emphasized the immediacy of spiritual experience. Some of these were in fact heresies—grave imbalances in thought or devotion—whereas others represented completely new faith orientations that often assumed a Christian veneer. All these movements can be regarded as variations of religious enthusiasm, denoting a rapturous experience of being taken up into God (*en theos*) or being transported beyond materiality into the realm of pure spirit.[26] Religious enthusiasm in this sense is closely related to spiritualism, which makes the inner light rather than holy Scripture the indefeasible criterion. The appeal is often to new revelations that supplement or supersede Holy Writ. A religious enthusiast is also likely to be a perfectionist, since the promise of the Spirit is the complete transformation of the human psyche. In orthodox Catholicism we can anticipate in fleeting moments the glory of the eschaton that always lies ahead of us. In religious enthusiasm we can already arrive at this beatific state through the ecstasy of being lifted out of ourselves by a special bestowal of spiritual grace.[27] Enthusiastic movements are bound to be elitist, for only the few who purify and discipline themselves can attain the state of perfect beatitude. Catholic theology has often called this superspirituality illuminism or angelism, since it claims a premature possession of the glory or rapture that is the eternal reward for faithful service.

One of the most sinister threats to the early church was Gnosticism, which denied the reality of creation as the theater of God's glory.[28] Redemption lies in disengaging the inner person or the perduring self from its bodily encasement and rising to an altogether spiritual realm. The key to release from the weight of materiality is the attainment of gnosis, which signifies not rational knowledge but intuitive self-knowledge or insight. But self-knowledge is also knowledge of God, since the self and God are identical. The Gnostic teacher Monoimus taught that we should abandon the search for a God outside ourselves and simply take ourselves as the starting point.[29] For a great many of the Gnostics, rituals like baptism become irrelevant. Of far more value is the "baptism of truth," which is found in the "renunciation of (the) world."[30] Gnostics such as Valentinus and Basilides regarded Christ primarily as the exclusive revealer, but they denied the reality and necessity of the atonement. Their inclination was to negate or downplay the humanity of Christ, which speedily led them to docetism.

Gnosticism was a wider movement than has until recently been duly recognized, and it took Jewish as well as Christian forms. What the different Gnostic movements had in common was the denigration of the physical or material world and the call to descent into the inner recesses of the self. Unlike the Neoplatonists, the Gnostics regarded evil not as a privation of the good but as a cosmic reality, a kingdom of evil arrayed against the kingdom of light. Evil is something objectively real and threatening. It is identified with materiality rather than with nothingness. In these movements we find an ontological or metaphysical dualism that is anticosmic. By contrast, Platonic dualism was precosmic. Where baptism was practiced among the Gnostics it signified the gaining of immortality rather than the remission of sins.

Like most enthusiasts the Gnostics were incorrigible elitists. Valentinus, a second-century Gnostic, divided humankind into three categories: first the "pneumatics," who are destined to return to the realm of pure spirit out of which they emerged; second the "psychics," who have life but not spirit and are therefore barred from entering the higher spiritual domain; and finally the "hylics," who are totally absorbed in the material world and completely die when the body dies. Many Gnostics divided believers into "psychics" and "gnostics"—the carnal Christians and the truly spiritual. Valentinus along with Cerdo and the semi-Gnostic Marcion were excommunicated as early as A.D. 150.

One of the most significant expressions of Gnosticism was Manichaeism, which took its name from its founder Mani, a Babylonian who lived from c. 216 to 276. Mani claimed to have had several revelations, one of which disclosed that he was the Holy Spirit, the third person of the Trinity. His philosophy derived from various sources. Eminently Gnostic, it supposedly rested on a higher knowledge that led to salvation. It connoted an extreme form of metaphysical dualism. The Manichaeans had their own sacred literature, rejecting the Old Testament and most of the New. They viewed the body as evil and advocated a spurious asceticism. They also appealed to reason and claimed to offer a rational solution to the problems of life.[31] In their philosophy the saints or elect are called to follow a higher rule than the auditors or hearers, renouncing marriage and abstaining from meat and wine. While the saints are assured of gaining paradise at death, the hearers are condemned to undergo repeated reincarnations before they finally attain salvation. It appears that this cult had no sacramental rites. "Knowledge and virtue alone could win salvation."[32] Hans Jonas contends that Manichaeism represented "the most monumental single embodiment of the gnostic religious principle."[33]

Another spiritual movement more anchored in biblical and church tradition was Montanism, also called "the New Prophecy," which emerged after the middle of the second century.[34] Its founder Montanus regarded himself as the mouthpiece of the Paraclete who would bring in the final revelation. The Montanists heralded the new age of the Spirit and the fulfillment of Christian baptism in a baptism of the Spirit. They were eager to reclaim the charismatic gifts, including prophecy and speaking in other tongues (glossolalia). This movement was also characterized by an ascetic rigorism: fasting laws were severe, and second marriages were strictly forbidden. Virgins often accompanied Montanus wearing heavy veils so that their faces were hidden from all men until the eschaton. It was customary for wives to live apart from their husbands so that the Lord might find them pure. The Montanists believed they had received the office of prophecy in an order of succession, and after them prophecy would cease. They placed the writings of their own prophets on a par with holy Scripture and therefore affirmed an expanded canon. They also looked forward to the imminent end of the world, which included a millennial kingdom. Tending to combine pre- and postmillennialism, they held to a dispensation of the Holy Spirit prior to Christ's second coming and the millennium. After becoming a Montanist, Tertullian labeled the Catholics "psychics" or "animal men" and the Montanists "pneumatics" or Spirit-filled. The Montanists saw themselves as the *illuminati,* the specially enlightened. Like most sectarians they harbored a negative or judgmental attitude toward the rest of Christendom. Montanism was formally condemned by Asiatic synods before A.D. 200 and with some hesitation by Pope Zephyrinus. Some scholars maintain that Montanism has unfairly received a bad press through Christian history. According to Adolf von Harnack, Montanism recaptured the vitality and enthusiasm of the New Testament church. John Wesley and many Pentecostals have viewed this movement with respect and even admiration.

Still another aberrant Spirit movement in the patristic era was

Novatianism, which like Montanism stood solidly in the apocalyptic tradition. Novatian, a Roman presbyter in the third century, preached that the second coming of Christ was imminent. He was hailed as a lat-ter-day prophet, though Catholic theologians deemed him heretical. His followers took the name "Cathari," or pure ones, anticipating the later medieval heresy by the same name.[35] The Novatians were rigor-ous ascetics, refusing to grant absolution to the lapsed. While Novatian saw himself as fairly orthodox, he was very much a subordinationist, holding that the Son is less than the Father since the Son originated from the Father.

Similarly rigoristic and moralistic were the Donatists in the fourth century, who also sought a pure church here on earth. They believed that all who tried to return to the church after having wandered into heresy should be rebaptized. They also held that a minister who fell from grace could not perform the sacraments. Their leader Donatus maintained that his followers were the 144,000 foretold in the book of Revelation, and only these would finally be saved. One of the foremost critics of Donatism in the early church was Augustine.[36]

A movement that signaled a recrudescence of gnostic motifs was the Bogomils (tenth-fifteenth centuries), which flourished for many years in the Balkans.[37] Scholars see in this aberration a precursor of the Cathari, whose influence was much more pervasive. The Bogomils affirmed a baptism with the Holy Spirit occasioned by the laying on of hands but without water. They rejected the Christian conception of matter as a vehicle of grace. They also affirmed three grades of the faithful: the elect *(electi)*, the believers *(credentes)* and the auditors or hearers *(auditores)*. One moves from one level to the next by the cere-mony of laying on of hands. Teaching a rigorous form of asceticism, they omitted from their diet every product of coition, including milk.

Less removed from Christian orthodoxy was Joachimism, founded by Joachim of Flora (c. 1132-1202).[38] Joachim postulated three ages of history based on a historical-typological interpretation of Scripture: that of the Father, that of the Son and that of the Holy Spirit. While the

Age of the Father was dominated by married laypersons, the Age of the Son witnessed the ascendancy of priests. The Age of the Spirit, which was to begin in 1260, would be led by monks. Joachimism was a restoration movement intent on inaugurating a reformed church of the Spirit akin to the early church. In contrast to orthodox Catholicism with its graded hierarchy, Joachimism was radically egalitarian. It was also consciously Johannine, focusing more on John's than on the Petrine or clerical writings. The Sermon on the Mount was to be the rule of life. The Age of the Spirit would be an age of peace in which the spirit of poverty triumphed. It would also see the union of Eastern and Western churches and the conversion of the Jews to Christianity. There would be no more need for the Eucharist and other sacraments because the Holy Spirit would rule directly over his people. The model of the new age was St. Benedict, the founder of the first great monastic order. Sometime after the death of Joachim the Spiritual Franciscans sought to realize his vision, and his writings were revered as the "eternal Gospel." Under Pope John XXII some of the Spirituals were burned by the Inquisition in 1318. Joachim's vision reappeared in the philosopher Schelling, who posited three churches: the Petrine (Catholic), the Pauline (Protestant) and the Johannine (the new spiritual church).[39]

In the later Middle Ages a new threat emerged to challenge Christian orthodoxy—the Cathari or Albigenses (twelfth-fourteenth centuries).[40] Signifying a refurbished Gnosticism, the Cathari upheld the rite of "consolation" subsequent to baptism. It was conferred by the laying on of hands. Like baptism it was believed to work the forgiveness of sins and restoration to the kingdom of God. The one who submitted to this rite became a *perfectus* (a perfected believer) and having attained this higher status was expected to eschew marriage, war, possession of property, and eating of meat, milk and eggs. Such foods were related to the sin of reproduction. The Cathari embraced a dualistic metaphysics: the world was created not by God but by an evil principle. Like many other spirituals they had a distinct preference for the Gospel of John, which they held to be the most spiritual of the Gospels.

Finally, the Friends of God of the fourteenth century stood more in the tradition of classical Christian mysticism than Gnosticism.[41] While upholding the gifts of the Spirit they were not schismatic and sought to be a leaven within the wider church. At the same time they believed that the direct experience of the Spirit takes precedence over church tradition. Ecstasy, visions, prophecy and clairvoyance were common among them. Some of their number definitely leaned toward pantheism. Mystics who were associated with the Friends of God include Henry Suso and John Tauler. The original stimulus came from Meister Eckhart, though there is no evidence that he was directly related to this fellowship. They were never an organized body but a loose association of like-minded persons. As with so many kindred groups, the free movement of the Spirit was valued over external rites and rituals.

Christian Mysticism

The spirituality that has dominated both Roman Catholicism and Eastern Orthodoxy is aptly described as mystical rather than gnostic. Yet mysticism as a spiritual movement has always existed in tension with the institutional church, with its hierarchy and sacraments. Mysticism connotes a direct experience of the divine presence, one that is ineffable and ecstatic.[42] Mystics are not necessarily religious enthusiasts, since they generally hold that we are given only a foretaste of the glory that is yet to be revealed, not the splendor of its fullness.[43] They also do not counsel separation from the church but instead encourage deeper immersion in the life of the church. This has not prevented them from being suspect in the eyes of the prelates of the church who have rightly feared that an appeal to mystical experience constitutes a challenge to church authority.

Unlike the Gnostics Christian mystics teach not an anticosmic dualism but a moral dualism that seeks to reclaim the world for the gospel. They see grace as fulfilling nature rather than negating nature. The goal in life is not a higher kind of knowledge *(gnosis)* but love, demonstrated in lowly service. The mystics affirm the polarities of eternal and temporal, spiritual and material, inside and outside, but they do not view these as dichotomies (as in gnosticism). In sharp contrast to enthusiasts and gnostics, the mystics tend to harbor a profound distrust of ecstasies and visions (though they do not spurn them), believing that these things are usually left behind in the higher stages of faith.

Among the noted mystics of the church in the East were Origen, John Cassian, Evagrius Ponticus, Gregory of Nyssa, Macarius the Great, Maximus the Confessor, Symeon the New Theologian, Pseudo-Dionysius and Gregory Palamas. In the West we have Augustine, Catherine of Genoa, Catherine of Siena, Walter Hilton, Meister Eckhart, Henry Suso, John Tauler, Bernard of Clairvaux, Bonaventure, John of the Cross and Teresa of Ávila, among others. Protestants who have embraced a mystical spirituality include Jakob Boehme, Gerhard Tersteegen, William Law, Hans Denck, Eberhard Arnold, Evelyn Underhill and Douglas Steere. A spiritual writer like Pseudo-Dionysius exerted a profound influence on both West and East.

While the mystics, unlike most religious enthusiasts, affirm the efficacy of the sacraments for faith and the spiritual life, they nonetheless call an exclusively sacramental spirituality into question. Mysticism involves a direct experience of God, which means that the mediation of the church can be bypassed. Moreover, mysticism calls us to trust in a God beyond the reach of the senses, and this implies beyond outward signs and rites. Meister Eckhart concluded: "To seek God by rituals is to get the ritual and lose God in the process."[44] Indeed, "All the sacraments point only to one spiritual truth. For this reason, do not cling to the symbols, but get to the inner truth!"[45] Symeon in the Eastern church referred to a baptism of tears that is more efficacious than the first baptism of water and oil.[46] These are tears of compunction or penitence, but they are superseded by mystical tears of joy. One critic comments: "The 'baptism of tears' is more potent than ordinary Christian baptism; for if the latter purifies us from past sins, the former purifies us from all the sins we have committed since."[47]

Although the mystics were emphatic that faith involves experience, they generally maintained that faith may prosper even when felt experience is lacking. Revealing the influence of Neoplatonism, mystic writers tend to posit four stages in the spiritual life: purgation, illumination, union and ecstasy. Mysticism in this sense is thus a pathway to salvation. Grace enables us to make the mystical ascent, but it is up to believers to prepare themselves for grace and to cooperate with grace. The mystics also speak of initial consolations, which mark the beginning of the mystic way. Then comes a growth into dryness and darkness. The beginning of the illuminative stage is often marked by what is called a second conversion.

Like many mystics, Bernard of Clairvaux taught an experience of the Holy Spirit beyond that of conversion. In his view the Spirit "communicates himself" when he works miracles "in signs and prodigies and other supernatural operations which He effects by the hands of whomsoever He pleases, renewing the wonders of bygone times, so that the events of the present may confirm our belief as to those of the past."[48]

Without denying the validity of gifts and visions, Meister Eckhart echoed the reserve that many mystics harbor toward such experiences: "Aware of it or not, people have wanted to have the 'great' experiences; they want it in this form, or they want that good thing; and this is nothing but self-will. . . . We ought to get over amusing ourselves with such raptures for the sake of that better love, and to accomplish through loving service what men most need."[49]

John of the Cross (1542-1591) also manifested the mystic distrust of what religious enthusiasts most esteem: "In order to say a little about this dark night, I shall trust neither to experience nor to knowledge, since both may fail and deceive; but, while not omitting to make such use as I can of these two things, I shall avail myself . . . of Divine Scripture; for, if we guide ourselves by this, we shall be unable to stray, since He Who speaks therein is the Holy Spirit."[50] While recognizing the proper place for the charisms of the Spirit, John of the Cross warned of the dangers of deception and excessive attachment. God does indeed instruct the soul by means of visions and other supernatural communications, yet it is not these things that bring about union with God. Only faith does that, and a fascination with charisms might well undermine the obedience of faith.

Similarly Brother Lawrence (c. 1605-1691) cautioned that we should not love God because of the sensible favors that he imparts; such favors cannot bring us as close to God as faith does in one simple act.[51] At the same time we should always be open to "the gale of the Spirit" and not impede it by setting little value on it.[52]

Among the Quietists the gifts of the Spirit were viewed with considerable suspicion, since they were thought to foster an egocentric piety.[53] François Fénelon (1651-1715) advised resting on God "only in unpretentious and plain faith, in the simplicity of the gospel receiving the consolations which he sends, but dwelling in none of them."[54] He explained the reason for his caution:

> These supernatural gifts nourish in secret the life of the old nature. It is an ambition of the most refined character, since it is wholly spiritual. But it is merely ambition, a desire to feel, to enjoy, to possess God and his gifts, to behold his light, to discern spirits, to prophesy—in short, to be an extraordinarily gifted person. For the enjoyment of revelations and delights leads the soul little by little toward a secret coveting of all these things.[55]

Such warnings should not lead us to ignore the unassailable fact that the charisms of the Spirit have been very much in evidence among the mystics. I have already mentioned the gift of tears, which has a solid biblical basis.[56] Martin of Tours (fourth century) was a noted healer and exorcist and also received visitations from angels and departed saints. Bernard of Clairvaux was blessed with the charisms of healing, preaching, miracles and wisdom. According to tradition some persons were cured instantaneously when this saint made the sign of the cross over them. Hildegard of Bingen (1098-1179), abbess of a Benedictine convent near Bingen on the Rhine, was endowed with gifts of healing, counsel and administration. It was said that hardly a sick person came to her who was not healed.[57] Francis of Assisi (1182-1226) received the stigmata as well as heavenly visions and dreams. Catherine of Siena (d. 1380) possessed the words of wisdom and knowledge, healing, discerning of spirits and prophecy. She is also reputed to have healed her confessor of the plague and to have multiplied wine in a wine vat. Nicholas of Flüe (1417-1487) allegedly had the gift of miraculous fasting and lived as a hermit for nineteen years on eucharistic bread and water.[58] Teresa of Ávila (d. 1582) was gifted with visions, leadership and wisdom. Sometimes it was reported that she swooned in the Spirit, being literally lifted up from the floor.[59] John Tauler (c. 1300-1361) had the charismatic gift of preaching; he could set an entire region aflame by his fiery tongue. Another gifted preacher was Anthony of Padua (d. 1231), who was also a worker of miracles. Vincent Ferrer (d. 1419) had a ministry that included miracles, preaching, leadership, healing and prophecy. The noted Russian mystic Seraphim of Sarov (b. 1759) was acclaimed for his healings and miracles. The *Curé d'Ars* (Jean Vianney; d. 1859) through his prayers and exorcisms healed thousands of people who were crippled spiritually and physically. He also presumably had the gift of the word of knowledge (the reading of hearts).

Speaking in tongues was also in evidence among many of the mystics, and occasionally this took the form of *xenolalia* (speaking in a foreign language unknown to the speaker). In the medieval church there were in fact more reports of xenolalia than of glossolalia (ecstatic utterance in an unknown language) and heteroglossolalia (hearing one's own language when the speaker is communicating in his or her native tongue). The last was associated with the ministry of Vincent Ferrer and Anthony of Padua.

In the mystical tradition we also find the phenomenon of jubilation—prayer without words or prayer with sighs too deep for words (Rom 8:26).[60] If glossolalia is defined as preconceptual prayer, then jubilation as many of the fathers and mystics expressed it qualifies as glossolalia. Yet jubilation is not an actual spoken language but wordless, vocalized prayer. It consists basically of wordless sounds, the utterance of cries and exclamations of joy. My view is that jubilation may on occasion take the form of glossolalia, but it properly belongs to another genre. Significantly, the mystics never related their cries of jubilation to the glossolalia of Pentecost in the book of Acts. Many of them referred to jubilation as "spiritual inebriation," which usually pertains to the early stages of the Christian faith.

Evangelical theologians have frequently complained that mystics are prone to assign a much more decisive role to the human will than to divine grace in procuring the blessings of the Spirit. Mystics are themselves divided on what part the human will plays in the salvific process, but generally they have taught that the human will must be enabled by grace to make the mystical ascent. The final gift—contemplative union—is wholly a gift of grace, though our efforts can prepare the way for this union. The anonymous author of *The Cloud of Unknowing* held that "contemplative prayer is God's gift, wholly gratuitous. No one can earn it."[61] At the same time, before receiving this gift one is obliged to purify one's conscience of all particular sins. Seraphim of Sarov taught that one could "acquire" the Holy Spirit through prayerfully repeating the name of Jesus. According to Meister Eckhart our ultimate union with God would not be possible unless we had purified ourselves by doing good.[62] John Chrysostom was convinced that it is within our power to be filled with the Spirit:

> When we purify our soul from lies, cruelty, fornication, impurity and cupidity, when we become kind-hearted, compassionate, self-disciplined, when there is no blasphemy or misplaced jesting in us— when we become worthy of it, then what will prevent the Holy Spirit from drawing near and alighting within us? And He will not only draw near, but will fill our heart.[63]

It is fair to say that the predominant stance in Christian mysticism is synergism: God does his part and we do our part in procuring our salvation. Before we are illumined we must undergo self-purification, which makes us receptive to the Spirit. This implies that Christians are co-redeemers with Christ, since we attain eternal blessedness with the aid of the Spirit.[64] In evangelical theology all the merit for our salvation belongs to Christ since he works salvation within us by his Spirit, but we are made active by his Spirit in manifesting and demonstrating this salvation. Some in the mystical tradition also use this language, but evangelical Protestants nevertheless see in mysticism a dangerous compromise with philosophical wisdom.

In the contemporary restatement of the mystical tradition, we find an effort to bring together sacramental mediation, human cooperation and divine grace. Lev Gillet, a monk in the Eastern Church, shares these words of wisdom:

> The grace of the Spirit . . . is already active in the baptism with water, as well as the grace of the Father and the grace of the Son. But there is a special sending of the Spirit to man; and a Baptism with water not completed by the Baptism with the Holy Ghost would manifest a deficient Christian life. . . . The question of Paul to the Ephesian disciples, "Did ye receive the Holy Ghost?" (Acts 19:2) is asked of every one of us. It would not be enough to answer: I have received the mystery or sacrament of the Spirit after my Baptism, when I was anointed with the holy Chrism. The question is whether and how this seed of the Spirit has been afterwards developed within the soul.[65]

Gillet contends that just as baptismal grace extends beyond the sacrament of baptism in the strict sense, so "the gift of the Holy Ghost cannot be exclusively identified with Chrisma."[66]

For the most part the mystical tradition, to its credit, seeks to hold together the gift of conversion, water baptism and the baptism of the Holy Spirit. This last is not so much a completely new experience as a renewal of grace already given to us in the sacrament. This renewal cannot be reduced to a single experience, however, but it is something that happens again and again. According to John of Ruysbroeck God perpetually visits us with new comings, with new instreamings of the brightness of his eternal birth.[67] For Meister Eckhart the spiritual person experiences anew the "outflowing of divine love" that conforms us more and more to the image of God.[68] The mystics have kept alive the New Testament call to perfection and the hope of real progress in the Christian life through the working of the Holy Spirit.

·FIVE·

REFORMATION
PERSPECTIVES

The Holy Spirit has called me through the Gospel,
enlightened me with his gifts,
and sanctified and preserved me in true faith.
LUTHER'S SMALL CATECHISM

God grants His Spirit or grace to no one,
except through or with the preceding outward Word .
SMALCALD ARTICLES

If we come to Jesus Christ by faith . . .
we shall receive gifts of His Spirit so abundantly
that we shall be able to communicate them to our neighbors.
JOHN CALVIN

For Reformation Christians,
the most important activity of the Holy Spirit
is not raising the dead here and now,
but raising to spiritual life those who "were dead in trespasses and sins."
MICHAEL HORTON

T he Protestant Reformation of the sixteenth century signaled the recovery of a theology of Word and Spirit, so evident in Irenaeus and Augustine in earlier centuries. In their treatment of both Christ and Scripture the Reformers propounded a sacramental view that distinguished between the sign and the thing signified while at the same time regarding them as inseparable. Countering a major strand in Roman Catholicism, they warned against ritualism, which made mystical union with Christ wholly contingent on ritual performance. Against the Spiritualists and enthusiasts of their time they insisted on God's deigning to meet us through external signs—baptism, the Lord's Supper and preaching in particular. The Anabaptists agreed with the magisterial Reformers that Word and Spirit belong together, though the Spiritualists tended to elevate the Spirit over the Word, thus rendering external rites superfluous.

The Twofold Baptism

Martin Luther was adamant that the work of salvation involves a twofold baptism—with water and the Spirit. Baptism with water and the Word is the channel or sign of baptism with the Spirit. It is the divinely ordained means that the Spirit uses to cleanse our hearts. Therefore water and the Word are veritable means of grace. In his comments on John 3 he contended that the new birth takes place through water and the Holy Spirit. "We are baptized in God's name, with God's Word, and with water. Thus our sin is forgiven, and we are saved from eternal death."[1]

It might appear that Luther endorsed the Catholic doctrine of baptismal regeneration. Yet he was convinced that baptism has no salvific effect unless it issues in repentance and faith. What regenerates or revivifies us is not the outward sign but the spiritual baptism that endures throughout life:

> The sacrament, or sign, of baptism is quickly over. . . . But the thing it signifies, viz., the spiritual baptism, the drowning of sin, lasts so long as we live, and is completed only in death. Then it is that man is completely sunk in baptism, and that thing comes to pass which baptism signifies. Therefore this life is nothing else than a spiritual baptism which does not cease till death.[2]

One should keep in mind that Luther distinguished between the validity of baptism and its benefit. Baptism does not benefit us until the promise is received in faith. The relation of baptism to salvation is that of promise and fulfillment, not cause and effect. The promise may not take effect until many years later.

Scholars tend to agree that Luther was not always consistent in his theology of baptism. He sometimes referred to baptism itself as the means of incorporation into the body of Christ and at other times to the Spirit as the bond of living fellowship with Christ. It seems that for him baptism with water is the beginning of a salvific process that includes repentance, faith and sanctification.

John Calvin also strongly adhered to the inseparability of the sign (baptism) and the thing signified (the gift of the Spirit). For Calvin baptism is the seal and sign of the outpouring of the Spirit. To be fully effectual baptism must be received in repentance and faith, and this involves a definite experience of God's love and grace. Children are baptized into future repentance and faith. They have the seed of faith but not yet faith in its fullness. By the seed of faith he meant the Holy Spirit, not a spiritual or metaphysical substance. Calvin more than Luther stressed the incapacity of the sign of baptism to bring about forgiveness of sins and regeneration through the Spirit. The sign must be united with the Word of proclamation and the openness of a believing heart if it is to effect salvation. Calvin insisted that the children of believers belong to Christ even before their baptism. The ground of their salvation lies in their eternal election to the covenant community of faith. Baptism and faith are confirming realities of their prior election revealed and fulfilled in Jesus Christ.

While Calvin believed that conversion and faith are the fruits of the gift of the Spirit, he nevertheless made a place for human preparations for receiving this gift. Yet these preparations are themselves possible only through the prior work of the Spirit.[3] Calvin allowed for a legal repentance that prepares the way for true repentance; only the latter proceeds from the awakening to faith. In gospel repentance we feel not only the sting of sin but also the consolation and assurance provided by the Spirit as we look to Christ alone for our salvation.

For Calvin the primary purpose of the Holy Spirit is to engraft us into the body of Christ.[4] His mission is to bring us "into the light of faith in his gospel," "regenerating" us so that we become "new creatures."[5] The

Spirit is poured out so abundantly for no other purpose than that "we might all be converted together to be the people of God and to receive Him."[6] Yet while the principal things the Spirit conveys are "the remission of sins and newness of life," the Spirit was also given to demonstrate the power of Christ by some visible gift.[7] Although the miracles of Pentecost have long since ceased,[8] the Spirit continues to energize the people of God so that they may "believe with the heart unto righteousness" and their "tongues may be framed unto true confession."[9] Spiritual power is still given by the Spirit of God to equip us to communicate the blessings of God to others.[10]

For Ulrich Zwingli the baptism of the Spirit is something quite different from water baptism. It signifies "inward enlightenment and calling when we know God and cleave to him."[11] He allows that Spirit baptism has an outward side as well—the gift of speaking in tongues—but it is given "infrequently and only to a few."[12] Only the inner baptism of the Spirit saves. The sacramental signs (water, bread, the cup) are not so much means of grace as outward testimonies to grace. Zwingli actually taught a threefold baptism: immersion in water, "whereby we are pledged individually to the Christian life"; Spirit baptism, by which we are inwardly enlightened and called; and teaching baptism, which denotes the external teaching of salvation that follows the rite of baptism. All three may be called "baptism," but only the baptism of the Spirit is indispensable for salvation.

Philipp Melanchthon was often cast in the role of a mediator between the various factions in the Reformation, and this perhaps accounts for ambiguities in his theology of baptism and salvation. By viewing faith as primarily intellectual assent to the promises of God, he separated faith from the regenerating work of the Spirit. The baptism of the Spirit becomes the inner assurance that what faith holds is true. When the mind is persuaded on the basis of rational evidence it then moves the will and heart to certainty. The Holy Spirit works through the mind to grant that certainty to the heart. Melanchthon tried to combine Luther and Erasmus so that faith becomes partly a gift of God and partly a human work.[13]

As his theology took shape Melanchthon came to understand justification in exclusively forensic terms—as a legal verdict that needs to be acknowledged by faith.[14] The indwelling of Christ by his Spirit follows justification. Faith is both induced by the Holy Spirit and at the same time prepares the way for the renewing work of the Spirit in a person's life. He could declare that "when the heart is encouraged and quickened by faith . . . it receives the Holy Spirit."[15]

Theodore Beza, Calvin's successor in Geneva, diverged from his mentor at several points. Beza distinguished between two works of grace: the first is the gift of faith and the second is sanctification.[16] Faith moreover is rendered void if it is not ratified by the second. It is the second work of grace that brings assurance, since the first grace may not persist. This contrasts with Calvin, who referred to a twofold grace (duplex gratia) rather than two separate blessings. In Calvin's view there is no forgiveness without inward cleansing, no salvation without assurance. We are summoned not to pin our hopes on a new outpouring of grace but to take refuge in the one outpouring in Jesus Christ that effectuates our redemption.

In the left-wing or radical Reformation the balance of the Reformers was further challenged by the revolutionary Spiritualists (Thomas Müntzer and the Zwickau prophets), who heralded the dawning of a new age of the Spirit. They hoped to establish a theocracy as an anticipation of this age. Müntzer and his followers spoke of an inner baptism of the cross that alone is the key to our salvation. What is crucial for our faith is not any external rite but only the inner baptism "in water and the Holy Spirit."[17] Müntzer tried to replace Scripture with the direct enlightenment of the Holy Spirit and justification by faith with the experience of the cross. He upheld the "bitter Christ," which he contrasted with the "sweet Christ" of Luther.

Evangelical Spiritualists like Kaspar Schwenckfeld and Sebastian Franck also spoke of a baptism of the Spirit and a new age of the Spirit. For them the inner Word, not the letter of Scripture, is the sole authority for faith. Their emphasis was on both the experience of the indwell-ing Christ and the demonstration of the fruits of faith in a Christian life. The spiritual baptism alone is decisive for our salvation. They did not accept the outward rite as divinely constituted or redemptive.

Andreas Karlstadt, who was at first allied with Luther but then embraced Spiritualist ideas, contended that the sacrament is not a means of grace because forgiveness is to be found only in the cross of Christ.[18] Karlstadt refused to baptize infants and regarded the Lord's Supper as only a memorial of Christ's death. Baptism should follow rather than precede the inner experience of regeneration. Karlstadt charged Luther with being lax on moral reform and called for "a faith rich in love and a love rich in faith."[19] Ministers who do not aspire to a holy life should be barred from public preaching. Karlstadt's theology shows the influence of German mysticism, especially of John Tauler and the anonymous author of the *Theologica Germanica*. Karlstadt pro-pounded an evangelical theology of the Spirit in which the Spirit was not even subject to the Scriptures.[20]

Finally we come to the Anabaptists, who affirmed with the mainline Reformers that salvation is wholly by the grace of God and yet remained open to certain Catholic themes and emphases. Theological luminaries in this movement include Melchior Hoffmann, Hans Denck, Leonhard Schiemer, Hans Hut, Menno Simons, Jacob Hutter and Bal-thasar Hubmaier.[21] Besides water baptism the Anabaptists taught a baptism of the Spirit and in addition a baptism of fire and blood. [22] The last generally refers to martyrdom, though it may also involve ongoing persecution under the cross. The baptism of the Spirit is the inward baptism to be followed by a public baptismal espousal. For Hoffmann the inner baptism is the most important and indispensable for salva-tion. Some Anabaptists thought the spiritual baptism involved a life-time of suffering; others envisioned a much briefer period, perhaps only an hour of intense anguish. The emphasis eventually came to be placed on the baptism of blood, outward suffering in the world. The baptism of blood was not infrequently regarded as the baptism with which Christ himself was finally baptized. Sometimes it was understood corporately more than individually: the suffering of the righteous remnant.

In Anabaptism the three Catholic sacraments of baptism, penance and extreme unction were transformed into three actions of grace: adult repentance, a life of contrition and penitential suffering, and the benediction of martyrdom. The last was seen as the oil of the Holy Spirit. All three acts were called baptisms.

Like the Spiritualists the Anabaptists tended to deny that baptism is a means or sign of grace. For Menno Simons Christ alone, prefigured in the Old Testament, is the preeminent sign of grace. Baptism signifies what takes place in us, or even what we do. It is a pledge of the obedience of the believer rather than a rite in which we receive the forgiveness of sins.

Many Anabaptists held that children are innocent before they come to distinguish between good and evil. Here we discern a major break with the Augustinian tradition, which was basically affirmed by the magisterial Reformation. Again, it was not uncommon among Anabaptists to contend that children are saved by virtue of Christ's atonement without baptism.

Anabaptists are sometimes portrayed as forerunners of the Pentecostal movement of the twentieth century. Yet there are marked differences. For the Anabaptists the baptism of the Spirit is essentially a salvific experience that entails much suffering. For the Pentecostals this baptism is primarily for ministry and involves an effusion of power. It is a joyful experience more than an experience of endurance under trial. As in Pentecostalism the Anabaptists spoke of human preparations for Spirit baptism—seeking, praying, obedience to God, renouncing sin, believing and separation from the world. The Spirit comes not only through hearing the Word (as in Luther) but also through bearing the cross in faith.

Like the revolutionary Spiritualists many of the Anabaptists believed that we are now entering the new age of the Spirit, which is a preparation for the eschaton itself. Melchior Hoffmann saw himself as one of two witnesses foretold in Revelation who are called to prepare people for the last judgment. Like Thomas Müntzer the Anabaptists incorporated in their theology a postmillennial motif, perhaps inherited from the Joachim movement.[23]

A New Kind of Confirmation

The Reformers strenuously objected to the Catholic sacrament of confirmation, which signaled an additional grace of the Holy Spirit for service in the name of Christ. For Luther this rite should be rejected first because it was not instituted by Christ and second because it detracted from baptism. He avowed that no further gift of the Spirit is necessary after baptism. We are sealed with the Spirit in baptism, and there is no need to be sealed again in confirmation. At the same time Luther saw the need for catechetical instruction, even culminating in a benediction of laying on of hands, which he could describe as a *ceremonia sacramentalis*. He wrote in 1520:

> Would that there were in the church such a laying on of hands as there was in apostolic times, whether we choose to call it confirmation or healing! But there is nothing left of it now but what we ourselves have invented to adorn the office of bishops, that they may not be entirely without work in the church.[24]

While Luther was adamant that the Holy Spirit is given in baptism, he did not break completely with Catholic tradition in its affirmation of a further work of the Spirit in the life of the baptized Christian. He sometimes made a distinction between *gratia* and *donum*.[25] Through the awakening to faith by grace we receive the forgiveness of sins. Through the gift of the Spirit we are enabled to fight against sin and master it. The Spirit is an agent in bringing us faith but also a gift that animates faith.

Like Luther, Calvin allowed for additional works of the Spirit beyond the gift of faith. In his interpretation of Acts 8 he opined that the Samaritans had received the Spirit with baptism but had not yet received the charismatic gifts or "visible graces" of the Spirit. With regard to the Ephesians in Acts 19 he advanced the view that they had received the Spirit of regeneration when they were baptized but still lacked the "visible graces" that confirmed and ratified their baptism. Calvin regarded the baptism of John the Baptist and his disciples as a legitimate baptism effecting the remission of sins, but Jesus' baptism with the Spirit and fire gives empowering for ministry.[26]

Calvin shared Luther's antipathy to sacramental confirmation and for the same reasons. He could disclaim confirmation as "an overt outrage against baptism, which obscures, indeed, abolishes, its function; it is a false promise of the devil, which draws us away from God's truth."[27] At the same time, he desired to return to what he believed to be an earlier practice consisting of instruction in the faith, laying on of hands and a solemn benediction. Both Luther and Calvin were mistaken regarding the earlier practice of confirmation. In the early church, confirmation was an integral part of the baptismal ceremony of initiation. The Reformers were actually the innovators, but this does not imply that their suggestions were not in accord with the intention of Scripture.[28]

Other Reformed theologians also manifested a desire to retain the form of confirmation even while altering its content. John Knox favored a refurbished rite of confirmation that included a benediction with the laying on of hands. Martin Bucer was the first to develop a liturgical rite of evangelical confirmation. He emphasized the necessity for a public reaffirmation of the baptismal vows. Anglican theology, which was markedly influenced by Bucer and Calvin, retained confirmation but as a rite of reaffirmation of faith. It basically consisted of a renewal of baptismal vows. The Prayer Book of 1549 required all confirmation candidates to be able to say the Creed, the Lord's Prayer and the Ten Commandments, and to answer the questions in the catechism. Richard Hooker tended to speak of "the illumination of God's Spirit" given at confirmation rather than a second gift of the Spirit.

The Gifts of the Spirit
The mainline Reformers affirmed the decisive role of the Holy Spirit in

creating faith and holiness, but they generally downplayed the role of the Spirit in empowering for ministry. While they had much to say on the gift of the Spirit, they regarded the gifts or charisms of the Spirit with considerable reserve. Although making a place for the Spirit's sanctifying work they were not convinced that the Spirit's miraculous work continued past the apostolic age. The Reformers rediscovered the charisms of preaching and teaching, though these did not remain charisms but became offices. The Holy Spirit became an auxiliary of the Word rather than a catalyst for the revitalization of the church.

Luther in particular was profoundly skeptical concerning claims of visions, dreams and ecstatic experiences.[29] His theology of the Word refused to grant such phenomena a revelatory status. While not denying that such things occur, he contended that we must test them to ascertain their agreement with the Word and faith. Luther acknowledged that signs and wonders accompanied the ministry of the apostles, but he insisted that they were restricted to that period. If the need arose and the gospel was threatened, the Lord might work such signs in our midst once again, but this is not the prerogative of the church. Luther was especially disturbed by the claim to such gifts by the Anabaptists and Spiritualists, whom he denounced as self-appointed "heavenly prophets." Miracles and signs do not prove the genuineness of faith:

It is true that such gifts and deeds certainly have occurred in the name of Jesus and that they will be given to none except the church of Christ. Nevertheless not all persons who have such gifts are righteous but can indeed be false Christians. For such things are given to the church not by the persons but rather by the Holy Spirit in order that those in the office and in relation to the church do many and great things which do not profit them but rather others.[30]

At first glance Calvin seemed to be more open to the gifts of the Spirit: "God does not disappoint us when he promises us his gifts. Hence both pardon of sins and newness of life are certainly offered to us and received by us in Baptism."[31] Therefore, "Let us not doubt that the Son of God displays the power of His Holy Spirit over us, that He makes us to experience His gifts, according to our need."[32] Calvin urges us to "fill our-selves fearlessly with the gifts of God's Spirit, and with his spiritual ben-efits, by which he feeds us in the hope of the heavenly life, for in so doing we cannot do amiss."[33] Yet the context of such statements indi-cates that Calvin was thinking of the salvific gifts of forgiveness and the new life in the Spirit rather than the preternatural or extraordinary charisms of the Spirit.[34] With regard to the office of prophets Calvin con-cluded that "we do not have it now to such excellent degree as it was then, as is evident. For God has diminished his gifts, because of the ingratitude of the world."[35] The gift of healing "was a temporary gift, and also quickly perished partly on account of men's ungratefulness."[36] On the sign of miracles he argued that "though Christ does not expressly state whether he intends this gift to be temporary, or to remain perpetu-ally in his Church, yet it is more probable that miracles were promised only for a time, in order to give lustre to the gospel, while it was new and in a state of obscurity."[37]

When we come to the Anabaptists we are in a different spiritual atmosphere. The charismatic gifts, also sometimes called mystical phenomena, were much in evidence in the various Anabaptist sects: miracles, healings, prophecy, tongues, dancing in the Spirit and so on.[38] Yet these gifts were ordinarily not elevated above the demands to live a Christian life. The gifts were intended for the service of ministry and the building up of the body of Christ. J. Heinrich Arnold of the Bruderhof (Society of Brothers), an Anabaptist religious community originating in the twentieth century, accurately mirrors his tradition:

The experience of the Holy Spirit can never remain an individual experience: it leads to community. . . . If we ask God for the gifts of prophecy, healing, and other gifts described in 1 Corinthians 12 and 13, we need to be watchful of wanting to receive honor for having them. We should not ask for these gifts for ourselves, but only on behalf of the whole Body of Christ on earth. For ourselves we ought to ask for pure hearts, wisdom, faith, hope, and love; for more patience and more compassion.[39]

Call to Holiness

The Reformers retained the apostolic call to holiness but sharply differentiated it from the medieval conception. Luther warned, "He who tries to get to heaven by means of a holy life, good works, and personal merits, deceives himself. He who does not confess himself a sinner, can find no access to the Lord Jesus; for Christ did not die for His own, but for the sinner's sake."[40] Luther and Calvin were adamant that salvation is a free gift of God—going out to the undeserving. We receive it only by faith, and faith itself is a work of the Spirit within us. Once we have faith, however, we are challenged to demonstrate our faith in a life of good works. Our works do not earn or procure our salvation, but they show whether our salvation is genuine.

Luther contrasted personal holiness, which is always incomplete, with the alien righteousness of Jesus Christ that covers our sinfulness, thereby making us acceptable to God. We can be assured of salvation, for our hope lies in Christ, whose righteousness is imputed to all who call on him in faith and repentance. Inwardly we remain sinners, but in faith we have the power to battle against sin and overcome it. The Christian is therefore both a sinner and righteous at the same time (*simul peccator et iustus*). Our sin is within ourselves though it is being driven out by the Spirit of God. Our righteousness is outside ourselves in Jesus Christ.

Luther insisted that both our justification and sanctification are hidden from ourselves with Christ in God (cf. Col 3:3). The Spirit works sanctity within us, but this is a matter of faith and hope rather than assured possession. The saints of God will always appear to themselves as common and profane.[41] Their growth in sanctity is measured by their heightened consciousness of their own sin. Progress in sanctification is not the same as an increase in empirical piety. Sanctification involves a constant return to the alien righteousness of Christ, on which our hope of salvation rests.[42]

Calvin too sounded the call to holiness, but he held out the hope that the Christian could make demonstrable progress in sanctification. "Ours is a holy calling. It demands purity of life and nothing less; we

have been freed from sin to this end, that we may obey righteousness."[43] Personal holiness is not the condition for faith but "the true
evidence of our faith."[44] Our goal is Christian perfection, though we
must never presume that we have arrived at this blessed state. Holiness involves an unceasing struggle against sin, death and the devil.

The Anabaptists placed even more emphasis on the holy life, which
was seen as not only the fruit of grace but its crown. The medieval tendency to posit levels of spiritual attainment reappeared in Anabaptist
spirituality. Leonhard Schiemer referred to three kinds of persons: the
carnal person, the lethargic or inert person and the spiritual or alert
person.[45] These are correlative to three kinds of grace. The "first grace"
occurs when we experience "the light of the spirit" and try to resist sin
but cannot do so through our own resources. The "second grace" is
given to cause us to hunger and thirst for righteousness. The "third
grace" enables the believer to overcome all carnal tribulations and to
be victorious in every trial. The Anabaptists held out the hope of a
higher righteousness that was attainable through the sanctifying work
of the Holy Spirit, but always involving human effort and cooperation.

The Decisive Role of Experience

While the mainline Reformers emphasized the objective character of
both Christ's atonement and the sacramental sign of baptism, they
nevertheless stressed that the fruits of Christ's salvific work must be
experienced and appropriated in faith and repentance. Just as important as the promise of redemption given in baptism is the evangelical
experience of an awakened heart. Luther could say that our faith is
certain because it places us outside ourselves in the promises of Christ
that never deceive.[46] At the same time, he was equally convinced that
Christ's saving work also takes place inside ourselves through the indwelling of the Holy Spirit.[47] In his words, "No one can correctly understand God or His Word unless he has received such understanding
immediately from the Holy Spirit. But no one can receive it from the Holy
Spirit without experiencing, proving, and feeling it."[48] Yet for Luther

experience is not the basis or source of faith but its medium. Faith can exist even when experiential confirmation seems to be lacking. He could even describe faith as "a sort of knowledge or darkness that nothing can see. Yet the Christ of whom faith takes hold is sitting in this darkness as God sat in the midst of darkness on Sinai and in the temple."[49]

Like Luther, Calvin sometimes left the impression that the rite of baptism has saving efficacy. It is in baptism that God "regenerates" us and "engrafts us into the society of his church and makes us his own by adoption."[50] Yet he also insisted that "the literal baptism avails hypocrites nothing, for they receive only the naked sign: and therefore we must come to the spirit of baptism, to the thing itself."[51] We cannot claim to be saved unless we experience this salvation through the power of the Spirit. "It is not enough to know Christ as crucified and raised up from the dead, unless you experience, also, the fruit of this." We must "feel how powerful his death and resurrection are, and how efficacious they are in us."[52]

The Anabaptists were emphatic that baptism with the Spirit is not an external rite but an internal experience. Even more important than outward baptism by water is the inward or spiritual baptism, which involves faith, repentance and suffering. Their unique contribution was the conviction that spiritual baptism is not a momentary uplift but a life of endurance under trial. It involves not only the joy of salvation and the consolation of the Spirit but dying with Christ in the bearing of the cross.

David Yeago admirably summarizes the teaching of the magisterial Reformation regarding the relation of the sign and the thing signified. "The preaching of the word and the celebration of the sacraments do not justify merely by their sheer ritual performance. They justify and confer salvation insofar as they evoke the faith which relies on what they promise."[53] Yeago also seeks to counter the tendency in Lutheran circles to reduce the gospel to justification: "The content of the gospel is not justification, not forgiveness, not acceptance; the content of the gospel, what it talks about, what it promises, is Jesus Christ."[54]

As a Reformed theologian I would argue that the gospel cannot be reduced to either justification or election. The gospel is the good news that Jesus Christ came into the world to save sinners by placing them in a right relationship to God through his substitutionary sacrifice on the cross and by engrafting them into the righteousness of Christ by the purifying work of his Spirit. This gospel needs to be received in faith and repentance and demonstrated in a life of lowly service, faith working through love. It also needs to be manifested in the practice of the spiritual gifts, which both build up the church and empower the church to reach the spiritually lost for the gospel. The life of the Christian should be one of unstinting devotion to Jesus Christ in the freedom that comes to us through the outpouring of the Spirit, whose generosity is evidenced in the proliferation of spiritual gifts and an abundance of fruits of love and obedience.

A theology firmly rooted in the mainstream Reformation will also insist that the Spirit establishes the believer in a mystical union with Jesus Christ through personal faith and repentance, sealed by the rite of baptism. The Spirit is the Spirit of Christ's Sonship, not an immanent, all-pervasive World Spirit that abides in the inner recesses of nature and humanity. The Spirit calls us not to a life of unceasing introspection but to one of sacrificial service grounded in faith in the living Savior, Jesus Christ. Jesus Christ is not the core of the soul (as in an ahistorical mysticism) but the Son of God confronting us from without by his Spirit, engaging us in personal dialogue with him. We who appeal to the Bible and celebrate the Reformation affirm not a universal Spiritual Presence that can be tapped into by prescribed repetitions but a personal, living God who remains hidden until he makes himself known in Jesus Christ. We affirm not a God who is waiting to be discovered in the depths of our being but a God who takes the initiative by confronting us as Master and Teacher, Lord and Savior. We affirm a God who does not remain distant from us but who reaches out to us by his Spirit, calling us to mission in the world in the name and for the sake of Jesus.

·SIX·
POST-
REFORMATION
RENEWAL
MOVEMENTS

Let us labor to have our souls sealed with the Spirit of God,
to have further and clearer evidence of our estate in grace.
RICHARD SIBBES

I conclude that a little grace, a little love, a little of the true fear
of God are better than all the gifts.
JOHN BUNYAN

The Holy Spirit, in his indwelling, his influence and fruits,
is the sum of all grace, holiness, comfort and joy.
JONATHAN EDWARDS

Every step of progress in the Christian life
is taken by a fresh and fuller appropriation of Christ by faith,
a fuller baptism of the Holy Spirit.
CHARLES FINNEY

A burgeoning interest in the spiritual life is reflected in the rise
of movements of spiritual purification after the Reformation
in the late sixteenth through the nineteenth and early twentieth centuries. My focus in this chapter is on Puritanism, Pietism, Evan-

gelicalism and the Holiness movement. These are convergent rather than divergent currents of renewal, and they often overlap. Yet each one has distinctive emphases, and this is why I treat them separately. Though emerging in the past they continue in new forms.

A common strand in all these movements is the emphasis on heart religion. It is not enough to subscribe to the tenets of the faith. One must have a palpable experience of the object of faith if one is to be regarded as a true believer. A purely theoretical knowledge of Christ must give way to an existential knowledge, often called the knowledge of acquaintance. Many of these people manifested an appreciation for the mystics of the faith, though they generally steered clear of mystics who gravitated toward pantheism.

The need to prepare the heart for the gift of grace as well as the role of disciplines of devotion that enable us to remain in the state of grace are also conspicuous in these ventures of renewal. The Puritans, Pietists and Evangelicals were united in affirming the Reformation doctrine of salvation by grace alone *(sola gratia)* and justification by faith alone *(sola fide)*, though they wished to unite these themes with the biblical call to holiness. An exclusive emphasis on faith alone was treated with grave reservations by many of the revival leaders, including John Wesley. Faith must prove itself in a life of outgoing love.

While holiness was a salient motif running through all these movements, it often lapsed into a legalistic rigorism that brought disrepute to the movements as a whole. Holiness was generally portrayed as ethical conformity to the precepts of true religion. It also contained the note of separateness from the ways of the world united with total dedication to the living Lord. In the eighteenth and nineteenth centuries holiness came to be understood as a higher happiness, reflecting a subtle accommodation to the Enlightenment. Self-denial was frequently treated as a means of self-realization, and the eros motif thereby overshadowed the agape motif. That is to say, the desire for the perfection of the self came to take precedence over the willingness to lose self in the service of the Master. Biblical themes were never eclipsed in any of these movements, however, and for the most part they remained true to the biblical imperative to deny self and take up the cross and follow Christ. The doctrine of the Holy Spirit assumed pivotal importance, for it is the Holy Spirit who enables us to believe and to serve in self-sacrificing love.

Puritanism

Puritanism is the name given to the spiritual renewal within Anglicanism that began toward the end of the sixteenth century and continues even to our day.[1] Like its kindred movement, Pietism, Puritanism emphasized the experiential dimensions of the faith. In addition it contended for purity in worship as well as in life, seeking to counter the trend toward formalism and ceremonialism. With a spirituality imbued with an iconoclastic thrust it decried images and symbols in worship, regarding the preaching of the Word as the high point in worship. At the same time, the Puritans generally held a high view of the sacraments, believing that the sign and the thing signified go together. Richard Baxter could refer to holy Communion as "the Blessed Sacrament." Lewis Bayly confessed that the sacramental bread and wine are "not bare signifying signs" but the "very body and blood" of Christ.[2] John Preston tied the baptism of the Spirit to the rite of baptism and made this rite the condition for effectual faith. For William Ames baptism is "the very beginning of regeneration," the "embryo of spiritual thirst."[3] The Puritans also encouraged self-examination before Communion.

One of the major debates in Puritanism revolved around the assurance of salvation. Whereas the Reformers taught that faith itself brings assurance, the Puritans sought a confirmatory experience that assures us that we are indeed in a state of grace. They encouraged believers to look for signs and evidences that attest the genuineness of their commitment to Christ.

The Puritans also taught the need to prepare the heart for the coming of grace.[4] Richard Sibbes contended that even a reprobate person could turn toward God's love, though this turning would not be effectual for salvation apart from the work of the Holy Spirit. Many Puritans appealed to the law of God as a means of preparing men and women for faith in the gospel. Calvin also sometimes referred to the law in this way, but he insisted that the law can prepare us for faith only when the Spirit works through it and unites it with the gospel.

Richard Sibbes is of special interest because of the significance he assigned to the role of the Holy Spirit in our salvation. He distinguished between an inward and an outward seal of the Spirit. The first indicates the regenerating work of the Spirit within us and the second the sacrament that is the sign of the gift of the Spirit.[5] But he also referred to a superadded seal in which the Spirit pours on us his power and gifts.[6] In Sibbes's theology sealing is a process. As we respond to the Spirit he does new work within us. Boldness in prayer, sanctification and assurance are the fruits of the seal of the Spirit. Sibbes acknowledged that some people are within the sphere of the Spirit but not yet sealed. He cautioned against giving too much attention to the gifts of the Spirit: "A natural man delights more in God's gifts than in his grace. If he desires grace, it is to grace himself . . . making him like unto God."[7] It is better to be with Christ in eternity than to enjoy the blessings of the Spirit in the here and now. "Why? Because they are all stained and mixed. Here our peace is interrupted with desertion and trouble. Here the joys of the Holy Ghost are mingled with sorrow."[8] Sibbes reflects the Catholic view that there is a second work of grace that confirms the gift of salvation: "Those that are in the state of grace already, they need a second grace. Those that have initial grace to be set in a good course, they need confirming and strengthening grace."[9]

Whereas Sibbes continued to work within the Anglican Church, most Puritans, including John Owen, chose the way of independence. Owen posited a preliminary work of the Spirit before his regenerating or sanctifying work. Those who seek for God already have the seeds of regeneration within them. While the law is prior to the gospel, the law does not lead to the gospel except when the Spirit is at work pricking the conscience of sinners. Owen entertained the idea of a twofold sanctification or a twofold holiness, consisting of separation from sin and the implanting of a new principle in one's heart. He was especially alert to the perils of religious enthusiasm:

> The work of the Holy Spirit in regeneration does not consist in enthusiastical raptures, ecstasies, voices, or any thing of the like kind. Such things may have been pretended to by some weak and deluded persons: but the countenancing of such imaginations, or teaching men to expect them, or esteeming them as conversion to God, while holiness was neglected, is a calumny and false accusation, as our writings and preachings fully testify.[10]

Thomas Goodwin (1600-1679), aligned like Owen with the Congregational wing of Puritanism, referred to "a light beyond the light of ordinary faith": It "cometh and overpowereth a man's soul, and assureth him that God is his, and he is God's and that God loveth him from everlasting."[11] He enjoined believers to "wait for a further promise of the Holy Ghost as a sealer. . . . You shall find, Acts 1:4, that the apostles were to wait for the promise of the Spirit: so do you."[12]

The radical Puritans or Separatists, who appeared in both Britain and America, were incorrigibly congregational and often baptistic. In the first half of the seventeenth century they practiced prophecy in many of their churches. Any member of the congregation who felt moved by the Spirit would rise and deliver a spiritual message to the church. "The proper purpose of public worship was not to engage in formal prayer or to listen to pre-concocted sermons"; it was rather "to provide opportunity for the outpouring of the Spirit through the prophesying of inspired believers."[13] Some congregations held meetings for prophecy on midweek evenings. All agreed that baptism alone does not make one a member of the true church. It is necessary for regenerate Christians to form their own assemblies.

John Bunyan, claimed by both Baptists and Congregationalists, was a staunch defender of the Puritan and Reformation doctrine that we are saved wholly by grace through faith. In opposition to sectarian enthusiasts he contended vigorously that even the sanctified Christian stands in need of the remission of sins. He was also convinced that "a little grace, a little love, a little of the true fear of God are better than all the gifts."[14] He adds:

> I perceived that although gifts are good to accomplish the task they are designed for . . . yet they are empty and without power to save the soul unless God is using them. And having gifts is no sign of the man's relationship to God. This also made me see that gifts are dangerous things, not in themselves, but because of those evils of pride and vainglory that attend them. . . . Gifts are desirable, but great grace and small gifts are better than great gifts and no grace.[15]

Charles Spurgeon, who has been aptly described as the heir to the Puritans,[16] was adamant that all saving knowledge of God comes from the Spirit enlightening the mind as it reflects on holy Scripture. He disputed the claims of rationalists that "an honest and willing mind" can "learn all the truth that is in Scripture without the teaching of the Holy Spirit."[17] Indeed, to the contrary, "the Bible without the Spirit of God is but a lantern without a light."[18] An avowed opponent of the doctrine of baptismal regeneration, he emphasized the necessity for an experience of personal conversion. External rites are not insignificant, but what is of crucial importance is being baptized by the Spirit into the body of Christ. After undergoing this spiritual baptism we still need to seek "the power of the Holy Spirit" in order to make our preaching and teaching effective.[19]

While the Puritans urged their hearers to seek confirmatory signs and evidences of having received the Spirit, it is well to keep in mind that they were thinking not of miraculous gifts but of such things as a continual fighting and striving in the soul, zeal for the faith, fortitude and boldness in witnessing. They emphasized the importance of knowing the frailty and corruption of our being, and the need for supernatural regeneration and redemption. The power of God is made perfect in the recognition of our weakness. Their expectation was that the Holy Spirit might so inspire us that "by his illumination and effectual working, we may have the inward sight and feeling of our sins and natural corruptions."[20] They remained with the Reformation in expounding a theology of the cross, but supplemented it with a theology of glory, acknowledging the rightful and necessary place in the Christian life for the manifestation of power and joy in the Holy Spirit.

Pietism

A comparable force of renewal was Pietism, which signaled the rekindling of experiential religion in the Lutheran and Reformed churches in Europe.[21] Its heyday was the seventeenth and eighteenth centuries, but the movement as a whole has continued into the nineteenth and twentieth centuries, constituting a major core element in the wider constellation of evangelicalism. The key emphasis of the Pietists was on the need for a new birth *(Wiedergeburt)* through the power of the Holy Spirit. Whereas Protestant orthodoxy regarded rebirth as one element in the order of salvation *(ordo salutis)*, the Pietists saw it as encompassing the entire process of salvation. While orthodox Lutherans gained their security by looking back to their baptism, the Pietists underlined the need for a new experience, a new regeneration. They generally acknowledged the objective regenerative work of the Spirit in baptism, but anyone who falls away from baptism can only be reclaimed through a personal conversion to Christ. They affirmed the regenerative but not the continuing power of baptism. Another hallmark of Pietism was its passionate concern to live the Christian life in an era of encroaching secularism. Our salvation is meaningless unless it produces fruits of obedience that attest whether we belong to Christ. The accusation is sometimes made that Pietism tended to downgrade external preaching, that the Word became mere clothing for the Spirit.[22] This may be true of radical Pietism, but these critics overlook the indisputable fact that Pietism produced a revival of biblical, evangelical preaching.

Johann Arndt (1555-1621), whom some scholars consider the father of Pietism, was a staunch defender of Lutheran doctrine, but he also underlined the need for personal appropriation of the truths of faith. In baptism we are "adorned and beautified with the Lord Christ's own righteousness,"[23] but the Holy Spirit does not remain with us if we persist in disobedience. We may have been anointed and baptized by the Spirit in times past, but we need a fresh anointing if we are to remain faithful to our Lord. It is incumbent on us to be reborn daily through the energizing power of the Spirit. "The Holy Spirit, which enlightens the heart, flees from the godless and continually gives itself to holy souls and makes prophets and friends of God."[24] Arndt also made a place for the gifts of the Spirit in the ministry of the church: "Through the supernatural light of the Holy Spirit a higher grade of gifts can be reached than the natural heavens can bring forth. Such gifts were given to prophets and apostles."[25]

Philip Jacob Spener (1635-1705), who held Lutheran pastorates in Strassburg and Frankfurt, became engaged in ongoing controversies with Lutheran confessionalists.[26] Though maintaining a high view of baptism, he regarded baptism by itself as insufficient for salvation. It is not enough either to hear the Word with the outward ear or to receive the water of baptism. We must "feel the sealing of the Spirit and the power of the Word."[27] Spener made a distinction between "keeping the law" and "fulfilling the law." While only Christ fulfills the law, the Christian by virtue of the indwelling Holy Spirit can keep the law. In opposition to those who taught that revelation ended with the apostles in the New Testament, Spener asserted that the prophetic light of God continues to shine, though not in the same measure.[28]

August Hermann Francke (1663-1727), who was influenced by both Arndt and Spener, was an avowed defender of the religion of the heart. We must not only be baptized but also converted, and conversion is often accompanied by a decided inner struggle *(Busskampf)*. While our righteousness is in Christ alone, we can make progress toward Christian perfection with the aid of the indwelling Spirit. Yet we must never claim to be free from sin, for such presumption only prepares the way for a deeper fall. "As soon as the heart exalts itself and neither seeks nor finds its salvation purely in the forgiveness of sin, it enters upon a false way which is full of unrest."[29] It is not sufficient simply to hear or read the Word. We "must penetrate the Word and come to Christ, because without Christ as the kernel, the Word would be . . . an empty shell."[30] Francke drew on Thomas à Kempis, John Tauler and the anonymous author of the *Theologica Germanica*.[31] Unlike Spener, Francke had a crisis experience of conversion. Before that he acknowledged that he had known "little of the new reality of the Spirit."[32] With many Pietists Francke contended that once we have received the forgiveness of sin by grace, the Lord will not deny us "further assurances and fruits of his grace."[33] He was also convinced of the continuing reality of divine healing, that Christ bears our sins not only to heal us of spiritual disease but also of physical disease.[34] Francke's ministry included pastoring, teaching and works of social reform.

The colorful Moravian leader Nicholas Count Zinzendorf (1700-1760) was another luminary of Pietism whose zeal for a servant-missionary church was contagious. In contrast to Lutheran orthodoxy Zinzendorf held that saving faith includes the impetus to love. "Even if one believes, yet he will not be saved, if he does not love. . . . There is no saving faith which is not simultaneously love for Him who laid down His life for us."[35] Zinzendorf distinguished between being awakened by the Holy Spirit and being converted. The Word will be effective only if it falls into prepared soil. Zinzendorf's theology was inimical to the Wesleyan idea of inherent perfection. We are perfect only in Christ through faith. Assuredly we grow in grace, but we do not grow in holiness. Against the enthusiasts, Zinzendorf warned that "doing miracles does not belong at all to the essence of a Christian; it does not belong at all to the Gospel. It is a gift which is usually bestowed either in condescension to this or that person or from the nature of the matter, because a miracle is necessary just at that point."[36] Zinzendorf founded the Herrnhut community, a Christian communal venture dedicated to mission and renewal. At a crucial moment in its history the community experienced an outpouring of the Spirit in which feuds and hostilities were dissolved. One of its leaders, Augustus Spangenberg, wrote:

"There were we baptized by the Holy Spirit himself to one love."[37] Zinzendorf referred to this day of outpouring at Herrnhut as "its Pentecost."[38]

Gerhard Tersteegen (1697-1769) embarked on a vocation to the single life in which he became a counselor to many restive souls. While he remained in the Reformed faith, his ministry reflected aspects of both Pietism and mysticism. Faith that justifies is not the assent of the mind but the experience of being drawn to Christ. It consists in the fact that "a poor and humble sinner believes he finds forgiveness, help and salvation in Christ alone, that he draws near him with all the strength of his heart."[39] What makes us holy and blessed is not our spiritual expertise or our form of devotion but what God does in us. Tersteegen contrasted the way of pure faith with seeking higher experiences or extraordinary gifts:

> It must be admitted that the way of pure faith—the way by which the soul, following the commitment of the spirit to Jesus, lets itself be led outside itself and all created being so as to attach itself to God in spirit and in truth and serve him and partake of his communion— this is the surest way, the truest and most indispensable way; whereas the way by which souls experience extraordinary gifts, visions, ecstasies and revelations or other supernatural communications is subject to many pitfalls and misunderstandings.[40]

One of the shapers of radical Pietism was Jakob Boehme (1575-1624), German Lutheran theosophist and mystic. For many years a shoemaker, he was self-taught in theology. His commitment to the spiritualist tradition is evident in his claim that "the entire Bible lies in me." He envisaged Jacob's ladder not as the mystical hierarchy of stages but as the struggling path of obedience made possible by grace. "I did not climb up into the Godhead . . . but the Godhead climbed up in me."[41] The baptism of the Spirit occurs in conjunction with water baptism, but the process of regeneration must continue. Although married and blessed with children, he entertained a high view of celibacy. He also taught that we are about to enter the seventh age of peace and unity, after which there will be tribulation before the second coming of Christ. Boehme was influential among the Romantics and German idealists.[42]

A kindred catalyst for renewal in the Catholic Church was Jansenism, which penetrated France and the Low Countries in the seventeenth and eighteenth centuries. It was based on the writings of Cornelius Jansen, Antoine Arnauld and Saint-Cyran. Its most famous supporter was Blaise Pascal, who taught that it is the heart, not reason, that experiences God. One critic alleges that Jansenism sought "to reduce the life of grace to the experience of irresistible inner sentiments of the heart."[43] The movement was characterized by a legalistic moralism, a rigoristic penitential spirit and a gnostic sense of the mystery and inaccessibility of God. It nevertheless exuded a warm piety and a profound seriousness regarding matters of salvation. Under repression Jansenist communities experienced an outpouring of the gifts of the Spirit, including miracles, prophecy and glossolalia.[44]

Pietist spirituality reappeared in the ministries of Johann Christoph Blumhardt (1805-1880) and his son Christoph Blumhardt (1842-1919).[45] The elder Blumhardt first taught at the Basel Mission and then served pastorates at Moettlingen in 1838 and at Bad Boll in 1852. He became noted for his miraculous cures, sometimes involving exorcism. Crowds flocked to him seeking not only healing but also forgiveness of sins. Through open confession of sins many experienced healing and release. Blumhardt sought to counter the temptation common among Reformed Christians in particular of simply resigning oneself to the will of God. We should not wait with folded hands for the miraculous kingdom but participate now in God's work in fashioning a new world order. He admonished, "It is much easier to get used to a resignation to God's will, than to push aside the barriers which hold up God's help."[46] Blumhardt recovered the biblical awareness of the reality of demonic powers in the universe and the necessity to extricate ourselves and others from their grasp. He also retrieved the holy optimism of New Testament faith that the future belongs to God and that Jesus' triumph over the powers of evil will encompass the whole creation. He looked forward to a new time of grace on earth before Christ's second coming. His motto was "Jesus is Victor!" later adopted by Karl Barth, who expressed deep appreciation for Blumhardt's ministry.

Christoph Blumhardt continued the ministry of his father but regarded the coming of the kingdom as tied not only to miracles of faith but also to the battle for social justice. For a time he became involved in the socialist movement, but toward the end of his life he recognized that only God can bring in his kingdom and that our feeble efforts at social reform must not be confounded with the new order of reality inaugurated by Jesus. Blumhardt's break with a certain kind of Pietism is evident in these words: "You are God's helpers, and you will perish miserably if you do not want to help. Long enough you have called on the Savior for His help. He has done His duty from the beginning. You need not remind Him. Now it is *your* turn to stand by Him and to do something to help *Him*!"[47] Both Blumhardts emphasized the role of the Holy Spirit in bringing redemption and deliverance. As the younger Blumhardt phrased it, "There is absolutely no obstacle that can prevail against the Holy Spirit; space, time, death—all come to an end. . . . Send us the Holy Spirit! Send us the Spirit of truth, the Comforter, the Teacher! We need Him even more than thy disciples who saw Thee!"[48]

While the Pietist movement had its beginnings in Germany, Switzerland and the Low Countries, it also penetrated Scandinavia and Eastern Europe. Of special interest to this study is Ole Hallesby (d. 1961) because of the impact of his theology on the charismatic and Pentecostal movements in Scandinavia, particularly in Norway.[49] Hallesby taught systematic theology at the Free Faculty in Oslo for a number of years and was active in the Inner Mission movement. He propounded a twofold bestowal of the Spirit: first regeneration, the sign of which is baptism, and second the charismatic filling of the Spirit mediated through the laying on of hands. He also postulated a state of awakening before conversion, which typified the disciples before Pentecost.

Hallesby sought to combine the Lutheran doctrine of baptismal regeneration and the Pietistic emphasis on an experience of personal conversion. He called the entry of divine life into sinful humanity the "baptism of the Holy Spirit," and this ordinarily takes place at water baptism. But those who fall away from their baptism or whose faith is eroding need a new experience of the Spirit whereby they receive both the assurance of sins forgiven and power for service. He was emphatic that the gifts of the Spirit have not ceased and that they should be manifest in any vital church. We should not, however, regard the gifts as infallible signs of having received the Spirit, nor should we focus attention on any particular gift.

Evangelicalism

Evangelicalism in this context refers first to the awakening movement in England, Wales and the American colonies in the mid-eighteenth century and second to the wider movement of evangelical revival in the nineteenth and twentieth centuries. In both cases Evangelicalism has drawn on both Puritanism and Pietism as well as the Protestant Reformation. Evangelicalism in its later development is notable for its emphasis on salvation by free grace to be received by faith, the authority and primacy of Scripture, the substitutionary atonement of Christ, the indispensability of personal conversion, the urgency of mission and the expectation of the imminent personal return of Christ.[50] Two opposing strands in modern evangelicalism are the Calvinistic and the Arminian, the latter making room for human cooperation in the attainment of salvation.[51] In the eighteenth century the Calvinistic emphasis was prominent in George Whitefield, Daniel Rowland, Howell Harris and Jonathan Edwards, whereas Arminian motifs were conspicuous in John and Charles Wesley and Francis Asbury.

John Wesley (1703-1791) is most significant for our study, since he laid the theological foundations not only for Methodism but also for the Holiness movement and Pentecostalism.[52] Wesley envisaged salvation as a process beginning with seeking for salvation, leading to justification and sanctification, and culminating in entire sanctification or Christian perfection. The salvific process finally ends in absolute perfection or glorification, but this takes place beyond the pale of death. Wesley insisted as did many Puritans that we are justified the instant we are born again, born of the Spirit. He drew an important distinction between preliminary faith, which includes the free response to God's prevenient grace, and justifying faith, which is a sure trust and confidence in Christ. The former is the faith of a servant, the latter the faith of a son. According to his own testimony he had only preliminary faith before his Aldersgate experience, when he felt his heart "strangely warmed" after listening to a reading of Luther's preface to the Romans. Wesley believed that we can cooperate with God before and after justification. We can prepare ourselves for justification, but justification itself is an undeserved gift of God. And we can prepare ourselves only by God's Spirit.

In a palpable break with Reformation spirituality Wesley subordinated justification to sanctification, faith to love. He regarded the experience of sanctification as "a still higher salvation . . . immensely greater than that wrought when [one] was justified."[53] He called it "perfect love," "entire sanctification," "Christian perfection," "holiness" and "full salvation." This state of blessedness is not beyond the reach of sin, however, for we can still fall because we are still vulnerable. We can overcome conscious or deliberate sin, but we can never be free of involuntary sins and sins of omission. We must therefore continue to pray even as sanctified Christians, "Forgive us our trespasses." The state of holiness is a "perfecting perfection" rather than a "perfected perfection." Wesley himself never claimed to have attained this higher state, though various of his followers made the claim. He argued that sanctification is both a process and an event. Before the moment of the experience of perfect love we are moving toward it, and after this moment we continue in it. He once described sanctification as a "progressive work, carried on in the soul by slow degrees, from the time of our first turning to God."[54]

Wesley carefully refrained from calling the experience of the second blessing the baptism of the Holy Spirit. He allowed that people might refer to this second change as "receiving the Holy Ghost," but the phrase in that sense is "not scriptural and not quite proper; for they all 'received the Holy Ghost' when they were justified."[55] Wesley regarded the baptism of the Holy Spirit as incorporation into the body of Christ through repentance and faith. Water baptism was "both a means and seal of pardon," and so could be claimed as "the beginning of that total renovation, that sanctification of spirit, soul, and body."[56] Wesley also distinguished between "the witness of the Spirit" and the born-again experience. The first generally accompanies or follows the new birth and brings assurance of salvation. He did not consider the experience of assurance necessary for salvation.

Wesley was remarkably open to the gifts of the Spirit and had a high regard for the Montanists, whom he designated as the "real, scriptural Christians." Yet he never made a claim to new revelations nor did he believe that the gifts of the Spirit would necessarily reappear as the church approached the "restitution of all things." At the same time, he recorded in his *Journal* no less than 240 cases of divine healing in his ministry. While rejecting rituals of exorcism as found in the Roman Church, he would pray over people for release from their spiritual bondage. On one occasion two women who, he believed, were tormented by the devil, experienced "deliverance" after he and several brothers prayed over them.[57] Against those who asserted that glossolalia had ceased with the passing of the apostolic age, he contended that it was not only possible but "absolutely certain" that many of his converts spoke in new tongues.[58] Yet Wesley was not a religious enthusiast, for he was adamant that the focus should always be on Christ, not on our own experience. With regard to the practice of "leaping up and down" in gospel services, he remarked that such people are "honest and upright men who really feel the love of God in their hearts. But they have little experience either of the ways of God or the devices of Satan." The evil one takes advantage "of their simplicity, in order to wear them out and to bring a discredit on the work of God."[59] At the same time, Wesley was unwilling to condemn outbursts of emotion in his services and allowed that there may well be something of God in them.

Although Wesley was reluctant to identify the higher experience of salvation with Holy Spirit baptism, his followers and colleagues were not so reticent. John Fletcher acknowledged that he differed from his mentor by distinguishing "more exactly between the believer baptized with the Pentecostal power of the Holy Ghost, and the believer who, like the Apostles after our Lord's ascension, is not yet filled with that power."[60] In one of his hymns Charles Wesley petitioned the Holy Spirit to attest that we are born again and to come and baptize us with fire. He also asked for a reappearance of the gifts of the Spirit, confessing that the believer cannot rest simply on the forgiveness of sins.[61] One of the early Methodist preachers who worked with Wesley, Thomas Walsh, noted in his diary: "This morning the Lord gave me a language I knew not of, raising my soul to Him in a wondrous manner."[62] Adam Clarke (d. 1832) made a place for charismatic endowments after conversion, but he did not equate this kind of divine intervention with Spirit baptism or with sanctification. He saw it as a new work of the Spirit but was equivocal on whether charismatic gifts continue in our day.

When Methodism was transplanted to America the doctrine of entire sanctification came with it. The first Methodist preacher to come to British North America, Thomas Webb, bluntly admonished his hearers:

> The words of the text were written by the Apostles after the act of justification had passed on them. But you see, my friends, this was not enough for them. They must receive the Holy Ghost after this. So must you. You must be sanctified. But you are not. You are only Christians in part. You have not received the Holy Ghost. I know it. I can feel your spirits hanging about me like so much dead flesh.[63]

Jonathan Edwards, the chief luminary of the Great Awakening in

America, insisted that true religion must be experiential religion. It is "impossible for men to have a strong or lively trust in God when they have no lively exercises of grace, or sensible Christian experiences."[64] At the same time, our experiences of God rest not on our own strivings but on the free outpouring of God's Spirit. Edwards held to seeking prior to believing, but seeking has salvific promise only when the Holy Spirit leads us to Christ.[65] We do not receive the seal of the Spirit until the Spirit attests our election and justification through an awakening to conversion. The witness or seal of the Spirit does not consist of only one experience, that which occurred at the supposed time of conversion. Assurance is never to be enjoyed on the basis of past experience; it must be anchored in the present and continuing work of the Spirit. Moreover the Spirit ordinarily makes use of external means, such as preaching and baptism. To hold to private revelations of the Spirit is "enthusiastical." We must be cautious in pointing to external manifestations of the Spirit as infallible evidences of our state of grace. The only sure way to gain assurance is through action, daily obedience to Christ under the cross. "Christian practice is the sign of signs, in this sense that it is the great evidence which confirms and crowns all other signs of godliness."[66]

While Edwards looked forward to a great outpouring of the Holy Spirit in the latter days, he firmly believed that the extraordinary gifts of the Spirit cease when the church advances. The gifts of prophecy, miracles and tongues belong to the childhood of faith, whereas the practice of divine love is the earmark of the church in its maturity. He declared, "I had rather enjoy the sweet influences of the Spirit, showing Christ's spiritual divine beauty, infinite grace, and dying love . . . one quarter of an hour, than to have prophetical visions and revelations the whole year."[67]

In later evangelicalism the division between those who defend a second blessing and those who attribute all blessings to justification has continued. "Are we all to possess the power of 'working miracles, and speaking divers kinds of tongues?'" Charles Simeon replied categorically: "No; the time for such things is long since passed. . . . No such power exists at this day, except in the conceit of a few brain-sick enthusiasts."[68] Although experiencing an evangelical conversion, Abraham Kuyper was severely critical of an exaggerated pietism and perfectionism.[69] At the same time, he held that in addition to the Spirit's indwelling we need the Spirit's shedding abroad of love in our hearts, though these always happen together.[70] He saw the Spirit's out-pouring of love not as a single crisis experience but as a perpetual, ongoing work in the life of the believer. The evangelist Dwight L. Moody experienced an infilling of God's love after his conversion, viewing it as an empowering experience that greatly enhanced his ministry, though he recorded nothing about glossolalia.[71] R. A. Torrey contended that every Christian is entitled to receive the gifts of the Spirit, there being no essential difference between the primitive church and our day. He termed this endowment with power the baptism of the Holy Spirit and distinguished it from conversion. Against the Holiness position he insisted that Holy Spirit baptism does not take away our sinful nature. The carnal nature is held in check as one walks daily in the power of the Spirit.[72] The intrepid Presbyterian missionary to India, John Hyde (known as "Praying Hyde," d. 1911), referred to the baptism of the Spirit as a crisis experience after conversion.[73] Yet if we are to have an effective ministry we must receive the constant infilling of the Spirit that follows this baptism. John Nelson Darby (1800-1882) and other early leaders in the Plymouth Brethren movement differentiated between being born of the Spirit and being sealed with the Spirit—infused with the love of God.[74] Later evangelicalism (fundamentalism) came to distinguish between the crisis of repentance and faith, and the crisis of consecration or full surrender. The latter is the condition for receiving the fullness of the Spirit.

The Holiness Movement
The Holiness movement, which flowered in the nineteenth century and continues to advance in our day, was bent on recovering the biblical

imperatives to follow Christ in costly discipleship, to walk in scriptural holiness. This revival movement was a facet or extension of the Third Great Awakening following the Civil War, which included Dwight L. Moody, R. A. Torrey and Billy Sunday. The theological roots of the Holiness movement lie in John Wesley, who used the term "the second blessing" to denote the experience of entire sanctification after conversion. As already noted, some of Wesley's followers, including John Fletcher, referred to this experience as "the baptism of the Holy Spirit." In the words of John Oliver, a convert to Methodism in 1748: "The Lord was conquered by our instant prayer, and we had the petition we asked of Him. I was baptized with the Holy Ghost and with fire, and felt that perfect love casteth out fear. Great was our fellowship with the Father, the Son and the Holy Spirit. . . . If ever I had access to the throne of grace, it was on this memorable day."[75]

The immediate historical roots of the Holiness movement reach back into the early decades of the nineteenth century.[76] In 1832 the bishops' pastoral address to the General Conference of the Methodist Episcopal Church called for a revival of holiness. In the later 1830s Mrs. Phoebe Palmer began to conduct her famous "Tuesday Meetings for the Promotion of Holiness."[77] She was instrumental in leading hundreds of Methodist ministers to claim that grace. She referred to the experience of holiness as "the full baptism of the Holy Ghost." In 1867 the first general Holiness camp meeting was held in Vineland, New Jersey, from which came the National Association for the Promotion of Holiness.[78] In 1971 the National Holiness Association became the Christian Holiness Association. Holiness theology in Britain was modified by a distinctly Reformed emphasis, as we see in the Keswick Convention, which taught that the second blessing increases love but does not eradicate sin. This blessing involves being anointed by the Spirit for the ongoing battle against the flesh. Fellowships like the Keswick Convention and the Torchbearers urge their people to press on to a life of victory over sin, but they do not teach sinless perfection.

In the mainstream Holiness movement the baptism of the Holy

Spirit is understood as a crisis experience of sanctifying grace after conversion. This experience has been variously called "the second blessing," "heart purity," "full salvation," "scriptural holiness," "Christian perfection," "perfect love," "entire sanctification" and "the fullness of the blessing." A distinction is also sometimes made between conversion and consecration or full surrender. Holiness leaders generally follow Wesley in associating holiness with happiness, though this is always thought of as the higher happiness. In the later nineteenth century the radical wing of the Holiness movement began speaking of a third blessing—"the baptism of the Holy Ghost and fire." The ground was thereby laid for Pentecostalism, which encouraged seeking after charismatic endowment in addition to sanctifying grace.

While definitely rooted in Wesleyan theology, the Holiness movement diverges from Wesley in certain critical areas. First, it often portrays the second blessing as the complete transformation of the sinner, not a relative state of perfection that needs to be supplemented and fulfilled in sacrificial service. Wesley held that even in perfect love we can never be free from "sins" of infirmity and ignorance. He tended to avoid the term "sinless perfection," though he was accused of teaching this.[79] Second, Wesley as an Anglican maintained a higher view of the sacraments, regarding baptism as a veritable means of grace, not as a mere outward symbol of an inner experience, as is the fashion in Holiness circles. Wesley warned against religious enthusiasm—seeking an immediate encounter with God outside the structures of church and sacrament, a spirituality that is sometimes evident in Holiness churches. Third, Wesley was adamant that both justification and entire sanctification are gifts of free grace, and though we can prepare ourselves for these blessings we can never earn them or induce God to impart them to us. In contrast to this evangelical emphasis, some Holiness thinkers have advocated the attainment of a certain degree of holiness as a necessary condition for either gaining justification (John Morgan) or retaining justification (C. W. Ruth). One should note that there is presently a rethinking of Holiness theology with regard to its relation to Wesley and an attempt to recover the catholic vision of Wesley.[80]

Holiness ideas arose within Methodism but also penetrated Reformed and Presbyterian churches and even some Baptist and Quaker churches.[81] The Holiness revival gave birth to new and sometimes separatist churches, including the Salvation Army, the Christian and Missionary Alliance, the Church of the Nazarene, the Free Methodist Church, the Wesleyan Methodist Church (which later became the Wesleyan Church), the Pilgrim Holiness Church, the Pillar of Fire, the Fire Baptized Holiness Church, the Faith Mission Church, the Evangelical Friends Alliance and the Church of God (Anderson, Ind.). [82] It also gave rise to interdenominational movements of spiritual renewal including Camps Farthest Out, the Disciplined Order of Christ,[83] the Keswick movement, E. Stanley Jones's Christian Ashrams, the Torchbearers and Bethany Fellowship.

Although Holiness teaching was not an integral part of General William Booth's original position, it has penetrated deeply into the theology of the Salvation Army. Booth's emphasis was on conversion to Christ and regeneration by the Holy Spirit, but he also taught that we should seek "the fiery baptism which burns up hatred and grudges and self-seeking and self-will, and purifies all our motives and affections."[84] Catherine Booth cautioned that sanctification does not imply "final attainment," that Christian character always needs to be deepened.[85] The early motto of the Salvation Army was Blood and Fire, indicating a twofold salvation: removal of sin by the cleansing power of Jesus Christ and the baptism of Pentecostal fire.

Holiness themes were very pronounced in Samuel Brengle:

The first blessing in Jesus Christ is salvation, with its negative side of remission of sins and forgiveness, and its positive side of renewal or regeneration—the new birth—one experience. And the second blessing is entire sanctification, with its negative side of cleansing, and its positive side of filling with the Holy Ghost—one whole, rounded, glorious epochal experience.[86]

As a true Salvationist Brengle underscored the need for lowly service as a sign of our conversion and sanctification: "You who have visions of glory and rapturous delight, and so count yourselves filled with the Spirit, do these visions lead you to virtue and to lowly, loving service?"[87]

Many Salvationists did not make the kind of distinction we find in Brengle. Brigadier Albin Peyron of the French Salvation Army described his baptism with the Spirit as being awakened as if "billows of divine love were passing and repassing over him."[88] "I cannot doubt, after ten years, that I received that morning the baptism of the Holy Spirit and that the Lord in this way wished to show His approbation of my obedience in entering the path He had opened for me."[89] Yet it appears that Peyron equated this experience not with entire sanctification but with effectual conversion. Later he records that he was delivered from both sickness (bronchitis) and the very root of sin. Before his conversion he had begun seeking for Christ and had offered his services to the Salvation Army.

Perhaps no one has made a more lasting impact on revivalism in the American scene than the Presbyterian evangelist Charles Finney (1792-1875).[90] Finney posited three steps in conversion: awakening, conviction and faith. Unlike his Puritan forebears he contended that "a change of heart is the sinner's *own* act."[91] The Spirit of God invites the sinner to change, but the human subject must do the changing. Finney described his own conversion as "a mighty baptism of the Holy Ghost" that "like a wave of electricity going through and through me . . . seemed to come in waves of liquid love."[92] He later pointed to the necessity for a second baptism of the Spirit that brings sanctification. While perfectionist themes were only mildly apparent in his early preaching, they came to full flower in his later preaching and in his teaching of theology at Oberlin. In accord with the spirit of the Enlightenment, Finney regarded happiness as the highest good and holiness as a means to happiness.[93]

Also prominent in the development of a new spiritual climate that emphasized the promise of holiness beyond conversion was Joseph H. Smith (1855-1946).[94] A Methodist Holiness minister, he saw the baptism of the Spirit as empowering as well as sanctifying, a "Pentecostal baptism" that augments one's effectiveness in soul winning. Smith identified the baptism of the Spirit with the sealing of the Spirit, but not with the witness of the Spirit, which follows the new birth. As was characteristic of the major strand in the Holiness movement, he opposed healing and tongues, though he made a place for prophecy and the discerning of spirits. Smith held to the second advent of Christ but not to the promise of the millennium.

Another formative figure in the shaping of Holiness theology was the Quaker Hannah Whitall Smith (1832-1911), who was much in demand as a speaker at Holiness meetings in the nineteenth century.[95] She taught that we have everything at conversion, but we do not have it experientially until by faith we claim it. The "sanctification the Scriptures urge, as a present experience upon all believers, does not consist in maturity of growth, but in purity of heart; and this may be as complete in the early as in our later experiences."[96] She spoke of "the baptism of the Holy Ghost" as the blessing of union with God through total surrender. In her judgment "if we will only surrender ourselves utterly to the Lord, and will trust Him perfectly, we shall find our souls 'mounting up with wings as eagles' to the 'heavenly places' in Christ Jesus."[97] The disciples of Jesus are the pattern for the Christian life. They followed and believed in Jesus but were not sanctified and empowered in his service until Pentecost. The baptism of the Spirit is the revelation that the Spirit already dwells within us. Sanctification is both an event and a process. It is "not a thing to be picked up at a certain stage of our experience, and forever after possessed, but it is a life to be lived day by day, and hour by hour."[98] With Wesley she acknowledged that we can never be entirely free from sins of omission and sin in human nature, but we can be free from conscious, known sin. With many of the saints in the mystical tradition of the church, she placed being in Christ over feeling. "Pay no regard to your feelings . . . in this matter of oneness with Christ, but see to it that you have the really vital fruits of a oneness in character and walk and mind. Your emotions may be very delightful, or they may be very depressing. In neither case are they any real indications of your spiritual state."[99]

Yet another noted proponent of holiness was Andrew Murray (1828-1917), South African Reformed devotional writer and revivalist preacher. While his focus was on the inner life, he was active in South African politics, sternly opposing both British imperialism and Afrikaner nationalism. He urged people of faith to strive for the "full blessing of Pentecost," which he also called the baptism of the Holy Spirit and the indwelling of the Spirit. He distinguished between the preparatory work of the Spirit in which he acts on us and the baptizing work in which he makes his abode within us. The ideal of Christian perfection must be our goal, but it does not involve the expulsion of the presence of sin. "The holiest believer must each moment confess that he has sin within him—the flesh, namely, in which dwelleth no good thing."[100] Like Wesley and Spener he made a distinction between "having sin" and "doing sin." We have the power to refrain from committing sins, but we can never be free from tendencies within us to sin. It is through faith and repentance that revival comes. "Men would fain have a revival as the outgrowth of their agencies and progress. God's way is the opposite: it is out of death, acknowledged as the desert of sin, confessed as utter helplessness, that He revives."[101]

Daniel S. Warner (d. 1895), founder of the Church of God (Anderson, Ind.), also merits serious consideration.[102] Originally a minister in the Churches of God founded by John Winebrenner in Pennsylvania in 1830, he joined the Holiness Association after accepting Wesley's doctrine of Christian perfection. Warner distinguished between the second work of grace (sanctification) and the anointing with power, which happens ever again. He tended to refer to both experiences as the baptism of the Holy Ghost. With most other Holiness writers he regarded justification as the precondition for sanctification. Warner became a noted evangelist, healer and exorcist, though he distrusted speaking in tongues and cautioned against such bizarre manifestations of religious fervor as jerking, dancing and loud moaning. He called for a revival of spiritual disciplines, including fasting. He harbored a deep concern for Christian unity and vigorously opposed all sectarianism. A person becomes a member of the true church by a decision of faith, not by joining an institutional church.

One who has had an enduring impact on the wider evangelical movement is Oswald Chambers (1874-1917), English Baptist minister and missionary. In his theology the new birth precedes the baptism of the Spirit, salvation is prior to sanctification. He himself experienced the baptism of the Spirit after a period of depression and anxiety, but he believed that he was born again while still a child. The baptism of the Spirit brings both freedom from the tyranny of sin and the power to witness. Chambers differentiated between carnal and spiritual Christians; the latter become so by the baptism of the Spirit. At the same time he distrusted an emphasis on experiences and raptures and sternly warned against works righteousness. He also cautioned against separating Christ and the Holy Spirit. "The baptism of the Holy Ghost is not an experience apart from Jesus Christ: it is the evidence of the ascended Christ."[103] He was adamantly opposed to the tongues movement on the grounds that it denigrates rationality. "When I receive the Spirit of God, I am not lifted out of reason, but into touch with the infinite Reason of God."[104] For Chambers repentance and conviction of sin are the outcome, not the cause, of salvation. "We usurp the place of the Holy Spirit when we try to convict a man of sin first."[105]

Equally influential in the shaping of Holiness thought was A. B. Simpson (1843-1919), founder of the Christian and Missionary Alliance. Born of Scottish Covenanter Presbyterian parents on Prince Edward Island, he had a conversion experience before his ordination as a Presbyterian minister and afterward a higher life experience that he called "the baptism of the Holy Spirit." He coined the phrase "Christ our Savior, Sanctifier, Healer, and Coming Lord," which became known as "the Fourfold Gospel."[106] On the subject of spiritual gifts he warned against seeking after such experiences. Tongues are a possible manifestation of the Spirit but by no means an infallible sign or definite evidence:

One of the greatest errors is a disposition to make special manifestations an evidence of the baptism of the Holy Ghost, giving to them the name of Pentecost, as though none had received the Spirit of Pentecost but those who had the power to speak in tongues; thus leading many sincere Christians to cast away their confidence, and plunging them into the perplexity and darkness of seeking after special manifestations other than God Himself.[107]

Another prominent figure in the Christian and Missionary Alliance was A. W. Tozer (1897-1963), who transcended the Holiness tradition in various respects, though he was convinced of the need to be filled and infused with the Holy Spirit after conversion. Sometimes he envisioned this as a crisis experience; at other times as a process. Yet the filling of the Spirit is only a means to something deeper—"the life-long walk in the Spirit."[108] He was sharply critical of much popular revivalism: "By trying to pack all of salvation into one experience, or two, the advocates of instant Christianity flaunt the law of development which runs through all nature. They ignore the sanctifying effects of suffering, cross carrying and practical obedience."[109] The primary work of the Holy Spirit is not empowering for witness (though this is not to be disregarded) but the restoration of the lost soul "to intimate fellowship with God through the washing of regeneration. . . . He then goes on to illumine the newborn soul with brighter rays from the face of Christ and leads the willing heart into depths and heights of divine knowledge and communion."[110] In the tradition of many of the Christian mystics, whom he greatly admired, he emphasized being over doing. He also stressed the importance of worship, communion with God, prayer and meditation. Like so many other Holiness writers he constantly veered toward perfectionism. While affirming the death of the old nature with the infusion of the Spirit, he continued to maintain that the possibility of sin still resides within us.

As he put it in one of his hymns:

Out of the depths do I cry,
O God, to Thee!
Hide now Thy face from my sin!
Fountains of tears flow in vain;
So dark the stain
Tears cannot wash it away.[111]

He would probably have difficulty saying with Luther that the Christian is both righteous and a sinner at the same time. In Tozer's theology the Christian is forever threatened by the power of sin, but insofar as one remains in Christ one can resist and overcome this power. It is possible to be tempted and fall into sin, but it is also possible not to commit sin.

Tozer can be commended for his perspicacious critique of popular or cultural evangelicalism:

Christ calls men to carry a cross; we call them to have fun in His name. He calls them to forsake the world; we assure them that if they but accept Jesus the world is their oyster. He calls them to suffer; we call them to enjoy all the bourgeois comforts modern civilization affords. . . . He calls them to holiness; we call them to a cheap and tawdry happiness that would have been rejected with scorn by the least of the Stoic philosophers.[112]

He also scores evangelicals for their reduction of Christianity to the cerebral or rational and their neglect of mystery in worship and the mystical dimension of faith.

A similar note can be detected in Theodore Hegre (d. 1984), founder of the religious community Bethany Fellowship in Bloomington, Minnesota, which is also a training center for world mission. Hegre distinguished between the new birth (being born of the Spirit) and the crisis of sanctification (being baptized with the Spirit). The baptism of the Spirit makes us mature Christians, but we must never claim to have sinless perfection. The baptism with the Spirit brings both power and purity. "All true Christians have been baptized by the Holy Spirit into the body of Christ . . . but not all have been baptized *by Christ* with the Holy Spirit."[113] Yet Hegre insisted that even power for personal victory is not enough. He urges us to "go on into the still-deeper step of the fellowship of the sufferings of Christ."[114] The hallmark of the Christian life is "brokenness," not rapture. He posited four stages in salvation: awakening, conversion, baptism with the Holy Spirit and the fellowship of sufferings. Bethany Fellowship regards tongues-speaking as a gift that is not to be despised, a manifestation of the Spirit, not as the proof of having been baptized with the Spirit. The gifts of the Spirit are a tool chest to be used, not gems to be displayed. For Hegre the infallible evidence of Spirit baptism is the desire to glorify God in outgoing love.

No less provocative is J. Sidlow Baxter, Baptist evangelist and Bible teacher, who was trained for the ministry at Spurgeon's College in London. Baxter is critical of Wesley and the Holiness movement for teaching that sin is eradicated by the Spirit in the life of the sanctified Christian. He defines holiness as moral likeness to God—having a saintly or transfigured character. For Baxter sin is an infection that permeates our whole being, not simply an outward transgression of the moral law. Yet he contends for a second blessing after regeneration: entire sanctification. This does not imply the eradication of sin, however, but a suffusion of the Holy Spirit. This deeper work is not intrinsically different from regeneration but a maximum present development of it. "Sanctification is the *river* (in deeper or shallower degree). '*Entire* sanctification' is the river in *fullest flow*."[115] Baxter is critical of the Victorious Life theory, which stresses substitution over sanctification. Christ works holiness not in our stead but in and through our action. He also disputes the doctrine of the two natures in redeemed humanity. There is one human nature, restored and renewed by grace.

Finally, we need to give some attention to Frank Buchman (d. 1961), the charismatic Lutheran pastor who founded the Oxford Group movement, which has sought to bring spiritual renewal to nations as well as churches.[116] While attending a Keswick Holiness conference, Buchman had an evangelical experience of conversion in a small mission chapel in northern England (1908). Upon hearing a sermon on the message of the cross by a woman preacher, he came to know for the first time the transforming reality of God's love and forgiveness. He immediately sought to make restitution for his sin and to share his newfound faith with others. Buchman visited various university campuses (including Oxford, Yale, Harvard and Princeton) bringing a message of hope for a changed life to countless young people troubled by personal sin and guilt. The way to release from sin is open confession of sin and total surrender to God. It is not enough to break with sinful habits; we must then resolve to live by four absolutes—honesty, purity, unselfishness and love. We can do this through the power of the Spirit of God.[117] In 1938 the Oxford Group became Moral Re-Armament, and the emphasis shifted from changing individuals to changing nations. Yet Buchman continued to maintain that the key to social reformation lies in personal transformation. Not without some justification, Buchmanism has been accused of both moralism and perfectionism, though it has won a measure of support from such formidable theologians as Karl Heim, Sigmund Mowinckel and Emil Brunner. The famed American evangelical theologian Carl Henry attributes his conversion to Christ to the ministry of the Oxford Group.[118] One should note that Buchman continued to speak of sin and the necessity for personal moral change even in his later period when he was seeking support from leaders of the world religions. He may have underestimated the syncretistic thrust that would challenge his christocentric faith in the wake of these efforts. His own evangelical conviction was still apparent toward the end of his life, as can be seen in these words included in one of his letters:

Thou, O Christ, art all I want;
More than all in Thee I find;
Raise the fallen, cheer the faint,
Heal the sick, and lead the blind.
Just and holy is Thy Name,
I am all unrighteousness;
False and full of sin I am,
Thou art full of truth and grace.[119]

* * * * * *

Despite its signal contribution to the recovery of a robust Christianity, the Holiness movement can justly be criticized on a number of points. First, it has often fostered legalism or works righteousness because of the importance it attaches to human preparation for the gifts of salvation and sanctification. Its tendency to define holiness as conformity to a set of legal standards has created an atmosphere of rigorism that focuses on law rather than grace. Another bane of this movement is perfectionism in which claims to holiness are belied by a blatant self-righteousness.[120] It is indeed regrettable that the public prayer of confession of sin is generally absent in the worship services of Holiness churches. Holiness teaching also opens the door to subjectivism in which immediate experience of the love of God renders superfluous the role of sacraments in mediating divine grace.[121] Ironically we see in many Holiness circles a return to the Catholic conception of grace as a God-given quality that adorns the human soul rather than the disposition of mercy and favor in God's heart. The righteousness of God is then reduced to moral virtue and attainment rather than the forgiveness of sins (as in Pauline and Reformation theology). Finally, in many but not all Holiness churches the search for signs of God's favor replaces the confidence of faith in the mercy of God revealed in Jesus Christ. Private revelations—visions and dreams—sometimes obscure the sufficiency of the revelation found in the Bible.

In my judgment the strengths of the Holiness movement far outweigh its weaknesses. It has recovered the biblical call to holiness, even though the emphasis on moral conduct sometimes overshadows the celebration of mystical union with the risen Christ. It also reminds us that there are blessings of the Holy Spirit after conversion—gifts of empowering and healing. Again, it shows that in addition to the Word and sacraments, the fellowship of love and the urgency of mission properly belong to the life of the church and indeed may be regarded as necessary marks of the true church. The Holiness movement has given tangible expression to the Reformation doctrine of the priesthood of all believers through its encouragement of lay evangelists and missionaries and women in ministry. Finally, this movement has powerfully demonstrated a passion for social holiness as well as personal holiness, thereby attesting its Wesleyan credentials.[122] Holiness preachers and laity have been actively involved in such worthy causes as women's suffrage, the abolition of slavery, prohibition, civil rights and right to life.[123]

In my opinion the theology of the Reformers presents a more realistic picture of the Christian life in that the emphasis is on daily struggle rather than on final attainment. Calvin here states my own sentiments: "Those who walk after the Spirit are not such as have wholly put off all the emotions of the flesh, so that their whole life is redolent with nothing but celestial perfection; but they are those who sedulously labor to subdue and mortify the flesh, so that the love of true religion seems to reign in them."[124] At the same time, the note of victory was often eclipsed in the churches of the Reformation, and the confession of free grace sometimes became an excuse for the practice of sin. The Reformation in its dark side occasionally abetted moral defeatism, whereas the Pietists and Holiness proponents held out the possibility of triumph over sin. We are not only sinners saved by grace but also ambassadors and heralds of the advancing kingdom of God. Faith not only justifies, but faith working through love sanctifies. We are not yet in the kingdom of glory, but we are already participants in the kingdom of grace, and we are in debt to the Holiness revival for reminding us of this exhilarating truth.

·SEVEN·

NEW

CHALLENGES TO

TRADITIONAL

FAITH

God is tempted in religion itself,
when signs and wonders are demanded of him,
and are desired not for some wholesome purpose
but only for experience of them.

AUGUSTINE

Beware of that daughter of pride, enthusiasm.
Oh, keep at the utmost distance from it!

JOHN WESLEY

There is a mysticism, and there are miracles, which are worldly
and serve the "Prince of this world."

SIMON TUGWELL

The sects arose as gifts of God to the Church.
They rose for a churchly need and purpose. They were appointed to recall
the Church to this or that neglected point in the fullness of the Gospel.

PETER T. FORSYTH

I n the modern period in particular, spirituality has taken multifari-
ous forms, some that lie outside the compass of historical Christianity, others that seek to return Christianity to its roots.
Innovations do not have to be aberrations, but the former often lead

into the latter. The fire of the Holy Spirit can bring new life into a moribund church, but it can also be misunderstood and give rise to forms of faith and commitment that mirror the biases of the culture more than Christian tradition. New streams of spiritual life hold both promise and peril, and Christians sorely need the gift of discernment to make the proper evaluations.

New challenges to religious tradition do not serve the cause of truth merely by appealing to the guidance of the Spirit. Nor do they become a source of renewal simply by displaying zealous commitment and dedication. Evil spirits can also endow people with enthusiasm and vivacity. The Holy Spirit brings his resources and power to those who acclaim Jesus Christ as Lord and Savior of the world and submit to Holy Scripture as the authoritative interpretation of God's self-revelation in Christ. The work of the Spirit must always be related to the christological norm if it is to bear fruit in faith and obedience. Some of the protest and reforming movements of our time recognize this fact, but others seem oblivious to it.

Definitions

As the church establishes itself in the surrounding culture, compromises in both faith and practice are inevitable. New movements arise that are bent on recovering the zeal and fervor of an earlier period, but some of these end by distorting and undermining the faith they were designed to safeguard. Heterodoxy seeks a restatement of the faith that intentionally or unintentionally tends to obscure or call into question certain parts of the heritage of the faith. Heresy contends for a substantial revision of the faith so that the way is prepared for a new faith. Heterodoxy signifies the elevation of what is peripheral over what is essential in the faith, while heresy leads to a denial of what is essential. Apostasy as distinct from both heresy and heterodoxy represents an abandonment of the faith—either for a new faith or for unbelief.[1]

Closely related are the terms *cult* and *sect.* While a sect indicates an unbalanced emphasis on some tenet of the faith, a cult connotes a basic departure from the foundations of the faith. A sect is a theological misunderstanding; a cult is a theological aberration. A sect is a new way of understanding the faith; a cult is a new faith orientation. Sects are inclined to be too narrow; many of the cults appear to be too broad. The marks of a sect are exclusivism and fanaticism.[2] Cults are often inclusive but no less fanatical.[3] In the early church period a representative cultic movement was Gnosticism. Sectarian movements in that period included Arianism, Montanism and Donatism.[4]

In this chapter I focus on movements that are commonly identified as either sects or cults. Yet one must keep in mind that many of these are not really heretical but heterodoxical in that they foster serious though sometimes mild distortions of truth rather than outright error. Some of these bodies have a sectarian origin but are moving steadily toward orthodoxy (such as Seventh-day Adventism). By contrast, mainline denominations like the United Church of Christ and the United Church of Canada had a solid anchor in orthodoxy in their beginnings, but are now gravitating toward heterodoxy and even heresy. Some of the new ventures could possibly be classified as dissenting movements rather than cultic or sectarian movements.[5] I do not wish to offend any constituency among my readers who are aligned with any of these groups. They should keep in mind that I speak as a Reformed theologian and that my standard for orthodoxy (right thinking) may well be somewhat different from theirs.

Quakerism and Kindred Movements

The Quakers represent one of the major Spirit movements in the modern era. Founded by an intrepid English layman George Fox (1624-1691), they have made an indelible imprint on modern Christian spirituality. Fox preached that a new age of the Spirit was dawning and urged his hearers to come out of the apostate churches and form fellowships of true devotion that would cross all denominational lines. The final criterion for faith, he taught, is not the creeds nor even Scripture but the inner light, the indwelling presence of the Spirit of God in all humanity. The Quakers rejected imputed righteousness, total depravity and the Trinity. They also did away with sacraments, maintaining that the true baptism is a spiritual one that takes place in the resolve to obey Christ as Lord of all of life.[6] The true church meets in silence waiting for the Holy Spirit to move people to pray and prophesy. In a manner indicative of the sectarian bent of the early Quakers, Fox and some of his companions abruptly interrupted services of worship in the established churches in order to call people's attention to the truth of the inner light. The early Quakers often trembled in awe as the Spirit of God moved upon them, and this is how they received their name.

Their story is rooted in the story of Fox, who spent a number of years in prison because of his courageous witness to the truth as he defined it. He was endowed with many remarkable spiritual gifts, including discerning of spirits, the word of knowledge, prophecy, preaching and healing. In his *Book of Miracles* he reported over 150 healings in his ministry. He seemed to be able to read the character of people simply by looking at them. He called for a rediscovery of the gifts of the Spirit and invited all people, women as well as men, to exercise these gifts, even in meetings of public worship. Fox condemned organized religion as being devoid of spiritual power and advocated fellowships in which people would pray and sing in the Holy Spirit.[7]

Quakerism is properly classified as a spiritualistic movement in that it makes the inner witness of the Spirit the final norm for truth.[8] In a considerable segment of the Quaker community the meetings of worship do not include either sermon or sacrament; instead the worshipers sit in silence interrupted only by sporadic words of encouragement or admonition. At the same time, a strong evangelical movement has emerged in Quakerism and now accounts for most of the growth of Quaker churches, especially in the Third World. The Evangelical Friends Alliance, founded in 1965, was influenced by Holiness thought. In this group biblical preaching and hymn singing play a major role in worship, though there is no attempt to restore the sacraments to the church. Outstanding Quaker leaders and theologians after Fox include Robert Barclay, William Penn, Joseph Gurney, Hannah Whithall Smith, Anthony Benezet, John Woolman, Rufus Jones, Douglas Steere and D. Elton Trueblood.

Many of the early Quakers came out of the Seekers, a kindred spiritualist movement in the seventeenth century. The Seekers had no formal organization and refused to be led by trained or ordained ministers. They had no sacraments, creeds or defined ritual. Their informal Sunday meetings for worship consisted of unbroken silence except for prayers and messages given by laity. They championed the inner light as the only infallible source of knowledge of God. The Seekers waited for a new revelation that would bring in Christ's kingdom. They also looked forward to a new outpouring of the Holy Spirit that would include a generous bestowal of spiritual gifts. Fox had some contact with the Seekers and derived some of his ideas from them.[9]

Another colorful expression of religious enthusiasm in the seventeenth century was the Ranters, who decried church, Scriptures, ordination and regulations of any sort. In their teaching God the Father reigned under the law, the Son under the gospel; now the Father and Son are delivering the kingdom to the Holy Ghost, who will be poured out on all flesh and reign in a new world order. A pantheistic bent is discernible in this description of their beliefs by a contemporary: "A man baptized with the holy Ghost, knows all things even as God knows all things, which point is a deep mystery and great ocean, where there is no casting anchor, nor sounding the bottome."[10] They were also perfectionistic and antinomian, some of them apparently holding that the Spirit-filled cannot sin. Their appeal was neither to church nor to Scripture but to the inward experience of Christ. They also broke with traditional beliefs concerning the last things, describing heaven as a state of the soul. Some of their leaders declared that they had been "'wholly and lastingly absorbed into the divine unity' having passed beyond good and evil and thereby risen above the normal human condition."[11] The Ranters were duly criticized by both Richard Baxter and John Bunyan.

Enthusiasm in the Roman Catholic Church was conspicuous in the Convulsionaries[12] and the Quietists in the sixteenth and seventeenth centuries.[13] The Quietists held that God works best in our lives when we are completely passive and quiet. In the experience of union with God we are translated into a state of "pure love" or "mystical death." God becomes everything, the believer nothing. Quietists aimed for a wholly disinterested love, a love "without hope." In this state of "holy indifference" the Christian lives above sin and stands in need of no external aids or props, not even sacraments. Among the noted exponents of Quietist spirituality were Miguel de Molinos (d. 1697), Madame Guyon (d. 1717) and Archbishop Fénelon (d. 1715). Quietist ideas have exerted some influence on the Protestant Holiness movement, evident, for example, in the "let go, let God" emphasis of the Keswick Convention.

One of the most spectacular movements coming out of Quakerism was Shakerism, led in most of its formative years by Mother Ann Lee, an itinerant English preacher.[14] Founded by Jane and James Wardley in 1747, the sect was at first known as the Shaking Quakers and then finally as the Shakers. Its name was derived from the shaking and trembling evident in people believed to be possessed by the Holy Ghost. Out of intense religious yearnings Ann Lee was drawn to the sect and rapidly assumed full leadership. Fleeing to America with a band of devotees in order to escape religious persecution, she inspired the formation of "the United Society of Believers in Christ's Second Appearing" in the 1780s. She taught a communal ownership of goods, celibacy and a purely spiritual worship. The Shakers became organized in religious communities that included single men, single women and children, many of them orphans. After 1837 spiritism flourished, with believers seeking the aid of discarnate spirits in living a life of pure love. In the early years of the Shaker communities spiritual gifts abounded, including prophecies, visions, tongues and healings. One of their distinctive beliefs linking them to Gnosticism was that God is both male and female. The female principle was manifested in Mother Ann Lee, who was seen as the second appearance of Christ. In their view the millennium began with the founding of the Shaker church. In the 1840s twice-yearly love feasts were held during which believers were visited by American Indian spirits and the spirit of Mother Ann. Like the Quakers the Shakers believed only in the spiritual baptism, not the sacrament of water baptism. Shaker communities, which thrived in the mid-nineteenth century in America, are now practically extinct.

Swedenborgianism

Another movement oriented around new revelations from the Spirit of God is the Church of the New Jerusalem, founded by Emanuel Swedenborg (1688-1772).[15] The son of a Lutheran minister and court chaplain to the king of Sweden, he embarked on a vocation as a scientist. In his later years he suddenly gave up his scientific career and became a mystic, receiving direct, insightful information on the spiritual world that surrounds us. He described Jesus being presented vividly before his internal eyes and the power of the Holy Spirit coming upon him. As a Spirit-filled man of God, he regarded his own writings as a revelation from God, superseding the authority of the Bible. He accepted only those books in the Bible that lent themselves to a spiritual interpretation. Most scholars acknowledge that Swedenborg had unusual psychic powers, demonstrated especially in the gift of prophecy. He also allegedly entered into communication with the World of Spirits, the intermediate state between heaven and hell—the abode of most mortals after death. He claimed to have conversed with Luther, Calvin, Augustine and Paul. Interestingly, as a bachelor he taught that marriage would take place in heaven, though it would be a spiritual marriage. Swedenborg rejected the orthodox doctrines of the Trinity and the atonement. He seemed to hold to a trinal monism or christomonism, identifying Jesus Christ with Jehovah. In his teaching God was the true Man from the beginning, indeed "the eternal God-Man." Sin is eradicated not by expiation but by personal repentance, and this is a possibility available to anyone who wills it. Heaven and hell are states of consciousness rather than physical places. Spirits can move from one realm to the other if their strength of character permits.

Swedenborg stands in the tradition of Montanism and spiritualism, in which private revelations are elevated above the authority of both church and Scripture. He declared, "I have written entire pages, and the spirits did not dictate the words, but absolutely guided my hand, so that it was they who were doing the writing . . . it being allowed me only to tell such things as flowed from God Messiah mediately and immediately."[16] Swedenborgian theologian Wilson Van Dusen addresses the question of other authoritative words from God besides the Bible: "Just as the New Jerusalem is everywhere, I believe the Word of God is also, for after all, it is our very lives, which are here, handy, to be read. This is the Word of God written on the heart."[17]

Paradoxically Swedenborg was both a rationalist and a mystic.[18] He drew on the rationalism of Descartes and the empiricism of John Locke as well as the transcendentalism of Immanuel Kant. He has exerted a profound influence on the modern cult movements of Spiritualism (also called "Spiritism"),[19] Theosophy, Transcendentalism and New Thought. He has been praised by Kant, Johann Wolfgang Goethe, the radical Pietist Friedrich Christoph Oetinger, William Blake and Ralph Waldo Emerson. The most famous convert to this new religion was Helen Keller. To his credit Swedenborg tried to conceal his psychic powers, which were discovered by friends and acquaintances almost by accident. While he worked many miracles, he believed that they "have a coercive effect on belief and destroy the free will in spiritual matters."[20]

New Light from Russia

Russia has been the home of various Spirit movements that have rebelled against the formalism and rigidity of the established church.

One of these is the Dukhobors, which began in the eighteenth century.[21] A Russian Orthodox bishop called them "Spirit-wrestlers," since
it was believed that they wrestled against the Holy Spirit. They
accepted this term but insisted that they fought with the Holy Spirit
against the entrenched powers of the world rather than resorting to
the sword. In the later nineteenth century (1899-1900) seven thousand
Dukhobors emigrated from Russia to Saskatchewan, Canada, under
their leader Peter Verigin. A sizable body later moved to British Columbia.

For Dukhobors truth lies not in books but in the Spirit within the
human subject. It is not the Bible but the Living Book—spiritual experience—to which they appeal. While denying the unique deity of Jesus,
they contend that Christ dwells in all believers. What is vital to our salvation is not baptism but Christ being born again in the human soul.
They claim that the Christ-Spirit descends on certain privileged individuals anointing them to become charismatic leaders of the community.
An early leader in Russia, Savely Kapoustin, declared, "Now, as truly as
heaven is above me and the earth under my feet, I am the true Jesus
Christ your Lord."[22] On one occasion Peter Verigin announced to a
Dukhobor assembly: "I am your Christ, your leader, and your Tsar."
Indeed, the Dukhobors have seen the emergence of many Christs or
Messiahs, each of whom has had twelve apostles. Being more radical
than most higher critics, they regard large parts of the Bible as myth.
The virgin birth of Christ is a fairy tale. Like most cult movements they
deny the Trinity and view only the Spirit as God. Revealing their bent to
enthusiasm they claim that Spirit-led members are free from tempta-
tions to sin.

The Dukhobors live communally. The radical elements disrobe as a
sign of protest against burdensome laws. All reject water baptism and
accept only the baptism of the Spirit. God alone knows who are the
truly Spirit-baptized. The charismatic gifts in evidence among them
include prophecy, miracles and on occasion tongues. The symbols of
their faith are a pitcher of water, representing the spirit of life; a dish of

salt, representing the essence of life; and a loaf of bread, the staff of life. Their services consist of singing, praying and prophecy. There is no preaching of the biblical word nor any sacraments. The Dukhobors hold that the human soul is immortal and undergoes metempsychosis (reincarnation). They are confident in the hope that the kingdom of God will finally be established on earth.

More perceptibly Christian are the Molokans, founded in Russia in the later eighteenth century.[23] They refer to themselves as the "True Spiritual Christians." While rejecting sacraments they affirm the gift of the Holy Spirit with the sign of new tongues after conversion. In contrast to the Dukhobors they accept the Trinity but contend that the Word and Spirit are subordinate to the Father. They hold to a spiritual baptism and a spiritual Communion. They look forward to a peaceful millennial reign of Christ on earth. Their worship services consist of singing, reading of Scripture, preaching by the elders and free prayer. In the more radical groups the service is considered incomplete without a manifestation of the Holy Spirit, who activates and moves various members in joyful, exuberant spiritual jumping. This wing of the movement, not surprisingly known as "the Jumpers," is the larger group in North America. The book that the Molokans hold in highest esteem after the Bible is *The Book of Spirit and Life*, composed of the writings of their prophets. The Molokans reject participation in war, oaths, alcohol, gambling, theatergoing and social dancing. In the nomenclature of this study they should properly be regarded as a sect rather than a religious cult.[24]

The Inspirationists

In America, a number of utopian and separatist communities have appeared in which private revelations have become a major source of authority.[25] Some of these have come out of German Pietism (such as the Amana Society, the Society of Separatists at Zoar and the Rappites); others reflect the influence of the Enlightenment (such as the Icarians, the Oneida community and Robert Owen's New Harmony

Society). The Amana Society, also known as the Community of True Inspiration,[26] traces its origins to the eighteenth century, drawing on the spirituality of Jakob Boehme, Philip Spener and Paul Gieseberg Nagel. Its immediate founders were Eberhard Ludwig Gruber and Johann Friedrich Rock, who gathered a small body of believers in Himbach, Hesse, Germany, in 1714. Rock would begin to prophesy whenever he heard the voice of God in his heart. Wherever he went he was accompanied by a scribe who recorded his utterances when he "fell under the spirit." Gruber claimed that he could discern whether a false spirit was present at the meeting when he was overcome by uncontrollable shivering and shaking of his head.

The final authority for the Inspirationists is the inward illumination of the Spirit, imparted to the prophets and apostles in biblical times and to sensitive spiritual souls in subsequent times. Jesus is deemed the greatest Inspirationist, but others are also acclaimed as mouthpieces of God. While the Inspirationists see Jesus Christ as the unique Mediator and accept the idea of Christ's sacrifice for sin, they contend that our salvation is contingent on our free response to God's love manifest in Jesus. The leaders of the community have been the divinely attuned individuals *(Werkzeuge)* who show forth the works of the Lord. Such persons fall into trancelike states and utter prophecies with authority. The most famous of these charismatic leaders was Christian Metz, who led a group of German Inspirationists to America in 1842. Eight hundred devotees settled in Iowa in 1855, founding the Amana colonies. The Amana community disintegrated when the last *Werkzeug* died. The Inspirationist church still continues, but its followers no longer live in community. In the past they celebrated footwashing and the love feast (comparable to the Lord's Supper). They no longer practice the former, and the latter is celebrated only every two years. Like many spiritualistic movements they have abandoned baptism with water in favor of baptism with the Spirit: "Since baptism by water is only external and hence not essential for salvation, so has God exempted us from its observance and directed us to the baptism by fire and by the spirit, through which alone we can become children of God."[27]

Unlike many sect groups the Inspirationists do not consider themselves the only true church. Instead, they see themselves as a sign of the kingdom of God, a sign that has now become a tourist attraction. The Amana communities are a powerful testimony that the elevation of the Spirit as the final authority leads ultimately to the dissolution of sacraments and thereby severs continuity with the tradition of the wider church. At the same time, one can admire the depth of their dedication and their rediscovery of the communitarian dimension of the Christian faith manifested in their commitment to care for one another in the area of worldly as well as spiritual needs.

Mormonism

One of the most influential of the neo-Montanist movements is Mormonism, the main branch being called the Church of Jesus Christ of the Latter-day Saints. Mormonism speaks of new revelations; the outpouring of the Spirit in the latter days; the spiritual gifts, including tongues and prophecy; the millennium; and the baptism of the dead. Many of the early Mormon choirs sang in tongues and in complete harmony. The spiritual vision of Mormonism is captured in the hymn "The Spirit of God Like a Fire" by William Phelps:

The latter-day glory begins to come forth;

The visions and blessings of old are returning,

And angels are coming to visit the earth.[28]

The Mormon church was founded in 1830 by Joseph Smith, who received a call to become "a prophet of the Most High God." Guided by the angel Moroni to a hill in upper New York State, he purportedly found golden tablets written by the prophet Mormon and buried by his son, the same Moroni, in A.D. 421. These tablets supposedly contain the history of the Latter-day Saints. The *Book of Mormon* claims that Jesus Christ appeared in America after his resurrection, establishing the gospel in the New World. The Mormons faced persecution and migrated west. Opposition intensified when polygamy was introduced.

Joseph Smith was murdered in Carthage, Illinois, in 1844 and was succeeded by Brigham Young, who led the main company of Mormons to Utah, whose capital, Salt Lake City, has become the spiritual center of this new faith.

It is not the purpose of this study to present a detailed repudiation of Mormon claims, but it is well to note that a movement that argues for an open canon on the basis of new revelations from the Spirit invariably sunders the faith from its theological heritage. While the Mormons accept the Bible as the Word of God (though parts of it have been corrected by the prophet Joseph Smith), they adhere to a number of other sacred books as well, including *Doctrines and Covenants*, which speaks highly of plural marriages. The Mormon presidents also give inspired utterances, which are added to the canon of authoritative writings.

Sociologically Mormonism is a church, given its elaborate hierarchical structure with ritual and sacraments. Theologically Mormonism is close to being a cult, since it represents a new faith orientation that radically challenges the Reformation and also classical Catholic emphasis on the priority of grace over works.[29] One of its key slogans is, "As man is, God once was; as God is, men may become." Reminiscent of ancient Greek mythology, its gods have bodies of flesh and bones and give birth to spirit children who are subsequently born in human bodies. Mormons affirm both a Father God and a Mother God and the Son as the first of many spirit children who will inhabit the earth. The millennium will occur when all preexistent spirits have taken bodily form. At the end of the millennial period will come the battle of Armageddon followed by a general resurrection and final judgment. No one will be lost except a few incurables. The guiding symbol of Mormon religion is not the cross but the angel Moroni blowing his trumpet. Also prominent is the beehive, symbolizing industry and diligence.

Like many cult movements Mormonism is a system of works righteousness. In addition, various rites and ceremonies are made prerequisites for salvation, one of these being baptism. This is why the church promotes the baptism of the dead, a vicarious baptism undertaken by living Mormons for their dead ancestors. Baptism usually takes place at the age of eight and is immediately followed by the rite of sealing, which imparts the gift of the Holy Spirit. In the words of Charles Penrose, a former Mormon president: "As baptism is the birth of water, so confirmation is the birth or baptism of the Spirit. Both are necessary to entrance into the Kingdom of God."[30] The Montanist hue of Mormonism is evident in this confession of Joseph Smith: "We believe in the gift of the Holy Ghost being enjoyed now, as much as it was in the Apostles' days. . . . We also believe in prophecy, in tongues, in visions, and in revelations, in gifts, and in healings."[31] However, the spontaneity and enthusiasm that marked the early Mormon church have been largely supplanted by prescribed rituals, a situation denoting the subordination of charisma to sacrament.

Restorationist Sects

Time and again Christians have been tempted to return to the practices of the apostolic or New Testament church and restore the offices of prophets, apostles, evangelists and so on. Mormonism has a restorationist hue, but it bears the imprint of novelty more than continuity with apostolic faith. A more authentically restorationist movement is the Catholic Apostolic Church, founded in the early nineteenth century by Edward Irving (1792-1834), a Presbyterian minister in London. Originally called "the School of the Prophets," the new denomination heralded the imminent return of Jesus Christ. Irving developed a doctrine of the baptism of the Holy Spirit whose standing sign was speaking in other tongues.[32] The sect holds to seven sacraments, including the rite of sealing whereby the Holy Spirit is imparted through the laying on of hands. It also has sacramentals, including holy water and incense. Twelve apostles were named to direct the new church, but with the death of the last apostle its membership has been dwindling. In its early days the gifts of the Spirit, including prophecy and healing, were in abundance. The church is premillennial and expects the end of the world in a very short time. This fellowship was the first to advance the idea of the secret rapture of the saints. The Catholic Apostolic Church is commonly considered a forerunner of Pentecostalism, though most Pentecostals would not accept the emphasis on church hierarchy and sacraments.

A breakaway from the Catholic Apostolic Church is the New Apostolic Church, which is based on a continuing order of apostles. This denomination has three sacraments: baptism, Communion and sealing. The last is identified with the baptism of the Holy Spirit and fire, and is "the most exalted sacramental impartation of grace that a human being can receive."[33] In New Apostolic theology the hundreds of years between the death of the original apostles and the new work of the Holy Spirit were a period of spiritual darkness. Then came the restoration of the apostolic office and the beginning of the latter days. Jesus or the Spirit of Jesus is believed to be incarnate in each apostle, a note that one also finds in the early Christian sect of Montanism. The New Apostolic Church is mainly German and Swiss in composition, but it is also found in Holland, England, the United States and various other countries. The charismatic gifts that have been in special prominence in its history are tongues, healings and prophecy, though the last is less frequent today. Unlike its parent body, the New Apostolic Church is slowly gaining in membership.

Another restorationist movement is the Christian Catholic Church, founded by the controversial John Alexander Dowie (1847-1907). Born in Edinburgh, he went to Australia and pastored a Congregational church for a number of years. When he discovered that he had the gift of divine healing he embarked on a healing ministry. Coming to the United States in 1888, he organized the Christian Catholic Church in Chicago in 1896. In 1901 he founded Zion City north of Chicago, which for a time functioned as a theocratic community. He called himself Elijah III and Elijah the Restorer, claiming to be the first apostle of a renewed church in the end times. Like the Irvingites he sought the full restoration of apostolic Christianity. Dowie had been considerably influenced by the Keswick Holiness movement, though there is no clear statement of sanctification in the four articles of the Christian Catholic confession of faith. A candidate for membership is expected to demonstrate that he or she possesses a measure of the witness of the Spirit. Dowie was keenly aware of the social implications of the gospel and was an avid critic of both the injustices of capitalism and the excesses of the labor bosses. He was also a tireless advocate of racial justice and integration. He later lost control of the community to Wilbur Glenn Voliva, who continued the emphasis on the ministry of healing.

The Christian Catholic Church is not a cult but an evangelical sect that has been marked by a number of eccentric beliefs, including the belief that the earth is flat. Dowie affirmed the realities of heaven and hell but rejected the traditional idea of hell as a place of eternal punishment. The church is holding its own as it becomes more solidly evangelical as well as more broadly ecumenical.[34]

No survey of restorationism would be complete without considering the Christian Restorationist movement rooted in the teachings of Thomas Campbell, Alexander Campbell, Barton Stone and Walter Scott, all of Presbyterian background. The most significant bodies in this movement are: the Disciples of Christ, now a denomination rather than a sect; the Independent Christian Churches; the Churches of Christ; and the International Churches of Christ.[35] In this tradition one can discern a rationalist bent in that the gospel is often defined as a set of facts and rules that require intellectual assent. In addition it is believed that sinners can accept the gift of salvation apart from any special enabling activity of the Holy Spirit. Believers' baptism by immersion together with faith and repentance are necessary elements in receiving the remission of sins. The Campbellites are reluctant to affirm the doctrine of the ontological Trinity because it is not explicitly affirmed in Scripture. Many prefer to speak of the Godhead rather than of the Trinity. Campbellites are also prone to take issue with the doctrine of justification by faith alone because of its supposed lack of scriptural grounding. Moreover, they discourage seeking extraordinary gifts of the Spirit and view the charismatic movement with suspicion. Their mottoes are "No Creed but Christ" and "Where the Scriptures speak, we speak; where the Scriptures are silent, we are silent." This has led some to question the use of musical instruments in worship and organized missionary societies. At their best, Christian Restorationists unite ecumenical outreach with evangelical commitment. At their worst, they tend to foster a legalistic and sectarian mentality.[36]

Seventh-day Adventism

Like some of the sects previously discussed, Seventh-day Adventism, founded by Ellen White (d. 1915), bears the imprint of both Montanism and Donatism.[37] Its origins go back to 1831 when William Miller, on the basis of protracted studies of Daniel and Revelation, announced the exact time Christ would come again. At first he said this event would occur in 1843, then changed the date to 1844. When nothing happened his followers began to fall away, and Miller himself expressed no confidence in the movements that continued to build on his prophecy. Ellen White made the claim that 1844 did have unique prophetic significance because it marked the time Christ entered the sanctuary in heaven in order to begin the investigative judgment that determines who will enjoy the benefits of Christ's atonement. Adventists teach that those who obey the law, including the worship of God on the original biblical sabbath, will alone be received into the presence of God in glory. This sectarian motif has been muted in recent years.

It is not my purpose here to spell out the intricacies of Seventh-day Adventist doctrine, but we should note that the gifts of the Spirit, especially prophecy, have played a major role in this movement. Because the church has not yet reached "the unity of the faith and of the knowledge of the Son of God" (Eph 4:13), "it still needs all the gifts of the Spirit. These gifts, including the gift of prophecy, will continue to operate for the benefit of God's people until Christ returns."[38] Ellen White laid claim to private revelations, which she regarded as equal in inspiration to that of the apostles. Some Adventists have viewed her writings as a third testament, but this has never been the dominant position. Her prophecies are nevertheless regarded as the hallmark of the remnant church, and Scripture is read in the light of these prophecies. Ellen White's words are indeed revealing: "In ancient times God spoke to men by the mouth of prophets and apostles. In these days he speaks to them by the Testimonies of his spirit."[39]

Seventh-day Adventists have frequently been accused by orthodox Protestants of legalism, the idea that one is finally saved by keeping the law. While teaching salvation by grace through faith, Adventists also hold that the characters of those who are forgiven must be found to be in harmony with the law of God before their sins can be blotted out in the investigative judgment. In recent years a controversy has erupted in the church concerning the relation of justification and sanctification. Those who hold to the full sufficiency of justification emphasize that grace means favor extended to undeserving sinners. The Adventist establishment tends to subordinate justification to sanctification and to make the keeping of the law the condition for final acceptance by Christ.[40]

Although Adventists teach that the gifts of the Spirit will be in evidence in the last days, they generally have reservations regarding the charismatic movement in the churches. They readily admit that Ellen White possessed the gifts of prophecy and healing, but they resist the Pentecostal doctrine of tongues as the mark of receiving the gift of the Spirit. Glossolalia did appear in early Adventism, and in some Adventist congregations it is emerging again. The deliverance ministry involving the exorcism of evil spirits is also in evidence in contemporary Adventism.[41] While Adventists object to an emphasis on only some of the extraordinary gifts of the Spirit, they believe that all of the charismata will play a role in the dawning of the millennial kingdom. According to Adventist theologian Richard Hammill, "The necessity for God to communicate directly with His people did not end when the New Testament canon was closed. In the crises of the last days the church of Christ especially needs particular divine guidance."[42]

Seventh-day Adventism signifies a spiritual movement that began in unbalanced speculation and has been moving to reclaim the treasures of Christian orthodoxy. Some of the early Adventists were Arians, but today the church is solidly trinitarian. It also views itself as essentially an evangelical church, though it has not shaken free of legalism.[43] Ellen White herself was an avowed admirer of the Protestant Reformation; and despite her sometimes unwise speculations, her teachings reveal an evangelical thrust. In an effort to counter religious enthusiasm she declared, "The world will not be converted by the gift of tongues, or by the working of miracles, but by preaching Christ crucified."[44] Just as Seventh-day Adventism has moved from heresy toward orthodoxy, so many mainline Protestant denominations today are moving from orthodoxy toward heresy. We are indeed living in interesting times!

Jehovah's Witnesses

Perhaps no cult has been entrapped by biblical literalism more than the Jehovah's Witnesses, one of the most rapidly growing religions of our time.[45] Founded by a Congregationalist layman, Charles Taze Russell, in 1879, it was originally known as Zion's Watchtower Society. Other names it assumed were the International Bible Students Association, the Associated Bible Students and the Millennial Dawn. Markedly influenced by Seventh-day Adventism in his early years, Russell announced that the millennial kingdom will shortly be upon us; therefore, "millions now living will never die." He also taught that there is no hell and that heaven would be on earth. A prolific writer and ingenious organizer, he was said to have traveled thirty thousand miles a year making pastoral calls. His successor, Judge J. F. Rutherford, was instrumental in leading the cult to adopt the name "Jehovah's Witnesses" in 1931.

What marks the Watchtower movement as a clear deviation from historic Christian faith is its denial of the Trinity and the deity of Jesus

Christ. Christ was essentially an angel and was raised not as a man but as a spirit being. The Holy Spirit is not a person but an active force or influence. There is also no immortality: the dead will sleep until the final resurrection. Unbelievers will be annihilated, not resurrected. Salvation is not by grace alone but is contingent on our obedience not only to the commandments in the Bible but also to the injunctions of the Watchtower Society.

The Jehovah's Witnesses represent a reemergence of both Arianism and Montanism. Like the Adventists they include in their gospel an extraordinary outpouring of the Spirit in the latter days, which are even now upon us. In addition to water baptism, symbolizing one's dedication to be God's minister, they speak of "the baptism of the holy Spirit" or "the baptism with the holy Spirit," which Christ administers as Jehovah's servant.[46] This is a baptism into Christ's death, into a life of total sacrifice for the cause of the kingdom. Only those who are the anointed members of Christ's body will inherit God's kingdom in heaven. The Jehovah's Witnesses distinguish between the "anointed class" (the Spirit baptized) and the other sheep, who enjoy "a measure of God's spirit" and who will survive the battle of Armageddon. The other sheep will be subjects of God in his kingdom, but they will not reign with the anointed. On the whole the Jehovah's Witnesses do not encourage the spectacular gifts of the Spirit and are therefore outside the charismatic movement. In the 1930s the Watchtower movement in Rhodesia and neighboring territories broke away from the parent body. This movement is anti-white, anarchistic and glossolalic.

Like all heresies the Jehovah's Witnesses have uncovered some truth that was hitherto buried in Christian tradition. Its rediscovery of the biblical doctrine of the priesthood of believers is especially to be applauded. Every member is a minister and every minister has the vocation of being a witness to the truth of the gospel. An orthodox Christian can also appreciate their zeal and discipline, their willingness to suffer and even die for their faith. I would implore them to be more open to the free movement of the Spirit. Their services have a rigidity that stifles the spontaneous expression of joy and faith. The sermons are actually read presentations prepared by the central headquarters of the Watchtower and Tract Society in Brooklyn, New York. Scripture, it seems, is not allowed to judge the teaching authority of the church. In this respect they are more Catholic than Protestant.

Jehovah's Witnesses are staunch biblical inerrantists and literalists. The third article of their statement of faith affirms that the "Bible is the inerrant, infallible, inspired Word of God as it was originally given, and has been preserved by Him as the revealer of His purposes."[47] The significance of this declaration is that belief in biblical inerrancy is no guarantee of orthodoxy, that it is possible to have faith in the Bible without faith in Jesus Christ, the living Word of God incarnate in human flesh.

The Unification Church

Also standing in the tradition of millennialism and Montanism—and definitely cultic in orientation—is the Unification Church or, as it is more formally called, "the Holy Spirit Association for the Unification of World Christianity."[48] Its founder, Sun Myung Moon of North Korea, allegedly received a revelation from Jesus Christ in 1936 instructing him to complete the work Jesus began. Moon came to believe that Korea is the promised land that will function as the world center for the coming reign of the Messiah. While not presenting himself directly as the Messiah, he has left little doubt that he himself is the new Elijah or "Lord of the Second Advent." Moon teaches a version of postmillennialism in which the kingdom of God will be realized within earthly history. The church told its followers that the millennium would begin in 1967 and then changed the date to 2001. Christ succeeded in providing humanity with the key to spiritual redemption, but redemption is not complete until there is physical restoration as well. In Unification theology salvation is realized through the sacrament of marriage. Our supreme earthly goal is to marry and fructify and thereby extend the family of God across all ethnic and racial barriers. The Unification

Church occasionally sponsors arranged mass marriages, which are designed to build a new humanity, a kingdom of God on earth.

The Moon cult rejects the doctrine of the Trinity and envisages God as binitarian—masculine and feminine. The feminine side of God is represented by the Holy Spirit. A pantheistic view of God supplants biblical theism. God is not a person but a "perpetuating, self-generating energy." Christ is not God himself in human flesh but a prophetic figure who carries out God's purposes. Just as Christ was the second Adam, so Moon is the third Adam, and his book *The Divine Principle* is seen as the third testament. The Holy Spirit enables us to grow in the grace and knowledge of Jesus Christ, but there is no perfection in this life. We continue working out our spiritual destiny in the life beyond. Messages are relayed to mortals from the spirit world by channeling. As members of the spirit world assist the growth and achievement of people on earth, they themselves are "spiritually benefited and progressively resurrected."[49]

Salvation is a matter of achieving spiritual maturity and character with the assistance of the Holy Spirit and spirits from the beyond. The church teaches the indemnity principle in which we clear our account before God through specific acts of penance. We need "to re-earn the privilege to fellowship and communion with God."[50] Christ shows us the way, but he did not suffer and die in our place. It is up to us to cooperate with God in building his kingdom, and without our efforts God's program would be frustrated.

Unification theology signifies a blend of traditional Christianity and shamanism. The church does not accept baptism and Communion but is amazingly open to clairvoyance, automatic handwriting and mediumship. The cross is a tragedy because it prevented Jesus from marrying and thereby preparing the way for physical redemption. The Bible is subordinated to new revelations, especially to those given to Sun Myung Moon. In the founder's words, "Scripture can be likened to a lamp which illuminates the truth. Its mission is to shed the light of truth. When a brighter light appears, the mission of the old one fades."[51]

The Unification Church represents an attempt to retrieve a holistic vision of faith in which physical salvation is deemed as important as spiritual salvation. Indeed, the spirit of a person can grow and become perfect only through a physical body. Despite its emphasis on the physical, the church denies the bodily resurrection of Jesus and, like the ancient Gnostics, teaches that his body remained in the grave. The Moonies do not pray to Christ or Jesus but to "Heavenly Father" (God) and sometimes to "Father" (Rev. Moon) or "Mother" (Hak Ja Han, Moon's fourth wife).

Unification leaders consistently throw their support to politically conservative causes. Besides its enormous real estate holdings in this country, the church owns the *Washington Times, Insight* magazine and Paragon House, a New York publishing firm. The Moon empire also includes printing presses, newspapers, banks and farmland in Uruguay, a conference center in Brazil and lesser holdings in some other countries.

This religion fits into the New Age ethos, for its god is the surge to life in all things, one that can be blocked or facilitated by human effort.[52] In contrast to the apocalyptic sects, it sees the kingdom of God emerging through human experimentation and social engineering rather than breaking into human history from the beyond.

The New Age Movement

The New Age is not only a new way of viewing reality but also a new way of life dedicated to the realization of human potential through discovering the secrets that lie dormant in the human psyche. It embraces many seemingly diverse movements, both secular and religious, and is anchored in some respected philosophical traditions. Its doctrines are taught in many churches and cults and have given rise to various experiments in community life, education and holistic health care. The New Age is the tip of an iceberg that I choose to call "the new spirituality," which connotes the dawning of a mysticism of the earth that sharply challenges both classical Christian mysticism and biblical, prophetic religion. God in this new perspective is "the total energy field of the universe" (Alan Watts), "the flowing river of Nature" (Emerson), "the Life-Force" (Bergson) or the "infinite abyss" (Tillich). Those who hew closer to traditional Christian tenets make a place for the Holy Spirit, but he is now depicted as "the Stream of Life," "the germinal power in nature," "the power of creativity" or "the Fire of the Cosmos." God is generally defined as spirit in the generic sense, since the Trinity is foreign to the greater part of the New Age movement. Jesus is esteemed not because he is the Word made flesh but because he is one of the prime manifestations of the Cosmic Christ—the bond of energy that ties all things together.[53] The message of the new dispensation is that the Cosmic Christ or the Spirit of Life is waiting to be born within us.[54]

The New Age signifies the convergence of the new science, modern pragmatism, American transcendentalism, German idealism and Eastern mysticism. It also shows traces of gnosticism and Platonism. Among the host of thinkers it draws upon are Ralph Waldo Emerson, William James, Henri Bergson, D. H. Lawrence, Nikos Kazantzakis, Carl Jung, Joseph Campbell, Aldous Huxley and Teilhard de Chardin. Theologians who have been attracted to New Age ideas include Matthew Fox, Sam Keen, Morton Kelsey, Geddes MacGregor, Miriam Simos (Starhawk), Charlene Spretnak, Margot Adler, Jay B. McDaniel, Ernest Larkin and Harmon Bro.[55]

Although not a monolithic movement, the New Age generally holds to the affirmation of life in all its fullness but on the basis of the cultivation of occult powers that accelerate the evolution of the human species to a higher level of existence. New Agers see the world not as a machine but as a living organism. The universe is also sometimes depicted as "a great thought." New Age writers often lend support to the Eastern ideas of reincarnation and karma, though they tend to affirm that the law of karma can be overcome through the will to life and power. Whereas the older cult of Spiritualism taught communication with departed spirits, the New Age teaches communication with

ascended masters, a higher order of beings, through shamans or channels. While many of the classical mystics envisage the world as a crucible in which we are tested and refined, New Age devotees consider the
world filled with infinite possibilities and opportunities for personal
growth and happiness.[56] In contrast to the theocentric or christocentric
perspective of biblical religion, New Age spirituality is biocentric (life-
centered) and holocentric (centered in the whole of reality). Its symbols include the rainbow, the globe, the pyramid, the lotus flower and
the crystal.

This movement encompasses seminars and workshops on creative
living, meditation centers, bookstores, retreat houses and religious
communities. It also includes a number of cults, among them the I Am
movement, the Church Universal and Triumphant, the Collegians
International Church, Transcendental Meditation, the Unity School of
Christianity, the Aquarian Light Church and the Light of Christ Community Church. A New Age ethos is also discernible in kindred cult movements such as Theosophy, Anthroposophy, New Thought, the Church
of Illumination, the Holy Order of MANS, Foundation Faith of the Millennium, the Esalen Institute, Silva Mind Control, the Nirvana Foundation, Eckankar and Scientology. One can even detect convergences
with Mormonism, the Unification Church and Swedenborgianism.[57]
Communities inspired by a New Age vision include Sparrow Hawk Vil-
lage, the Findhorn Community, the Lama Foundation, the Tara Center,
the Renaissance Community and the Institute in Culture and Creation
Spirituality of Matthew Fox. In addition, New Age notions have penetrated spiritual renewal movements like Camps Farthest Out, the Disciplined Order of Christ and the Spiritual Frontiers Fellowship. Hannah
Hurnard, a Quaker mystic and frequent speaker at Camps Farthest Out
for many years, endorses the gnostic idea of preexistent spirits who
are struggling to return to unity with God through successive reincarnations.[58] Albert Day, who stands much more forthrightly in the mainstream of Christianity, sees salvation and the kingdom of God as
dependent on human effort and ingenuity: "God needs our sympathy

for others. His heart is athrob with loving concern for every troubled, anxious, breaking heart in the world. But what He wants to do for them cannot be done until some human heart offers itself for the deed."[59]

The New Age teaches neither creation by the will or decree of God nor emanation from the overflowing being of God but progression or evolution toward unity with God. It basically sees God and the world as inseparable. Its metaphysics can be called pantheistic, or better panentheistic, rather than theistic. The human spirit and the Spirit of God are continuous with one another rather than discontinuous. The Spirit no longer resides in the historical Christ or in the Bible but in the inner recesses of the human self. The Holy Spirit is not God in action in biblical history but the "Slumbering Deep" within us waiting to be discovered. Sacraments are superfluous in this kind of spirituality, since the Spirit encounters us not through external means or signs but immediately, in the depths of our being.[60] The baptism of the Spirit can only mean the alteration of consciousness through meditative techniques, including visualization. Empowerment by the Spirit is at the same time self-empowerment, since God or Spirit is the core of the soul.

Dispensationalism

It should be recognized that challenges to traditional faith include movements that seek to hew to orthodoxy, some receiving inspiration and support from Bible conferences. One of these is dispensationalism, which has penetrated the bastions of evangelical Protestantism.[61] In stark contrast to cults such as the New Age, Spiritism, New Thought and Theosophy, dispensationalism sees itself as a new articulation of biblical Christianity. In this respect it is comparable to the original Quakers, Anabaptists, radical Pietists and restorationist movements like the Churches of Christ. In common with these bodies it manifests a sectarian thrust evident in its call to separation from established Christendom. In addition it has been led into unwise speculation on eschatological themes. *Dispensationalism* is a fluid term and includes many devout believers who identify with the Reformation. It nevertheless constitutes a marked departure from Reformation faith when and insofar as it makes the dispensations a part of the gospel proclamation. The concern of evangelicals like myself who wish to transcend sectarianism is that pious opinions not be elevated to the status of gospel truth.

Dispensationalism refers to a mode of theologizing based on the way God relates to his people in the different stages of salvation history. This kind of speculation is most conspicuous in Bible churches, conservative Baptist congregations, Pentecostal churches and Plymouth Brethren assemblies. It is resisted in Anglican, Lutheran, Reformed and more orthodox Presbyterian bodies, though it has found a lodging among some Presbyterians. The spiritual roots of dispensationalism go back to Montanism, Tertullian, Joachim of Flora and Cocceius.[62] In the eighteenth century dispensational ideas emerged in the writings of Pierre Poiret, John Edwards, John William Fletcher and Isaac Watts.[63] Dispensationalism was systematized by John Nelson Darby (1800-1882), a former priest of the Church of England, and popularized by the American Congregationalist Cyrus I. Scofield in the Scofield Reference Bible. It was further amplified by Lewis Sperry Chafer, a teacher at Dallas Theological Seminary for many years.

In this theology a dispensation is "a period of time during which man is tested in respect of obedience to some *specific* revelation of the will of God."[64] The dispensational mainstream holds to seven dispensations—innocency (Adam before the fall), conscience (Adam to Noah), human government (Noah to Abraham), promise (Abraham to Moses), law (Moses to Christ), grace (Pentecost to the rapture) and the millennial kingdom in which Christ will reign on earth from Jerusalem. This last dispensation will see the fulfillment of the messianic promises to the people of Israel. In the present dispensation believers live under grace, but in the coming millennial kingdom there will be, so it seems, a partial reversion to meritorious obligation (though this conclusion is vehemently resisted in some circles). The blessed hope is the secret rapture of the church that will occur prior to the great tribulation and the second coming of Christ. Most dispensationalists speak of two comings of Christ—the rapture and the millennium. A great many dispensationalists have held that the establishment of the present State of Israel in 1948 was the "blooming of the fig tree" (cf. Lk 21:29-30), thus heralding the return of Christ within one generation. Dispensationalists generally distinguish between the kingdom of God and the kingdom of heaven, basing this on the fact that most of the parables of the kingdom of heaven (as found in Mt 13) are not in Mark or Luke. The kingdom of heaven (in Scofield's view) is Jewish, messianic or Davidic. The kingdom of God is universal and embraces all dispensations.[65]

Dispensationalists usually make a place for baptism and the Lord's Supper but as ordinances of the church, not as sacraments or means of grace. The baptism of the Spirit alone ensures our entrance into the kingdom of God. The more extreme dispensationalist theologies abandon water baptism, though as a rule they retain Communion as symbolic of Christ's sacrifice.[66] Some ultradispensationalists (such as the Grace Gospel Fellowship and the Berean Bible Society) distinguish between "baptism with the Spirit" (Acts 1:5) for miraculous power and "baptism by the Spirit" into one body (1 Cor 12:13). In their view the church began not at Pentecost but in Paul's ministry to the Gentiles sometime after Pentecost. Plymouth Brethren are inclined to distinguish between the incoming (or sealing) of the Spirit and being filled with the Spirit daily.

Reformed theology has criticized dispensationalism for underplaying the normative role of the Old Testament in the living of the Christian life and for failing to see that at least many of the promises to Israel in the Bible have a spiritual fulfillment in the establishment of the church. Reformed Christians also have difficulty with the tendency to spiritualize the sacraments and thereby empty them of salvific significance. In addition they have taken vigorous issue with the supposition that Christ will come prior to the great tribulation at the end of the age and that the church will be exempt from this tribulation. Some dispensationalists argue that Christ will come after the tribulation and others in the middle of the tribulation period.

Dispensationalism has attracted a measure of support from Pentecostals, though orthodox dispensationalism teaches that the "sign gifts" are confined to the apostolic age. Pentecostals overlook this particular teaching and generally embrace the schema of dispensations because of the prominence given to the imminence of Christ's return and the promise of future glory in the millennial kingdom.[67]

Critics of the movement should recognize that dispensationalism has the ring of biblical truth even though its basic message is flawed by an extreme literalism. Its followers remind us that God has not abandoned his promises to his beloved people of Israel and that salvation history will not be complete until Israel is engrafted into the body of Christ (cf. Rom 11). Dispensationalists are also sound in their insistence that biblical revelation constitutes an unfolding of salvation history and that some of God's promises will be realized on earth as well as in heaven.

Today in dispensational circles there is a movement to integrate some of their past claims with the broader evangelical consensus. For example, dispensational theologians are giving renewed attention to the unity of the Testaments and to the unity of the Gospels and the Pauline epistles. There is also rethinking concerning the nature of the church in which the church is interpreted not simply as a federation of local assemblies but as the manifestation of the mystical body of Christ through the ages.[68]

The wider evangelical community owes a debt of gratitude to groups like the Plymouth Brethren who have remained true to the gospel of free grace in a time of accommodation to works righteousness in the guise of social engineering. From its very beginning there were elements in the Brethren that took issue with the theory of dispensations (e.g., B. W. Newton, Anthony Norris Groves and George Müller). One cannot but admire the role of the Brethren in the formation of new interdenominational seminaries (Regent College and Ontario Theological Seminary), Bible colleges (Emmaus Bible College, Ontario Bible College, now Tyndale College), publishing companies (Marshall, Morgan & Scott and Paternoster Press) and missionary societies (Operation Mobilization and Christian Missions in Many Lands).[69] They have also produced a number of eminent scholars, such as F. F. Bruce, who speak first of all not as Brethren but as evangelical Christians. A sectarian bent is conspicuous especially among the closed or exclusive Brethren, who view themselves as the only true church and who discourage fellowship with other Christians. A departure from biblical Christianity is also noticeable when the gospel is reduced to biblical prophecy and when the Bible is used to provide a ready explanation of the hand of God in contemporary events.[70] Among many Brethren today the dispensational note is muted, and the gospel of God's free redeeming grace through the vicarious atoning sacrifice of Christ is being sounded anew.[71]

Postscript

One might well pose the question: Why include a discussion of modern sects and cults in a study of the Holy Spirit? First, it should be obvious that many of these new movements represent the reemergence of ancient heresies that we have already dealt with, heresies that compromise the historical Christian understanding of christology and pneumatology. Second, nearly all of these movements assign a prominent role to the Holy Spirit. Third, the distortions of God, Christ and the Spirit that we encounter in sects and cults are instructive in helping us reformulate the doctrine of the Spirit for the contemporary context. From these minority religions we can learn where the field mines lie in reassessing the role of the Spirit in Christian thought and practice.

Cults and sects are based on selected truth that clouds or obscures other truths equally essential to faith. Such imbalances yield an erroneous understanding of God, Christ and the Spirit. Most of these movements swing toward either sectarianism, a narrowness or rigidity that is closed to new truth, or eclecticism, which renders people gullible in the quest for inclusivity. Again, one can detect in these religious aberrations an inability to hold together the biblical polarity of the holy life and free grace. They invariably land in either the quagmire of works righteousness or the pitfall of cheap grace and its corollary, antinomianism. The penchant for legalism can be seen in the indemnity principle of the Unification Church and the law of sowing and reaping stressed in Theosophy and the New Age movement.

Finally, cultic and sectarian movements manifest an incapacity to steer clear of the Charybdis of spiritualism and the Scylla of sacramentalism. Either the Spirit is elevated above the rites of initiation and celebration of the Lord's passion and death, or the Spirit is confined to these rites so that water baptism becomes the equivalent of Spirit baptism and the bread and wine in holy Communion become virtually identical with the body and blood of our Lord. A closely related aberration is rationalism, which treats the Word by itself as the sole or exclusive authority for faith, the result being a lapse into a wooden literalism and obscurantism.

It should come as no surprise that *cults* and *sects* are slippery terms, and because they are almost always used pejoratively it is an open question whether they fit my purposes here. I contend that they are adequate for this kind of discussion so long as we distinguish between the sociological meaning of *sect* and *cult* and their theological meaning. Theologically speaking, any group that tendentiously holds that it is the only true church or that it has a corner on the truth is a sect. Theologically speaking, any group that bases its claims on new revelations that supersede biblical revelation is a cult. In this sense the Roman Catholic Church as well as Lutheran and Reformed churches have functioned as sects or even cultic movements at certain stages in their history. By contrast, the Moravians are a sect in sociological terms in that they maintain a degree of separation from the mores of the wider society. They are nonetheless a branch of the church in theological terms because of their openness to dialogue and willingness to cooperate with other Christians based on a common allegiance to the

Word of God in the Bible. One should also note that groups that have been labeled cults in the past such as the Seventh-day Adventists and the Worldwide Church of God have moved toward the mainstream of Christian orthodoxy and are now closer to being churches. On the other hand some sects have slid into deeper heresy and have indeed become cults. I am thinking of that segment of the Quakers who became Shakers and of the Children of God who at one time were an integral part of the Jesus movement but now rest on the private revelations of their founder.[72] Mainline denominations like the United Church of Christ, the Presbyterian Church USA and the Disciples of Christ often bear the marks of a sect through their alignment with social ideologies that brook no criticism or deviation from the party line of political correctness.

The founders of various sectarian movements, such as George Fox, John Nelson Darby and Ellen White, were for the most part good people and often fairly orthodox in their theological subscriptions. At the same time when they urged fellow Christians to leave "apostate churches" and form new communities of faith, they veered toward sectarianism, since they contributed to sundering the unity of the church. The biblical stance is to remain within the parent body as long as possible and seek to bring renewal to old structures and thought patterns. The Reformers did not set out to found new churches, but they were finally forced out of the Roman Church because the parent body could not assimilate their new insights, which nevertheless had an anchor in Catholic tradition as well as in Scripture. John Wesley did not devote his energies to building the Methodist Church, but he preached revival for the whole church and remained a member of the Anglican communion till the end. One should nevertheless keep in mind that sometimes God does call us to separation (cf. 2 Cor 6:17), but this call ordinarily comes only after we have made strenuous efforts to reform the church from within. To leave the parent church means to give up on that church, and this is a decision that should be made with some fear and trepidation.

Cults and sects are the unpaid bills of the church.[73] Because the doctrine of the communion of saints has fallen into eclipse in Protestantism, cults seek to fill this void with their weird conceptions of the spirit world beyond death that become a source of sustenance for believers on this side of death. Various cults and sects have rediscovered the gifts of the Spirit, especially healing and prophecy, which have been sorely neglected and even denied in the mainline denominations. The new religions also remind us that fellowship is an integral part of the true church and that unless we demonstrate a caring concern for the material as well as the spiritual needs of our people we will invariably lose members to groups that work assiduously to satisfy these needs.

In the light of Christ we can discern glimmers of light in spiritual movements and groups outside the church (cf. Ps 36:9). The Spirit is at work outside as well as inside the parameters of the church, though only those with the eyes of faith can discern how the Spirit is working to draw people to Christ. Some of these new movements appeal to the Spirit to bolster their claims to a superior knowledge of the mysteries of faith. We who stand in the tradition of evangelical orthodoxy are right to challenge these claims, but we are nevertheless obliged to ask whether they know something about the Holy Spirit that we do not know. While there is salvation only in the Jesus Christ attested in holy Scripture, there may be pathways leading to this salvation that exist within cult or sect movements but are often buried under fantastic speculation born out of the stubbornness and intransigence of their misguided leaders. Most of these movements still make the Bible available to their adherents, even if it is in spurious translations, and the Spirit can and does work within the Bible to lead people back to the holy catholic faith, even if they are presently ensnared in deceptive ideologies.

In this whole discussion the very important distinction between cult and sect should be kept in mind. A sect can evolve into a church, whereas a cult can only be replaced by the church. Born-again Christians can live, though hardly thrive, in sects, but they need to break away from cults if they are to maintain the integrity of their faith commitment. As biblical, evangelical Christians we need to sound the call to fellow believers in these various new movements to come back to the fold of the one holy catholic and apostolic church;[74] yet before making this call we must make sure that the denominations we are presently affiliated with are themselves sound vehicles for the saving truth of the gospel of reconciliation and redemption through the vicarious atoning death of Christ and his glorious resurrection from the grave. We also are obliged to ask ourselves whether we too as individuals are fully faithful to the revelation of God in Jesus Christ, bearing in mind that there is an element of heterodoxy in every orthodoxy just as there is a remnant of orthodoxy in most heterodoxy.

What distinguishes the mature in faith from carnal Christians (1 Cor 3:1-4) is that the former acknowledge the limits of their horizons and the tentativeness of their formulations. They are willing to be reformed and corrected by the light that comes to us from the Spirit of God as he speaks to the church in every age, clarifying and deepening what he has already communicated to the biblical prophets and apostles in the past. We are assured of a full comprehension of the mysteries revealed to us in Scripture, but this is a future reality that we can only wait and hope for (cf. 1 Cor 8:2-3; 13:12; 2 Cor 5:7; Phil 3:12; 1 Jn 3:2). At the same time, we are granted sufficient knowledge of God and his will for us that we can live lives of meaning and purpose, and for this we can only be grateful.

To its credit a sect will always strive to keep intact the boundaries between church and world, though the way it delineates these boundaries will vary depending on how open it is to self-correction in the light of holy Scripture and sacred tradition.[75] If a church is to maintain its doctrinal integrity and evangelistic passion, it must always contain something of the sectarian impulse within it. I have sometimes described myself as an ecumenical sectarian in that while vigorously defending that side of the truth that is given to me I wish to be led into the fullness of truth through dialogue and cooperation with other

Christians. The ideal is a believers' church that seeks to be as inclusive as possible while still sedulously maintaining the exclusive claims of the gospel. Orthodoxy is not a possession or achievement but a goal that is yet to be realized, a promise that is still to be fulfilled. The pathway to orthodoxy lies in sharpening the distinctiveness of the teachings of the church, even while seeking to infuse the whole of the culture with the grace of the gospel.

It is well to recognize that true orthodoxy can be undermined in a denomination just as easily as in a sect. A denomination more often than not signifies an inglorious attempt to accommodate to cultural mores and values in order to ensure institutional survival and expansion. Its goal is no longer world evangelization but its own preservation as a socioeconomic unit. This is why it is often preoccupied with shoring up its boards and agencies rather than winning souls for Jesus Christ. The wind of revival can blow through a denomination as well as a sect; but when revival comes sectarian and denominational loyalties will be loosened, and fidelity to the gospel will again become the overriding concern.

·EIGHT·

PENTEC<u>O</u>STALISM

If it is a choice . . . between the uncouth life of the Pentecostals
and the aesthetic death of the older churches, I for one choose uncouth life.

JOHN MACKAY

The latter-rain outpouring of the Holy Spirit is God's final great movement
of power to provide a strong witness to the church and the world
before the coming of the Lord Jesus Christ.

J. A. SYNAN

As a young Christian I liked these noisy, shouting, singing meetings.
I couldn't stand Bible teaching; it was too dry.
Now singing and shouting bores me, and I want the Word.

DAVID J. DU PLESSIS

Conversion without empowering is not enough—it is sub-normal Christianity.
The pentecostals have been right about this—the rest of us had better listen.

CLARK PINNOCK

Together with ecumenism, Pentecostalism is probably the most important spiritual movement of the twentieth century.[1] The doctrine of the Holy Spirit has been given tangible reality in the emergence of a religion that appeals to Pentecost as well as to Calvary for its inspiration and motivation. The Pentecostal churches presently constitute the largest family of churches in Christendom after Roman Catholicism. Including believers within other denominations, Pentecostalism is now approaching 250 million adherents.[2] In Latin America Pentecostals easily comprise the largest grouping of Protestants, totaling 20-25 percent of the population in some countries. By the year 2010 they may well represent a majority of Christians in a few Latin

American countries.[3] Pentecostalism is also growing rapidly in Africa and Asia and is even altering the religious scene in Europe. In sub-Saharan Africa there are now over five thousand independent Christian denominations that reflect Pentecostal spirituality. From 1985 to 1990 the mainline churches in Britain (including Anglican and Roman Catholic) registered significant losses, while in the same period independent Christian churches (mainly Pentecostal) gained nearly 30 percent. The largest congregation in the world is the Yoido Full Gospel Church in Seoul, South Korea, a megachurch of 800,000 members. Henry P. Van Dusen, a past president of Union Theological Seminary in New York, made this astounding confession: "I have come to feel that the Pentecostal movement with its emphasis upon the Holy Spirit is more than just another revival. It is a revolution in our day . . . comparable in importance with the establishment of the original Apostolic Church and with the Protestant Reformation."[4]

Pentecostals deserve special treatment in a book on the Holy Spirit, since their understanding of the works and gifts of the Spirit reflects emphases that diverge markedly from traditional or mainline Christianity. At the same time, their appeal to holy Scripture as well as to the renewal and revival movements in the history of the church is sufficient to keep most of them within the purview of orthodoxy. This is not to discount cultic movements within Pentecostalism that have caused considerable embarrassment among ecumenical Pentecostals, and I examine some of these in this chapter. The principal challenge confronting the student of Pentecostal history is to ascertain whether this movement can bring rejuvenation to the whole of Christendom.

Theological Background

Pentecostalism is not a radical innovation on the Christian scene, for it can be shown to have deep roots in Christian tradition. Its emphasis on a new outpouring of the Holy Spirit and the imminent end of the world was anticipated in Montanism, Anabaptist spiritualism, Quakerism and fundamentalist millenarianism. Glossolalia (speaking in tongues) reappeared among the radical Anabaptists in Germany and Switzerland and the Camisards and Jansenists in seventeenth-century France. It was also evident among the Shakers, the Mormons and the Irvingites, mainly in the nineteenth century.

Setting the stage for the Pentecostal revival was the Holiness movement, which viewed the baptism of the Holy Spirit as a crisis experience subsequent to conversion. This experience was sometimes called "the Pentecostal experience" or "the baptism with fire." The grace of the second blessing (purification) was occasionally referred to as "pentecostal grace."[5] The gift of tongues was sometimes part of this experience, though it generally was not seen as the proof or evidence of receiving the Spirit.

Significantly, nearly all the leaders of the original Pentecostal movement were Holiness preachers. A prime example was Smith Wigglesworth in England, who was converted at a Wesleyan Methodist revival meeting in his early years. After attending a Wesleyan Methodist church in Bradford, he began working with the Salvation Army at the age of sixteen. He relates that he and his coworkers would often stay up all night in prayer. "Many would be prostrated under the power of the Spirit, sometimes for as long as twenty-four hours at a time. We called that the baptism in the Spirit in those days."[6] In 1910 or 1911 he received the Pentecostal baptism of the Spirit with the evidence of tongues at a revival meeting in the Episcopal church in Monk Wearmouth, Sunderland (England). He went on to become an international Pentecostal evangelist and renowned spiritual healer.

Within the Holiness movement was the Fire-Baptized Holiness Church, which began in Iowa in 1895. Founded by Benjamin Hardin Irwin, it held to an experience following sanctification called the "baptism of burning love" or the "baptism with the Holy Ghost and fire." Those who received the message of sanctifying grace would often shout, scream, jerk and speak in tongues. This church later joined the Pentecostal family of churches.

The evangelical revival known as the Third Great Awakening also created a climate that prepared the way for Pentecostalism. Dwight L. Moody received an empowering experience of the Spirit after his conversion, which greatly enhanced his ministry. R. A. Torrey contended that "every true believer has the Holy Spirit."[7] Every Christian receives the gift of the Spirit at the time of conversion, but beyond this blessing there is still the filling of the Spirit.

James H. McConkey wrote the best-selling work *The Three-fold Secret of the Holy Spirit* in which he made a distinction between the incoming of the Spirit (through repentance and faith), the fullness of the Spirit (through surrender and faith) and the constant manifestation of the Spirit (through love and faith). The term "baptism of the Holy Spirit" is equivalent to his "incoming."[8] McConkey was adamant that all of God's children have received the gift of the Spirit, but we need to press on to the Spirit's fullness and his constant manifestation. McConkey contended that there are two conditions for receiving the Holy Ghost: repentance and faith.

Once blessings after conversion were postulated, it was but a short step to label one or other of these blessings as the baptism of the Holy Spirit. When this experience was linked to the evidence of speaking in tongues, Pentecostalism was born. There were many in both the Holiness and the wider evangelical movements who vigorously resisted this identification. A. B. Simpson, founder of the Christian and Missionary Alliance (1897), acknowledged tongues as one of the evidences of the gift of the Spirit but not as a proof or sign of having the Spirit. Alma White, founder of the Pillar of Fire Holiness Church, attacked the practice of tongues as coming from the devil.[9] In her movement the "holy dance" was widely regarded as the evidence for sanctification. The Pentecostal Church of the Nazarene remained opposed to Pentecostal doctrine and subsequently changed its name to the Church of the Nazarene.

As Pentecostalism developed it subordinated the pursuit of perfection to the power for witness. Missions came to take precedence over individual sanctification. Yet the element of perfectionism persisted in the Pentecostal movement, thereby attesting its Holiness roots. Pentecostals coming directly out of the Holiness movement still looked forward to the crisis experience of "entire sanctification," defined as freedom from the very desire to sin. The Assemblies of God and kindred churches preferred to speak of progressive sanctification.

It is well to note that sanctification was often linked to Pentecost in church tradition.[10] According to the Catholic scholar C. Friethoff, "the constant tradition of Holy Church has been that after the first Pentecost the Apostles were unable to sin, at least mortally."[11] The consensus of the church has been that the Holy Spirit brings purity as well as power. Church theologians have also generally held that there will be a tremendous outpouring of the Holy Spirit before the second advent of Christ. Pentecostals speak of this as "the latter rain revival" (cf. Joel 2:23).

Historical Development

The origin of Pentecostalism as a spiritual movement of renewal can be traced to the beginning of the twentieth century. In 1900 a former Methodist minister, Charles F. Parham, opened a Bible college in Topeka, Kansas, and encouraged his students to search the Bible to ascertain whether there is any evidence for the baptism of the Holy Spirit. When they subsequently began speaking in tongues, a new revival movement was born. Parham now began to bring "the Pentecostal message" or "the full gospel message" to various other cities. In 1905 he founded a Bible school in Houston, Texas. Among those who attended the school was W. J. Seymour, a black Holiness preacher. In 1906 he was invited to preach in a black church in Los Angeles, but he was barred from this church because of his Pentecostal message. Those sympathetic to his doctrine began meeting in a house and then in a larger building on Azusa Street. The Azusa Street Mission began to attract national attention as thousands received the baptism of the Holy Spirit.

Some scholars hold that the Pentecostal movement originated in

1896 at a revival in Cherokee County, North Carolina, led by William F. Bryant, a layman. Charles Conn writes that "some of the worshipers were 'so enraptured with the One to whom they prayed that they were curiously exercised by the Holy Spirit,' speaking in languages unknown."[12] The origin of Pentecostalism can perhaps be attributed to a convergence of ideas and events that sired the hope for an eschatological outpouring of the Holy Spirit, which would bring new life to a church that had lapsed into formalism and creedalism.

Pentecostalism was unified in its expectation of a second Pentecost, but it has never been a monolithic movement. One of the major divisions revolves around the doctrine of the Trinity. What is not generally known is that almost one-fifth of American Pentecostals are unitarian. The so-called Oneness movement stresses the unity of God, though seeing this unity in Jesus Christ, who is equated with Jehovah. This movement is now known as "Jesus Only," and baptisms are administered not in the name of the Trinity but in the name of Jesus. Some Pentecostals—like the Bible Way, a charismatic Jesus communal movement—envisage God as the eternal Spirit who is everywhere present. Jesus, in whom the Spirit dwelt, is acknowledged as the Son of God. Cultic Pentecostals like the Way hold to a unitarianism of the first person.[13]

Pentecostals have also been divided over the second blessing. Those following W. H. Durham deny sanctification as a distinct work of grace. One is sanctified at conversion and has no need for a further change later. They espouse the finished work of grace rather than a second work. In their view Christian experience involves only two steps: conversion and baptism with the Holy Spirit, which brings power for witnessing. The Assemblies of God and the Four Square Gospel are among the churches that hold to the finished work of grace, conceiving of sanctification as progressive rather than instantaneous. A distinction is often made between baptistic Pentecostals (holding to the finished work) and Methodistic types (holding to the second blessing of sanctification).

Some Pentecostals speak of a third stage beyond salvation and Holy Spirit baptism: the experience of "ascension." A few even hold to a fourth stage: "total shattering" whereby there is complete redemption from one's religious ego. Others teach the experience of being "slain by the Spirit," which takes place after Spirit baptism. In this experience one is physically knocked down or overcome by the Spirit. David du Plessis speaks of a "baptism of fire" subsequent to "the baptism in the Spirit," resulting in inward purification.[14]

Pentecostalism arose in the United States, but it has expanded far beyond its country of origin, and the great majority of its adherents are in foreign lands. Among the largest Pentecostal denominations in the United States are the Church of God in Christ (over seven million members), the Assemblies of God, the Church of God (Cleveland, Tenn.), the Church of God of Prophecy, the Pentecostal Assemblies of the World and the United Pentecostal Church (the last two being Oneness churches). Other significant denominations are the Pentecostal Holiness Church, the Apostolic Faith movement, the Open Bible Standard Church, the International Church of the Four Square Gospel, the Pentecostal Free Will Baptists, Inc., the Apostolic Overcoming Holy Church of God[15] and the Vineyard Christian Fellowship. The leading Pentecostal churches in Britain are the Elim Pentecostal Church, the New Testament Church of God and the Church of God of Prophecy. In Scandinavia the Philadelphia Churches are prominent; in Germany, the Mülheim Association of Christian Fellowships (now known as the Union of Christian Assemblies). Pentecostal churches in Brazil include the Evangelical Pentecostal Church, formerly known as Brazil for Christ; the Congregation of Christ; and the Assemblies of God. In Chile, which like Brazil has experienced rapid Pentecostal growth, we find the Evangelical Pentecostal Church and the Methodist Pentecostal Church.

Pentecostalism encompasses a variety of beliefs and practices. Most Pentecostals practice believers' baptism, but a few denominations adhere to infant baptism. Jonathan Paul, founder of the German Pentecostal movement, defends infant baptism. In some fellowships speaking in tongues is marginal. In the Chilean church less than half of the pastors speak in tongues. In Haiti the bridge-burning experience is not speaking in tongues, which is common in Voodooism, but the burning of the Voodoo idols.

Significant leaders in the wider Pentecostal movement include T. B. Barratt of Norway; Lewi Pethrus of Sweden; Donald Gee, English Pentecostal pastor and author; George Jeffreys and Stephen Jeffreys, founders of the Elim Pentecostal Church in Britain; David du Plessis, ecumenical Pentecostal who has worked closely with the World Council of Churches; Oral Roberts, healing evangelist and founder of Oral Roberts University; Gordon Fee, Pentecostal biblical scholar teaching at Regent College in British Columbia; Pat Robertson, founder of the 700 Club; Paul and Jan Crouch of the Trinity Broadcasting Network; William Branham (d. 1965), healing evangelist who aligned himself with the Oneness movement;[16] and Reinhard Bonnke, international evangelist and head of Christ for All Nations, which is dedicated to worldwide mission.

Another growing phenomenon is neo-Pentecostalism, often known as the charismatic movement. The movement began in 1960 when Dennis Bennett, rector of St. Mark's Episcopal Church in Van Nuys, California, received the baptism of the Spirit and the gift of tongues.[17] The church divided over the issue, and he subsequently moved to Seattle to become pastor of St. Luke's Episcopal Church. The charismatic movement has infiltrated Episcopal, Presbyterian, Methodist, Baptist, Disciples, United Church of Christ and Roman Catholic churches. Even Eastern Orthodox churches have been affected. Various paraparochial fellowships have felt the impact of the charismatic movement: the Blessed Trinity Society (now defunct), the Order of St. Luke the Physician and Camps Farthest Out. Magazines that have emerged out of neo-Pentecostalism include *Trinity, Logos, New Covenant, Charisma, Charisma Digest* and *New Wine*. Prominent among the leaders in the charismatic movement have been Agnes Sanford, spiritual healer and author; J. Rodman Williams, Presbyterian theologian now at Regent University (Virginia Beach); Harald Bredesen, Reformed pastor; Theodore Jungkuntz, minister and teacher at Valparaiso University; Larry Christenson, Lutheran minister;[18] Ralph Martin and Stephen Clark, Roman Catholic laymen formerly associated with the Word of God community in Ann Arbor, Michigan; Kevin and Dorothy Ranaghan, originally of the People of Praise community in South Bend, Indiana; Edward O'Connor and Donald Gelpi, Roman Catholic priests and well-known authors; and Francis MacNutt, former Catholic priest and spiritual healer.[19]

Catholic Pentecostalism is especially significant, for it reveals the breadth of the Pentecostal revolution. It began at Duquesne University in 1967 and spread rapidly throughout the country and then overseas. Tongues are accepted as one of the gifts of the Spirit but not as a proof of having the Spirit. Some Catholic Pentecostals see the baptism of the Spirit as the fulfillment of conversion. They regard the practice of laying on of hands for Spirit baptism not as a new sacrament but as a catalyst that makes baptism and confirmation operative. For them Holy Spirit baptism comprises the ontological reality given in the sacrament of baptism and the experiential moment when this reality comes to conscious realization. Religious communities that have grown out of the Pentecostal revival in the Catholic Church include the Word of God community in Ann Arbor, Michigan; People of Praise community in South Bend, Indiana; Emmanuel community in Paris; and the Maranatha community in Brussels.

Pentecostal spirituality has also penetrated evangelical religious communities: the Brethren of the Common Life, the Evangelical Sisterhood of Mary, Bethany Fellowship, the Community of Celebration, the Jesus Army, Jesus Abbey in Korea, and the Community of Jesus. Mother Basilea Schlink, founder of the Evangelical Sisterhood of Mary in Darmstadt, Germany, distinguishes between conversion and the gift of the Spirit but contends that tongues are only one of the evidences or manifestations of the Spirit. She is severely critical of the perfectionism that characterizes much of Pentecostalism and insists that conversion is not simply an event but a lifelong process. While appreciative of the spiritual gifts as promoting the common good, she is quite firm that "they were never the decisive factor of our spiritual life, the source of which lies in repentance, and love for Jesus."[20]

Cultic Pentecostalism is still another movement or complex of movements that deserves consideration. I have already alluded to Oneness Pentecostalism, which denies the Trinity and rejects the trinitarian formula for baptism. In the United Pentecostal Church baptism in the name of the Lord Jesus Christ is a condition for salvation. Speaking in tongues is seen as the prime sign that one is really baptized in the Spirit. The Holy Spirit is only a power or influence, not a person. Churches that appeal to new revelations that are often valued over the Bible include the Church of the Living Word, founded by John Robert Stevens, and the United House of Prayer for All People. Stevens teaches that the Bible is outdated and needs to be supplemented by prophecies inspired by the Spirit for our time.[21]

Much more alluring is the Faith movement in Pentecostalism, also called the Word of Faith and Positive Confession.[22] The movement has its philosophical source in the writings of E. W. Kenyon (1867-1948), who attended the Emerson College of Oratory in Boston, a spawning ground for New Thought ideas.[23] Kenyon began as a Congregationalist, then switched to Unitarianism and then to New Thought. He finally ended in Christian Science, but he sought to relate the insights of the so-called metaphysical movement to the burgeoning Pentecostal revival.[24] One of his chief converts was Kenneth Hagin, founder of the Rhema Bible Training Center. Other Pentecostal leaders who teach the Faith confession theology include Kenneth Copeland, Fred Price, T. L. Osborn, John Osteen, Robert Tilton, Charles Capps, Charles Cowan and Marilyn Hickey. To some degree the Faith philosophy has intruded into the ministries of Paul Crouch, Oral Roberts and Pat Robertson, though the evangelical note is much more prominent. The Faith movement teaches that the universe runs by spiritual laws, and it is up to us to discover and apply these laws to our own situation. The way to be healed is to confess that we are healed and not waver in this belief. One "conquers error by denying its verity."[25] Faith becomes a superhuman effort to alter human consciousness and thereby dispel sickness. As in the New Thought movement, pain is overcome by denying its sensory evidence and affirming the goodness of God and the efficacy of Christ. Fred Price declared in a chapel service at Oral Roberts University (Sept. 19, 1980), "It's not God who heals you, it's your faith."[26] We simply need to confess the beneficence of God and then claim this beneficence for our healing. A gnostic element is apparent in this movement, whose adherents regularly "base their teachings on truths revealed directly by the Spirit, things they 'never saw before' in the Bible."[27] They claim that "difficulties are only suffered by Christians when they fail to exercise the laws of faith."[28]

The Faith movement and indeed the New Thought movement on the whole are not bereft of biblical support. The Psalms urge us to meditate on the law of God (77:12; 119:15; 143:5), which will be a source of healing for us (Prov 3:8; 4:20-22). Paul enjoins us to fix our mind on those things that are edifying and uplifting (Rom 8:5-6; Phil 4:8; Col 3:2). Faith teachers correctly discern the power of thought to affect the way we meet the challenges of life. But they gravely misunderstand the character of faith, which has its basis not in the human will but in God. By contending that health and prosperity follow inevitably from a right faith attitude, they deny the salutary role of cross bearing, which often involves the sacrifice of the comforts and goods of this world.[29] They rightly remind us, however, that sickness does not belong to the new order of the kingdom of God and that the fullness of salvation involves the overcoming of sickness as well as sin. Yet the Bible teaches that we can triumph over sickness inwardly and that physical healing is not the essence of salvation (cf. Lk 17:11-19).

Pentecostal Distinctives

The one denominator that links all Pentecostals together is the Pentecostal experience, often called the baptism *in, with* or *of* the Holy Spirit. This experience is interpreted in several different ways, however, so that it tends to be a barrier to Pentecostal unity. Most often it is seen as an energizing or empowering experience that equips the believer for mission. Some circles identify it with the experience of full sanctification; others sharply distinguish it from this experience. Some Pentecostals hold that the Holy Spirit is only *with* the believer at his or her conversion and that the Spirit comes to dwell *in* the believer at a later time. Others contend that the Spirit comes to dwell within us at conversion, but we are then urged to seek the fullness or "infilling" of the Spirit. A few Pentecostals, such as David du Plessis, make a distinction between the baptism *of* the Spirit (which occurs at conversion) and baptism *in* the Spirit, which is subsequent to conversion. The Mülheim Association of Christian Fellowships in Germany rejects the view that the baptism of the Spirit is a second experience after the new birth and affirms the Reformation doctrine that in conversion we are baptized into the body of Christ. Arnold Bittlinger, who has been active in the charismatic movement in German Lutheranism, contends that there is only one baptism—of water and the Spirit. Our task is to realize this blessing in our personal experience.[30] United Pentecostals are inclined to regard the new birth as including repentance for sin, immersion in water in the name of the Lord Jesus Christ and the baptism of the Spirit.[31]

A second hallmark of Pentecostalism is its emphasis on glossolalia as the confirmatory sign of the gift of the Spirit. Yet even here there are noteworthy differences among Pentecostals. Some contend that speaking in tongues constitutes *the* evidence of Spirit baptism and others that it is only *an* evidence or even a possible evidence. A number of Pentecostal leaders such as T. B. Barratt of Norway and Lewi Pethrus of Sweden have been willing to admit that Spirit baptism may occur without glossolalia. Pastor Samuel Edestav of the Philadelphia Church in Sweden has held that the primary evidence of the reception of the Spirit is the power to witness. The Elim Pentecostal Church in England rejects the doctrine that tongues is the initial sign of receiving the Spirit. The Mülheim Association of Christian Fellowships asserts that tongues is a natural human gift and that the Spirit may use it as he wishes. The Church of the Living God permits tongues but only in recognizable languages and disclaims the view that tongues is the initial evidence for Spirit baptism.[32] Alan Walker reported that 60 percent of the ministers in the Methodist Pentecostal Church in Chile confessed that they had never spoken in tongues.[33] At the same time, one cannot deny that original or classical Pentecostalism assigns a prominent role to speaking in tongues and that the experience of Spirit baptism is commonly assumed to be a glossolalic experience.

Perhaps nothing so exemplifies the Pentecostal movement as the urgency of mission. The Holy Spirit imparts not only sanctification but missionary power and fervor. The baptism of the Spirit enables one to bear witness to Christ in the world. Even the critics of Pentecostalism marvel at the ability of untrained laypeople to share their faith with total strangers. While Pentecostals assign a prominent role to preaching, they also make a place for other kinds of evangelistic outreach: caring fellowship, robust singing, Bible study groups, prayer cells and dancing in the Spirit. It is rightly said that the Pentecostals communicate the gospel not simply through verbal concepts but also through social embodiment.

Pentecostals are also agreed that the gifts of the Spirit did not cease with the apostolic age but were intended to fortify and edify the Christian community throughout its history. Besides glossolalia the gifts that are given special attention among Pentecostals and charismatics are healing; prophecy, speaking a direct word from God that has bearing on the present or future situation; the discerning of spirits, which enables one to know whether a prophecy or witness comes from God or the devil; the word of wisdom, which brings divine illumination to the issue at hand; the word of knowledge, which allows one to penetrate the deeper recesses of another person's being; and the working of miracles, which equips one to transmit the life-giving energy of the

Spirit to those in need. These gifts are generally viewed as manifestations of the Spirit rather than permanent endowments.

A special word should be said about divine healing, an important element in the Pentecostal ministry. Except for cultic Pentecostalism this healing can be described as "messianic" rather than "metaphysical," since it is a sign of the inbreaking of the kingdom of God in its messianic glory. It is not the power of thought or ultimately even the power of faith that brings about healing but the living Christ who responds to the petitions of his people in grace and mercy.[34] One will often find magical practices in Pentecostal healing services, such as the blessing of handkerchiefs, scarves or vials of oil that supposedly enables these finite objects to transmit divine power. The Pentecostal emphasis on healing must be seen in the context of a theology that regards sickness as a prime manifestation of sin. The call for healing is therefore at the same time a call for battle against the powers of sickness and death. Pentecostals do not always perceive that sickness can be used by God for his glory. They would find it difficult to empathize with P. T. Forsyth's "sacrament of pain."[35] J. Oswald Sanders, a non-Pentecostal, gives a balanced view when he argues that God overcomes sickness either by removing it or granting us the strength to bear it.[36]

Closely related to the healing ministry is the ministry of deliverance, which is based on the supposition that the ultimate adversary of humanity is Satan or demonic powers. Sickness is attributed not only to sin but often to demonic incursion. What is needed is not simply a prayer for healing but the exorcism of the demons that pull us down into the depths of misery and depravity and render us helpless to help ourselves. Demons are often conceived of animistically, as discarnate spirits seeking bodies to inhabit. Pentecostals are prone to see demons as radically different from angels in that they come from the netherworld rather than from heaven.[37] The exorcism of demons frequently takes the form of the laying on of hands and includes commands to the demons to depart from the accursed individual in the name of Jesus Christ.

The Phenomenon of Glossolalia

Because Pentecostals commonly regard speaking in tongues (glossolalia) as not only a gift of the Spirit but an evidential sign of receiving the Spirit, this phenomenon deserves special consideration. The pivotal question is the nature of glossolalia. Pentecostal scholar Russell Spittler describes it as "the religious phenomenon of making sounds that constitute, or resemble, a language not known to the speaker. It is often accompanied by an excited religious psychological state."[38] Many Pentecostals regard tongues as an actual language unfamiliar to the speaker (xenolalia). Some portray it as an ecstatic language, a state of rapture that the mind cannot grasp or contain. According to Charles W. Conn, a former Church of God executive, "The unknown tongue is not the stammering of excited vocal organs, but rather the clear utterances of spiritual ecstasy. When the Spirit speaks through you, it will be exalted praise or convicting exhortation."[39] A number of Pentecostals dislike the term *ecstatic* when applied to tongues, for this seems to connote the elimination of the personality. The Holy Spirit enables us, but he does not so overwhelm us as to abrogate our personality. Pentecostals are inclined to attribute any sign of the complete transcendence of personality to demonic influences.

At Pentecost there was probably a mixture of glossolalia and xenolalia. The miracle of Pentecost was that every person heard the apostles speaking in his or her own language. There is a miracle here beyond what can be psychologically explained. The "tongues" in the churches of Corinth were very probably ecstatic speech, not foreign languages.

Scholars are indeed divided on the nature of the tongues experience. According to William James and Frederic W. H. Myers "glossolalia" is an automatism similar to automatic writing.[40] Ira Martin sees it as a form of psychic catharsis, symptomatic of a personality readjustment.[41] Morton Kelsey regards tongues as a type of somnambulism, a trancelike state analogous to dreams and visions. Whereas in hypnotism one has rapport with others, somnambulism is characterized by lack of rapport with others.[42] William J. Samarin, a linguist, contends that "glossolalia is a perfectly human, perfectly normal (albeit anomalous) phenomenon."[43] Glossolalia is *sometimes* associated with *some* degree of altered state of consciousness," and "this *occasionally* involves motor activity that is involuntary. . . . In any case subsequent use of glossolalia (that is, after the initial experience) is *most often independent* of dissociative phenomena."[44] Wayne Oates, a pastoral care theologian, holds that tongues may be a form of "parataxic speech" expression corresponding to Jean Piaget's egocentric speech.[45] Those who begin to speak in tongues "have no language but a cry." On both the psychological and spiritual levels maturation can be traced from private unintelligibility to social communicability.

George Barton Cutten claims that glossolalia may involve the utterance of foreign words, but always words with which the speaker has had some contact. He also asserts that the glossolalist's capacity for rational thought is undeveloped.[46] Similarly James Lapsley and J. H. Simpson contend that glossolalia should be understood as a dissociative expression of a truncated personality development.[47] Against this view Morton Kelsey argues persuasively that it may actually aid one in achieving deeper personal integration.[48] Virginia Hine also gives a more positive assessment of glossolalia: "One of the remarkable things about tongue speakers is the degree to which they can communicate both the quality and the effect of their subjective religious experiences."[49]

From the theological perspective one might say that this phenomenon has two sides, the psychological and the supernatural. Only the first is open to direct empirical investigation. One can admit that the Spirit may be present in the unconscious guiding of a person who prays in tongues. Yet this fact can be discerned only in faith. The evidence of the genuineness of one's experience lies in the fruits of a Christian life.

Glossolalia may be viewed as a type of prayer, since the one who so prays addresses God (1 Cor 14:2, 14). Yet it is not full or complete prayer because prayer in the deepest sense involves the understanding as well as the spirit (1 Cor 14:15). It could be regarded as preconceptual prayer. When accompanied by interpretation it becomes complete prayer. It enables one to give voice to concerns that have not yet been conceptualized.

For the apostle Paul speaking in tongues serves private edification. It should not be practiced in public unless it is followed by interpretation. A person who prays in this manner should also pray for the power to interpret (1 Cor 14:13). Paul discouraged tongues in public meetings under any circumstances (1 Cor 14:34). Yet on the basis of Pauline theology tongues are certainly permissible for private devotion and in small groups. Paul boasted that he spoke in tongues more than all of them (1 Cor 14:18). Luke associates tongues with missionary power. The gift of tongues equips one for service to the gospel. It is a sign of total surrender and openness to the Spirit.

In my opinion tongues are given for private edification, but they may benefit the church indirectly by leading to the gifts that build up the body of Christ—such as prophecy, teaching, service and preaching. They may also enable us to draw closer to God and thereby give us power to witness. Tongues are mysterious but not necessarily miraculous. The miracle is the movement of the Holy Spirit on us and in us, and this is imperceptible. Tongues should not be celebrated as a higher kind of prayer. I take exception to Merlin Carothers, who contrasts glossolalia to prayer with the understanding: "When we speak in tongues, we communicate directly from our spirit to God."[50]

Catholic Pentecostals tend to take a more reserved attitude toward tongues and other spectacular charisms of the Spirit. Donald Gelpi believes that "it is dangerous and misleading to demand that the divine response be the gift of tongues, just as it is dangerous and misleading to call the gift of tongues, which is the least of the gifts, the 'fullness of the Spirit.'"[51] Catholic Pentecostals stress that the Holy Spirit will calm as well as arouse the heart. What the Spirit imparts is not only exuberant joy but also inner peace. Josephine Ford sees tongues as a step to a deeper, interior life—a means, not an end. Similarly Edward O'Connor regards the charisms as "neither the source, the goal nor the substance of Christian life; they are an aid—a powerful one indeed, but one which needs to be integrated into the life of prayer and fraternal service which this aid is meant to foster."[52] Among Catholic Pentecostals there is a noticeable inclination to portray faith as insufficient for sealing our union with God. In O'Connor's words: "Not simple faith, but faith irradiated by the gifts . . . is what gives us that contact with God that justifies our speaking of a new presence."[53] For Cardinal Suenens baptism with water only sets us on the way. We need to experience a release of the Spirit in our lives in order to belong completely to Christ.[54]

I believe that tongues should be related to the childhood of faith or to new beginnings in faith. Carl Jung is helpful here in reminding us that the invasion of the unconscious commonly occurs prior to the integration of the personality. In his view "the strangeness of the unconscious contents not yet integrated in consciousness demands an equally strange language."[55] This is how he explained the frequency of glossolalia among the early Christians. Christianity demands a break with established patterns of living and thinking. It gave rise to a new experience that could not be entirely absorbed by the consciousness.

Those who speak in tongues seek a readjustment to a new horizon, a new way of living and coping. Jesus apparently never spoke in tongues because he was never a child in the faith. He did not need conversion. Tongues results when we try to integrate past memories embedded in the unconscious with the new vision. For Paul tongues can sometimes be helpful to children in the faith, but when we press on to maturity they can be set aside (1 Cor 13:8, 11, 13). Yet Paul himself spoke in tongues for the purpose of the service and adoration of God (1 Cor 14:18).

There is also the ministry of holding one's tongue, as Bonhoeffer points out in his *Life Together*.[56] James praises those who hold their tongues in check, for they can control both mind and body (Jas 1:26; 3:2-12). Silence under the Word is characteristic of the later stages of faith. Love sometimes entails the inhibition, even the suppression of one's feelings. Having had a transforming experience of the living Christ, Paul referred to "things that cannot be told, which man may not utter" (2 Cor 12:4). This is not to discount or underplay the positive benefits that accrue from speaking in tongues, and those whose prayer life is going nowhere may be encouraged to experiment in new methods of conversing with God so long as they are solidly grounded in Scripture.

Dangers in Pentecostalism

Every vital and dynamic religious movement is constantly threatened by excesses and imbalances on the part of its followers. Pentecostalism is surely not exempt from these pitfalls. One danger that besets this movement is legalism, the vain expectation that one can make oneself worthy or morally acceptable to God. Frederick Dale Bruner observes: "In the majority Pentecostal view, as the converted sinner increases in sanctification he progressively qualifies for the special gift of the Spirit. The Christian is understood as quite another kind of person by the time he is ready to receive the subsequent spiritual baptism."[57] Faith itself is often understood as a spiritual work, a superhuman effort rather than the despair of all effort.[58] It is not a "mere trusting" but an "absolute surrender." The steps to salvation are removing all known sin, then heart purification by faith, and finally the Pentecostal baptism of the Holy Spirit. Some Pentecostals teach that we must first make sure that we are "right with God" before we apply for the gift of the Spirit. In a manner reminiscent of semi-Pelagianism, Pentecostals sometimes suggest that justification is produced "by the cooperation of divine and human activities."[59] On the credit side one can perhaps say that Pentecostals have rediscovered another dimension of faith—faith as obedience.[60] Yet I would insist that the obedience of faith is not what justifies us but is a consequence of the inward awakening produced by the Holy Spirit. Nonetheless we need to remember that Christians are not to remain passive but must actively seek the fulfillment of the promises of God in their lives.

Reformed Christianity contends against Pentecostalism that our task is not to find God through a heart experience but to confess that God has already found us in Jesus Christ. New outpourings of the Holy Spirit will surely follow the work of the Spirit in conversion, but we must maintain the biblical fact that the converted person has already received the Spirit in faith.

Something is terribly amiss in the theology of a Swedish Pentecostal leader who declared, "We have in our assemblies many more people, perhaps even members, who only have the forgiveness of sins, but are not born again and have not received the Holy Spirit."[61] But if we have the forgiveness of sins, then we must assuredly have the Holy Spirit as well as the new birth.

Illuminism or spiritualism is another bane of the Pentecostal movement. In this aberration the inner light or private revelations become more authoritative than sacred Scripture or sacred tradition. The Church of the Living Word confesses that there are truths yet to be revealed by the Holy Spirit that will enable us to continue our walk with God and witness the full restoration of his church for our time.[62] Such a position does not contravene biblical revelation, but it prepares the way for "truths" that go beyond the parameters of Scripture. The Brazilian Congregation of Christ sometimes portrays the Spirit as a higher criterion than Scripture. When faced with biblical truths contrary to their position, some of these people reply: "The Holy Spirit has not revealed this to me in this way."[63] The now defunct Daystar community in Minneapolis allowed for the possibility of new inspired writings and new prophets. The Full Salvation Union, a Pentecostal Quaker group, regards the writers of the Bible but not the book as inspired. It asserts that God's direct guidance of an individual takes precedence over the Bible. In Reformed theology the Holy Spirit is not a second criterion alongside the Word but one aspect of the one criterion—the Word enlightened by the Spirit. Some Pentecostal groups err in the opposite direction by stressing the empowering work of the

Spirit but not his illuminating work so that divine revelation is portrayed as directly accessible to human reason and imagination. This rationalistic strand does not belong to original Pentecostalism but signifies the infiltration of fundamentalism in this movement.

Pentecostals remind the wider church that worship is something deeper and richer than sermonic proclamation, but too often the much sought after spontaneity in worship services results in attempts to manipulate the emotions of those present. A disdain for worship forms prescribed by tradition leads to ad hoc worship forms that often lack biblical substance and grounding. Ironically in many cases the new format solidifies into a pattern at least as rigid as any of its predecessors. Worship sometimes degenerates into performance, and it is human dexterity and technology that are celebrated rather than the glory of God. Praise choruses take the place of the great hymns of the church, and the sermon in the sense of biblical exposition is supplanted by inspiring testimonies and prophecies. David du Plessis confesses, "I have seen too many shouting Christians go to sleep when the Word is preached. They live on 'milk' and choke on the 'meat' of the Word."[64] Edward O'Connor warns against "charismania"—"expecting charismatic activity to take the place of the natural exercise of the human faculties or the ordinary workings of Church office."[65] J. Sidlow Baxter, a sympathetic critic of both traditional Pentecostal and charismatic movements, gives this timely admonition:

> Where has the Bible got to in many charismatic gatherings? To my own way of thinking, in every such meeting the Word of God should be heard. Where has the hymnbook gone? The people are not given hymnbooks; so none of the richer-quality hymns can be sung (such hymns have much to do with the spiritual tone or level of Christian gatherings). The hymnbook is forsaken in favor of lilting choruses—chorus after chorus, with repetition after repetition, meeting after meeting. Where has Bible teaching gone? Instead of enriching, challenging, edifying Bible exposition and application there is a platform-engineered stir up of emotion. There is a place, of course, for

stirred emotions; but emotional*ism* is bad, and there is far too much of it.[66]

This brings us to the anti-intellectualism that characterizes not only Pentecostalism but the wider movement of conservative evangelicalism.[67] A disdain for theology is manifest in many Pentecostal assemblies, including the electronic church. Some Pentecostals complain that their pastors neglect theological study and sermon preparation. Although Pentecostalism has given birth to many flourishing Bible colleges, it has produced little lasting theological and biblical scholarship, though this may be changing.[68] Many Pentecostals appeal to 1 John 2:27: "You have no need that any one should teach you," since the anointing teaches one about everything. Yet the New Testament makes clear that the church needs teachers as well as evangelists and prophets. Teaching and study are gifts of the Spirit just as much as tongues and miracles. If theology is "the sanctification of the mind" (J. Edward Carnell), then we do not have entire sanctification unless we have engaged in theological reflection. Both Catholicism and the Reformation have honored the doctors of the church, and without such teachers the church would be severed from its spiritual and theological moorings.

Pentecostalism also needs to be wary of spiritual sensualism, the search for higher experiences of the divine. When signs and wonders become the principal focus of ministry, faith begins to erode. Although faith involves feeling, our mandate is not to cultivate feelings but to grow in faith. Faith itself is an experience but one that is not accessible to psychological observation. It is an experience that bypasses the senses. Luther put it well: "Faith directs itself towards the things that are invisible. Indeed, only when that which is believed on is hidden can it provide an opportunity for faith."[69] Calvin concurs: "It is His will that we should shut our eyes to what we are and have, in order that nothing may impede or even check our faith in Him."[70] This same reservation toward experiences is found in Kierkegaard: "Now, Spirit is the denial of direct immediacy. If Christ be very God, He must be unknown, for to be known directly is the characteristic mark of an idol."⁷¹ The Pentecostal Barratt once wrote that glossolalia is a "palpable proof of God's influence on man."⁷² Is not Luther closer to the biblical witness when he describes faith as "impalpable" and "insensible"?⁷³ To be sure, the Christian can have foretastes and anticipations of the glory that lies ahead, but basically we must walk by faith. Pentecostals often point to Acts 4:29-30 to show that signs and wonders belong to the ministry of the church. Yet what we have in these verses is a petition not for the performing of signs but for the preaching of the Word with the recognition that signs and wonders would follow. Speaking in tongues may be a consequence of the baptism of the Spirit, but it is not an unequivocal sign. The pagan can also be moved in this way (1 Cor 12:2). Pentecostal worship is sometimes more *seelisch* (emotional) than *geistlich* (spiritual). Forsyth presciently warned that "the deepening of spiritual life" should not be confused with "the quickening of spiritual sensibility."⁷⁴

Yet having made these criticisms a fair observer must acknowledge that many Pentecostal services do manifest the awesome presence of God. When healings take place most Pentecostal pastors immediately give God all the credit and confess that in and of themselves they can heal no one. Too often in mainline Protestantism the worship service is encased in ritualized forms that allow no free expression of faith, no unexpected manifestation of the Spirit. There are many Pentecostal worship services in which reverence and joy are held together. Presbyterians are often associated with the maxim that things should be done decently and in order, but this can become a pretext for blocking the free movement of the Spirit in a worship assembly. The Word of God is not only to be heard but also to be seen (cf. Acts 2:22; 4:20; Rom 15:19), though one must be cautious here, for the real seeing is with the eyes of faith.

Perhaps the most frequent criticism of Pentecostalism by the religious establishment is that it substitutes a theology of glory for a theology of the cross. Sometimes Pentecostals appear to be overly familiar with God, thus creating the impression that they live no longer by faith but by direct sight with an instant understanding of God's will. Jeremy Taylor (d. 1667) warned, "Let no man be hasty to eat of the fruits of paradise before his time."[75] David du Plessis admonished his fellow Pentecostals that we are in dangerous heresy when we speak of "shaking, trembling, falling, dancing, clapping, shouting, and such actions as manifestations of the Holy Spirit. These are purely human reactions to the power of the Holy Spirit and frequently hinder more than help to bring forth genuine manifestations."[76] Many in the charismatic movement seek the rapture of Pentecost without first submitting to the cross of Calvary. Holiness becomes a "cherished delight" rather than a cross to be borne.[77] On the other side of the ledger, we must not downplay or deny the place in the church for the experience of Pentecost, which can enliven and embolden us in the practice of our faith. One should note that Paul sought the redirection, not the suppression, of the zeal of the Corinthians. He did not denigrate tongues but endeavored to regulate and subordinate them.

Sectarianism is another pitfall in Pentecostalism, though this temptation is found in all branches of Christendom, including Roman Catholicism and Eastern Orthodoxy. In this regard Pentecostals are inclined to be more open to ecumenical initiatives than many conservative Presbyterians and Lutherans. At the same time, a sectarian propensity has often been manifest in the Pentecostal movement in its history. Many early Pentecostals taught that while all believers constitute the church, only the Spirit-baptized comprise the Bride of Christ. At the marriage supper of the Lamb the role of the other believers is to serve the Bride.[78] The Church of God of Prophecy has claimed to be "the one, true 'Church of God.'"[79] William M. Branham, who was associated with Oneness Pentecostalism, insisted that believers baptized with the trinitarian formula be rebaptized in the name of Jesus.[80] Every denomination must struggle to curb and suppress its schismatic side and try to be a church rather than a sect.

The doctrine of the Trinity is not always confessed or rightly understood among Pentecostals. Too often Christ is separated from the Spirit, and the baptism of the Spirit into the body of Christ is portrayed as qualitatively different from the baptism of Christ with the Spirit. Sometimes Pentecostals speak of two faiths, a "faith toward Christ for salvation" and "a faith toward the Holy Spirit for power and consecration."[81] Some say that the Holy Spirit is only *with* the person who has given his or her heart to Christ. The Spirit allegedly does not yet abide in that person. The Spirit is frequently likened to electricity or a magnetic force. Hans Küng rightly claims that the Spirit is neither "some magical, mysteriously supernatural aura of a dynamistic kind" nor "a magical being of an animistic kind." He is "God himself in his especially personal and self-giving aspect: as a power which gives itself to man, but cannot be controlled by man, as a power which creates life."[82] Pentecostals too readily gravitate toward either an almost polytheistic tritheism in which the Father, Son and Spirit have independent personalities or a unitarian monotheism that celebrates the unity of God but does not allow for different modes of being within God himself.[83] This problem does not pertain only to Pentecostals, for the doctrine of the Trinity is being debated anew within Christendom.

Finally we must note the danger of secularism in the Pentecostal movement. When a group disdains theology it becomes ever more vulnerable to the values and pressures of the world. A major wing of Pentecostalism has embraced the cultural values of health, wealth and prosperity and sees faith as a means for gaining the goods of this world. Many thoughtful Pentecostals are embarrassed when people of affluence and power boast of how their faith helped gain their enviable status in society. Pentecostalism is too quick to celebrate power (physical and spiritual) as a Christian virtue and misses the New Testament emphasis on the powerlessness of the cross. At the same time, does not faith bring us a power for service and witness, and have not Pentecostals grasped this reality more than the mainliners? Karl Barth was even willing to speak of a will to power that grows out of faith, but this is always power for service, not for dominion over others.

Luther astutely perceived that wherever Christ builds his church, the devil builds his chapel. We need to keep these words in mind as we examine the shadow side of Pentecostalism. Pentecostalism may contain more heat than light, but the communities of God's "frozen chosen" (the mainline churches) need heat as well as light, the Holy Spirit as well as the Word of God. In this discussion we of the mainline must confess that the Spirit of God is speaking to us through this movement, and for this we can only be grateful.

Enduring Contributions

At this juncture in history the wider church should treat Pentecostalism not as an adversary but as a challenge to reclaim the fullness of the gospel. While we need to be on guard against certain grave imbalances in this movement, we must try to ascertain what we can learn from the Pentecostal awakening.

First, Pentecostals remind us that there are blessings of the Spirit beyond conversion. People in mainline churches too often appeal simply to baptism or confirmation as assuring them that they have the blessings of the Spirit, not realizing that Pentecost must be an enduring reality in the life of the Christian.

Second, Pentecostals have rediscovered the vital role of the charismatic gifts for private edification, public worship and the ministry of evangelism. They are wrong to limit the gifts to the nine or twelve referred to in 1 Corinthians 12—14 and to elevate the spectacular gifts above those that seem more ordinary. The story is told that David du Plessis at a Presbyterian Conference on Evangelism in Cincinnati (Sept. 1971) reproved another Pentecostal minister who complained that the gifts of the Spirit were not in evidence in a certain unnamed Presbyterian church. Du Plessis took exception to this judgment and proceeded to list gifts that he had observed—none spectacular but nevertheless very important: teaching, hospitality, lowly service, leadership and so on. The spiritual gifts should be seen as tools for ministry rather than rational evidences of having the Spirit. In this light it is not wrong to seek for spiritual gifts, especially the higher gifts that build up the church (1 Cor 14:1-5).

Pentecostalism has also drawn attention to the energizing or empowering work of the Holy Spirit. In the Reformed tradition the emphasis has often been on the Spirit's illuminating work, especially in reference to understanding the Bible. The regenerating and sanctifying work of the Spirit has also received due consideration. But the Spirit not only regenerates and illumines but also energizes and thereby equips the Christian for a missionary vocation. God is not only the loving heavenly Father who forgives but also the power of creative transformation who makes alive that which was dead.

Fourth, Pentecostals teach us that the marks of the church include mission and fellowship (koinonia) as well as Word and sacraments. A church that may have right preaching but lacks the fellowship of love is likely to have only the form and not the content of Christian faith. One reason why Pentecostalism has experienced such spectacular growth is that people are drawn to the fellowship of love that is manifest among many of its adherents. The local Pentecostal congregation is more often than not a family that cares for the physical and material as well as the spiritual needs of its members.

Fifth, Pentecostalism has given poignant expression to the priesthood of all believers. The Reformation had rediscovered this biblical concept but was unable to avoid a hierarchical church in which all major responsibilities are assumed by the pastor. Pentecostals remind us that all Christians share in the ministry of Christ, including laity and women. The question of women in ministry has not been a divisive issue in most Pentecostal churches. The Catholic charismatic theologian Edward O'Connor warns that we must also be alert to the danger of "paraclericalism" that results in the laity usurping the prerogatives of the pastoral office.[84]

Sixth, Pentecostalism has powerfully rediscovered the moral dualism of the New Testament: the conflict between Christ and the adversary of God and humanity, the devil or Satan. When this dualism becomes a metaphysical duality between the material and spiritual worlds, however, we see the intrusion of gnosticism into Pentecostal theology.

Seventh, Pentecostals have succeeded in recovering the role of signs and wonders in the evangelistic ministry of the church. People are brought to faith not only by hearing the Word but also seeing the power of the Word in action (Acts 14:3; Rom 15:18-19; Heb 2:4). Yet miraculous signs must never become an end in themselves and must never be regarded as evidences of godliness or authentic faith (cf. Deut 13:1-5). Jesus himself was not enthusiastic about the quest for signs (Mt 12:38-39; Lk 11:29; Jn 4:48).

I cannot go along with many critics of Pentecostalism who score them for classifying Christians on the basis of their level of spiritual maturity. All Christians are justified sinners, but some are making progress toward becoming saints. Paul makes a helpful distinction between babes in Christ and spiritual persons (1 Cor 3:1), and we must not discount this important insight. None of us can earn our salvation or make ourselves worthy of God's grace. But we can demonstrate and manifest God's grace in our daily lives, and if we do so we will be rewarded, not because we have achieved a higher level of holiness but because we have been more open to the moving of the Spirit. Even then we can take no credit, since our openness is irrevocably tied to our election. We do good works because we have been separated by God for a life of service. If we cease to do good works we will be judged for having quenched and grieved the Spirit who lives within us and strives to perfect our union with Christ.

Finally, Pentecostals give powerful reaffirmation of the evangelical thesis that the most important fact in the Christian life is crossing the divide that separates the state of sin and lostness from the state of grace and redemption. Where they are prone to err is in claiming too much for the Spirit-filled Christian, in identifying the gift of the Spirit with the eschatological fullness of the Spirit. They should pay heed to Karl Barth's keen observation on the work of the Spirit in the lives of

Christians: "The love of God which has been shed abroad in their hearts through the Holy Spirit will never be for them a self-evident, settled fact and occurrence."[85] Yet we must not discount the fact that the decision of faith is something settled and completed even while it is at the same time something to be renewed in daily experience. We have been saved, but we are also still being saved, and we will be saved when Christ comes again in his glory.

The Spirit of Self-Criticism

What gives the Pentecostal revival some promise is that it has fostered a spirit of self-criticism among many of its leaders. There is now a growing reluctance to view tongues as the primary evidence of having received the Spirit. Du Plessis considers much speaking in tongues as chaff: "It looks bad when adults act like children. Some must come to maturity."[86] In his opinion, "love, not tongues, is truly a sign that one is full of the Holy Spirit."[87] Michael Harper in the charismatic renewal movement admits that "it is tragically possible to receive a baptism in the Spirit and yet remain basically self-centered—a person out for kicks and the sensuous enjoyment of meetings, rather than the costly following of our Lord in self-denying zeal."[88] Don Basham writes that "it is primarily the fruit of the Spirit which produces character, and character—not miracles—is the major issue in determining whether a man is a true or false prophet."[89] R. Hollis Gause, dean of the Church of God Graduate School of Christian Ministries, makes this remarkable confession: "We sometimes exalt the secondary benefits of the Spirit-baptism to a primary level. . . . Charismatic manifestations are made the tool of the individual and are subjected to his will."[90] And in the words of Larry Christenson: "Without the Christ-ordained ministries of authority, without Spirit-given structures to direct and shepherd the life, the fire of the Spirit can too easily become wild fire, and burn itself out in a short display of spiritual pyrotechnics."[91]

One pastor in the wider charismatic revival movement makes this trenchant observation:

There are many who exercise spiritual gifts (even as the Corinthians did) who are exceedingly carnal. We have allowed our people to assume that gifts are an evidence of being spiritual, when really they are given to babes that they might become spiritual. Proof of this misunderstanding is evident in our pentecostal churches where fleshly fads and fashions hold sway instead of a godly simplicity of life; where we can only hold attendance by using soulish entertainment; where people live on a constant diet of glamorous personalities who give unique testimonies of their experiences. Yet all the while our folk manifest so little true hunger or appetite for revealed truth from God's Word.[92]

Another critic from within Pentecostalism, Bernie L. Gillespie, shares this candid admission:

Growing up as a Pentecostal I learned to think that the more miracles, dreams, healings, visions I had, the more it showed I was spiritual. I felt good whenever I could manifest the supernatural. . . . For some, the absence of the "supernatural" is their evidence that truth and faith in God's presence are absent. The Scriptures declare that we are right with God by faith in Jesus Christ. For some, as it was for me, this truth has been either muted or replaced by a "faith" in the miraculous.[93]

Pentecostalism has inherited two traditions: Montanism and Protestant evangelicalism. While both claim to be biblical, Montanism is prone to elevate new revelations over the Bible and substitute the direct vision of God for simple trust. It also tends to foster spiritual elitism, whereas evangelicals stress the equal worth of all believers. As Pentecostals face the future I would encourage them to choose the way of the holy catholic faith over divisive enthusiasm. They must reaffirm the gospel of free grace and resist the pull toward works righteousness. They should respect prophecy, healing, discerning of spirits and the other spiritual gifts, but the gifts must be subordinated to the preaching and hearing of the Word of God. On the one hand, Pentecostals need a salutary dose of Calvinism to remind them that God is in control and that the coming of the kingdom is assured to us by God's promises and does not rest on our evangelistic strategies. On the other hand, Calvinism could benefit from a dose of Pentecostalism, for divine predestination does not take place except through the obedience of faith. Predestination is not divine determinism but divine liberation for service and witness through the exercising of spiritual gifts and the living out of a vocation of self-giving love.

Appendix B: Battling the Demons

For many decades the ethos of modernity relegated the demonic to the background, but with the collapse of an unwarranted faith in reason and the rise of postmodernity, the demonic is coming back into fashion. The flourishing of shamanism and animism in the wider culture, manifested in the Satanist and New Age movements, attests the emergence of a new cultural paradigm that makes a place for the demonic powers of chaos that threaten cultural stability and integrity.[94] The Pentecostal revolution reflects and promotes the fascination with the demonic, though contemporary academic theology has been slow to incorporate this theme in its enterprise.

While the demonic played a prominent role in Reformation theology (particularly with Luther),[95] the Enlightenment (from the late seventeenth to early nineteenth century) treated the demonic as a relic of our mythological past. It could be tolerated so long as it was understood poetically. For Schleiermacher reference to the devil belongs to "our treasury of song" but should not be a theme in dogmatics.[96] The deists tended to deny the existence of the devil: in their theology "the spiritual world was depopulated and God stood alone, his truth made known by the powers of rational man."[97]

Rudolf Otto (d. 1937) powerfully challenged the rationalism of the modern era by focusing attention on the nonrational aspects of faith and the eschatological nature of the kingdom of God. He also contended that the exorcism of demons was a pivotal theme in Jesus' ministry. Yet he could not escape the spell of the Enlightenment, insisting that the healings and exorcisms of Jesus could largely be explained in psychosomatic terms.[98]

Paul Tillich, who was markedly influenced by Otto, gave still more credence to the idea of demons but viewed them as symbolic of dark and sinister powers within the structures of being. The demonic side of reality could be apprehended only by cultivating a mythic consciousness that sees below the surface of things. He defined the demonic as the "form-destroying eruption of the creative basis of things."[99] Demons in mythological vision are "divine-antidivine beings. They are not simply negations of the divine but participate in a distorted way in the power and holiness of the divine."[100] Whereas the main mark of the tragic is the state of being blind, the main mark of the demonic is the state of being split.[101]

James Luther Adams gives this astute interpretation of Tillich's demonology:

> The principal opposition to the divine unity is not a satanic principle of mere negation; it is rather a demonic power that perverts the creative power into a mixture of form-creating and form-destroying energy in history. A demon is something less than God which pretends to be God. The demonic operates not only in the individual's wilful yielding to the temptation to give rein to the libido of sensuality, of power, and of knowledge. It operates even more powerfully in human institutions.[102]

Much of what Tillich says can be incorporated into a biblical, evangelical vision. His error lies in reducing the demonic to an "it" rather than a "he." For Tillich the demonic is a creative-destructive force that subverts human integrity and stability. Yet do not we also have to contend with an overarching intelligence who masterminds a strategy of evil that affects the whole cosmos? Just as Tillich fails to do justice to the personal dimension of the divine, so he depersonalizes the demonic, though he acknowledges that the demonic "comes to fulfillment in personality, and personality is the most prominent object of demonic destruction."[103]

Karl Barth interpreted the demonic as symbolic of the nothingness or chaos that constantly threatens creation. Demons are not angelic persons but forces of disruption that can only unravel and destroy. They exist through the act of divine negation, which accompanies the act of divine creation.[104] Their power is that of the lie, which is unmasked when exposed to the light of truth. The demons can be formidable adversaries to humans, but they are no match for the living God and have already been conquered through the victory of Jesus Christ.

More recently theologians are beginning to recognize how dismissal of the demonic has contributed to the vacuity of theology. In the words of Walter Sundberg, "To expurgate the Devil from the core of faith is to cut ourselves off from the nerve of biblical religion concerning the teaching of evil. It is to ignore both the Christian tradition and crucial aspects of contemporary reality."[105] James Stewart complains of the deleterious effect of demythologizing the devil: Such theologies "have failed to take seriously the New Testament's concentration upon the demonic nature of the evil from which the world has to be redeemed. They have misunderstood as secondary and extraneous elements in the primitive Christian proclamation what in fact are integral and basic components of the gospel."[106] William Manson asserts that "the supernatural demonological element of the gospel is not a mere veneer. It is not a temporary trapping which can bestripped away from the gospel. It is engrained in its very substance."[107] According to the Lutheran theologian James Kallas salvation in the original context of the New Testament meant much more than the mere remission of sins: it involved being saved from "the scourges and afflictions of Satan."[108] Salvation was therefore not a purely spiritual occurrence but deliverance from disabling illnesses and compulsions that have their source in demonic assault and oppression.[109]

In light of the new attention to the demonic, some theologians are cautioning against any return to the animistic view. Walter Wink warns, "The attempt to bring back belief in demons repudiates one of

Christianity's greatest victories: the de-demonization of the world."[110] Wink reinterprets the demonic in existentialist and psychological categories.[111] Vernon McCasland argues that the belief in demons has been exploded by modern psychology and medicine, but we must not therefore dismiss the New Testament accounts of exorcisms and healings as fictional. The demon-possessed are to be understood as abnormal personalities who achieve personal integration through faith in the healer and the assurance that the demon has been driven away.[112] This psychological interpretation is sharply challenged by Michael Welker and Ernst Käsemann, who contend that we need to uncover the "metaphysical depth and cosmic breadth" of the New Testament accounts of liberation from demons.[113]

The ancient worldview. In order to understand the central thrust of New Testament demonology it is necessary to examine the ancient worldview, which provided the background and imagery for the preaching of the apostles. This worldview was both utilized and countered by divine revelation. The task is not to demythologize the New Testament narratives but to interpret them in the context of a reconceptualization inaugurated by Jesus himself.

In the primitive or animistic worldview demons are wandering, disembodied spirits seeking bodies to inhabit. Some are mischievous, others benign. Moreover, demons act randomly and capriciously. They are more or less autonomous beings, though they may be bound together in a kingdom. Yet "there is no unity of will in this kingdom, nothing but planlessness, capriciousness, independent activity."[114] Demons are also omnipresent. They hover over or dwell within almost all animate objects. In the popular culture of the time "they were to be found everywhere, but particularly in ruined houses, marshes, the shade of certain trees," even "in lavatories."[115] Every person is vulnerable to demonic assault and possession. Animals too are not exempt from demon incursion. "Among the humans those whom they most frequently attacked were chronic invalids, engaged girls and the best man, or groomsman, at a wedding. . . . It was exceedingly unwise for a man to sleep all alone in a house: he would be the victim of Lilith, the she-devil, and anything at all might happen to him."[116] In the ancient worldview demon possession was regarded as a misfortune, not a consequence of sin. The demons were more active in the periods of darkness than in the light of day. The "terror of the night" and the "pestilence that stalks in darkness" (Ps 91:5-6) probably refer to specific demons. Because the demons were generally thought to have existed before the present cosmos was organized, their natural habitat was commonly regarded as the desert and sea, symbols of primordial chaos. Finally, the ancients often postulated "a chaotic, uncoordinated fraternal strife among the demons; the stronger ones driving out the weaker ones,"[117] an assumption, as we shall see, flatly contradicted by Jesus' preaching.

The animistic conception of demons infiltrated Jewish thought and religion and led to ministries of exorcism. One critic comments, "Apocryphal literature, especially the Book of Enoch, did much to fasten animism in the popular thinking of late Judaean and early Christian times."[118] A case can be made that Judaism absorbed ideas of demonology from Assyrian, Babylonian, Iranian and Greco-Roman cultures as well as developing its own. What is important to recognize is that the demonic was radically rethought in the apostolic church in the light of God's self-revelation in Jesus Christ. While much of the language was drawn from the primitive or mythological worldview, the meaning-content was drastically altered.

Pentecostalism has powerfully reaffirmed the New Testament picture of demonology but has not always discriminated between what is purely cultural and what belongs to the essence of revelation. Demons are sometimes depicted as spirits from the netherworld rather than fallen angels whose origin is the realm of pure spirit rather than a primordial chaos. Some Pentecostals speculate that demons are spirits of a pre-Adamic race of beings who were corrupted by Satan and his angels. They seek embodiment in human and even animal form because they long "to escape the intolerable condition of being unclothed."[119] Sometimes evangelicals and Pentecostals portray demons as scum and filth, thereby insinuating that they belong to a lower order of beings, subhuman more than superhuman.[120] The practice of repeated exorcisms in Pentecostal circles belies the apostolic doctrine that once we become Christians we are then protected against demonic possession.[121] Jesus insisted that no one is able to snatch us out of the Father's hand (Jn 10:28-29), and Paul was adamant that nothing can separate us from the love of Christ (Rom 8:38-39).

Reformed theologian and biblical scholar Thomas A. Boogaart scores what he calls "the kick-the-devil theology" rampant in Pentecostalism for reducing the devil to a malignant force that can be expelled by ritual techniques rather than an angelic adversary of God and humanity who can be adequately dealt with only by Jesus Christ himself.

> The preaching of Benny Hinn, Stephen Hill, Frank Peretti, and others today depersonalizes the forces of evil and in the process legitimates violence against them. [Unlike Jesus] they do not ask the demons for their names; they do not converse with them; and they do not grant any requests for mercy. Their engagement of evil borders on sadism: "Kick the Devil in the face tonight. He is already down and all beat up. Kick him one more time." The faces of Hinn's audience . . . register pleasure when they are stomping on the floor and symbolically inflicting pain on the devil. Are they also not being encouraged to stomp on the faces of people who are supposedly under the influence of the devil? . . . Their engagement of evil is also naïve. Hinn, Hill, and many other preachers zap evil spirits in their great gatherings as if they were playing a video game in the local arcade. They do not seem to understand that demons are children of God, and, as such, have names and tremendous power. In fact, ignorance of their true names is itself an unmistakable sign of their ultimate power, the power to hold people in darkness.[122]

Where the Pentecostals are right is in their contention that the kingdom of God delivers from disease as well as from guilt and sin. Indeed, in the New Testament disease is often related to sin; both belong to the kingdom of evil or nothingness that is being driven out by the advancing kingdom of Christ. Adolf von Harnack is surely correct in claiming that "Jesus does not distinguish rigidly between sicknesses of the body and of the soul; He takes them both as different expressions of one supreme ailment in humanity."[123] At the same time it is much too simplistic to assert that devils are the cause of sickness,[124] since this tends to exonerate humans from personal culpability in their predicament.[125] Humans are not simply victims of evil but willing participants in evil.[126] Moreover, the origin of many illnesses is shrouded in mystery and is therefore inexplicable, and it would be a profound mistake to attribute these afflictions to either human or demonic sin, though we would not be vulnerable to sickness had not sin weakened us from the beginning.

Faith's transformation of myth. The history of demonology in the Bible consists in a progression from the animistic idea of demons to a prophetic mysticism in which demons become agents of Satan or the devil and are overthrown by the cross and resurrection victory of Christ. The concept of Satan changes from being a messenger and servant of God to being an adversary of both God and mortals. He is still wholly subordinate to the living God, who alone directs the course of world history. In Revelation 20:1-2 the devil, Satan, the dragon and the ancient serpent are all identified as the anti-God power that holds the human race in bondage. The idea of demons as fallen angels took root in the intertestamental period and was a prominent theme in the apostolic church.[127] The demons represent not simply inhuman forces of evil but superhuman powers with tremendous insight and cunning. This conception is especially prominent in Paul, who warns that we are contending not against flesh and blood but "against the principalities, against the powers, against the world rulers of this present darkness, against the spiritual hosts of wickedness in the heavenly places" (Eph 6:12).

In the teaching and ministry of Jesus demons are no longer wandering disembodied spirits seeking bodies to inhabit but agents of Satan who seek to advance an anti-God agenda for the human creation. According to the New Testament scholar Anton Fridrichsen, "Jesus does not consider the demons as more or less free and independent beings, but as *the servants of Satan*: it is his will they further, his commissions they perform."[128] Each of Jesus' exorcisms signaled the defeat of Satan and the unraveling of his kingdom.[129] Demons were not ghosts or spirits from the netherworld but spiritual beings who, created in light, chose to turn to darkness and therefore must be dispelled from God's good creation.

In the New Testament demons belong to the powers that enslave the human race: sin, death and hell. The battle against the demons is at the same time a battle against sin and death. Sin provides the entry of demonic power into one's life, and to be under the curse of sin is also to be under the power of Satan. The devil entered Judas because of his sin. The devil was not able to master Jesus because he defied the temptation to sin (Mt 4:1-11; Lk 4:1-13).

Sickness also belongs to the kingdom of chaos that is now passing away in light of Christ's resurrection triumph. Already in the Old Testament being stricken with disease is linked to the bearing down of a demonic hand.[130] In the popular culture that comprised the zeitgeist of the New Testament, mental illness was commonly associated with demon possession. Yet a close reading of the text discloses that Jesus treated the demonically possessed in a different way from those who were merely sick either in mind or in body. One scholar observes:

> Jesus was accustomed to touch a sick person in a way which symbolized his pity; in the presence of the possessed, he stood at a distance as though to repudiate someone unworthy of his presence, a being whom he did not wish to touch. He spoke in command, but briefly and mordantly: "Be still, and go out of this man." He exercised absolute dominion without mercy or discussion. He would not even allow the demon "to tell what he knew." Only after the deliverance would he speak to the man or take him by the hand. No purely psychological explanation of possession can justify this radical difference in the attitude of Jesus.[131]

To be sure, some pathological states might indeed have their source in demon possession, but one must be careful in routinely ascribing demonic influences to people who are emotionally distraught or unduly agitated. Bernard Ramm shows perspicuity in his contention that "the demonic is not the psychopathic person but the person who is unusually closed in and internally split."[132] Yet this insight fails to provide the clue to the nature of demon possession in biblical perspective. The demon-possessed are those who are unable to help themselves in any moral or spiritual sense. They are not only disabled in the sense of being unable to extricate themselves from their precarious predicament, but they are also under a compulsion to do evil. Demon possession is a state of self-destructiveness that leads eventually to disintegration and perdition. At the same time, demon possession is not always visible to the observer and can finally be detected only by those who have the gift of discerning of spirits (1 Cor 12:10). It is not the physician or psychotherapist but the holy person or spiritual sage who is most able to help in such cases. Demons are ultimately driven out not by medical treatment or psychological counsel but by prayer and fasting (Mk 9:29 KJV). To be demon-possessed is to be spiritually bound to falsehood. The answer to demon possession is the ministry of spiritual deliverance, which consists not in magical incantations but in the proclamation of the Word and fervent prayer in the Spirit. It entails not just the repetition of the name of Jesus but the confession of this name as the victor over sin and death.[133]

Demon possession must be clearly differentiated from demonic subjugation. All of unredeemed humanity is in the grip of demonic control. This is what theologians mean when they speak of the bondage of the will. Since the Fall the whole of humanity has been in captivity to forces and powers beyond our control—the devil, sin and death. But demon possession in the narrow or technical sense refers to a state of bondage in which our freedom is not only impaired but entirely subverted. In demon possession our actions and even our words are directed if not dictated by the devil.[134]

It is also helpful to differentiate between hidden and manifest demon possession. In many cases the average observer will note that something is radically wrong and that the afflicted person needs deliverance. In other cases the demon-possessed will appear perfectly normal, but those who have eyes to see will discern a grave imbalance that needs to be rectified. Demon possession is not so much an internal split as an external invasion that can be dealt with only by a power superior to the invasive power. The solution lies in both an external act of reparation and liberation by the Son of God and an internal cleansing and empowering by the Spirit of God.

The New Testament does not dismiss belief in demons but corrects the popular conception by seeing demon possession in the light of the perduring conflict between the eternal God and the angelic adversary of God. Deliverance from the demons becomes an integral part of salvation history in which the kingdom of God triumphs over the kingdom of evil. The theological task is not to demythologize in the sense of abandoning the concept of the demonic. Instead it is to reinterpret the ancient world picture not in the light of a new scientific picture but in the light of divine revelation itself as we see it unfolded in the life, death and resurrection of Jesus Christ. In the apostolic church the mythological understanding of the demons is transformed into the kerygmatic proclamation of the cross in which the demonic powers are dethroned by the victorious Jesus Christ (Lk 10:18).

Overthrow of the demons. The life, death and resurrection of Jesus are incomprehensible apart from his victory over the devil. It is incontestable that Jesus regarded his healings and miracles as the means by which the demons were dislodged and routed.[135] In a text that even Bultmann acknowledges to be authentic, Jesus declares, "If it is by the finger of God that I cast out demons, then the kingdom of God has come upon you" (Lk 11:20). In looking ahead to his approaching death and resurrection, Jesus reveals that he "saw Satan fall like lightning from heaven" (Lk 10:18). And again: "Now is the judgment of this world, now shall the ruler of this world be cast out" (Jn 12:31). First

John finds the key to the incarnation in the battle against the kingdom of evil: "The reason the Son of God appeared was to destroy the works of the devil" (3:8). I heartily concur with James Kallas: "The simple fact is that when we fail to take seriously the demonological motif of the gospel not only do the miracles become obscure but the resurrection becomes insignificant."[136]

Not only the message of the cross but the success of apostolic Christianity is tied to the victory over the demons through the atoning work of Christ and the demonstration of this victory in the ministry of his followers. Alan Richardson makes an important point: "Christianity conquered the other religions of the ancient world partly because of its success in casting out the fear of demons, and the Christians rapidly ousted the Jewish exorcists from their position of supremacy. The early Church saw in the power of Jesus over the demons the earnest of His triumph over Satan, His power to bind the 'Strong Man.'"[137]

Jesus came to establish his kingdom in the very midst of the spiritual darkness that engulfs the human race, but the demons have not meekly submitted to his sovereignty. Jesus suggests that angelic agents of evil are counterattacking, even though their power is being taken from them: "The kingdom of Heaven has been subjected to violence and the violent are taking it by storm" (Mt 11:12 NJB).[138] Even after the resurrection—in which Christ demonstrated his victory over sin, death and the devil—the spiritual forces of darkness prepare to fight on. Even though they have been divested of their ontological power, they still possess the power of the lie, which becomes lethal only when we fail to perceive that it lacks any enduring basis. This is why Christians are warned to be sober and watchful, for our "adversary the devil prowls around like a roaring lion, seeking someone to devour" (1 Pet 5:8).

The church errs either when it ascribes more power to the devil than is warranted by Scripture or when it treats the threat of the devil too lightly. I have difficulty with the idea of a demonized world, which we find in Frank Peretti[139] and to a lesser degree in James Kallas.[140] On the other hand I do not believe we are doing full justice to the biblical witness when we describe the world as already liberated (as in Barth and Wink). The New Testament picture is of a world that is being liberated and therefore one in which sin and evil still continue. The devil is still "prince of the world" but only on the basis of a false claim that has already been exploded by Jesus Christ. Yet the victory of Christ is not complete until his lordship and saviorhood are acknowledged in faith and repentance. In a world of darkness Christ by his Spirit has established islands of light, centers of Christian renewal, that testify to the coming of a new kingdom that is basically in the future but whose power and impact can already be felt and whose eventual victory is completely assured.[141] This world is no longer demon controlled, but it continues to be demon oppressed, since the demons do not acknowledge their defeat. The war against the demons therefore continues, but its outcome is not in doubt. The principalities and powers that appear to exercise control are not reconciled servants of Christ (as Cullmann maintains) but enslaved powers that are made to serve God's kingdom unwillingly and continue their rebellion covertly.[142]

We must avoid drawing the conclusion, rooted in Gnostic and Iranian dualism, that the world is basically divided between two comparable kingdoms. I fully agree with Walter Lüthi:

> It is not true that there are two equal kingdoms in this world, Christ's kingdom and Satan's kingdom. Even though time and again it may seem that the kingdom of the Devil is superior to Christ's, it is not even equal to it. It is not true that the course of the world is an undecided tug-of-war between Christ and the Devil, and that we men are pulled to and fro between them. The tug-of-war has been decided, decided in Christ's favour, and therefore in ours.[143]

Jesus Christ is alone Lord of the world, though his lordship is not universally acknowledged and respected. The devil vehemently challenges Christ's lordship, but this challenge rests on the insubstantiality of chaos. Wherever Christ builds his church, the devil mounts a campaign to infiltrate and subvert. The devil vents his fury even more against the saints than against unbelieving sinners, but it is precisely the former who have the weapons to combat demon assault and oppression (cf. Eph 6:10-17).

It is perhaps most biblically correct to describe this world as besieged rather than either demonically controlled or divinely liberated. The world is besieged by the advancing church that storms the very gates of hell (Mt 16:18). It is not the demons who are on the offensive but the angels and saints of God. The powers of darkness do make repeated forays into areas that now belong to the victorious kingdom of Christ but only in order to conceal their overall retreat. These sinister powers are basically on the defensive and already in flight, even though they plot and scheme to overthrow what cannot be overthrown because its foundation is the irreversible will of God.

Bultmann would very probably describe my demonology as remythologization, since I appear to be replacing animistic mythology by a mythology spawned by the early church.[144] While it is true that I continue to use symbolic or mythopoetic language to describe the kingdom of the devil and his legions, I am not proposing a new mythology but articulating a vision of reality that has a solid basis in prehistory and history. There is a real devil and there are real demons, though not as animistic thought describes them but as divine revelation redescribes them. The language of poetry and myth is the best available tool to delineate the cosmic warfare between Christ and Satan, which concerns not inner conflicts of the soul but invisible conflicts in objective history. In this discussion I am reaffirming orthodoxy but at the same time recognizing that narrational language is best for describing realities that transcend the reach of discursive reason. Just as God himself is not myth but fact, so the angelic adversary of God is not the product of human imagination but the embodiment of realities objective to the observer. The narrative of the Bible rests not on idealistic speculation but on a realistic portrayal of what has actually transpired in superhistory and history.

·NINE·

RECENT
DEVELOPMENTS
IN THEOLOGICAL
THOUGHT

The Spirit, who is both one and transcendent,
is able to penetrate all things without violating or doing violence to them.
YVES CONGAR

The Father acts through His Spirit
beyond the boundaries of the Christian Church.
PHILIP ROSATO

God the Spirit is also the Spirit of the universe,
its total cohesion, its structure, its information, its energy.
JÜRGEN MOLTMANN

Baptism in the Spirit, which is sacramentally symbolized in water baptism,
gets worked out over a lifetime, whether it begins in infancy or later life.
CLARK PINNOCK

The contemporary scene is marked by a continuing tension between revelational theology and experiential theology. Do we gain knowledge of God through his past revelation in Jesus Christ as found in the Bible, or does our knowledge of God derive from an experience of the Spirit who dwells within us? We should recognize that revelation itself contains an experiential or mystical dimension. Otherwise revelation would be reduced to the communication of concepts that affect the mind but not the whole human being.

A closely related polarity in contemporary theology is that between Logos christology and Spirit christology. Theologians who espouse the former tilt toward rationalism, whereas those who defend the latter lean toward mysticism or spiritualism. The challenge today seems to be to rediscover the complementarity of Logos and Spirit while still maintaining the subordination of Spirit to Logos (which is the biblical pattern). A Logos christology does not necessarily preserve the transcendence of God, for the emphasis could be on the continuity rather than the discontinuity between the divine Logos and human reason (as in evangelical rationalism). A Spirit christology is always in danger of forfeiting transcendence by its stress on the immanence of God in history and nature.

Current theology is also divided on the relation between Spirit baptism and the sacrament of baptism. A sacramentalist position tends to equate Spirit baptism and water baptism or to regard them as inseparable. Those who stand in the tradition of spiritualism are prone to treat the sacraments as purely symbolic. The divine reality is thought to be internal rather than externalized in sacramental rites. Quakerism is the most authentic representation of spiritualistic religion.

Finally, contemporary theologians debate the role of the spiritual gifts in the life and ministry of the church. These gifts have gained prominence through the emergence of Pentecostalism and the charismatic renewal within the mainline churches. A quintessential question is whether the gifts of the Spirit belong to the being *(esse)* of the church or simply to its well-being *(bene esse)*. A related issue is whether they belong to the present ministry of the church or ceased with the end of the age of the apostles.

The dialectical theology associated with Karl Barth and Emil Brunner—and continuing with some modification in John Thompson, Thomas Torrance and Donald Bloesch—signifies a reaffirmation of Logos christology but without denying the experiential element. Most current theologies stand in the tradition of Schleiermacher and Romantic idealism and emphasize the interdependence of God and the world. The battle today seems to be between a biblical or trinitarian monotheism and a mystical panentheism that sees the world as the body of God rather than a separate creation of God.

The theologians I have chosen for this discussion represent different traditions and generally divergent positions. Obviously many worthy scholars have been omitted, partly because their approach is anticipated or embodied in one of those selected for this study.

H. Wheeler Robinson

H. Wheeler Robinson, principal of Regent's Park College in Oxford from 1920 to 1942, stands solidly in the tradition of Friedrich Schleiermacher and Wilhelm Herrmann, though he tries to steer clear of a religion of pure immanence (as found in the early Schleiermacher).[1] For Robinson the fundamental ontological category is Spirit, which encompasses both humanity and nature. Spirit is the unifying center of the universe but is most powerfully revealed in the life and teachings of Jesus. The Bible is a normative criterion for Christian faith, but it must be read through the lens of religious experience. The final court of appeal is the Christian consciousness of God.

Robinson rejects the idea of "three *hypostases* and one *ousia*, three 'centers' on one plane equidistant from the believer."[2] He reaffirms what he regards as the intensive approach of Paul, which focuses on divine interaction rather than separate divine persons. This view speaks of our being in the Spirit, always through Christ and to the Father.[3] He proposes that we substitute *pneuma* (Spirit) for *ousia* (substance) and *parousia* (presence) for *hypostasis* (person).

Robinson begins with the work of the Spirit and then proceeds to a discussion of his person. We know the person only through the work. This theologian affirms one God who is Creator, Redeemer and Sanctifier. In these different activities we see one all-encompassing Spirit. He accepts "Father" and "Son" as metaphors for divine reality, yet considers "Mother" as a possibly richer metaphor.

This scholar takes stern issue with the so-called social doctrine of the Trinity—three subjects who are consubstantial with one another. Such a doctrine gives us one Godhead but not one God. In the social doctrine one ends in the "corporate personality of a community."[4] Robinson upholds a strict monotheism but affirms a threefoldness in the operations of the one God.

While endorsing "the personality of the Holy Spirit," he is adamant that this personality is not separate from the Father and the Son. The Holy Spirit is "the personal presence of God through Christ" rather than an individualized subject who interacts with other such subjects. The Holy Spirit is "the whole activity of the divine in relation to the human personality, as mediated through Christ."[5]

For Robinson the first postulate of Christian experience is "the reality, the dignity, the eternal value of human personality."[6] He seems to project God as the ground and goal of human personality. In faith we enter into a relation with a "higher and larger personality."[7] Although striving to maintain the otherness of God, he contends that there is a natural kinship between divine and human personality. The relation of Spirit to human spirit entails "the heightening of all human powers, the clarifying of human vision and judgment, the strengthening of the human will, the discovery of latent and unsuspected possibilities of endurance."[8] He rejects Schleiermacher's identifying of the Holy Spirit with the spirit of the community but is insistent that the Spirit creates community and sustains community.

Robinson sees the Spirit working outside the confines of the institutional church, and this is equivalent to prevenient grace. God includes "all Nature" and "all created spirits" within "the circle of His being."[9] All people are in contact with the Spirit of God, though not all recognize the reality of the Spirit. Human personality is not absorbed into the divine but is activated by the divine. With Herrmann he sees Christianity rooted in "moral experience."

Robinson can be appreciated for his vigorous defense of monotheism and for his timely warnings against tritheism. It is questionable whether he has remained true to the biblical and catholic vision of a God who exists within himself as a triune community or fellowship. By beginning with human personality and then trying to relate this to divine personality, he loses sight of the utter transcendence of God, of what Kierkegaard called "the infinite qualitative difference" between God and humanity. I agree with Alasdair Heron:

> Too highly "personalized" language—as in the slogan of the "personality of the Holy Spirit"—may encourage a misleading sense of the Spirit as a "personality" external to and even competing with our own. It can indeed *reduce* the divine Spirit to too human dimensions and hide the greatness in humility of the God who searches, answers and hopes even in us as our search, answer and hope.[10]

Karl Barth

The experiential approach of Schleiermacher and H. Wheeler Robinson was called into serious question by Karl Barth, who insisted that we gain valid knowledge of God only through God's self-revelation in Jesus Christ. The Holy Spirit plays a pivotal role in bringing this revelation home to the biblical prophets and apostles and also to believers in every age. Barth could therefore describe the Spirit as the subjective possibility of both salvation and revelation. Yet he was also emphatic that the Spirit not only illumines men and women concerning the truth of Jesus Christ but also empowers God's elect to bear witness to this truth. The Spirit not only has a noetic function in opening our eyes to the eternal significance of Christ, but he is also the catalyst for an inward ontological change—the new birth or regeneration.

The baptism that saves us has already taken place in Jesus Christ, who is both our substitute and representative, in Christ's virgin birth, in his anointing by the Spirit and finally in his cross and resurrection. A momentous change or conversion *(Umkehr)* took place for all humankind and all human history in the events associated with Christ's life and death. "The world and every man exist in this alteration."[11] This general baptism in Christ is "the divine preparation of man for the Christian life in its totality."[12] In Christ's suffering and death we see "the washing, renewing and rectifying of all mankind."[13]

Yet Barth was insistent that the baptism with the Spirit must also take place in people's lives if the death and resurrection of Christ are to be fully efficacious for them. Barth had in mind not a rite of the church but a revivifying experience in which we are converted to faith and empowered to live out a vocation of being a herald and disciple of Christ. Spirit baptism is an awakening to the fact that we are already called to be children of God through the dying and rising again of Christ and his intercession for us in heaven.

The Bible makes clear that there must be a human response to the gift of salvation accomplished in Christ and sealed within us by the Holy Spirit. This response does not procure our salvation, but it demonstrates our commitment to live a life of obedience to this salvation. "Christian baptism is the first form of the human answer to the divine change which was brought about in Him."[14] The human decision follows and corresponds to the divine act in Jesus Christ manifested in the lives of men and women by the Holy Spirit. Yet the human decision is not the instrumentality by which the change in humanity is effected. Baptism acknowledges and proclaims the crisis of salvation, but it does not bring it about. In baptism we recognize and confirm for ourselves "the renewal of the world which has taken place in Jesus Christ" and which has led to our "personal cleansing in the outpouring of the Holy Spirit."[15]

For Barth baptism by water is not a sacrament, a means of grace, but a public testimony concerning the fact that salvation has already been wrought for all people in Jesus Christ. Our response is basically ethical, not soteriological. Baptism is best viewed as an act of moral and spiritual obedience. It is the first step in living out the Christian life, which testifies to our salvation but does not accomplish it. What is absolutely necessary for our salvation is not the rite of baptism but the baptism of the Spirit, for it is the Spirit who communicates the fruits of Christ's sacrifice to every believing person. The Spirit may make use of outward means, but he does not *need* any outward rituals or signs. Basically he confronts us directly and immediately, though ordinarily in conjunction with the biblical and apostolic testimonies to Jesus Christ.

The Spirit both enlightens and empowers us for service and witness. He not only brings down our pride by humbling us but also delivers us from our sloth by energizing us. For Barth "the empowering to speak of Christ" is "the decisive" operation of the Spirit.[16] The Spirit does not simply communicate information about Christ but imparts the power to live in the freedom of Christ. He is the bestower not only of faith but of charismatic gifts and powers. "The Christian community can and must be the scene of many human activities which are new and supremely astonishing to many of its own members as well as to the world around because they rest on an endowment with extraordinary capacities."[17] Barth makes a place for healing, evangelism, miracles and even speaking in tongues. The last is "an attempt to express the inexpressible in which the tongue rushes past . . . the notions and concepts necessary to ordinary speech and utters what can be received only as a groan or sigh, thus needing at once interpretation or exposition."[18] We are to think of this not as "bizarre stuttering and stammering" but as an ecstatic overflow of irrepressible joy. Sometimes speaking in tongues is better than "illegitimate silence."[19]

All the gifts of the Holy Spirit are designed to empower the people of God for their pilgrimage. "This is the greatness but also the limit of these gifts. They are exercised in works which have to take place between the times, in this time of the ministry of the community."[20] Gifts are to be exercised, but we must not claim a premature possession of our redemption in special illuminations. "Ecstasies and illuminations, inspirations and intuitions, are not necessary. Happy are they who are worthy to receive them! But woe be to us, if we wait anxiously for them."[21] Special manifestations of the Spirit are not to be seen as "indispensable preconditions, verifications or tests of the presence of the Spirit."[22] Yet this does not imply that we should not seek for charismatic endowment. "Only where the Spirit is sighed, cried, and prayed for does He become present and newly active."

Barth is convinced that the work of the Spirit begins in creation, for Christ creates through the power of the Spirit. All people are in contact with Jesus Christ by means of the *Spiritus Creator*, but only some are adopted as sons and daughters of the most high God, because only some believe. The Spirit of creation is also the Spirit of redemption, and this means that creation leads to redemption. For Barth theology is both christocentric and pneumatocentric. He strongly adheres to the *filioque*, the Western addition to the Nicene Creed that the Spirit proceeds from both the Father and the Son, adopted by the Third Council of Toledo in 589. The Spirit brings not new revelations but a deeper grasp of the revelation accomplished once for all in Jesus Christ. We cannot appeal to private illuminations in order to come to God apart from the church and Scripture. Jesus Christ is the only way to salvation, and the Spirit reminds us of this fact. John Thompson rightly observes, "Barth's theology is not merely a logos christology from above; it is a christology of reconciliation based on God's action in Christ which is both from above to below and at the same time from below to above, and centered on the crucified and risen Lord Jesus Christ."[23]

Barth has presented a theology that can possibly overcome the cleavage between Reformation and Pentecostal churches by powerfully showing that our salvation is dependent finally and entirely on God's grace manifested in Christ as opposed to the performance of ecclesiastical rites such as baptism and confirmation. He also keenly perceives that faith necessitates a personal decision and act of obedience, and cannot be routinely passed on from one generation to another. Here we see Barth's indebtedness to the tradition of evangelical revivalism.[24]

The only question is whether Barth does justice to the important role of human mediation in the communication of the gifts of God, including the gift of salvation. God is not bound to the Bible, church proclamation and the sacraments, but does not God make use of these earthly vehicles to reach a fallen humanity for the kingdom of his Son? God is not limited to external means, but does not God limit himself as he works to realize the eternal plan of salvation? It seems that in Barth's theology God's appearance in the Word is "an unpredictable, extrinsic occurrence" without continuity with either sacred Scripture or sacred tradition.[25] Here Barth palpably diverges not only from Catholicism but also from Calvin and Luther. Yet we need to hear Barth's reservations about a sacramentalism that binds the Spirit to rituals performed by the clerics of the church and that confounds the role of the church and the role of the Spirit. Once we lose sight of the infinite qualitative difference between the divine and the human we exempt the human from judgment by the divine. Once we confuse the kingdom of God with the institutional church we exempt the church from reformation and purification by the Spirit. The challenge is to grasp the paradoxical inseparability of sign and thing signified and at the same time their radical disjunction. Barth's theology can be immensely helpful in this regard, but it needs to be held in balance with the witness of Augustine, Calvin, Luther, Forsyth and other theological luminaries who succeeded in maintaining a high view of both church and sacraments.

Paul Tillich

Paul Tillich, who freely took issue with Barth in so many areas, presents a Spirit theology that reveals a kinship to German idealism (especially Hegel and Schelling) and Platonic and Neoplatonic mysticism (especially Meister Eckhart and Jakob Boehme).[26] For Tillich the source of revelation includes not only the Bible and church tradition but also the history of religion and culture. Our task is not to proclaim a definite message of a particular revelation in history that routinely excludes other truths and claims but to probe the depths of human spirituality and share insights from our spiritual quest. Tillich gives Jesus preeminent status in the galaxy of the saints, but he does not regard him as different in kind from the holy prophets and sages of the great world religions. The Christian mission consists not in imposing archaic dogmas on others but in making clear to people how their deepest needs and questions are answered in the universal revelation of the Spirit, especially as we see this in Jesus Christ. Like many of the noted Christian mystics, Tillich contends that it is "in listening and waiting" that we "experience the Spirit."[27]

Tillich sees the value of sacraments as bearers of the Spiritual Presence. Indeed, he regards the whole world as sacramental, since any word or happening can be seized by the Holy in his self-manifestation. Tillich distinguishes "sign" from "symbol."[28] A symbol participates in the reality to which it points and can thereby lead us into experiential contact with the numinous. Symbols do not automatically convey divine power and frequently need to be recharged with spiritual dynamism. Tillich contends that the truths of biblical religion can be grasped only by the cultivation of a mythic consciousness that tries to ascertain how the revelatory events in Scripture throw light on the universal human condition.

For Tillich Spirit is the inclusive term for God. It is "the most embracing, direct, and unrestricted symbol for the divine life. It does not need to be balanced with another symbol, because it includes all the ontological elements."[29] He frequently refers to God as the divine Spirit or the Spiritual Presence. The trinitarian formulation is simply a formal way of holding together the transcendence of God and his concreteness. Tillich opposes a monarchial or exclusive monotheism, which separates God from creation, in favor of a trinitarian monotheism, which regards God as both transcendent and inseparable from the world. He is more tolerant of a mystical monotheism but believes that it too easily devolves into pantheism.

Tillich could be justly accused of upholding a unitarianism of the Spirit, since Spirit is the commanding symbol in the Godhead. He can even say, "The Son *is* the Spirit."[30] Jesus Christ is important because he points to the Spirit. In him we are confronted with the awesome presence of the Holy. The trinitarian names are simply metaphors that describe the way God relates to the world.

Predictably Tillich is warmly supportive of Spirit movements that sporadically emerge in the history of the church. When office replaces charisma as the focal point of church life, the Spirit is quenched or suppressed.[31] When doctrinal or moral structures replace ecstasy, the church experiences a palpable loss in vitality. Yet Tillich warns that the church cannot rest on charismatic experiences alone. The ideal is the unity of ecstasy and structure. He admonishes the church to "prevent the confusion of ecstasy with chaos."[32] A vital church needs structure, but it must allow for structures to be changed and renewed in the light of a fresh visitation of the Spirit.

The future of religion lies in an attempt to get beyond parochialism and sectarianism to a global perspective that does justice to the universal working of the Spirit. Tillich looks forward to a "Religion of the Concrete Spirit" that will supersede the dogmas and forms of institutional Christianity.[33] Such a religion will be marked by the unity of ecstasy and knowledge, love and prophecy. Tillich's expectation reflects Schleiermacher's vision of a purer form of religion that will break through the confines of fossilized religious traditions.[34]

For Tillich Jesus is the final revelation of God but not the only revelation. He can declare that "every new manifestation of the Spiritual Presence stands under the criterion of his manifestation in Jesus as the Christ."[35] Yet the Spirit is not confined to Christ nor to the Bible as a whole. God's Spirit is working in all religions and even in the secular arena seeking to move people toward deeper communion with the living God and more vigorous commitment to the cause of justice and peace.

Tillich can be appreciated for his valiant protest against theologies that deliver the Spirit into the hands of the church. "If religious devotion, moral obedience, or scientific honesty could compel the divine Spirit to 'descend' to us, the Spirit which 'descended' would be the human spirit in a religious disguise."[36] Against the enthusiasts he sternly warns that the Spiritual Presence is "not an intoxicating substance, or a stimulus for psychological excitement, or a miraculous physical cause."[37] Yet he allows for extraordinary manifestations of the Spirit in the lives of people of faith, including "knowledge of strange tongues, penetration into the innermost thoughts of another person, and healing influences even at a distance."[38]

Tillich can be faulted for subordinating doctrine to experience, for understanding revelation as the impartation of power more than of knowledge. For him the Spiritual Presence "is not that of a teacher but of a meaning-bearing power which grasps the human spirit in an ecstatic experience."[39] The Spirit does indeed revivify and transform us, but does not he also teach us with regard to what faith requires? Does he not lead us into a fuller understanding not only of God but also of the world and of ourselves?

My greatest difficulty with Tillich is in his championing of an "ecstatic naturalism" over biblical supernaturalism. In his view God is not the supreme being who calls the worlds into being but the depth and ground of all being. He can speak of the "mutual immanence" between the divine Spirit and the human spirit. The divine Spirit becomes the dimension of depth in the human spirit. He envisages a "God above God" who transcends the differentiation of the Trinity, but this God proves to be the ground and depth of the human self. He calls his position an "eschatological panentheism" in which all things are embraced and graced by the Spirit of God. The question is whether he sacrifices the utter transcendence of God in his affirmation of the inseparability of God and the finite creation.

Rudolf Bultmann

Like Paul Tillich, Rudolf Bultmann, professor of New Testament for many years at Marburg University, was engrossed with the problem of myth in the Bible.[40] Unlike Tillich, who believed that we need to think mythologically in order to grasp the meaning-content of Scripture,

Bultmann contended that in today's secular milieu myth constitutes an insuperable obstacle to understanding the gospel; therefore we need to translate myth into existentialist and psychological categories in order to make it intelligible.[41] Bultmann's demythologizing program has significant implications for his doctrine of the works and gifts of the Spirit.

Bultmann alleges that the mythical worldview, which constitutes the background of divine revelation, contained elements of both *animism* (belief in spirits) and *dynamism*, which posits an impersonal spiritual force communicated through sacramental rites and magical incantations.[42] Bultmann is quite firm that the New Testament, especially Paul and John, strives to reinterpret the biblical myth in ethical and existential categories so that the gift of the Spirit is seen no longer as paranormal power but as obedience under the cross. The impartation of the Spirit does not alter the human psyche but liberates the human will for service to our neighbor. Miracles are not suspensions of natural law but wonders that significantly expand the human horizon. Demons are not unclean spirits that take possession of a human personality but destructive forces in human personal and social life. Jesus is not the preexistent Son of God who incarnates himself in human flesh (a mythological concept) but instead the exemplar of freedom who challenges people to heroic action. The Holy Spirit is not a vital force that is transmitted through sacramental rites but the power of freedom that enables us to embark on a new way of living, the creator of authenticity.

Bultmann has virtually nothing to say about the Trinity, since such a dogma signifies an accommodation to the Hellenistic ethos. God cannot be thought of theoretically—as a transcendent monarch—but only existentially—as the power of the new life within us. He refers to God not as Father, Son and Holy Spirit but as "the Occurrence of Transcendence," "the Wholly Other," "the Beyond in Our Midst" and "the Darkness of the Future." He does not dispense entirely with trinitarian imagery in depicting the workings of God, but it is clear that metaphysical speculation concerning the eternal nature and plan of God has no place in his theology. Like his mentor Immanuel Kant, he was convinced that reason cannot penetrate the noumenal, but moral commitment can give meaning to the phenomenal. We can assume *that* God is but not *what* God is.

Miraculous events really happened in biblical history, but they need to be reinterpreted as "abnormal psychic phenomena."[43] Bultmann hails Paul as one of the few in the New Testament who grasped the ethical implications of the cross of Christ. For Paul "the might of the Spirit is not a magically (mechanically) working power, but is one that equally demands and presupposes a transformation of the will."[44] In the demythologized version of the gospel we still see Christ as the source of salvation but only because he makes it possible for us to face up to the realities of life and shape a new future. We make use of myth to get to the truth, but we do not preach myth. Instead we proclaim the kerygma—that God's forgiveness is available to those who break with the old way of living and embrace the call to a higher form of existence, a life of self-giving love.

Against sacramentalism Bultmann warns that Christian existence cannot be built on "Hellenistic sacramental magic"[45] but only on the free movement of the Spirit, who brings us new possibilities that enable us to live creatively and responsibly in the world. Salvation does not mean the payment of a penalty of sin but the breakthrough into freedom. Bultmann laments the triumph of clericalism and sacramentalism in the early church in which charisma was conveyed no longer by the free outpouring of the Spirit but now through the rite of ordination and the elements of the sacrament.[46]

Evangelical Christians can appreciate much of what Bultmann says about the loss of spiritual power in the catholicizing of the early church. But they must take exception to Bultmann's dismissal of the supernatural claims of Christian faith. In his theology God is reduced to an invasive creative energy and Jesus to the model of authentic human selfhood. Bultmann often gives an honest exegesis in which he freely

admits that the text tends to support the traditional or orthodox interpretation. Yet he insists that we are not bound to this interpretation,
since the changing situation of the church calls us to adopt a new language that resonates with the ethos of modernity. Here Bultmann in
effect gives up his claim to be a biblical theologian and becomes
instead an existentialist philosopher.

Jürgen Moltmann

In marked contrast to Bultmann, German Reformed theologian Jürgen
Moltmann offers a trinitarian theology that emphasizes the congruity
rather than the distance between God and humanity. Formerly allied
with the theologies of hope and liberation, Moltmann now identifies
himself as an ecological theologian, one who addresses the current
environmental crisis. He still wishes to be known as a liberation theologian, since the growing gulf between rich and poor continues to be a
prominent theme in his theology. The plight of the poor indeed is
aggravated by environmental pollution and the depletion of natural
resources.

Moltmann draws on a variety of philosophical systems in building
his case for revolutionary action on behalf of the poor and disenfran-
chised. He is unabashedly Hegelian when he speaks of "the creative
and life-giving Spirit" arriving at "consciousness of itself in the human
consciousness."[47] A Whiteheadian perspective is conspicuous in his
contention that "the God who rests in face of his creation does not
dominate the world . . . he 'feels' the world; he allows himself to be
affected, to be touched by each of his creatures."[48] He readily acknowledges his indebtedness to the early philosophy of life (Wilhelm Dilthey,
Henri Bergson, Georg Simmel and Friedrich Nietzsche) and to the
Christian mystical tradition (Dionysius the Pseudo-Areopagite, Hildegard of Bingen, Meister Eckhart).

Moltmann characterizes his worldview as panentheism (God is in
all) as opposed to pantheism (God is all) and atheism (God is dissolved
in the all).[49] Unlike neo-orthodox theologians, Moltmann does not

envisage God breaking into history but instead sees history in God. God is not separate but inseparable from the world. Creation derives from the creative resolve of God to create, but this creative resolve is inherent in the very being of God. Creation rests on the necessity of love to share itself. Although this seems to be a moral rather than a metaphysical necessity, the lines between the two are often blurred. God does not need the world in order to exist but desires the world in order to satisfy his inner longing for the "other." Creation is "the outcome of the rapturous abundance of his divine Being, which longs to communicate itself and is able to communicate itself."[50] In the creative and life-giving power of the Spirit, God *pervades* his creation. In his sabbath rest he allows his creatures to exert an influence on him. Moltmann views the relationship of God and the world as "a perichoretic relationship"—one of mutual indwelling.[51] Prayer is making contact with the creative energy that sustains us rather than petitioning a God outside us who is projected in the heavens.

This theologian is amazingly open to the Neoplatonic concept of emanation, which he seeks to relate to the biblical *creatio ex nihilo*. God creates by producing a space for the world and then filling this space with the energy of his Spirit. Creation in the Spirit of God does not merely set creation over against God. "It also simultaneously takes creation into God, though without divinizing it."[52] He accepts the Neoplatonic language of "the emanation of all things from the All-One, and their remanation into the All-One."[53] Light breaks forth from God and then flows back into God.

Moltmann is quick to defend the doctrine of the Trinity but reinterprets it to connote a process of unfoldment culminating in an eschatological fullness of glory. Instead of the polarity of the immanent and economic Trinity, Moltmann posits a primordial Trinity that evolves toward a future fulfillment. He also speaks of an open Trinity—open to the sufferings and agonies of the creation. It is the Spirit who relates the Father and Son to the created order and who thereby gives Father and Son their concreteness and dynamism. He calls the Spirit "the principle of creativity" and "the principle of evolution."[54] He sometimes describes the Trinity as an eschatological process in which "all created beings are drawn into the mutual relationships of the divine life, and into the wide space of the God who is sociality."[55] God is not detached or removed from the created world but constitutes the vital force that moves this world to completion. In the cross of Christ we see not only the human suffering of Jesus but also the divine suffering of Jesus.

While Moltmann is heavily dependent on philosophical ideas and terminology in elucidating his seminal insights, he is by no means uncritical of philosophy. He takes Hegel to task for viewing the self-movement of the Absolute into human history as the action of a single subject rather than the interaction of three subjects.[56] Unlike Hegel he sees the evolutionary world process in terms not of the transformation of matter into Spirit but of the transformation of the cosmos into the spirit of love. He is critical of Whitehead and process theology for erasing the distinction between God and humanity, for denying the first creation of the world. Although seeing much promise in Whitehead's philosophy, he complains that Whitehead conceives of God in "curiously impersonal terms."[57]

My principal difficulty with Moltmann is that his theology regrettably proves to be a subtle accommodation to the zeitgeist (the spirit of the times) rather than bringing God's judgment to bear on the times (as in Barth). In an era of inclusivism and pluralism Moltmann views the non-Christian religions as integral components of the history of salvation. The coming of the redeeming kingdom rests partly in their "potentialities and powers."[58] He also sees promise in the nature religions, which remind us of the beneficence of "nature's cycles and rhythms" and the desirability for "harmony with the earth and with the moon."[59] He even contends that out of the different religions "a 'religion of the earth' will emerge that will teach us the spirituality of the earth in order that we may recognize ourselves as 'children of the earth.'"[60]

To be sure, Moltmann affirms the Trinity, but a probing examination of his position shows that he is veering unnervingly toward tritheism. In contrast to Barth he postulates three different subjects, each one being a "unique personality."[61] While he does not regard these subjects as autonomous selves, he frequently describes them as interacting divinities or constellations of divinity.[62] At the same time, they are not separate beings but beings in relationship. Sometimes it appears that Spirit is the all-inclusive metaphor that ties the members of the Trinity together. He can even describe God as "a Fatherly-Motherly Spirit."

I share some of Moltmann's reservations regarding the impassible God of classical theism, but it seems that he unnecessarily downplays God's almightiness in order to promote a picture of God more congenial to the modern consciousness. He prefers to speak of God not as Lord and Master but as Friend and Companion. Like Whitehead he contends that just as the world is dependent on God, so God is dependent on the world. In Moltmann's theology God is enriched and fulfilled by the creation. In the struggles of humans for justice and peace God waits for the redemption of himself.[63]

Moltmann's spirituality is based on eros rather than agape.[64] Eros is the love of the beautiful, the urge to satisfy our desire for union with the highest. Eros is the acquisitive love that seeks the realization of the self, as opposed to agape, which willingly sacrifices the self for the good of the other.[65] The model for the right love of God is to be found "in the vitality of true human love."[66] Self-love is not something to be overcome but indeed furnishes "the foundation for a free life."[67] There is, of course, a wrong kind of self-love that uses the other person to pursue selfish ambition, but there is also a right kind that gives us the strength to love our neighbor as ourselves. In this area, as in many others, one can discern the affinities of Moltmann's spirituality with mysticism.[68]

Moltmann gives the impression of taking the Bible seriously when he depicts God as making himself vulnerable both in creation and in redemption. This can be accepted if it means that God opens himself to the pain and suffering of creation. But if the meaning is that God gives up control of the world in order to have real relations with his people, then I must take vigorous exception. Moltmann sees the world process as being partly dependent on chance, an interplay of forces that render something wholly new and underivable.[69] It seems that in Moltmann's scheme God gives up the plenitude of his power in order to allow the human creature a determinative role in bringing the kingdom to fruition.

While Moltmann is sound in his concern that Christians exercise their divinely given obligation to be stewards of the creation, he comes dangerously close to divinizing the creation by seeing it as totally filled with the presence of God. He even declares that the adoration of God will involve the *veneration* of nature.[70] He also avers that salvation entails not only the justifying of sinful humanity but also its deifying. Yet he does not wish this concept to be taken literally. We do not actually become gods but "partakers of the divine nature."[71] Deification means that "the divine characteristics of non-transience and immortality . . . become benefits of salvation for human beings."[72]

Evangelical theology can appreciate Moltmann for his emphasis on the healing dimension in salvation, the important role of the gifts of the Spirit in the church's ministry, and the desirability of regulative discipleship groups that will feed life into the institutional church. He is also to be applauded for his call for a charismatic church as opposed to a hierarchical church and for his contention that the real apostolic succession rests not on a mechanical laying on of hands but on fidelity to the gospel of God through the ages.[73] He even tries to guard against patripassianism by viewing the cross of Christ not as the death of God but as death *in* God. The Father suffers with the Son but not in the same way. Moltmann is right to seek for an alternative to the God of classical theism, who is not related to the world in any positive way, but he regrettably loses sight of the sovereignty of God in stressing God's dependence on human effort and initiative in shaping a new world.

Yves Congar

Much more respectful of church tradition is the French Catholic theologian Yves Congar (d. 1995), who is nevertheless poignantly aware of cultural accretions in tradition that need to be excised in order to achieve full catholicity. He laments the denigration of the Holy Spirit in much popular Catholicism in which Mary and the pope assume the role formerly given to the Spirit: guiding the church into all truth and nurturing the faithful on the bread of life.[74] He also deplores the almost total subordination of the Spirit to the person and work of Christ, which subverts trinitarianism in favor of christomonism. Congar contends that the time has come to envisage the Spirit not as a subsidiary principle within the Trinity but as the "ultimate principle."[75] He is also ready to acknowledge the feminine side of the sacred, which we see in the Holy Spirit's work of nurturing and comforting the people of God.

Unlike many orthodox Catholic theologians, Congar welcomes the charismatic renewal as a potential catalyst for Christian unity. He appreciates the concern of charismatics to relate sacramental reality to personal life and experience. He pays tribute to Symeon the New Theologian, who insisted that the sacramental rite apart from the work of the Spirit is ineffectual for our salvation. Similarly, faith understood as mere intellectual assent does not cleanse and renew humanity but only leaves us with the illusion that we are in the right before God. At the same time, Congar perceives in Symeon a tendency to downplay objective sacramental grace in order to do justice to the need for personal appropriation of grace.

Congar remains a sacramentalist but regards it as highly important that the sacrament be fulfilled in an act of decision and commitment. He can speak of "two supernatural causes" in the miracle of rebirth—water baptism and the descent of the Spirit. The two are not the same, yet they ordinarily occur together. Because baptism is above all a sacrament of faith, he acknowledges that the practice of infant baptism is problematical.[76] The way confirmation is performed in the life of the church should also be subjected to critical scrutiny, especially in light of the fact that it is often nothing more than a perfunctory rite. His recommendation is that baptism and confirmation still be assigned a prominent role (he believes the two should be celebrated in close proximity with each other) but that a place be made for a new rite of personal consecration to Christ within the Christian community to mark the fulfillment of baptism and sacramental confirmation.[77]

What charismatics call the baptism of the Spirit Congar sees as a renewing work of the Spirit that does not replace baptism and confirmation but carries them to a new level in Christian experience. Baptism in the Spirit signifies an adult reaffirmation of the sacramental grace given in baptism and confirmation as well as in other sacraments, including penance and ordination.

Congar also endeavors to build bridges to Eastern Orthodoxy by reopening the question of the *filioque*, which asserts that the Spirit proceeds from the Father and the Son, not from the Father alone. The *filioque* was a later addition to the Nicene Creed by the Western church but never accepted in the Eastern church. Orthodox theologians reject the *filioque* on the grounds that it undercuts the monarchy of the Father, who is the fount of unity in the Trinity. Congar appeals to writings of the church fathers to show that it is possible to rephrase the intertrinitarian relationships in such a way that the Father is still seen as the primary source of the Spirit, but the Son too is given a role in the hypostatic procession of the Spirit. For example, we can say that the Spirit proceeds from the Father *with* the Son or *through* the Son. Congar is unhappy with monopatrism, which views the Father as the sole cause within the Trinity, for this seems to deny the reciprocity of love that exists within the Godhead. At the same time, too much emphasis on reciprocity could lead in the direction of tritheism. Congar agrees with Augustine that the Holy Spirit is the bond of unity between Father and Son. Yet he is willing to suspend the *filioque* from the creed if this would facilitate fraternal relationships with Orthodoxy.

According to Congar, the Holy Spirit is active in creation as well as in redemption. The Spirit holds all things together in unity. He is "both one and transcendent . . . able to penetrate all things without violating or doing violence to them."[78] We cannot presume to know "the frontiers of the Spirit's activity in this world, nor the ways in which he acts. We can only be sure that they are related to Christ, whose spiritual body is formed with men by the Spirit."[79]

Congar opposes both ecclesiocentricism, associated with traditionalist Catholicism, and fundamentalism, pervasive in the charismatic movement. The first blurs the lines of distinction between the actions of the church hierarchy and the Holy Spirit. The second denies the usefulness of historical-critical methods in understanding the text of Scripture, resulting in a barren literalism that prevents us from discerning the deeper levels of meaning in the text. The church is not "the incarnation of the Holy Spirit," as some conservative Catholic theologians have alleged, but instead the channel through which the Holy Spirit carries the message of redemption to the world.

Evangelical Protestants can appreciate Congar's warning against a hyper-sacramentalism that views the sacraments as automatically efficacious apart from personal faith and repentance. He continues to affirm the principle of means of grace but wishes also to allow for the free movement of the Spirit within the sacramental life of the church. At the same time, he can still speak of the sacrament as conferring grace and as a cause of grace.

Congar's disavowal of Mariolatry is also helpful in cementing ecumenical relations with both Orthodox and Protestants. He faults Bernardino of Siena for teaching that Mary has at her disposal "a certain jurisdiction or authority over the temporal procession of the Holy Spirit, to such an extent that no creature has ever received the grace of any virtue from God except through a dispensation of the Virgin herself."[80] Mary is a witness to Christ's redemption, but it is the Spirit who applies the fruits of this redemption to an unbelieving world. It is the Spirit who "makes life 'in Christ' real, personal and inward."[81] The Spirit leads us to the Son, who then proceeds to lead us to the Father.

Regin Prenter

Danish Lutheran theologian Regin Prenter has made a substantial contribution to the discussion on the Holy Spirit in his groundbreaking *Spiritus Creator*.[82] While his intention is to give a creative restatement of Luther's position, he makes it abundantly clear that he stands with Luther on the critical questions of faith and life. In elucidating Luther he shows himself at odds with other Luther interpreters such as Karl Holl and Reinhold Seeberg, who understood Luther to be teaching that justification is a real, progressive process in righteousness.[83]

Prenter seeks to counter both Protestant orthodoxy with its exclusively forensic understanding of justification and the mystical-pietist view that mortification is a precondition for justification. He sets forth a "theocentric-evangelical" spirituality as opposed to one that is "anthropocentric" and "nomistic," as in Pietism and liberalism.[84] The emphasis should be not on the imitation of Christ, where Christ is merely an example for right living, but on conformity to Christ in the trial of bearing the cross through faith in his redemptive grace. The work of the Holy Spirit should be postulated not from below—from the universal experience of the Spirit—but from above—from God's self-witness in Jesus Christ. It is not human striving after God but the searching of the Spirit in the interior depths of the believer that brings a right understanding of the mystery of salvation and the new birth.

Prenter contrasts his biblical-theocentric view, which focuses on God's descent to a broken humanity in Jesus Christ, with what he terms "*caritas* idealism," where the emphasis is on the mystical ascent of the soul to God with the aid of grace. He is particularly insistent that Luther and Augustine were not saying the same thing. The former stressed the justification of the ungodly whereas the latter viewed justification as the process by which we are made righteous. Our hope lies not in the cultivation of personal holiness through the power of the Spirit but in the alien righteousness of Jesus Christ that covers our sinfulness as we make contact with Christ through faith and obedience. Mortification, the ongoing struggle against sin, is not a preparation for justification, as the enthusiasts teach, but the consequence of justification as we try to conform our thoughts and actions to the new nature, the living Christ within us. Sanctification is not "a gradually increasing real righteousness" but "the constantly repeated putting to death of self and being raised with Christ."[85]

There is a place for "empirical piety," but our outward works of righteousness must not be confused with our inward sanctification and redemption. Empirical piety is always ambiguous. "It may in every moment be either an expression of the Spirit or of the flesh, according to whether the man in that particular moment is either Spirit or flesh."[86] Prenter does not deny that we may make progress in our attempts to live a holy life, but this progress is always hidden from the self. Moreover, our focus should never be on our own spiritual endeavors but on Christ's mercy and promise, which are daily communicated to us by the Spirit.

With Luther, Prenter affirms that Word and Spirit belong together. We must first hear the outward Word before we can believe and obey in the power of the Spirit. God deigns to impart his Spirit through external means—preaching, Scripture and sacraments—and we must not neglect these means in living the Christian life. Yet against the Roman Catholic view Prenter insists that the Spirit is completely free in his mastery of the means of grace. The work of the Spirit cannot be "calculated and guaranteed in advance."[87] The sacraments do not convey grace automatically or necessarily, but God may confront us with his grace as we hear his Word and partake of his sacraments. "The Word and the sacrament do not guarantee the presence of the Spirit. They do not carry the Spirit. It is, however, the Spirit that carries the Word and the sacrament. It is the Spirit that makes the Word the gospel of God and the sacrament God's sign of confirmation."[88] While Prenter clearly prefers Luther's "spiritual understanding of the divine" to the "sacramental-magical" understanding of ritualistic religion (as in Roman Catholicism), he stands with Luther in opposing an antisacramental, spiritualistic form of religion.[89]

Evangelical Christians can appreciate Prenter for his recognition that *gratia* (grace) precedes *donum* (gift), and that the gift of faith and the Spirit must be appropriated throughout one's whole life. He rightly reminds us that Luther affirmed a double motion: the Spirit gives rise to faith and faith leads us back to the Spirit. In Luther's understanding, passive sanctity, which is worked by the Spirit within us, must give rise to active holiness, in which we seek to demonstrate our faith in lives of outgoing love.

Where I have difficulty with Prenter is his almost uncritical appeal to Luther to the extent that Luther's writings practically function as a prolongation of the canon. There is a remarkable paucity of biblical references in Prenter's book on the Spirit. It seems that Prenter reads the Bible through the lens of Luther's theology rather than vice versa. Luther is also one of my mentors, but we should not assume that he was always correct in his interpretation of the biblical text.

Prenter's devaluation of empirical piety is also troubling. Granted that empirical piety is not to be confounded with either faith or love, it can certainly be a sign of whether faith or love is present. We must never place our hope and trust in empirical piety, but we are surely under some constraint to make ourselves fit vessels of the Holy Spirit. In his *Spiritus Creator* Prenter tends to disparage the endeavor to live a holy life, but in a later work he acknowledges that as Christians we can glory in a holy life so long as we see the source and wellspring of this life in the risen Christ who both sacrificed his life for us at Calvary and now lives within us by his Spirit.[90]

Despite his trenchant critique of sacramentalism, Prenter does not break completely with this aberration. He can declare that sacraments "are a necessary means for obtaining righteousness and holiness."[91] If this were true then nonsacramental Christians—Salvationists and Quakers—would have to be considered bereft of holiness, whereas I see in both of these movements outstanding examples of biblical holiness and sanctity.

Prenter's *Spiritus Creator* is one of the classics of evangelical spirituality and must be taken with the utmost seriousness in ecumenical discussions. Most evangelicals would concur with Prenter that Luther not only discovered the heart of the gospel but also laid the foundations for a this-worldly holiness that claims every area of life under the sovereign rule of God. At the same time, certain emphases in Luther's theology could easily lead to the heresy of cheap grace in which the demands of costly discipleship are subverted and the freedom of God's Spirit is dangerously compromised by tying his gracious work to the performance of sacramental rites. Prenter's book on the Spirit needs to be read with Kierkegaard's *Purity of Heart* and Bonhoeffer's *Cost of Discipleship*, which testify to the continuing consciousness in Lutheranism of the need for the demonstration of a holy life—not as a means to salvation but as a compelling witness to a salvation once for all achieved by Jesus Christ on Calvary.

Clark Pinnock

Much more open to pietism and the current charismatic renewal is Baptist theologian Clark Pinnock, who offers a Spirit christology that views Christ as "an aspect of the Spirit's mission" instead of the Spirit as a function of Christ's mission.[92] The Spirit is not subordinate to the Son, for the two are "partners in the work of redemption."[93] Their missions are to be understood in terms not of hierarchy but of equality and complementarity. The cross is not only a work of Christ but also a work of the Spirit, since it is the Spirit who brought Jesus to the cross and raised him from the dead.

Pinnock upholds what he calls the participatory model of redemption over the legal model. Redemption is a salvific journey in which Jesus Christ shows the way as well as furnishes the power to persevere on this journey. Christ saves not by offering satisfaction for sin (though this note can have a place in the fuller picture) but by conquering sin through self-effacing love. Salvation is completed not through the vicarious death of Christ on Calvary but through the outpouring of the Holy Spirit, who enables us to appropriate the fruits of Christ's death and resurrection. The Spirit endows us not only with charismatic power but also with deifying energy, which enables us to conform our lives to that of Christ. The salvific process continues beyond Pentecost and even beyond death. The author likens life to a process of education and character formation culminating in our transformation into the likeness of God.

Pinnock seeks to forge a global theology that takes into consideration the work of the Spirit in cultures and religions outside Christianity. He favors building "redemptive bridges" to other world religions, which enable us to appreciate elements of truth in those religions. Yet it would be wrong in his view to consider non-Christian religions as vehicles of grace, for they contain much that is fragmentary, questionable and even erroneous. His point is that we must not deny that the Spirit works universally and that no person, regardless of cultural background or religious affiliation, is bereft of the presence of the Spirit. Moreover, we must be prepared to recognize this presence when it appears in the words and lives of non-Christians.[94]

Pinnock is to be applauded for his contention that the Spirit is not opposed to the material, that physical signs and media can be used by the Spirit to impart divine grace. This insight has a firm anchor in the patristic tradition, which waged an unrelenting battle against Gnosticism with its false dualisms. Interestingly Pinnock not only sees the need for sacraments but regards sacraments as efficacious for redemption. In his theology baptism is "the moment when the Spirit is imparted and when people open themselves to gifts of the Spirit."[95] He views the laying on of hands as a separate sacrament through which we receive and rekindle the gift of the Spirit.

As one who fully supports charismatic renewal, Pinnock not surprisingly endorses the gifts of the Spirit, which make our ministry fruitful in the world. Speaking in tongues is "prayer without concepts, prayer at a deep, noncognitive level. We surrender to God when we pray in tongues and give control even of our speech over to him."[96] Yet he sees tongues not as the norm for life in the Spirit but as normal in the living out of this life. This theologian also recognizes the important role of prophecy, healing, miracles and exorcism.

Pinnock is sharply critical of the *filioque* in the Western version of the Nicene Creed, which affirms that the Spirit proceeds from the Father *and* the Son. This position tends to subvert the universal mission of the Spirit, the belief that the Spirit is at work, even redemptively, outside the confines of the community of faith. Pinnock here acknowledges his indebtedness to Eastern Orthodoxy. His affirmation of the social Trinity is another sign of the impact of the Eastern church on his thinking. Father, Son and Spirit comprise a divine community "unified by common divinity and singleness of purpose."[97] The question is whether Pinnock successfully avoids tritheism, particularly when he asserts three different consciousnesses in the Trinity.

Where I have the most difficulty with Pinnock is in his doctrine of salvation. It seems that in his theology we are saved not by grace alone but by grace assisting sinful humans to save themselves. Justification is a moment in salvation rather than the enduring basis of our salvation (as with the Reformers). Higher than justification is deification, in which we are literally raised into the glory of God and thereby participate in the inner life of the Trinity. Sometimes Pinnock leaves the impression that grace is a power infused through the sacraments rather than the gracious God himself extending his favor to unworthy mortals. Pinnock acknowledges that he stands closer to the Council of Trent in these matters than to the Reformation.[98] In light of his recent works he gives cause for concern that he may be slipping into Pelagianism and semi-Pelagianism in which the human will plays an indispensable role in gaining the remission of sins.[99]

Pinnock reveals his affinity to the mystical tradition of the church in viewing the goal of the Christian life as the transfiguration of the human spirit rather than the service of the glory of God.[100] The motivation for the spiritual journey seems to be egocentric: the acquisition of divine power and freedom rather than selfless service to the poor and downtrodden of the human race. This criticism may not be fair to Pinnock, however, since he makes an important place for evangelism and mission in the life of the church.

It is somewhat disturbing to hear Pinnock contend that "there are no formal criteria of truth, no absolute guarantees that we will not make a mistake."[101] Surely we as Christians are not guaranteed freedom from error in our understanding and articulation of the faith, but we do have access to the infallible criterion of divine revelation through the illumination of the Holy Spirit and the inspired testimony of Holy Scripture. This criterion is admittedly hidden from human perception in the earthen vessels of the proclaimed and written Word of God, but it becomes available to us in the gracious condescension of the Spirit as we arduously strive for further insight and deeper understanding in a spirit of prayer and openness to the transcendent. It seems that Pinnock is proposing a postmodern theology that finds truth in the narrative history of a community rather than in a divine revelation superimposed on the self-reflection of a community that needs always to look beyond itself for guidance into right thinking and right conduct.

Pinnock is right that we must come to know God experientially and not just cognitively. Yet rational cognition must not be downplayed, for we do not truly know unless we understand, unless we are able to express the truth conveyed to us in propositional or conceptual terms. Narrative itself, even the biblical narrative, does not yield revelatory or divinely given knowledge of the event or issue in question. In order to know we must ourselves be grasped by the Spirit of God reaching out to us and bringing our thoughts into conformity with the self-revelation of God in Jesus Christ. Pinnock intersects with this position, but he sometimes appears to compromise the sovereign freedom of God in his haste to adopt a sacramentalist approach that elevates the outward sign to almost the same prominence as the spiritual reality. Such an approach enables him to draw on Orthodoxy and Roman Catholicism, but he needs to keep in touch with the Reformed corrective that the finite cannot of itself grasp or carry the infinite, that the human must never be confounded with the divine, that salvation is never a cooperative affair between willing humans and the Spirit of God but always a surprising work of grace that does not merely negate our will but turns our will in a completely new direction so that we can act and believe—yet not to gain salvation but to give evidence that we are indeed recipients of saving grace.[102] According to Pinnock we are not dead in sin, but we are drowning and thereby still have the power to reach out when God gives us a helping hand.[103] Yet Scripture irrefragably teaches that the sinful human race is indeed dead in sin (Eph 2:1, 5; Jn 5:24) and that we need to be liberated before we can repent, believe and obey.

Paul Evdokimov

The survey would not be complete apart from a serious treatment of an Eastern Orthodox theologian, for that communion has given special attention to the critical role of the Holy Spirit both in the inner life of the Trinity and in the mission to the world. Paul Evdokimov (d. 1970) merits our consideration because of his welcome ecumenical thrust as well as his innovative contributions to the discussion.[104] A Russian Orthodox theologian, he was professor of moral theology at St. Sergius Theological Institute in Paris for many years and served for a time as director of the Ecumenical Institute in Bossey, Switzerland. He has appropriately been called "a theological bridge between East and West." In striking contrast to the reserved attitude of Protestant neo-orthodoxy toward seeking philosophical support for theology, he freely draws on a variety of philosophical traditions, including the life philosophy of Teilhard de Chardin and the naturalistic mysticism of Carl Jung, though his grounding in the patristic fathers keeps him from embracing the new spirituality. The impact of Platonism and Neoplatonism on his thought will be dealt with later.

Given his solid commitment to Eastern Orthodoxy it is not surprising that he strongly reaffirms the doctrine of the Trinity as three persons in one nature or creative energy. He contends that the monarchy of the Father is the foundation for the unity of the Trinity. The Son does not possess causality as does the Father. The Father alone is the cause of the Son and the cause of the Spirit. The Spirit like the Son proceeds from the Father alone, and this is why Evdokimov objects to the *filioque* of the Western church. At the same time, he tries to build ecumenical bridges to the West by restating the role of the Spirit in the economy of both the Trinity and salvation. The Spirit does not proceed from the Son, but he is the Spirit of the Son. The Spirit comes from the Father, rests on the Son and comes back to the Father in ecstatic embrace. Although the hypostatic procession of the Spirit is from the Father alone, his manifesting work cements the unity of the Father and the Son. The Spirit is not less than the Son or the Father in the inner life of the Trinity, but in his temporal mission to the world he gives glory to the Son and the Father. "The Son comes in the name of the Father to make him known and accomplish his will. The Spirit comes in the name of the Son to bear witness to him, to manifest him and complete with his gifts the work of Christ."[105] Evdokimov is convinced that in his creative work the Spirit precedes the incarnation of Christ, for he was already involved with the Father and the Son in the creation of the cosmos.

Evdokimov has an ultra-high view of the sacraments, interpreting them as agencies of salvation. In the sacrament of baptism the baptismal water becomes "the vehicle of divine energy, a tangible sign of God's vivifying power, and the creator of new life."[106] In language that would be offensive to many evangelicals, he contends that "water is not simply elevated by the Spirit to the level of becoming the agent of his operations, but the Spirit is infused into the water."[107] Confirmation or chrism is the sacrament that "supremely confers the gifts of the Spirit."[108] Following Symeon the New Theologian, he sometimes links the baptism of the Spirit to the gift of tears of repentance after water baptism in which we personally repent of our sins and throw ourselves on God's mercy.[109] The sacraments convey not only the remission of sins but also the deifying energy of the Spirit, which transposes us into godlike beings. Deification is pneumatization, "the penetration of the whole human being by the deifying energies of the Holy Spirit."[110]

Like almost all Orthodox theologians, Evdokimov assigns an important place to the gifts of the Spirit. In deification we are raised above the purely human level and endowed with capacities that often astound the unbelieving world. He strongly affirms gifts of prophecy, wisdom, knowledge, discerning of spirits, healing and miracles. "The fathers," he says, "could read souls, could tell the contents of a letter without opening it, and above all were able to bring men's hearts out of hiding. Long before the discoveries of modern depth psychology, they were masters of the amazing art of penetrating the subconscious."[111] These gifts have reappeared in the history of the church especially in the mystics and pneumatics, who are not necessarily part of the church hierarchy.

One of Evdokimov's distinctive emphases is his portrayal of Jesus as healer as well as Lord and Savior. Sanctification pertains to the body as well as to the soul. In the life of grace we should expect inner healing and even physical healing as a sign of God's favor to us expressed in the ministry of his angels and the prayers of the saints.

Much more daring is his exploration of the feminine dimension of the divine. The motherly aspects of God are best expressed in the Holy Spirit, whom he refers to as "hypostatic motherhood."[112] Evdokimov closely associates Sophia, the Spirit and Mary. He sees Mary as the archetype of the feminine and John the Baptist of the masculine. He here seems to open the door to the depiction of Jesus as bisexual or androgynous.[113] Although freely acknowledging the feminine side of God, he consistently refers to God in trinitarian terms and generally uses masculine pronouns in depicting God's activity.

Another distinctive mark of his theology is his circumscribing of the use of icons in the church, although he strongly adheres to the Orthodox claim that icons are veritable means of grace and are conducive to the worship of the believing community. Icons sensitize the emotions and acclimatize the mind to spiritual reality. But as we make progress in the spiritual life we are to leave the visual behind and go forward solely by faith. Here we see the influence of Neoplatonic mysticism, which upholds a God beyond images, a God who is ineffable and illimitable. In our prayers we should not try to discern any image or figure, for otherwise we could fall into madness. He combats the notion that some ontological presence is absorbed into the matter of the icon. The icon "neither captures nor retains anything."[114] The narrative illustrations that constitute the icon hide more than reveal the grandeur and reality of the living God, which is discovered only by faith.[115]

Evdokimov can nevertheless be faulted for seeing icons as parallel to Scripture, for not giving adequate recognition to the biblical principle that faith comes by hearing and hearing by the preaching of the gospel (Rom 10:17). Icons can perhaps have a place in enhancing the beauty of worship, but the essence of worship lies in the free movement of the Spirit through the oral witness of the messengers of God to the truth of the mystery of the gospel. Perhaps we need churches that make a place for icons on the grounds that creation can symbolically point to the Creator. But we also need churches that are iconoclastic on the grounds that icons can become a pretext for idolatry.

The author has many fine insights in his theology of love, but it is incontestable that he views love predominantly as eros, the upward unitive love of pure beauty that is exemplified in the living God.[116] This is the love that he can describe as "mad" and "ecstatic," that seeks the possession of the beloved. Love of self is not something to be overcome (except in its carnal phase) but a steppingstone to love of God. Here as in some other areas of his thought we see the profound impact of Platonic philosophy. In Platonism and Neoplatonism we strive to leave the material behind and ascend to the purely spiritual. Evdokimov reflects this emphasis when he contends that our royal dignity lies in "the mastery of the spiritual over the material, over the instincts and pulsations of the flesh, the freedom from all determination coming from the world."[117] A Neoplatonic note is evident in his quotation from

Symeon the New Theologian: "God comes into the soul, and the soul goes into God."[118]

Yet in our discomfort over the Platonic cast of his theology we would do well to recognize that all theology draws on some philosophy. The question is whether philosophical concepts and images are baptized into the service of the gospel or whether they alter the apostolic interpretation of the gospel. I confess my own indebtedness to Kierkegaard, Pascal and even Kant for furnishing insights and concepts that serve to elucidate the meaning of the gospel for the contemporary mind. Yet there is always a risk in this endeavor. The greatness of Karl Barth lies in his abandonment of his early reliance on Kierkegaard as he embarked on the writing of his *Church Dogmatics*. Evdokimov reveals his biblical commitment when he describes the mystical way of ascent as involving a descent into the trials and sufferings of our neighbor.[119]

Other areas of his theology arouse some uneasiness. One is an exaggerated sacramentalism that ties sacramental efficacy to ritual performance. Is not this closer to magic or fetishism than to a genuinely biblical theology that sees sacraments as only outward signs that can be used by the Spirit but are not themselves charged with spiritual energy? I am also disturbed by his proclivity to give human effort more weight than divine grace in the determination of our salvation. Yet at times he appears to grasp the biblical paradox that God does everything in us as we strive to our uttermost for God.[120] His Sophiology can also be questioned particularly when he speaks of Sophia as giving Yahweh a human face. Finally, his firm commitment to the doctrine of apocatastasis—the universal restoration of all things—contradicts the biblical teaching of the twofold outcome of human history.[121]

To Evdokimov's credit he regards the role of the Son as always central in the economy of salvation. The role of the Spirit is to bring to the world the message of salvation procured by the Word. The Spirit is not so much subordinate to the Son (except in a voluntary sense) as complementary to the Son in the divine plan of salvation. Within the Trinity itself he sees reciprocity and mutual service, and here we can perhaps attain some common ground in our understanding of this mystery.

Other Voices

That the doctrine of the Holy Spirit is probably the most pivotal one in Christianity today is attested by the growing number of books on this subject. We have already explored some important discourses on the person and work of the Spirit, but it behooves us to heed other voices as well. Hendrikus Berkhof, a Dutch Reformed theologian, is significant because he radically breaks with the trinitarian tradition in an attempt to reclaim the unity of God.[122] For Berkhof God is not a community of persons but an extension of activities. He upholds a dynamic monotheism rather than a trinitarian communitarianism. The Son and the Spirit are expansions of God's working rather than persons within an ontological Trinity. He speaks of "a movement of the one God" rather than "a static community of three persons."[123] In his view, "Jesus Christ, God, and the Holy Spirit are three ways of describing God's one saving reality."[124] The Trinity is not a self-enclosed order of being apart from or above the world of humanity but the covenantal event between God and humanity.[125] The Spirit is effectively conflated with the action of Christ. Berkhof upholds a revelational Trinity but not an ontological Trinity. "The Trinity is . . . not a description of an abstract God-in-himself, but of the revealed God-with-us."[126]

On the work of the Holy Spirit Berkhof explores the possibility of a third element in regeneration beyond justification and sanctification in which we are filled with the Spirit for active service in mission. He here seeks to build bridges to Pentecostalism. In this discussion he acknowledges an affinity with Barth's third work of the Spirit—vocation, whereby we demonstrate the efficacy of our justification and sanctification as we live in the everyday world.

Berkhof repudiates the notion embraced by many evangelicals of "the personality of the Holy Spirit," since this leads directly into tritheism. The Spirit is the name for "the exalted Christ acting in the world."[127] He calls for a pneumatic christology over a logos christology because the focus of our attention should be on the work of the Spirit within the historical Jesus rather than the generation of the Son from the Father or the hypostatic procession of the Spirit from the Father and the Son. We can have no knowledge of realities that completely transcend human experience. Berkhof recommends that we free ourselves from the categories of Hellenistic philosophy in order to recover the more dynamic vision of the New Testament. The question is, can the narrational language of the Bible be translated into conceptual discourse apart from some philosophical mediation? Berkhof appears to sunder the doctrine of the Trinity in order to clarify a mystery that cannot be neatly resolved in purely historical categories.

* * * * * *

Representing an almost diametrically opposite view is Wolfhart Pannenberg, who upholds a relational over an autocratic Trinity. The persons of the Trinity exist as persons only in relationship to the others. He still subscribes to the monarchy of the Father, but the Father has his monarchy or kingdom only through the Son and the Spirit. The unity of the persons is based not on the Father as the source of deity but on their concrete life relations. He is deeply critical of Barth's view of God's triune life as the unfolding of a single divine subject. Pannenberg contends that there are three subjects in the Trinity, yet not autonomous or independent but dependent on each other. There is no eternal essence of God that is a subject alongside the three persons; only the latter are subjects of divine action.

The Holy Spirit is the bond of unity that links Father and Son together. But he is more than the divine life that is common to Father and Son: he "stands over against the Father and the Son as his own center of action."[128] The Spirit allows the creatures to share in the relation of the Son to the Father. Pannenberg is unhappy with the *filioque* clause in the Nicene Creed. In his view the Spirit proceeds from the

Father and is received by the Son. He describes the Spirit as a life force or force field that activates the Trinity and rejuvenates the world. He affirms reciprocal relations within the Trinity as opposed to monopatrism in which the Father is the single cause of action.

Pannenberg is a severe critic of pietism, which he accuses of fostering unnecessary anxiety in the lives of believers. Instead of a penitential piety in which we constantly face anew the judgment of God through the proclamation of the law, he upholds a eucharistic piety in which we celebrate God's victory over sin in Jesus Christ and strive to bear witness to this cosmic reality in the structures of our common existence. The center of the church's worship is not the sermon but the Eucharist. The sermon serves the eucharistic celebration rather than the latter being an appendage to the sermon. The Christian life should be envisaged not as a repetition of personal crisis and surrender but as a process of continual transformation by Christ, beginning with baptism. The eucharistic celebration "encourages and inspires political commitment for the sake of peace and justice."[129] Missions should be conceived not as preaching for conversions but as influencing through example and dialogue.[130]

Pannenberg has made a solid contribution in his discussion of the Trinity. He rightly warns us not to understand the relations of Father, Son and Spirit as exclusively relations of origin, for then we cannot do justice to the reciprocity in the trinitarian relations. It seems, however, that he leaves the moorings of the Reformation to embrace the Catholic concept of the eucharistic sacrifice as central in worship. In his theology faith is continuous with prefaith existence on the part of those who grow up in the Christian community rather than a decision that marks an irrevocable turning point in our relation to God with bringing about a new creation.[131] Pannenberg is sound in his insistence that the doctrine of forensic justification must be united with an emphasis on mystical participation in Christ through the Holy Spirit if we are to do justice to the whole of the biblical witness.

* * * * * *

Peter Hodgson, professor of theology at Vanderbilt University Divinity School, presents a doctrine of the Spirit that is in tune with the traditions of German idealism and Anglo-American naturalism. He is especially indebted to Hegel, Tillich, Whitehead and Moltmann. Revealing a naturalistic bent, he chooses to define Spirit in terms of energy rather than of mind. He rejects the idea of Spirit as "a supernatural person of the Godhead" in favor of an emergent spiritual reality "generated out of the interaction of God and the world, in the process of which the world is liberated and God is perfected."[132] Instead of speaking of the Spirit as proceeding from the Father and the Son, he prefers to depict this procession as being from God and the world. Dismissing the traditional trinitarian formula of Father, Son and Spirit as too "hierarchical" and "patriarchal," he proffers in its place "God, World and Spirit."[133]

In this theology God is no longer almighty Lord of the universe but the creative force that directs the evolution of the universe. Hodgson redefines God as the "ultimate and inclusive event of communication,"[134] "the Alluring Cosmic Eros," who is both "primal energy" and "spiritual-erotic love." God is the organizing power that "makes creativity serendipitous rather than destructive."[135] Life is a risk, and God is involved in that risk. The human relationship to God is one of "radical openness" rather than "radical dependence."[136]

The liberal myth of progress is strikingly apparent in Hodgson's pneumatology, though he tries to do justice to the destructive as well as the creative side of cosmic reality. He speaks of the world growing into Christ through the power of the Spirit. Through the Spirit the world is progressively liberated from alienation into freedom, and God is perfected as the world unfolds back into the divine life. Hodgson describes his position as "holism" in that all of reality is seen to be interrelated. He is willing to accept the term *panentheism* because he regards God and the world as mutually dependent, though he seeks a vision that is "trans-theistic" rather than pantheistic, in which God and the world are coextensive.

Hodgson is alert to the dangers of both subordinationism (of the Spirit to Christ) and supersessionism (of Christ by the Spirit).[137] Yet it is incontrovertible that Spirit is the dominant category in his doctrine of God. He avers that "Spirit encompasses the whole, God and world together."[138] Jesus is simply one of the great sages of history in whom the Spirit is preeminently manifested. God's Spirit is active in all dimensions of the cosmos and in all religions. All of nature is God's self-revelation, and the idea of a unique intervention of God into the history of a particular people is flatly repudiated.

Hodgson offers us a postmodern theology where the accent is on diversity and indeterminacy rather than eternal verities and perduring congruities. The unifying strain in his theology is the all-pervasiveness of energizing or alluring eros that shapes the configuration of world history. With William James he espouses an open universe where nothing is predetermined. Both God and humanity are in the process of evolution, and the proper attitude regarding the outcome of history is hope that the forces of liberation will finally triumph. Hodgson's theorizing should be taken seriously but not as a viable option for thinking Christians who wish to remain true to the biblical vision of a God who both rules and saves the world through a decisive intervention in world history in the person of Jesus Christ.

* * * * * *

More biblically based, though still questionable, is Michael Welker's disquisition on the Spirit.[139] Welker, professor of theology at Heidelberg University, propounds a Spiritology from below—beginning with human experience.[140] Like Hodgson he theologizes in a postmodern way, avoiding totalistic metaphysics and respecting differences in cultural ethos. Similarly he draws on Hegel, Moltmann and Whitehead.

Welker maintains that the Spirit is not world-negating but life-affirming. The Spirit "is *not* a force that erodes, squelches, impairs, and deforms life *in* the flesh. Rather, the Spirit of God is a power that liberates life *in* the flesh from the power of sin."[141] The Spirit motivates us not to flee from the world but to overcome the world, "delivering and renewing life." The Spirit does not create solitaries but shapes community, one that embodies the ideals of justice and peace.

The Spirit is not a supplement to the written Word of God but the authority that establishes the Word. It is not the letter of the Bible but "the Spirit who through the texts produces a charged field of experiences."[142] By the action of the Spirit "inspired testimonies and inspired readers of the Bible become capable of experiencing, expressing, and communicating the presence and glory of God."[143]

Likewise the Spirit is over the church reforming and purifying the fellowship of those who follow Jesus Christ. It is "not the communion of the sanctified itself" but the Spirit of God who "recognizes, enlivens, and maintains the body of Christ in constantly new ways."[144] The Spirit leads the people of God in the struggle for righteousness and peace.

Welker takes seriously the healings and exorcisms of Jesus. He regards these as signs of the availability of freedom and integrity. While acknowledging the mythological cast of the battle with the demons, he adamantly contends that "the superior power that overwhelms the demonic powers, is the power of God that intervenes in earthly life relations: the Holy Spirit."[145]

Similarly Welker seeks to do justice to the charisms of the Spirit, interpreting them as force fields that communicate the power and freedom of the Holy Spirit. In these charisms "the Spirit becomes recognizable through the process of human beings receiving a share in the Spirit."[146] He acknowledges the therapeutic benefits of speaking in tongues but regards tongues as "an expressive religious form that in itself is empty, indeterminate, and in need of interpretation."[147] Tongues speech is subordinate to prophetic speech, which is comprehensible.

In his attempt to avoid metaphysical speculation Welker seriously calls into question the doctrine of the Trinity. Because he brooks no thinking back into the mystery of the Trinity, his theology lacks an explicit trinitarian foundation. He does not regard "Father" as a proper name for God, though he carefully refrains from romanticizing God as Mother. The Spirit is not a person in the sense of a self-related, autonomously active center of action. Instead the Spirit is "a network of relations," a unifying life force "in which we participate and which we help to constitute."[148] Jesus is not the preexistent Son of God but the bearer of the Spirit, the mediator of the power of the Spirit. Welker's theology has a certain biblical ring, but it signifies a palpable break with the apostolic understanding of both Christ and the Spirit as articulated in the ecumenical creeds.

* * * * * *

Also involved in constructing a Spirit christology is the Jesuit theologian Philip Rosato, who develops his argument in opposition to Barth. Rosato's approach is to view the Spirit "from below" as "the omnipresent Giver of life." We should begin not with a metaphysical analysis of intertrinitarian relations but "with an investigation of mankind's global search for a just human community which is marked by freedom and united in harmony as well."[149] Rosato seeks to place christology in a pneumatic framework. Jesus becomes the totally Spirit-filled man. Jesus' own experience of the Spirit must be shown to have relevance to our own encounter with grace.

Rosato accuses Barth of subordinating the Spirit to Christ, of seeing the Spirit "exclusively as the one sent from Christ, but not inclusively as the one leading all things to the glory of the end-time through the mediation of mankind's secular experiments."[150] In Rosato's view the Spirit is active in creation apart from the Christ revelation, guiding all things toward union with God. The Father "acts through His Spirit beyond the boundaries of the Christian Church."[151] Rosato is also critical of Barth's objectivism, which portrays humankind as already redeemed ontically by Christ. This means that "the Spirit can do no more than noetically realize this achievement. Thus the Spirit is incapable of adding any substantial gain to Christ's universal efficacy."[152]

Rosato also faults Barth for not recognizing a correlation between the divine Spirit and the human spirit. Salvation is not a work of Christ alone or of his Spirit alone but also a work of the human subject, who cooperates with Christ in carrying forward the drama of salvation. Rosato conceives of humanity as "reaching up to, seeking after God, in dialogue with him, and responding to him, so that while God is said to be sovereign and transcendent there is a form of mutual reciprocity."[153] He posits an "obediential capacity" within humankind that has its basis in the universal working of the Spirit, which causes human nature to long for and find rest "in the saving work of the same Spirit who meets him as Redeemer and Lord."[154] John Thompson astutely observes that Rosato here reflects the traditional Roman Catholic position that justification is contingent on human effort and cooperation with grace. Rosato would therefore be unable to affirm *solus Christus* (Christ alone) and *sola gratia* (grace alone).[155]

Following Moltmann, Rosato upholds an eschatological Trinity, which he contrasts with "the originative Trinity."[156] In this theology Father, Son and Spirit are fulfilled in the consummation of history when God will be all in all. The persons of the Trinity "will reach a three-in-oneness only at the point in time when man attains his own social and political goals with the aid of the incessant eschatological power of the Spirit."[157] The Spirit's role is not only to bring to completion the "Father-Son-Spirit" movement to humanity but also the "Spirit-Son-Father" movement with humanity toward the eschaton.[158] Thompson contends that "Rosato must end up with a highly dubious conception of the Trinity—a triune God who is only completed through his involvement with us."[159]

Rosato seeks to present a theology of the Christian life that is grounded in the universal working of the Spirit in creation as well as in his particular working in Jesus Christ. The role of the Spirit is to motivate us to open ourselves to the love and light that shine in Jesus so that we can be included in the trinitarian unfolding that is now taking place in history. In his theology we play a prominent role in contributing to the work of salvation. In contradistinction to Rosato I hold that

Christ alone performs the atoning work of reconciliation and redemption. Our task is not to add to his work or share in his work but to proclaim and manifest this work in our lives. It is not our reaching up to God but God reaching down to us that is decisive for our redemption. Rosato virtually ignores the human dilemma of being bound to sin and therefore appears not to see that God not only offers grace to humanity but also delivers humanity by his grace.

* * * * * *

J. Rodman Williams is a significant figure, having left a mainline denomination (Presbyterian) to embrace the Pentecostal or charismatic renewal. An authority on existentialism,[160] he is now professor of theology at Regent University in Virginia Beach, Virginia. In his theology the two great acts of the Holy Spirit are indwelling and effusion.[161] He occasionally refers to the latter as the baptism in the Spirit, the filling with the Spirit and the outpouring of the Spirit. It is an act distinct from regeneration in which we are incorporated into the body of Christ by faith. This second work of the Spirit provides power for witness and is always accompanied by upwelling love and joy. It constitutes an "interpenetration of the divine and the human, the supernatural and the natural."[162] Williams acknowledges that effusion can occur simultaneously with regeneration but ordinarily follows it.

The peculiar sign of Spirit baptism is speaking in tongues. This is not a necessary sign, but it generally forms part of the Pentecostal experience. Speaking in tongues is not speaking in foreign languages but "pneumatic speech—the speaking by the Holy Spirit through the mouths of human beings."[163] He regards it as an eschatological sign, a preparation for "uttering the word of God with new power."[164]

Water baptism is important, but it has no direct connection with Spirit baptism. It is "a tangible impression and certification of the reality of the remission of sins."[165] Spirit baptism on the other hand denotes a spiritual empowering that equips us for ministry. Williams vigorously disapproves of confounding the two baptisms, for the free gift of the Spirit is then eclipsed by the ritual of the church.

Williams deplores the functional subordination of the Spirit to Christ, which has dominated ecclesiastical history. "Not only does the Spirit point to Christ but also Christ points to the Spirit, and . . . beyond the Spirit's work in uniting [us] to Christ (the area of salvation) is Christ's mediation of the Spirit to others."[166] Williams takes issue with the *filioque* added to the Nicene Creed by the Third Council of Toledo. The sending of the Spirit is from the Son, but the procession is from the Father. The Son and Spirit are subordinate to the Father in relationship, but not in being.

My chief criticism of Williams is that he tends to separate the missiological and soteriological work of the Spirit (a common Pentecostal failing). When the Spirit brings us salvation he also imparts power and inward renewal, and I make a case for this position in the succeeding chapter. Williams can be appreciated for seeking to relate the Pentecostal revival to the witness of the Spirit in the church through the centuries.

Postscript

While there are still defenders of the orthodox position on the person and work of the Spirit, a perceptive observer can only conclude that a radical shift is taking place among theologians on this subject. For a growing number of scholars the Spirit is no longer the third person of the Trinity but the first person, in some cases the only person. The Spirit is no longer subordinate to Christ as a messenger carrying out his commands, but Christ now points to the Spirit as the transformer of nations and cultures. Instead of a Logos christology focused on the unity of the divine Logos and the humanity of Jesus, we are frequently confronted with a Spirit christology in which Jesus is portrayed as the man totally possessed by the Spirit. The point of departure is no longer the preexistent Trinity and the hypostatic procession but the impact of the Spirit of God on the quest for justice and peace. We begin not with abstract metaphysical speculation but with human experience and the role of the Spirit in this experience. There is also a marked tendency in contemporary theology to view the Spirit as working universally in history and experience even apart from the parameters of Christian faith. When the Spirit is no longer tied to Christ, interreligious dialogue takes on a new and disturbing significance.

Those who seek to draw on modern naturalism and idealism reconceive the Spirit as a field of force or power or energy rather than a person. Alasdair Heron recommends that in the new climate of discourse we refer to the Spirit as "it" rather than "he" or "she."[167] The Spirit is less a subject than an agent or force. Michael Welker urges that we avoid I-Thou terminology in our discussion of the Spirit and view the Spirit more as the power of cosmic rejuvenation and cultural transformation.[168]

A natural theology of the Spirit is increasingly usurping the understanding of the Spirit shaped by the biblical revelation. In natural theology we begin with the ecstatic experience of self-transcendence and then try to link this up with an encounter with the Spirit. Or we begin with the experience of human motherhood and then try to discover the motherly qualities in the activity of the Spirit. Or we focus our attention on the quest for justice and peace and then seek to discern the hand of God in this quest.

Instead of trying to find a biblically based coherent pattern in the working of the Spirit many theologians under the impact of postmodernism insist that the Spirit will act differently in different historical and cultural contexts. They contend that our theology of the Spirit should be shaped by experiences of the Spirit in Third World and primitive cultures that will force us to be less dependent on and more critical of our Eurocentric heritage. They advocate a crosscultural spirituality over a christocentric or bibliocentric spirituality that supposedly bears the mark of insularism.

One can also discern on the contemporary scene a growing discomfort with the *filioque* in the revised Nicene Creed that expresses itself in finding a pathway to the abysmal God from the Spirit alone—without the necessary mediation of the Son. Most of those in the Eastern Church who have difficulty with the *filioque* nevertheless assign a prominent role to the Son in our coming to a knowledge of God. Opposition to the *filioque* is often fed by a certain kind of mysticism that seeks an immediate experience of God through the Spirit rather than through historical mediation.

It should be noted that some theologians have resisted the trend toward a natural theology of the Spirit and have continued to uphold a Logos christology. Here I could mention Karl Barth, Eberhard Jüngel, John Thompson and Yves Congar. But even among these scholars one can discern sweeping innovations such as abandoning the concept of person for mode of being.

Others on the conservative side have been prompted to embrace a sacramentalism that contends that the Spirit works primarily through external signs and rites rather than immediately on the human soul in conjunction with preaching and hearing.[169] Those who are attracted to the sacramentalist position include George Montague, Frederick Dale Bruner, G. W. H. Lampe, William Hordern, Paul Evdokimov, Alexander Schmemann, Burkhard Neunheuser, Lindsay Dewar, L. S. Thornton, Dom Gregory Dix and Richard Jensen. Those who warn against sacramentalism include Karl Barth, Markus Barth, James Hull, James Dunn, G. R. Beasley-Murray, Rudolf Bultmann, Jürgen Moltmann and J. Rodman Williams. I deal with the role of sacraments in the distribution of the graces of the Spirit in the succeeding chapter.

Suffice it to say here that given the often fantastic speculation on the person and work of the Holy Spirit, it is by no means surprising that groups and seminars focusing on the seemingly benign subject of "spirituality" are frequently hotbeds of rampant heresy subtly undermining the tenets of biblical and apostolic faith. We need creative restatements of the doctrine of the Spirit but based firmly on the biblical testimony and on the witness of sacred tradition. I try to meet this challenge in the final two chapters of this volume.

·TEN·

THE HOLY SPIRIT: PERSON & MISSION

It is the Spirit who gives eternal life. Human effort accomplishes nothing.
And the very words I have spoken to you are spirit and life.
JOHN 6:63 NLT

Without the Spirit, the sacrament is empty,
and the same applies to the office of the priest.
SYMEON THE NEW THEOLOGIAN

The activity of the Holy Spirit has to be experienced and felt,
and it is by having these experiences that one is taught by the Holy Spirit.
MARTIN LUTHER

There can be a Pentecostal experience without any real commitment of faith,
without the basic determination that Jesus Christ
is to be the interpretative context for anything that happens.
SIMON TUGWELL

In these last two chapters I give an evangelical reappraisal of the person and mission of the Holy Spirit, particularly as the Spirit relates to the life of the church. I use the term *evangelical* in the sense of "centered in the gospel" rather than in any ideological sense. The apostolic interpretation of the gospel is considered normative, as is to a lesser extent the Reformers' elucidation of this interpretation. The consensus of the undivided church of the first centuries is also treated with the utmost respect, though the witness of the church is always secondary to that of Scripture. Here as throughout my works the Bible is seen as over church tradition and the Spirit in unity with Christ as the final authority regarding scriptural interpretation.

The Spirit in the Trinity

A particularly vexing bone of contention in the history of Christian theology has been the role of the Holy Spirit in the Trinity. Eastern and Western churches have taken different though not necessarily opposing approaches. The first tends to begin with the trichotomy of Father, Son and Spirit and then relate this to the Godhead, whereas the second usually begins with the unity of God and then proceeds to acknowledging a differentiation. While the Eastern Church affirms three persons united in one nature, the West is prone to speak of one God in three persons. Part of the problem lies in the definition of "person." In both the ancient and the medieval churches *hypostasis,* when applied to the members of the Trinity, did not mean an independent thinking personality but a mode of personal relationship or simply being-in-relatedness.[1] The Trinity does not constitute a society of individuals bound together in an inseparable unity but a tripersonal interaction within the life of God. *Hypostasis* especially in the Western Church indicates an agency of relationship rather than an individual center of consciousness.

From my perspective it is more felicitous to make the point of departure the unity of God rather than the trinitarian relations. The idea of a social Trinity, which presupposes three different subjects, leads more often than not into tritheism.[2] The Eastern Church affirms that the three persons are consubstantial, but the question is whether the peril of tritheism is in this way successfully averted.

In the contemporary discussion I must confess that I am closer to Karl Barth, Robert Jenson, Eberhard Jüngel and John Thompson than to

Jürgen Moltmann, Wolfhart Pannenberg, Vladimir Lossky and Clark Pinnock. I prefer to see one God in three events rather than three persons in one nature (though I have no qualms in accepting the latter when rightly interpreted).[3] God remains God, but he is God in a different way in each event. There is one subject but three modalities of action. There is one overarching consciousness but three foci of consciousness. God exists as one self but with three identities. The unity of God is differentiated though not individualized. I hold to one divine being in three modes of existence, not three beings who interact in a social unity. What we have in the Trinity is not separate selves that function in an indissoluble unity but an all-encompassing consciousness in three modes of relationship. God is will, thought and energy, yet not in temporal succession but always together. God is a thinking and willing being whose thought energizes and vivifies. The Trinity is not one God in three roles (this would be the economic Trinity only) nor three Gods in one inseparable unity (this would be tritheism) but one God in three subsistences or life histories. We should not speak of the will of the Father or the will of the Son unless we understand these as dimensions or stages of the one will of God. When we pray to the Son or the Holy Spirit we are praying to the one God in his existence as Son or Spirit. We are not praying to a separate divine subject. The relations between the members of the Trinity are relations within God, not external to him in any of his modes of being.

Those who espouse the social doctrine of the Trinity sometimes give the illustration of a family to clarify their position. But a family is composed of separate selves, and when we speak in this way we are probably departing from biblical monotheism. Theologians who build on the family metaphor are sometimes led to describe God as "a fellowship of beings," but this is clearly outside the parameters of orthodoxy.[4]

Church tradition is replete with metaphors and images that supposedly make the Trinity more comprehensible, and even though they invariably fall short of their goal they can nevertheless be helpful in bringing a measure of coherence to the discussion. Gregory of Nazianzus sought to bring illumination to this mystery by viewing God as the conjunction of three suns with a single combined radiance.[5] The divine nature is likened to one blazing torch. Here we see the tendency in the Eastern Church to begin with the triunity and then affirm the unity. Because this unity is fully affirmed and not obscured I can appreciate this metaphorical depiction. At the same time my own preference would be to envisage *one* sun with three dimensions—fire, light and heat. This way of understanding the trinitarian reality is also very much embedded in the ancient church and throughout church tradition.[6]

John Weborg of North Park Seminary in Chicago has shared with me an illustration that is perhaps still more promising, since it focuses on the creative speech of God rather than on God's essence or substance, which is more Greek than biblical.[7] For Weborg there is one act of communication involving thought, word and spirit. Both word and spirit occur simultaneously, and both are dependent on thought. There is no temporal succession but one event with three distinctive dimensions. In this image we not only hear but also see, since the spirit in which one speaks or communicates is perceptible to the senses as well as accessible to the mind. Weborg's illustration has more direct bearing on the economic Trinity (the way in which God relates to the world) than to the immanent Trinity (the manner in which God exists within himself).

Today the doctrine of the *filioque* (the Spirit proceeding from the Father and the Son) is under attack, even in evangelical circles. The common objection is that this formula easily leads to christomonism and calls into question the universal role of the Spirit—his presence in secular culture as well as in the world religions. In my opinion the *filioque* is not only based on a solid biblical witness but is also congruous with a broad line of patristic interpretation. The Spirit is spoken of in Scripture as being of the Father (Mt 10:20; Jn 15:26) and of the Son (Gal 4:6; Jn 14:26; 20:22; Lk 6:19; 1 Pet 1:11). The Spirit proceeds from the Father (Jn 15:26) and receives from the Son (Jn 16:14). Both the Father and Son give the Spirit and send the Spirit. Christ is both bearer and sender of the Spirit. Eastern Orthodoxy, of course, accepts the authority of these texts but insists that they refer to the temporal mission of the Spirit in the world rather than to the hypostatic procession of the Spirit that in its view is from the Father alone.

One of the troubling questions is whether the *filioque* implies one single procession (from the Father *through* the Son) or a double procession (from the Father *and* the Son). Orthodox theologians are inclined to reject both notions, but some have been open to a rephrasing of this processional event. For example, as I have indicated, one could say that the Spirit proceeds from the Father and receives from the Son, thereby preserving the monarchy of the Father but doing justice to the role of the Son in the work of the Spirit. Or one could say that the Spirit shines out from the Son but proceeds only from the Father. In my opinion we should strive to achieve some measure of agreement on this perplexing issue, recognizing that the *filioque* preserves a truth that is supportive of the gospel witness, namely, that the Spirit unites his own mission with that of Christ and thereby chooses to serve the mission of Christ. The *filioque* also lends support to the idea of the intratrinitarian communion between Father and Son.

Karl Barth perceived in the Greek view "an unsubjugated remnant of subordinationism, as though the Father were more and greater than the Son." He also raised the pertinent question of whether the denial of the *filioque* is "a reflection of the very mystically oriented piety of the East, which, bypassing the revelation in the Son, would relate man directly to the original Revealer, the *principium* or fount of deity." Barth did not lightly dismiss the Orthodox objections to the Western position, but he sincerely believed that the latter is more in accord with biblical intuitions.[8]

John Thompson, for whom Barth is a theological mentor, contends that the denial of the *filioque* could create the impression that there is a "real difference between God in his revelation and God as he is antecedently in himself." Because "the Spirit comes from the Father *and* the

Son in the economy of salvation it does so eternally in the life of God."[9] Thompson rightly conjectures that a pattern of activity in the economic Trinity surely reflects a similar pattern in the immanent or ontological Trinity.

I do not see the Father as the only actor in the Trinity, nor is he the sole source of action (monopatrism). The Father presents a plan and the Son carries through the plan with the aid of the Spirit. But the Son and the Spirit also contribute to this plan. The Spirit not only receives from the Father and the Son but also responds creatively. The Spirit is not only acted upon by the Father and the Son, but forges the bond of unity between Father and Son. He searches the depths of God and brings the intentions of God to fruition and realization (1 Cor 2:10-11).

There is an order of succession in the Trinity, though not of ontological subordination. There is no hierarchy of being but a distribution in action. There is a priority of function in that the Father initiates the action, but there is no ontological priority or superiority.

The essence of the Godhead is not mind, as rationalists suppose, nor simply energy, as vitalists believe. Instead, it is being in action.[10] God encompasses both mind and energy. God is a thinking being whose thought energizes and vivifies. In this sense the Spirit as well as the Father or the Son is a source and principle of the Trinity. The God of the Bible is neither the self-contemplating God of classical philosophy nor the dancing God of the new spirituality but the seeking and redeeming God who enters into the travail and pain of the world. He is ever at work and ever at rest (Augustine). He goes out of himself into the world of decay and death and yet remains within himself as the fulcrum and wellspring of everlasting love.

In any discussion of the Trinity it is necessary to affirm both the threeness and the oneness of God. God is both triadic and monadic, but he is not a dyad—Father and Mother, Light and Darkness, or Yin and Yang (as in Taoism). He has both one name (Yahweh or Lord) and three names—Father, Son and Holy Spirit. He is both one person (the living God) and three persons (God, Christ and Spirit).[11] There exist within God an interdependency and a dependency. Son and Spirit are both dependent on the Father, but the Father is also dependent on the other two for the implementation of his will. The Spirit is dependent on the Son, but the Son also needs the Spirit for the perfecting of his work. The Spirit is both person and force. He is both life-giving energy and one who speaks and prays. He utters prayers within us and helps us in our prayers (Rom 8:26-27). If we lose sight of any of these polarities we are then irremediably on the road to heterodoxy. The key to orthodoxy is to confess that the mystery of the Trinity can be only dimly apprehended, that our attempts to elucidate and expound will always fall short of a rational resolution. The mystery of the Trinity is best described in terms of paradox, and this perception is in full accord not only with the biblical witness but also with church tradition.

Spirit and Word

Both the biblical witness and sacred tradition attest that our knowledge of God as well as our redemption by God lie in the coalescence of the Word and the Spirit. I am thinking mainly of the living Word, Jesus Christ, but because this Word is reflected in Scripture and church proclamation, one can aver that the Spirit works not only in Jesus Christ but also through the human mediation of Scripture and sermon. Irenaeus referred to the two hands of God—Spirit and Word—by which our redemption is secured.[12] Paul affirms that Christ's atoning work must be united with the Spirit's interior work for people to become children of God. In Ephesians 1:13 the apostle contends that receiving the gospel is also being sealed with the Holy Spirit. In Ephesians 3:16-17 he prays that we be strengthened in our inner being by the Spirit so that "Christ may dwell in [our] hearts in love" (REB). In 1 Corinthians 2:12-16 receiving the Spirit is closely associated with having the mind of Christ. It is by the inner work of the Spirit that we perceive the mysteries of Christ. Church proclamation is ineffectual if it consists only in plausible words of wisdom: it must occur "with a demonstration of the Spirit and of power" (1 Cor 2:4 NRSV). The Word is animated by the

Spirit, and the Spirit always directs us to the Word. God sends his Spirit by means of the testimony of the prophets (Zech 7:12), and this testimony is clarified by the bestowal of the Spirit. The Holy Spirit reminds us of all that Christ says to us in Scripture (Jn 14:25-26) and confirms the witness of Christ that we are indeed children of God (Rom 8:16-17).

The Protestant Reformation strongly affirmed the complementarity of Spirit and Word, and gave special emphasis to the paradoxical unity of the living Word (Jesus Christ), the written Word and the proclaimed Word. Luther declared that we must first "hear the Word, and then afterwards the Holy Ghost works in our hearts; he works in the hearts of whom he will, and how he will, but never without the Word."[13] In Calvin's view "the Word is the instrument by which the Lord dispenses the illumination of his Spirit to believers."[14] He notes:

Holy Scripture is for us a dead and ineffectual thing until we have come to realize that God speaks to us and manifests His will to us therein. . . . The apostle calls his preaching "the ministration of the Spirit" (2 Cor. 3:8) meaning, doubtless, that the Holy Spirit so inheres in His truth, which He expresses in Scripture, that only when its proper reverence and dignity are given to the Word does the Holy Spirit show forth His power.[15]

There is no uniform scholarly consensus on the precise way in which Word and Spirit are related in Luther and Calvin. Is the Spirit immanent in Scripture, or does the Spirit descend into Scripture and into our inner being for Scripture to become the living Word of God?[16] I contend that a comprehensive analysis of the Reformation writings yields the conclusion that revelation was basically viewed as dynamic rather than static, that both the scriptural and sermonic witness are ineffectual apart from the special illumination of the Spirit. Calvin made clear that "there is no benefit from the word, except when God shines in us by the light of his Spirit; and thus the inward calling, which alone is efficacious and peculiar to the elect, is distinguished from the outward voice of men."[17] At times the Reformers virtually equated Scripture and the Word of God; at other times they insisted that the fount of authority is Scripture illumined by the Spirit, not the letter or word of Scripture by itself. Protestant orthodoxy was inclined to make the same kind of distinction, but it often failed to maintain the infinite qualitative difference between God's truth and the human expression of this truth.[18]

Does the present work of the Holy Spirit simply confirm and ratify the prior affirmations of Scripture, or does the Spirit add something new for the situation of the reader? Some interpreters of Calvin hold that he believed the witness of the Spirit "adds nothing to the Scripture; he tells us nothing about it that it does not already contain; in a word, that witness is no new revelation disclosed in addition to the scriptural texts."[19] On the other hand, both Calvin and Luther contended that the Old Testament authors unwittingly pointed to Christ, who was the fulfillment of their prophecies, though they did not understand this at the time. It is the Spirit who guides us to see how the Old Testament text is related to the New Testament revelation. While Calvin believed that God communicates with us by outward signs, God's Spirit also leads us "to grasp something transcendent beyond the sign."[20] Luther was convinced that the scriptural text remains law unless we see how it is related to Jesus Christ, the "star and kernel" of Scripture.[21]

The Reformers also sought to relate the work of the Spirit to the visible Word—the sacraments of baptism and holy Communion. Yet here again they did not wish to tie the grace of God to the sacraments. The sacraments do not contain the Word, but through the Spirit they can point us to the Word. The mainstream Reformers were unequivocally opposed to the Roman view that the sacraments confer grace through the mere act of being performed. In Luther's words, "It is a most pernicious error to say that the sacraments of the new law are efficacious signs of grace in such a way that they do not require any disposition in the recipient except that he should put no obstacle in the way."[22] In his understanding the Spirit is not immanent in either Scripture or the sacraments, but he works in, by and under the Word and the sacramental signs.[23]

Neo-orthodoxy (Karl Barth, Emil Brunner) rediscovered the patristic and Reformation doctrine of the complementarity of Word and Spirit and for a time recovered a dynamic view of revelation and mission. In his earlier writings Barth affirmed the perichoresis of the living, written and proclaimed Words of God. Later he came to regard Jesus Christ alone as the one Word of God and the only bona fide sacrament; the Bible and the sermon now became pointers to the living, transcendent Word—the exalted Christ. At the same time, Barth expanded the role of the Spirit to include not only the subjective possibility of revelation but the vibrant reality of revelation as well. He reclaimed the Nicene affirmation that the Holy Spirit is "the Lord and Giver of Life," but he failed to give adequate recognition to the fact that the Spirit ordinarily employs external mediation in connecting us with Christ.[24]

I see the Spirit as not only the means by which we receive revelation but also the source and agent of revelation. He is not merely an adjunct to the Word but the speaker of the Word. He is also the servant of the Word. He magnifies not himself but Jesus Christ and the gospel. The Spirit carries the Word and the sacraments; the latter do not contain or guarantee the Spirit (Prenter). The relation of Word and Spirit is a relation not of cause and effect but of promise and fulfillment. The Spirit brings to fulfillment the promises contained in holy Scripture.

With the Reformers and Barth I hold to the sovereign freedom of the Spirit in his dealings with humanity. The Spirit enters into our preaching, animating our words and convicting human hearts. Yet the Spirit is not bound to our preaching. We do not enclose the Spirit in our own words.[25] At the same time, we must not lose sight of the Reformation principle that the Spirit freely acts to relate himself to us through outward means—Scripture, sermon and sacrament. He is not bound to these means, but we as the people of God are so bound. The Spirit of God does not inhere in the means of grace except in the sense of a free decision to manifest himself in and through these means. But we cannot suppose that the Spirit necessarily binds himself to the means of grace. God is free to withhold his Word from the means of grace. There can be many preachers in the land, yet at the same time a famine of the Word of God (Amos 8:11-12).

The Holy Spirit brings us not a new revelation but new light on the once-for-all revelation given in Jesus Christ and attested in holy Scripture. The Spirit enhances our spiritual perceptivity so that we can discern in the scriptural text the Word of God for our time as well as for that time. The Holy Spirit communicates to us through the Letter as well as through the sacramental sign, but he is not a property of either the written Word or the sacramental elements. He is always the speaker and the actor. The preacher and the priest are only heralds and witnesses to what the Spirit secretly enacts and accomplishes.

My reservations regarding the special powers of the sacrament are not based on the Platonic notion of the inadequacy of material things to represent the spiritual. They are based rather on the sovereignty of God's grace. Divine revelation cannot be put into a sacramental box, but it can employ sacramental signs in bringing home to us the message of faith.

In relating Word and Spirit we must eschew the Scylla of spiritualism and the Charybdis of rationalism. In the first the Spirit becomes an independent criterion effectively separated from the witness of both Scripture and sacred tradition. In the second the Spirit is reduced to assisting the will to assent to what reason can know on its own concerning the revelation of God. In evangelical rationalism the Bible becomes a depository of divine revelation that is accessible to rational and historical investigation. In spiritualism the Bible becomes a cipher or symbol of inward realities that are unfolded by the Spirit. Barth is noted for his warnings against rationalism, but he was equally alert to the dangers of spiritualism:

> The Bible is one thing and revelation another. Nevertheless, we have revelation not in itself but in the Bible. For we have the witnesses of revelation, those upon whom its reflection rests, the prophets and apostles, only as they presented themselves, that is, in the Bible, in the texts of the Bible.[26]

My own position could be regarded as a fusion of biblicism and spiritualism. The Spirit not only certifies the truth of the biblical witness but brings this truth home to the contemporary situation. The Spirit illumines the Bible, but the Bible in turn points us to Jesus Christ, the goal and content of divine revelation. In biblical hermeneutics we begin with the natural sense of the passage but do not remain with this sense. We proceed to the spiritual sense—the relation of the text to the self-revelation of God in Jesus Christ, a relation that is unfolded only by the Spirit working with our spirits to lead us into the knowledge of the truth of the gospel.

The aberration of spiritualism is evident today not only in the New Age and New Thought movements but also in the Word of Faith movement in Pentecostalism. For these people "the Word that truly saves is not the written text of Scripture, proclaiming Christ the Redeemer, but is rather the 'Rhema' Word that is spoken directly to the human spirit by God's Spirit."[27] In my view the one who truly saves is Jesus Christ himself, and he does so by means of both the written Word of God *and* the interior illumination of the Spirit.[28]

Water and Spirit

One of the perennial controversies in the history of the church has been the mysterious relation of water and Spirit baptism. Lutheran theologian Richard Jensen succinctly expresses the sacramentalist view: "The giving of the Spirit stands in the closest possible relationship to baptism with water. To be baptized with Christian baptism (water and the Word) is to receive the gift of the Holy Spirit."[29] Some sacramentalist theologians relate the gift of the Spirit to the laying on of hands, which they contend was originally an element in the sacrament of baptism (Max Thurian, Lionel Thornton, Lindsay Dewar). In sacramentalism the rite of baptism by the very fact of being performed *(ex opere operato)*, conveys the grace that cleanses from sin.

The Bible is replete with allusions to water as the agent of spiritual cleansing and renewal. Already in the Old Testament water is seen in close association with the Spirit (cf. Ex 29:4; 40:12-13; Is 55:1; Ezek 36:25-26; Zech 13:1). Prior to the messianic ministry of Jesus Christ, John the Baptist preached a baptism of repentance for the forgiveness of sins (Mk 1:4; cf. Mt 3:1-12; Lk 3:1-22). Jesus came to baptize with the Holy Spirit, but water was an integral element in this new rite. The question is whether the various references to water in the New Testament canon refer to the inner cleansing work of the Spirit or to an outward rite that symbolizes this interior renewal. John's Gospel portrays the Spirit as living water that washes away the stain of human perfidy (cf. Jn 4:10-15; 7:37-39). Jesus' words in John 3:5-8, which make entrance into the kingdom of God contingent on being born of water and the Spirit, continue to be debated, but it is unlikely that these verses can be made to yield a sacramental interpretation.[30] In Revelation 21:6 the Spirit is depicted as the water of life that flows from the throne of God and of the Lamb (Rev 22:1). Many scholars see a sacramental allusion in Hebrews 10:22: "Let us draw near with a true heart in full assurance of faith, with our hearts sprinkled clean from an evil conscience and our bodies washed with pure water." Philip Hughes regards the outward ceremony of cleansing with water as pointing to "the inward reality of the cleansing of the conscience."[31] According to Donald Hagner, "bodies washed with pure water" does not refer to Jewish ceremonial washings for purification but "almost certainly to Christian baptism, which is the outward sign of the true, internal cleansing."[32] Similarly in Titus 3:5 we find an unmistakable allusion to water baptism: "He saved us, not because of deeds done by us in right-eousness, but in virtue of his own mercy, by the washing of regeneration and renewal in the Holy Spirit." Fred Gealy comments that this formula "undoubtedly reflects the pregnant meaning and central importance of baptism in the early church."[33]

It is a law of the religious life that the initial spontaneity and enthusiasm of a religious movement ineluctably give way to ritual performance in order to preserve continuity with the experiences of the first converts.[34] This indicates that the rite of baptism may well be implied in these relatively late epistles. At the same time, one cannot thereby conclude that renewal by the Holy Spirit occurs at the very moment of contact with the water of rebirth as in a full-blown sacramentalism.

The Pauline references to the seal of the Spirit are also relevant to this discussion. Does Ephesians 1:13, which declares that believers are marked with "the seal of the Holy Spirit," refer to the sacrament of baptism or to an inward work of regeneration and renewal? On the one hand, Markus Barth vigorously rejects a sacramental interpretation, arguing that sealing in this context indicates "the designation, appointment, and equipment of the saints for a public ministry—a ministry which includes the power to understand, to endure, to pray, to sing and to live in hope."[35] Calvin likewise viewed the event of sealing as a confirming work of the Spirit rather than an outward rite.[36] On the other hand, F. F. Bruce detects in this Ephesian text on sealing a reference to baptismal water as "the outward and visible sign" of an inward and spiritual grace.[37] We are confronted with a similar passage in 2 Corinthians 1:22: "He has put his seal upon us and given us his Spirit in our hearts as a guarantee." Immersion in baptismal water is the sign but not the content of spiritual regeneration by the Spirit. I agree with Lampe that in the Pauline corpus being sealed with the Spirit indicates "the inward experience of which Baptism is the effective symbol."[38]

The question remains how the two baptisms—by water and by the Spirit—are related in time. Ezekiel ties ritual purification by water and the gift of the Spirit very closely: "I will sprinkle clean water upon you, and you shall be clean from all your uncleannesses, and from all your idols I will cleanse you. A new heart I will give you, and a new spirit I will put within you" (36:25-26). The Qumran Essenes maintained in their rule of life that God will cleanse seeking souls through a holy spirit, and will sprinkle on them "a spirit of truth as purifying water." In Jesus' own baptism by water we see a close association with the gift of the Spirit: "No sooner had he come up out of the water than he saw the heavens torn apart and the Spirit, like a dove, descending on him" (Mk 1:10 JB; cf. Jn 1:32). James Dunn trenchantly argues that the Fourth

Gospel tends to use water as a symbol of the Spirit's activity and this activity is never tied to a sacramental rite.[39] In his view John never thought of the Spirit "as given through Christian baptism, let alone through the water of Christian baptism." At the same time, he acknowledges that in John 3:5-6 Jesus is speaking of two baptisms—by water and the Spirit—in close connection.[40]

The New Testament actually speaks of four baptisms: the baptism of John the Baptist, Christian baptism, Spirit baptism and the baptism with blood. The last is referred to by Jesus in Mark 10:39: "The cup that I drink you will drink; and with the baptism with which I am baptized, you will be baptized" (cf. Lk 12:50; Jn 18:11). John's baptism was supplanted by the baptism with water and the Spirit that Jesus instituted. It is important to understand, however, that baptism with water is always the outward sign of Spirit baptism, and what truly saves is the latter. It is possible to have the gift of the Spirit without baptism, as in the case of Apollos (in Acts 18:24–28).[41] Yet baptism with water can be used by the Spirit to strengthen and confirm faith, even to impart faith where faith is lacking.

According to James Dunn both Acts 2:38 and 22:16 indicate that the forgiveness of sins is conveyed not by baptism but by repentance and calling on the name of the Lord. Baptism, however, seems to have an instrumental role in these verses, and Dunn does not do justice to the sacramental dimension of coming to faith and repentance. For Dunn water baptism is the vehicle of faith but not the vehicle of the Spirit. "Faith reaches out to God in and through water-baptism; God reaches out to men and meets that faith in and through his Spirit."[42]

In striking contrast, Frederick Dale Bruner maintains that since Pentecost "Christian baptism becomes the locus of the Spirit's reception in response to the Spirit's pressure in preaching."[43] His thesis is that baptism and the reception of the Spirit are so synonymous as to be identical. "For Christian baptism . . . is spiritual baptism. There is only *one* baptism."[44] Bruner rightly points to the priority of grace over works of repentance and purification in coming to faith, but he ties the gift of grace to the ritual performance of baptism, thereby weakening the New Testament affirmation that we are saved by grace through faith alone (Eph 2:8).

My position is closer to that of Augustine, who held that "faith and conversion of heart can fill up what is lacking in baptism."[45] The later Augustine emphasized the objectivity of Christ's saving work and the efficacy of the sign of baptism through the Spirit. Yet even in his anti-Pelagian period he did not believe that the sign has "any actual power to effect grace."[46] Neunheuser attributes Augustine's reluctance to embrace a full-blown sacramentalism to Neoplatonic influences.[47] But it may also be due to Augustine's wish to preserve God's freedom in imparting grace and also the necessity for a personal appropriation of grace by faith.

In Luther too we detect a palpable tension between a sacramentalist and a personalist orientation. Sometimes Luther averred that baptism is not a mere sign but a garment. It does not merely point to Christ but presents Christ.[48] He could declare: "Baptism bears the Word of God by which the water is sanctified, and we are sanctified in the water."[49] Yet he stoutly opposed any automatic imparting of grace through ritual performance and insisted that the sign has no efficacy unless it is related to the proclaimed Word of God and the Spirit who implants faith within the seeking soul.

I find the position of Basil of Caesarea attractive, for he resisted the temptation to regard baptism as automatically effective—without any direct relationship with faith. In his view "faith receives its completion in baptism, but baptism is founded in faith. . . . The confession of faith which leads us to salvation precedes; then follows baptism and seals our assent in conclusion."[50] My inclination is to identify the seal with the gift of the Spirit and baptism as the external sign of this inward seal of grace.

Baptism, as I see it, carries the promise of the new life, but it does not insure the new life. Baptism can be used by the Spirit as a means of grace, but it is never effective unless it is accompanied by faith, which is itself a gift of God.[51] The relation of sign and thing signified is to be understood in eschatological terms. The seal of the Spirit is an anticipation of the glory that is yet to be revealed (cf. 2 Cor 1:22; Eph 1:3; 4:30). We can experience now the power of the coming kingdom of God through faith and baptism, but we do not fully enter into the new dispensation of glory until we are transfigured into the very likeness of God by the Holy Spirit in the eschaton or fullness of time.

The danger today, especially in ecumenical circles, is a new ritualism or sacramentalism that subverts the need for personal faith and repentance. Grace is not a supernatural fluid infused into us (akin to the mana of primitive religion or the *dynamis* of ritualistic religion), but it is the living God himself who reaches out to us in self-giving love. The water of baptism does not contain the Spirit of God (as alleged in some forms of gnosticism),[52] but it points us to the Spirit of God and reminds us of our utter dependence on God's grace.

On the other hand, we must take care not to dismiss the sacraments as mere symbols or regard them as simply public expressions of personal faith. They are indeed symbols of our commitment of faith, but they are also means by which God confronts us with the power of his personal presence. It is incumbent on us to be sacramental without being sacramentalist. There is a thin line between fetishism, a fascination with objects held to have supernatural power, and sacramentalism, which sees supernatural power conveyed by outward ritual acts. One cannot help but perceive the profound difference between biblical personalism, in which we are related to God through personal encounter, and sacramentalism and ritualism, which reduce the life of faith to prescribed rituals. Faith has need of ritual support, but it does not gain its vitality from ritual observance. Faith is a gift of the Holy Spirit, who reaches out to mortals through various means but never apart from the preached Word of God. Where the Word of God and personal faith are lacking, sacramental observance may promote both an idolatrous fixation and a false sense of assurance. Nonetheless, sacraments can build up our faith if they instill within us a passion to know Jesus Christ and his gospel and a love for sacred Scripture, whose primary author is the Holy Spirit of God.

Works of the Spirit

Scripture tells us that the Spirit of God does many works and that these works are indissolubly related not only to each other but also to the work and mission of the Son of God. While charismatic endowment is indeed a special work of God's Spirit, it is not wholly separate from his regenerating work or his revealing work. Anointing, filling, sealing, baptizing—all of these represent various aspects of the gift of the Spirit, yet with different nuances of meaning. It is common in Pentecostal circles to distinguish the awakening of faith from the gift of the Spirit, a practice that tends to reduce faith to a mere preparation for the coming of the Spirit, whereas faith in the fuller biblical perspective is the catalyst that enables us to grasp the Spirit. Faith does not merely point to a future victory over sin, but it is itself the victory that overcomes the world (1 Jn 5:4).

One thing is certain: the Holy Spirit is not uniform but multiform. His workings cannot be systematized, nor are his gifts ever in the control of the clerics of the church. He moves in a variety of ways and bestows a diversity of gifts. His work is always surprising and unexpected. God is not absolutely bound to give his Spirit even to those who repent of sin and are baptized, but he freely acts at his own discretion and in his own time.[53]

Especially vital for both faith and salvation is the revealing work of the Spirit. It is the Spirit who discloses the truth of Jesus Christ that alone can set us free from the bondage of sin and the horror of death (Rom 1:4; 1 Cor 2:9-16). It is the Spirit who probes "the depths of everything, even the depths of God" (1 Cor 2:10 JB). It is the Spirit who brings life and power to the written Word of God. The letter by itself kills, but the Spirit gives life (2 Cor 3:6).

The Spirit not only reveals the saving truth of the living Word of God but also inspires the prophetic and apostolic writing that mediates this

Word. All of Scripture is breathed out by the Spirit of God (2 Tim 3:16). "Men and women moved by the Holy Spirit spoke from God" (2 Pet 1:21 NRSV; cf. 1 Cor 2:13). Owing to the Spirit's superintending action, the mysteries of God are reflected in the Bible, but they are not revealed in all their splendor until the Spirit opens our inward eyes to their truth and significance (Eph 1:17-18).

The Spirit inspires the words of Scripture, and he also illumines the minds of the readers so that they may come to a saving knowledge of the Word of God. In addition the Spirit proceeds to guide the church into the right understanding of the gospel message, but the Spirit does not guarantee that the church will fully grasp the truth revealed. Nor does the Spirit guarantee that the church will unfailingly communicate this truth to its constituents. The Spirit does give assurance that the church that remains under the Word, that subjects itself to the scrutiny of the Word, will persevere in the truth through the power of the Spirit. The Spirit not only produced the written Word of God but also interprets this Word to the church in every generation. Our Lord makes clear that "when the Spirit of truth comes, he will guide you into all the truth; for he will not speak on his own, but will speak whatever he hears, and he will declare to you the things that are to come" (Jn 16:13 NRSV).

The Holy Spirit is known not only for his revealing and illumining work but also for his creative work. Indeed, these works are inseparable, for the Spirit in bringing us the knowledge of Christ creates within us the faculty for receiving this knowledge. The Spirit plays a crucial role in the creation of humanity and the world and in their renewal. He is *Spiritus Creator*—the source of both our existence and our renovation. He is the conveyer not only of redeeming grace but of sustaining or preserving grace. But he preserves in order to redeem. He keeps us alive and well in order to transform us in his image. The pivotal role of the Spirit in creation is powerfully attested in Psalm 104:29-30 (REB):

When you hide your face, they are dismayed.

When you take away their spirit, they die

and return to the dust from which they came.

When you send forth your spirit, they are created,

and you give new life to the earth.

In addition to God's preserving grace there is a prevenient grace that signifies the first stage in regeneration.[54] Our Puritan forebears called this the quickening work of the Spirit. Because of sin the natural person does not even seek for God (Ps 14:1-3; Rom 3:9-12), but when the Spirit acts on us our yearning for God is heightened and we begin to seek for his salvation—not on our own but through the power given to us from on high. The Spirit not only enables us to seek but motivates us to continue our seeking after conversion. Not all who seek will find, but no one will find who does not seek in the power of the Spirit. The one who truly seeks is no longer a natural or unregenerate person, but neither is that one a regenerate or born-again person. Before our new birth we who seek are best designated as pre-Christians rather than as non-Christians.

When the Spirit regenerates us he enters into us and makes his abode within us. He convicts us of our sin and empowers us to believe and obey. Our Lord declared, "He, when He comes, will convict the world concerning sin" (Jn 16:8 NASB). This is a key work of the Spirit, but it does not encapsulate the Spirit's mission. He also comes to console the people of God and to guide them into all truth (Jn 16:13). He teaches us to pray and bears witness with our spirit that we are children of God (Rom 8:16). The Spirit is the agent not only of salvation but also of rejuvenation. An astute observer can perceive an allusion to Pentecost in Malachi 4:2: "For you who fear my name the sun of righteousness shall rise, with healing in its wings. You shall go forth leaping like calves from the stall."

The Spirit comes not only to convict of sin but also to purify and cleanse from all unrighteousness. He is not only the Revealer and Comforter but also the Sanctifier (2 Thess 2:13). His mission is not only to empower but also to make holy (Rom 15:16; 1 Cor 6:11). He not only awakens us to the gravity of our sin but fills us "with all joy and peace in believing, so that by the power of the Holy Spirit" we may abound in hope (Rom 15:13).

His baptizing work, a pivotal focus in this study, is not a wholly new work. It is a dimension of the Spirit's activity as creator, revealer and sanctifier. Baptism is a fluid metaphor indicating immersion, power, endowment from on high, initiation and purification. In the New Testament baptism is related to fire, water and oil. To be baptized with the Spirit means to be submersed in and inundated by the Spirit. Water baptism is an outward sign of this inward cleansing and empowering. It is ordinarily synchronous but not synonymous with Spirit baptism.[55] Spirit baptism is not a second blessing after conversion but the experience that fulfills and confirms our conversion. To be "baptized with the Holy Spirit" is tantamount to "repentance unto life" (Acts 11:16-18). In the decision of faith we were "washed," "sanctified," and "justified . . . in the Spirit of our God" (1 Cor 6:11). Peter confesses that Pentecost was the time he received Christ (Acts 11:17). Baptism with the Spirit is equivalent to sealing with the Spirit (Eph 1:13; 4:30). One is not a Christian apart from Spirit baptism. Paul is adamant that "anyone who does not have the Spirit of Christ does not belong to him" (Rom 8:9).

Finally it is important to give some attention to what might guardedly be called the deifying work of the Spirit. Those who stand in the tradition of the Protestant Reformation have difficulty with this concept because it seems to blur the infinite qualitative difference between God and humanity.[56] From a biblical perspective it simply means that the one who is born from above will become not only more holy but also more victorious over the unruly passions of the flesh. Salvation entails not only the restoration of true humanity but also elevation to superhumanity. Through the power of the Spirit we are enabled to become not only more godly but also more Godlike. We can never possess the power of divinity, but we can reflect this power. By being channels of God's love we literally impart new life to others—not through our own powers but through the Holy Ghost working in us. This is why Luther could call Christians "little Christs." The Holy Spirit enables us to become not simply reformed selves but new selves. Those who are on the way to becoming saints will do works beyond human power and ingenuity. Jesus made this very clear: "The truth is, anyone who believes in me will do the same works I have done, and even greater works, because I am going to be with the Father" (Jn 14:12 NLT; cf. Mk 16:17-18). This is why we can speak of healing and deliverance ministries in the church as well as preaching and service ministries.

Deification may involve on occasion an alteration in the physical appearance of the saints of God. "When Aaron and the people of Israel saw the radiance of Moses' face, they were afraid to come near him" (Ex 34:29-30 NLT; cf. 2 Cor 3:7). Paul comments that if there is splendor in the dispensation of death how much more there will be in the dispensation of righteousness (2 Cor 3:7-11).[57] Stephen's face at the time of his martyrdom shone like that of an angel (Acts 6:15). Through the Spirit we become not only messengers of God's grace but also bearers of God's glory (cf. 2 Thess 2:14; 2 Pet 1:4). Sanctity involves not only fidelity to God but also transparency to God.

Like its practical equivalent glorification, deification should be understood eschatologically. Now we have only an earnest of the glory that is to be revealed to us (2 Cor 1:22; 5:5; Eph 1:4 KJV). Paul writes that "when Christ, who is your real life, is revealed to the whole world, you will share in all his glory" (Col 3:4 NLT). The word *deification* is probably best reserved for that eschatological moment when we are transfigured into the very likeness of God.[58] Now we participate in the sanctifying and revivifying work of God (2 Cor 3:18). Then we shall be transformed in his splendor (Rom 8:17; 2 Thess 2:14).

To be adopted into the family of God as his sons and daughters means to be baptized into the service of his glory. Such a baptism will cause us to radiate his glory if we truly draw near to him in repentance and faith. Yet even though submersed in his glory we remain mortals vulnerable to temptation and subject to all kinds of infirmities. The closer we grow toward God the more keenly we are aware of the infinite gulf that separates us from God, the more conscious we become that we are only sinners saved by grace.

Charisms and Ministries

As we have seen, the gift of the Spirit entails not only regeneration and sanctification but also charismatic endowment. This is best understood not as a second blessing but as a vital element in the one blessing—the gift of the Holy Spirit. Jesus' baptism was both a revelation of his entire sanctification and the occasion of his empowering by the Spirit for public ministry. While Luke's emphasis was on charismatic endowment, Paul's was on initiation into the body of Christ, but these emphases complement rather than exclude one other.

The charisms of the Spirit are multiform. Key passages that enumerate these gifts are Isaiah 11:1-3; 1 Corinthians 12–14; Romans 12:4-8 and Ephesians 4:11-12. A close examination of these texts reveals that the gifts are not always referred to in the same sense. In addition there are allusions in the Bible to other gifts such as craftsmanship (Ex 31:1-6; 35:30-33), shepherding (Ps 78:70-72 NIV) and hospitality (Gen 18:1-8; Rom 12:13; 1 Tim 3:2; Tit 1:8; 1 Pet 4:9-10). In the history of the church further gifts manifest themselves, particularly in the lives of the great saints.[59] The principal area of controversy is the role of the spectacular or so-called extraordinary gifts: tongues, prophecy, healing, miracles, wonder-working faith, reading of hearts, discerning of spirits, exorcism and so on.

Speaking in tongues is one of the more startling or sensational gifts. It is well to note that Paul himself spoke in tongues (1 Cor 14:18; 2 Cor 5:13), though he tried to regulate it in the service of worship. Tongues are mysterious but not necessarily miraculous. They properly belong to the childhood of faith, as Paul indicated (1 Cor 3:1; 13:11; 14:20), and in Catholicism are often related to the initial consolations of the Holy Spirit. A nun who was in summer school at Notre Dame University in 1967 observed: "The ones moved to speak in unknown tongues were using none of their own adult talent, learning, wisdom, or ingenuity.

They were closer to being like children learning by imitation and repetition, than to any mature adult formulation."[60] David du Plessis also associates tongues with the childhood of the born-again believer. In maturity, he says, we go on to prophecy and the higher gifts.[61] His remarks do not imply that the mature Christian should never speak in tongues. Yet they seem to indicate that one should not remain with tongues to the neglect of other spiritual gifts. Tongues can be regarded as a legitimate prayer gift, though not as full prayer or even less as a higher form of prayer. In spiritual maturation it becomes subordinated to other gifts. It is not an unequivocal sign of having the Spirit, though it may well be an authentic manifestation of the Spirit. The need for the gift might well disappear as one progresses in the spiritual life, and it should be set aside when it is no longer spiritually fruitful. Du Plessis likens glossolalia to chaff, and prophecy, teaching and preaching to wheat. Tongues itself may persist if it proves a blessing, but reliance on tongues recedes as we grow in maturity. As Forsyth put it, "The more spiritual we grow, the more we rise out of the subconscious or the unconscious."[62] Tongues at a later stage in the Christian life may signify a new beginning or new departure in the faith pilgrimage. It may even indicate a new resurgence of faith, but not a final stage in spiritual development.

Paul writes that in services of worship tongues should always be accompanied by interpretation, for otherwise it would constitute an offense to outsiders (1 Cor 14:13-19, 27-28). Interpretation is not a translation but the reproduction of the thoughts and feelings of the tongues-speaker. The purpose of tongues in Pauline theology is private edification. We should not frown on this goal, but our primary task is to seek the upbuilding of the body of Christ and the evangelization of the world. James Dunn argues persuasively that Jesus in all probability did not speak in tongues. He was a healer and exorcist but not an ecstatic.[63]

Scholars have been divided on whether tongues and other charismatic phenomena represent the heightening of natural powers and sensibilities or the appearance of wholly new powers. On the one hand Dunn contends that "charisma is not to be confused with human talent and natural ability; nowhere does charisma have the sense of a human capacity heightened, developed or transformed."[64] On the other hand Simon Tugwell argues that "miraculous, charismatic works are paranormal, but natural psychic phenomena, inspired by the Spirit of God, and so integrated into the mystery of Christ. But the same phenomena, as such, can be produced by spiritualists and magicians as well as devotees of other religions. What makes them christian is their context and their significance."[65] My own view is that the Spirit both heightens natural sensibilities and imparts new energies that equip the believer for service in ministry. In both cases the supernatural and the natural are intertwined, and we are indeed confronted by a miracle of grace.

The gift of prophecy is often confused with clairvoyance or mental telepathy. It basically represents the discerning of the will of God for a particular situation. It may involve both foretelling and forthtelling. The Spirit does not give a totally new revelation but causes what has been revealed to be seen in a new light. True prophecy contains an ethical dimension. In the Old Testament the sons of the prophets focused on extraordinary mystical phenomena whereas the major prophets voiced the moral demands of God. An example of a genuine prophet in the New Testament was Agabus, who predicted that a severe famine would come over the world, and Luke tells us that this took place during the reign of Claudius (Acts 11:27-28). Agabus also foretold the incarceration of the apostle Paul (Acts 21:10-11).

Pentecostalism reminds the church that the gift of healing is one of its essential ministries. According to D. S. Cairns we are accustomed to thinking of the action of the Divine Spirit "as confined strictly to the moral and spiritual life," but the early Christians thought of the Spirit as "working amid the whole range of human activities—bodily, mental and spiritual." He observes that "there is not one single instance recorded in which He [Jesus] refused the appeal of a sick man on the ground that it was God's will that he should continue to suffer."[66] He cites the Reformer Luther, "If we have faith enough to be healed, there is no disease from which we may not recover."[67]

Healing as a gift of the Spirit is not to be confounded with mental or magical healing. It is not the channeler or shaman who heals but the living God himself. Healing as a charism of faith is divine healing or spiritual healing. We heal not by magical incantations but by prayer and fasting (Mk 9:29). The key to healing lies not in the discovery of spiritual laws (as in the New Thought movement) but in the impartation of the Holy Spirit in response to the prayer of faith. It is wholly in accord with the biblical witness to contend that we can sometimes prevent genuine healing by striving to uncover some higher law. In the ministry of healing we must bear in mind that grace is not a supernatural fluid akin to the mana of animistic religion but the reaching out of the Holy Spirit, and therefore not within human control.

The word of wisdom (1 Cor 12:8) denotes insight into the mystery of God's providential working among his people. It enables one to discern the counsel of God in human history. The disciples were promised this gift so that they would know how to answer in the time of persecution (Lk 21:14, 15). Some people have a special endowment of wisdom, and it is these who are particularly adept in the care of souls. The gift of wisdom is closely related to the gift of counsel, which enables one to give the right advice to people who are torn by indecision.[68]

There are other so-called spectacular gifts. The word of knowledge (1 Cor 12:8; 13:2) signifies a mystical insight into the yearnings, thoughts and character of a person. In some cases the subject may not even be aware of these inner tumults of the soul. In Catholic theology this gift is often called "the reading of hearts." Closely related is the discerning of spirits, the ability to determine what is in agreement with God's will and what is opposed to his will. This gift includes the capacity to judge spiritual impulses and spiritual movements. The working of miracles can refer to such phenomena as the multiplication of food (cf. Mt 14:13-21; 15:32-39) and the exorcism of demons. The faith that produces wonders involves a capacity to believe that illness can be overcome and bondage can be broken.

The extraordinary charisms of the Spirit are commonly distinguished from the ordinary charisms, but this is a false dichotomy, since the latter also manifest the hidden working of the Spirit. The apostle Paul regards some of the so-called ordinary charisms as being among the higher gifts (1 Cor 12:27-31). We mistakenly attribute these ordinary gifts to natural powers, whereas they bear the mark of the supernatural, sometimes more than what might be designated occultic gifts. Among the gifts of the Spirit that are esteemed by the apostles in carrying out the general ministry of the church are preaching with boldness, teaching, evangelism, leadership, admonition and service. The last indicates more than charity: it signifies helpfulness that exceeds the call of duty.

With the mainstream of catholic tradition I contend that all of the charisms belong to the wider ministry of the church in every generation. Some have fallen into eclipse, but not because the gifts have ceased with the passing of the apostolic church. Rather, through its desire to control, the church has grieved and quenched the Spirit so that the Spirit's distribution of the gifts has been impeded. We need to seek and pray for wisdom, boldness and power, and only then will the Holy Spirit begin manifesting himself within us and through us (cf. Rom 8:12-27). I fully concur with Harold Fray's assessment of the situation:

> The Holy Spirit is conservative in the distribution of his gifts. He grants light only to those who demonstrate by their action that they need light. He gives strength only to those who are exhausting themselves in the struggle to do God's will. We may fervently pray for light, but if we remain in the safety of our sanctuaries, we shall remain in the dark. The gifts of the Spirit are only for those who will launch out into the deep and bear the risk.[69]

Hans Küng has a patently reserved attitude toward the more spectacular or occultic gifts, regarding them as lower in the hierarchy of gifts.

In addition to minimizing the importance of such charisms of enthusiasm, Paul criticizes the miraculous hellenistic "pneumatika," the powers of ecstasy and wonders and, instead of the very common hellenistic expression, he usually substitutes, on purpose we may suppose, the word "charisms." When he uses the word "pneumatika" (1 Cor. 12:1; 14:1) he points out their distinctive Christian features.[70]

Küng rightly observes that charisms are "not special marks of distinction belonging to a chosen few" but "a distinguishing mark of the whole Church."[71] Yet he minimizes the so-called extraordinary charisms of the Spirit and fails to underline the need for special ministries in the church, such as healing, exorcism and evangelism. He is sound in his conviction that all Christians are called to be charismatic personalities; yet I would add that not all are called to be leaders, guides, counselors or healers. I am convinced that the church should create special rites of commissioning for new kinds of ministry in the church.

In my estimation we may seek for manifestations of God (cf. Ps 17:6, 7; 86:14-17) so long as we do not place our security in these gifts. We may embark on a charismatic ministry so long as we do not try to subject God to a test and demand proofs of his reality. We should never seek gifts of the Spirit without at the same time praying that the fruits of the Spirit might be manifest in our lives. Gifts need to be exercised in order to continue. They may atrophy through disuse, and only a new movement of the Spirit will rekindle the fire that is now dormant.

While people of faith should be encouraged to embark on charismatic ministries, we must never base our confidence and assurance on ecstatic experiences and gifts. The words of our Lord are very apropos: "Nevertheless do not rejoice in this, that the spirits are subject to you; but rejoice that your names are written in heaven" (Lk 10:20). Our assurance is to be found in daily obedience, and the power of obedience is given in faith. Assurance is something that must be recovered again and again. Full assurance of salvation is a goal, but it can be anticipated now.[72] The apostolic writer shares these words of wisdom: "We want each one of you to show the same diligence so as to realize the full assurance of hope to the very end" (Heb 6:11 NRSV). Jonathan Edwards voiced a similar sentiment: "Assurance is not to be obtained so much by self-examination as by action." Paul "obtained assurance of winning the prize more by running than by considering."[73]

Pentecostals remind us that signs and wonders can also be means of grace. Paul confessed, "I will not venture to speak of anything except what Christ has wrought through me to win obedience from the Gentiles, by word and deed, by the power of signs and wonders, by the power of the Holy Spirit" (Rom 15:18-19; cf. Acts 5:12; 14:3; 15:12; Heb 2:4). The risen Christ told the disciples that miraculous signs would accompany those who believe, including casting out demons and speaking in other tongues (Mk 16:17-18). At the same time Jesus warned that seeking after signs could be damaging to the soul: it might very well reveal an attempt to base our confidence on sight rather than on faith (Mt 12:38-39; Jn 4:48). This admonition is echoed in Augustine, "God is tempted in religion itself, when signs and wonders are demanded of him, and are desired not for some wholesome purpose but only for experience of them."[74] Dostoyevsky astutely perceived that the desire for miracles may mask a rebellion against God and that a feverish quest for miracles kills faith.[75]

At the same time, I contend that to *see* miracles could be an evidence of faith, to be *open* to miracles could be an indication of faith. Signs and miracles are always equivocal, for they lend themselves to various interpretations. Yet God can and does make use of signs, as Scripture clearly testifies. Faith comes by hearing the Word of God proclaimed, but faith can be deepened and confirmed when the Spirit of God manifests his love and power in the midst of those who believe.

At the time of the Second Vatican Council Cardinal Suenens took sharp issue with Cardinal Ernesto Ruffini, who maintained that "charisms are very rare and altogether singular."[76] Suenens argued rightly that charisms of the Spirit are ordinary and essential to the life of the church. Indeed, if charismata are lacking it could be a sign that God is withholding or withdrawing his Spirit. The key to a revitalized and dynamic church lies in the outpouring of God's Holy Spirit, which necessarily involves the distribution of charisms.

Rethinking Pentecost

The controversy over the Pentecostal experience reveals the continuing impasse within the wider Christian community. Orthodox and Catholics see Pentecost as an experience communicated through the rite of confirmation with the laying on of hands. Pentecostals and Holiness adherents are prone to regard this experience as a second blessing in which we receive sanctifying and empowering grace after conversion.[77] Those in the Reformed tradition tend to view the Pentecostal experience as the sign of belonging to the covenant of grace, which is ratified at baptism. Lutherans see Pentecost as the gift bestowed on all persons at holy baptism.

In my perspective we should make a place for the Pentecostal experience, but we need to take exception to some aspects of Pentecostal doctrine. Likewise we should respect catholic tradition but not regard it as irreformable or infallible. The Bible takes precedence over tradition even as it is illuminated in tradition through the working of the Holy Spirit.

Pentecost remains an enigma and a source of contention unless it is seen as inclusive of faith and repentance. Faith is not prior to Pentecost but a vital element in Pentecost. Yet it is not the only element, for the Spirit imparts various blessings including power, wisdom, knowledge, fortitude and piety (cf. Is 11:2-3).

It is important to understand that the disciples were not believers until Pentecost. They were under the law but not yet under grace. They had been converted to the "way" of the cross, yet not to the gospel of the cross. They had accepted Jesus as Messiah in the Jewish sense, but they did not embrace him as the Savior of the world. The Holy Spirit was *with* them, not yet *in* them (Jn 14:17). They were in the sphere of the kingdom but not yet sealed in the body of Christ. Jesus declared, "I tell you this now, before it takes place, that when it does take place you may believe that I am he" (Jn 13:19; cf. 14:29). Even at the time of the ascension the disciples still regarded Jesus only as Messiah of Israel rather than God in human flesh, as is evident in their words; "Lord, will you at this time restore the kingdom to Israel?" (Acts 1:6).[78] The disciples before Pentecost were seekers rather than believers. They had an incipient faith but not the faith that is "the power unto salvation." They were faithful as servants but not as sons (cf. Heb 3:5-6). They received the gift of the Spirit when their hearts were purified by faith (Acts 15:8-9 JB).

Repentance and baptism are not the conditions for receiving the Spirit but the correlatives of the gift of the Spirit (cf. Acts 2:37-38).[79] Repentance, faith and the baptism of the Spirit happen concurrently in the Christian experience. There are no moral conditions for receiving the Spirit but only the struggle through to repentance and faith, and this occurs only in the power of the Spirit. Luther's distinction between the Spirit as agent and the Spirit as gift is helpful, but it is more felicitous to affirm that the Spirit's work as creator of faith and his charismatic empowering belong to the same event—the new birth. It is only when we believe in Christ that we receive the power of the Holy Spirit, but it is precisely this power that enables us to believe. Luther perceived it rightly: "To him who has the Holy Ghost is the power given; to him, that is, who is a Christian. But who is a Christian? Whosoever believes has the Holy Ghost."[80]

The tradition of the church universal gives added support to the biblical axiom that faith and the gift of the Spirit are inseparable. According to John Wesley, "Every man, in order to believe unto salvation, must receive the Holy Ghost."[81] Calvin contended: "Faith cannot lay hold of Christ for righteousness without the Spirit of sanctification."[82] When Pentecostals see faith as only preparatory for the gift of the Spirit, they tend to diminish faith. We need to realize that faith itself is an empowering, an inner renewal. I concur heartily with the Catholic theologian Karl Adam:

> If it be genuine divine faith, the faith of a Christian is in very truth a "showing of the spirit and of the power" of the Holy Ghost. It is not we who believe, but the Holy Ghost within us. The experience of Pentecost is continually repeated, and our faith is in its essence nothing else than the pentecostal faith of the apostles.[83]

R. A. Torrey reflected the mindset of later evangelicalism when he declared, "Every true believer has the Holy Spirit, but not every believer has the baptism with the Holy Spirit."[84] The truth in this statement is that every believer must have the Spirit in order to believe, though not every believer manifests the gifts of the Spirit in daily life. Yet we need to understand that if we truly believe we have indeed been baptized by the Spirit. This does not imply, however, that we have reached our full potential in living a Spirit-filled life.

The baptism of the Spirit is a metaphor that includes various dimensions of the Spirit's blessing and cannot be reduced to simply one kind of experience. Its hallmarks are wholehearted trust in Christ alone, a burning love for God and neighbor, indefatigable power to witness to others and deep-seated conviction of sin. Its constituent elements are endowment with power, initiation into the community of faith, loving concern for our neighbor in need and repentance of sin. If any of these elements is lacking in our life and witness we need to pray for a new filling of the Spirit, for a new anointing that will enable us to fulfill our vocation and mission as heralds and ambassadors of the Lord Jesus Christ. We should seek not a second baptism of the Spirit but an awakening to the significance of our one baptism by water and the Spirit.

Some theologians have used the term *baptism* loosely to refer to any infusion of the Spirit. According to Charles Hodge "any communication of the Holy Spirit is called a baptism, because the Spirit is said to be poured out, and those upon whom he is poured out, whether in his regenerating, sanctifying, or inspiring influences, are said to be baptized."[85] I believe it is more in accord with the pattern of the New Testament to restrict the term *baptism* to the experience of being incorporated into the body of Christ and to speak of subsequent communications of the Spirit as fillings, anointings, outpourings and so on. The truth we are obliged to maintain is that God's act is prior to sacramental baptism and repentance. The promise is given to all whom the Lord calls (Acts 2:39). God's call is the basis for both baptism and repentance. Divine election precedes human decision. Human decision, moreover, is made possible only through divine empowering.

We must beware of stereotyping any experience of the Spirit in order to make it conform to the expectations of our religious peers. The experience of conversion or of Pentecost may take many forms—the shedding of tears of joy, the welling up of outgoing love, conviction and repentance of sin. After her initial dedication to the Christian faith Catherine of Genoa experienced a deep infusion of love that enabled her to give of herself unsparingly to the sick and dying.[86] Stephen Grellet, an English Quaker (d. 1855), described the experience that enabled him to embark on a ministry of evangelism as one of "awfulness" and "reverence."[87] John Wesley felt his heart "strangely warmed" when he heard Luther's preface to the Epistle to the Romans read at a Moravian meeting on Aldersgate Street, London. Thérèse of Lisieux likened her experience of the Holy Spirit to the whisper of a "gentle breeze."[88] In the case of T. B. Barratt, Pentecostal minister in Norway, flames of fire were allegedly visible in his baptism of the Spirit.

It is imperative that we always distinguish between form and content in the experience of receiving the Spirit. There may be various physical as well as mystical phenomena, but the key elements in a Christian conversion experience are repentance of sin, joy and assurance of salvation through faith in Jesus Christ. It is not extraordinary gifts of the Spirit but the fruits of the Spirit (Gal 5:22-26; Col 3:12-15) that constitute the evidence of whether our conversion is genuine. If we manifest joy, love, wisdom and humility in our lives people will have some intimation that the Spirit is working within us and upon us. We need to take seriously Jesus' warning that signs and wonders will also accompany false prophets (Mt 24:24; Mk 13:22; cf. 2 Thess 2:9-11) and that salvation belongs only to those who endure to the end (Mt 24:13).

It is misleading to create dichotomies between the initial work of the Spirit and regeneration and empowering, or between faith and assurance. Every work of the Spirit is regenerative and transforming. It is also always new and surprising. Karl Barth phrased it well:

> In all its actions the work of the Holy Spirit is always and everywhere a wholly new thing. At each moment of its occurrence it is itself another change, a conversion, which calls for even more radical conversion. As the change to the Christian life was radical in its inception, so it must and will always be in its continuation.[89]

Jonathan Edwards uttered similar words of wisdom:

> As it is with spiritual discoveries and affections given at first conversion, so it is in all subsequent illuminations and affections of that kind; they are all transforming. There is a like divine power and energy in them as in the first discoveries; they still reach the bottom of the heart, and affect and alter the very nature of the soul, in proportion to the degree in which they are given. And a transformation of nature is continued and carried on by them to the end of life, until it is brought to perfection in glory.[90]

In the circles of revivalistic evangelicalism repentance is often located at the beginning of the Christian life, to be followed by growth in sanctification. Yet the fuller biblical picture is that the Christian is daily besieged by the powers of sin and death and must daily repent and believe. Paul confessed that even in his Christian life he fell back into sin and needed to throw himself ever again on the mercy of God (Rom 7). Luther was firm in his insistence that the entire life of the Christian is one of repentance. Samuel Rutherford testified: "New washing, renewed application of purchased redemption, by that sacred blood that sealeth the free Covenant, is a thing of daily and hourly use to a poor sinner."[91]

What insures our salvation is the *fact* of the new birth, not our response to it or our memory of it. Even so, a momentous event in one's personal history cannot occur without an experiential awareness of it. Repentance for sin is not a matter of the lips only but of the heart. The knowledge of our redemption is not an intellectual knowledge only but an existential knowledge. Yet the ground of our certainty does not lie in any particular experience or rite of the church. It lies in the living Christ himself who died for our sins according to the Scriptures (1 Cor 15:3). The Spirit gives us certainty by directing us outside ourselves to the atoning sacrifice of Christ on Golgotha.

In Lutheran tradition it is commonly asserted that the fact of our baptism gives us assurance of our salvation. Lutheran theologian Wilhelm Herrmann offers these cautionary words: "If . . . we point to baptism, as to the work of God that is guaranteed by His faithfulness, are we not dispensing with Christ as the basis of our confidence? This question certainly arises if we say that a miraculous change of the inner life results from baptism."[92]

Looking back to our baptism is helpful if it points us beyond our baptism to Christ's baptism into death and his glorious resurrection into life, for it is this baptism that saves us from sin, death and the devil. The sacrament of baptism communicates this knowledge to us and thereby enables us to participate vicariously in the death and resurrection of our Savior. But baptism works in this salvific way only when it is laid hold of by the Spirit and joined to the promises of Jesus Christ in Scripture.

It is finally only the Spirit of God who imparts assurance of salvation. It is the Spirit who witnesses with our spirit that we are indeed children of God (Rom 8:16). But the Spirit gives us this assurance ordinarily at the moment of faith and renews this assurance in us as we live out our faith. The Christian is not necessarily led into higher experiences of union with Christ but receives inner fortification in the daily struggles of faith. We may well be blessed with transforming and illuminating experiences of God, but these experiences will happen less and less as we progress in the life of faith. Our deepest life is hidden from ourselves (Col 3:3), and we go forward in the knowledge that Christ is both *for* us and *in* us, that no obstacle can block our perseverance in our vocation.

The gift of the Spirit to those who struggle in faith and serve in love is indeed the message of Pentecost. It is only by living outside ourselves in the needs of our neighbor that we receive power and certainty in our vocation and witness. But we can live outside ourselves only in the power that comes to us from the Holy Spirit. This reciprocal, ongoing relationship between the living God and the people of God is the paradox of Pentecost.

Appendix C: Some Difficult Texts

In this section I deal with some troublesome texts to which theological partisans often appeal to reinforce their biases. I do not give an exhaustive exegesis but simply share my own interpretation. In the process I draw on biblical and theological scholarship, but my principal emphasis is on ascertaining whether discordant testimonies can be reconciled. If we believe the Holy Spirit to be the primary author of Scripture, we then must presuppose some overarching unity, but this does not imply that every textual difficulty can be overcome, since our mortal interpretations can only dimly reflect God's self-interpretation in Jesus Christ. We should bear in mind that the scriptural authors themselves were not always interested in reconciling all the data or in giving an exact chronological account of what actually happened.

* * * * * *

John 3:1-15 is probably one of the most controversial texts in the entire New Testament.[93] When Jesus says to Nicodemus that one must be born of water and the Spirit in order to enter the kingdom of God, is he referring to water baptism as the condition for salvation, or is he speaking metaphorically so that "water" is practically synonymous with "Spirit"? John Calvin was convinced that "water" in this context meant "simply the inward cleansing and quickening of the Holy Spirit."[94] By contrast, Luther held that Jesus had in mind "real, natural water."[95] According to R. V. G. Tasker "water" and "Spirit" are to be understood conjunctively and are to be regarded as "a description of Christian baptism, in which cleansing and endowment are both essential elements."[96] F. F. Bruce saw a baptismal allusion in these verses, contending that the Evangelist was writing in a day that witnessed the completion and absorption of John's baptism by Christian baptism.[97] Bultmann regarded the phrase "water and Spirit" as an addition of a redactor reflecting the growing sacramentalism in the apostolic church.[98] Raymond Brown cautioned that there is not enough evidence in the Gospel itself to support a sacramental interpretation.[99] Ben Witherington suggests that John 3:5 associates water with physical generation, since water in biblical thought was "a regular metaphor for various facets of procreation—insemination, the child in the womb, childbearing, and childbirth."[100] "Water" and "Spirit" in verse 5 therefore refer to "physical and spiritual birth."[101]

I am led to conclude that "water" in this passage has a predominantly metaphorical use and that being born of water and the Spirit in verse 5 is synonymous with being "born of the Spirit" in verse 8. I agree with Leon Morris, Raymond Brown, F. F. Bruce and many other biblical scholars that these verses point to the exaltation of Jesus Christ on the cross and to his ascension into heaven.[102] The new birth does not take place until the Son of Man is lifted up (vv. 14-15), and it is only those who believe in him who have eternal life. To believe in Christ is tantamount to being born of water and the Spirit.

This interpretation does not preclude the view that verse 5 may have a sacramental allusion, since the sacrament of baptism was gaining in prominence in the late apostolic church. But water is then to be regarded as the outward sign of the spiritual reality that is the living water, the water of life (cf. Jn 4:10; 7:38). The sacrament does not of itself confer the Holy Spirit, but the Spirit makes use of the sacrament either to prepare the way for living faith in Jesus Christ or for a confirmation of faith in inner experience.

It is helpful to compare the passage under question with John 7:37-

39: "On the last and greatest day of the festival Jesus stood and declared, 'If anyone is thirsty, let him come to me and drink. Whoever believes in me, as scripture says, "Streams of living water shall flow from within him."' He was speaking of the Spirit which believers in him would later receive; for the Spirit had not yet been given, because Jesus had not yet been glorified" (REB). Here we see a clear reference to Pentecost as the time when those who would follow Christ are born of water and the Spirit.

* * * * * *

One of the perplexing problems in scriptural exposition is the relation of the Johannine Pentecost (Jn 20:22) to the Lukan Pentecost (Acts 1, 2). In John's Gospel, after his resurrection Christ appears to his disciples saying, "Receive the Holy Spirit" (REB). The problem is whether this event signifies a pre-Pentecostal blessing or another way of describing the one event of Pentecost. In both Luke and John the giving of the Spirit is depicted as taking place after Christ's ascension into heaven. Theodore of Mopsuestia speculated that Jesus did not really give the Spirit on Easter but acted only figuratively or by way of promise.[103] This view was condemned at the Second Council of Constantinople (A.D. 553). John Chrysostom held that the gift of the Spirit in John 20 relates to the forgiveness of sins, whereas the gift of the Spirit in Acts 2 is associated with the power to work miracles and raise the dead. Johann Albrecht Bengel argued that the gift of the Spirit on Easter was transitional or anticipatory. Along the same lines one could conclude that regeneration was begun at Easter and completed at Pentecost. Pierre Benoit advances the view that the visible departure of Christ at the end of the forty days in Acts was preceded by an invisible but real exaltation to heavenly glory on the day of his resurrection.[104]

I find most plausible Raymond Brown's contention that both authors are describing the same event: the one gift of the Spirit by the risen and ascended Lord to his followers.

In particular, there is no insurmountable obstacle in the fact that

John and Acts assign a different date to the gift of the Spirit. . . .
John's dating of Jesus' first appearance to his disciples is artificial, for
Galilee has a better claim than Jerusalem to be the original site of
this appearance, and that would obviously rule out Easter Sunday as
the date of the appearance. But there is also much that is symbolic
in Acts' choice of Pentecost, for Luke is using the background of the
Sinai covenant motif associated with that feast in his description of
the coming of the Spirit. Yet we do not discount the possibility that
Luke preserves an authentic Christian memory of the first charismatic manifestation of the Spirit in the community on Pentecost.[105]

I see John 20:22 as a theological reconstruction of a historical
report, whereas Acts 1 and 2 constitute what is basically a historical
rendition, though through the lens of a particular theological interpretation. It should be noted that on the matter of the ascension Luke
gives two different reports of the same event (Lk 24:50-53; Acts 1:6-
11). Norval Geldenhuys contends that Luke is not interested in reconciling the data, and that the two reports both bear witness to the fact of
the ascension of Christ into heaven.[106]

* * * * * *

Jesus' declaration that his disciples were already clean by the word
spoken to them (Jn 13:10; 15:3) has led some commentators to conclude that the disciples were regenerate before Pentecost. R. A. Torrey
argues that the baptism of the Spirit was not given to the disciples for
regeneration because they had already attained the regenerate state.[107]
I believe this position lacks exegetical grounding. In John 13:1-20 Jesus
washes his disciples' feet, an act that symbolizes their future cleansing
by the blood (the cross) and the Spirit. They were now clean by virtue
of being covered by the blood of Christ (1 Jn 1:7), but they were not
actually clean. They did not yet have regeneration because they were
not yet baptized into the death of Christ (Mk 10:35-45). Again Raymond Brown is helpful:

  The Johannine writer certainly does not think of the disciples at the

Last Supper as already fully united to Jesus and abundantly bearing fruit. All the questions attributed to them stress the imperfection of their understanding. But when "the hour" has been completed and the Paraclete/Spirit has been given to the disciples, he will bring the work of Jesus' word to fruition. Thus Jesus' word may be said to make them clean already because they have received his word and they are in the context of "the hour" which will make the working of that word possible.[108]

One might say that the disciples were given an intimation of their regeneration that was still to occur through baptism into the death of Christ. They were marked out for regeneration by the rite of footwashing, but they had yet to experience total cleansing, which is given by the Holy Spirit. Their hearts were not yet "sprinkled clean from an evil conscience" (Heb 10:22), which comes by the shedding of the blood of Christ (Heb 9:22). The disciples were justified like the Old Testament patriarchs and prophets were justified—by the promise of the blood, not by actual immersion or participation in the blood. Their justification and inner renewal had yet to be finalized or sealed. They were cleaned proleptically by virtue of the word addressed to them. They were on the way to regeneration but not yet totally cleansed. They had accepted the teaching of Jesus, which is "spirit and life" (Jn 6:63), but this was still only an outward acceptance, for even in the upper room after the crucifixion and resurrection of Christ, they still thought of Jesus as the political Messiah of Israel, not as the Savior of the world (Acts 1:6).

* * * * * *

A key passage that Pentecostals as well as Anglo-Catholics often cite to support their allegation that the gift of the Spirit is subsequent to faith is Acts 2:38-39: "Peter said to them, 'Repent, and be baptized every one of you in the name of Jesus Christ so that your sins may be forgiven; and you will receive the gift of the Holy Spirit. For the promise is for you, for your children, and for all who are far away, everyone whom the Lord our God calls to him" (NRSV). At first glance it seems that repentance and faith are the conditions for receiving the gift of the Spirit. Yet Peter has already made clear in his appeal to the prophecy of Joel that the pouring out of the Holy Spirit precedes calling on the name of the Lord for salvation (Acts 2:17-21). Indeed, the outpouring of the Spirit enables those lost in sin to respond and to believe. In verse 39 it is clear that "the promise"—the forgiveness of sins and the gift of the Spirit—is for all those whom the Lord calls to him. It is the call of God going out through the power of the Spirit that produces repentance and the forgiveness of sins. This is further confirmed in Acts 5:30-31, which speaks of God raising Jesus from the dead and exalting him as Leader and Savior "to give repentance to Israel and forgiveness of sins." Peter confesses that the apostles are witnesses of these things, "as is the Holy Spirit who is given by God to those obedient to him" (5:32 REB). This obedience, moreover, is the result, not the condition, of the gift of the Spirit.[109]

It is also instructive to compare Acts 2:38-39 to Acts 10:44-48 and 11:15-18, which describe the coming of the Spirit to Cornelius and his household. Here it is expressly stated that the Spirit fell on those who heard the Word of God, and they were then baptized with water as a sign of their dawning faith. They praised God saying, "God has given even to the Gentiles the repentance that leads to life" (11:18 NRSV). Peter declares that Cornelius's experience of salvation and forgiveness was precisely the same as that of the one hundred and twenty at Pentecost: "God gave the same gift to them as he gave to us when we believed in the Lord Jesus Christ" (11:17).

On the basis of the wider testimony in the book of Acts, one can only conclude that the gift of the Spirit is not contingent on faith and obedience but is correlative with them. For faith and obedience also come from the Spirit. What we have in Acts 2:38-39 are not precisionist elucidations but paradoxical affirmations. These texts point to the mystery that the Spirit is both gift and agent. They also certify that the human subject is both responsible for his or her actions and peculiarly endowed with the power to respond in faith and obedience. Faith is not the condition for receiving the Spirit but the catalyst that enables one to grasp and appreciate the manifestation of the Spirit.

According to Frederick Dale Bruner Acts 2:38 implies that "the future tense of the reception of the spiritual gift is as future as the baptism with which it is connected. The gift of the Spirit is here directly joined with and promised to the forgiveness which comes with baptism."[110] Peter is offering not a chronological sequence in Acts 2:38, 39 but a confession that all of these elements in the gift of the Spirit belong together—repentance, baptism, forgiveness and empowering.

If our text is taken in isolation, it is possible to infer that a charismatic endowment by the Spirit follows faith and repentance. Yet the fact that calling on the name of the Lord for salvation is preceded by the outpouring of the Spirit in the earlier part of the chapter and the fact that the call of the Lord is the basis for repentance and faith in our text lead me to conclude that salvation is both a gift and a work of the Spirit, that the Spirit works both upon us and within us giving us assurance of divine forgiveness as well as the power to witness. As I have already indicated, the texts in Acts 5 and 11 also underline the fact that repentance and faith arise out of the outpouring of the Spirit.

In the light of the fuller witness of the New Testament it is necessary to conclude that the human response follows the divine initiative (cf. 1 Cor 12:3, 13; 2 Thess 2:13 NASB; Tit 3:4-7; Heb 10:22 GNC). At the same time, the human response gives rise to new divine initiatives. Those who are touched by the Spirit can be touched again (2 Tim 1:6-7). Those who believe in Jesus Christ as Savior must believe again through the power of the Spirit. We cannot procure the baptism of the Spirit, but we can wait, hope and pray for the coming of the Spirit. We can prepare ourselves to receive the Spirit not just at the time of initiation into the Christian community but throughout our lives. For the Spirit is given again and again to those who cry out and pray for deliverance and forgiveness.[111]

* * * * * *

A favorite text that both Catholics and Pentecostals employ to support the supposed distinction between the dawning of faith and the bestowal of the Spirit is Acts 8:4-25. Here we read of the missionary Philip visiting Samaria in order to share the message of the gospel. His preaching is accompanied by miraculous signs including the exorcism of demons. The people respond positively to his preaching and are baptized. Yet surprisingly we are told that they had not yet received the Holy Spirit (8:16). When the apostles at Jerusalem heard of the openness of the Samaritans to the Word of God, they sent Peter and John to Samaria, where they promptly laid hands on the people, who then received the Holy Spirit. This narrative lends support to the view that faith and baptism in and of themselves are insufficient to impart the Holy Spirit. G. W. H. Lampe offers another explanation: The Spirit is withheld until the Samaritan church is brought into organic relationship with the church in Jerusalem.[112] Similarly Michael Green argues that the Spirit was freely given only when the mother church expressed solidarity with the Samaritan Christians.[113] Richard Dillon of Fordham University avers that the Holy Spirit operates only when there is communion with the apostles, the original witnesses of the resurrection.[114] Calvin's position was that the Samaritans were already regenerate but stood in need of charismatic endowment, which was communicated as the apostles laid their hands on the new converts.[115]

My own position on this matter is close to that of James Dunn and George Montague, who argue that the Samaritans lacked effectual faith or full conversion, since the text indicates that their belief was based on their fascination with the miracles and signs that accompanied Philip's ministry.[116] Indeed, we read that Simon Magus had believed and was baptized, yet his heart was not right before God (Acts 8:21), and he was therefore commanded to repent (Acts 8:22). Luke "makes it clear that Simon's faith and baptism were precisely like those of the other Samaritans."[117] The Samaritans were similar to the stony-ground hearers in Jesus' parable (Mt 13:20-21), who received the word with joy but then almost immediately fell away. Montague recognizes that an expression of solidarity with the Samaritans by the Jerusalem church is important in this story, but he also believes that the faith of the Samaritans was deficient: "Luke, aware of the Samaritans' fascination with magic and magicians, used the story at one level to distinguish authentic faith and the Holy Spirit from any possible confusion with the occult or with personalities."[118]

What is powerfully affirmed in Acts 8 is the sovereign freedom of the Spirit to act as he chooses. Richard Dillon argues that Luke is making the point that "the Spirit is not controlled by ritual or office" and the apostolic admonition to Simon underscores the "inviolable gift character" of the Spirit.[119] The Spirit works in and through baptism but always freely. Faith alone is the essential element in the Pentecostal experience. I agree with J. H. E. Hull that Acts nowhere claims

> that baptism of itself, or the laying on of hands as such, or even a combination of them both, confers or can confer the Spirit. If there is any *sine qua non*, and indeed there is, that is to be found in repentance and faith (trust) in Christ. For these two factors there is no substitute at all.[120]

A similar passage is Acts 19:1-7, which recounts the conversion of the Ephesian disciples through the ministry of Paul. Paul asked them whether they had received the Holy Spirit when they became believers, and they replied, "No, we have not even heard that there is a Holy Spirit." They then disclosed that they had been baptized only in the baptism of John the Baptist. Thereupon Paul baptized them in the name of Jesus and laid hands on them as the Holy Spirit came upon them in power.[121] Like the company of the believers at the time of Pentecost, they began to prophesy and speak in other tongues. It is obvious to me that the Ephesians when they first met Paul were not yet Christians, for they had received only the Johannine baptism of repentance.[122]

What was given through the ministry of the apostles to both the Samaritans and Ephesians was neither confirmation nor ordination but baptism into the body of Christ. This baptism involved the awakening to faith, water baptism and laying on of hands, and charismatic endowment. The outward rite or rites may have played a role in the mediation of the Spirit's power, but it is the inward commitment that is most important. It is calling on the name of the Lord in repentance as we submit to the rite in obedience that is the cardinal evidence that the Holy Spirit is reaching out to us and sealing our union with the sufferings of Jesus Christ.[123]

* * * * * *

The conversion of Paul reveals the inseparable relation of grace, faith, baptism and repentance (cf. Acts 9:1-19; 22:6-16; 26:12-20.). We read that Saul, the noted persecutor of Christians, was traveling with his companions on the road to Damascus, when suddenly he saw a light from heaven and "heard a voice saying, 'Saul, Saul, why do you persecute me?' And he said, 'Who are you, Lord?' And he said, 'I am Jesus, whom you are persecuting; but rise and enter the city, and you will be told what you are to do' " (9:4-6). Saul was then struck with blindness, which remained with him for three days. At the end of this period he was directed by the Spirit of God to a disciple in Damascus, Ananias, who laid his hands on him so that he could regain his sight and be filled with the Holy Spirit. The scales then fell immediately from his eyes, and he arose and was baptized. Between his Damascus road experience and his baptism Paul seems to have been a pre-Christian. He was seeking for salvation but had not yet found it. Still he was able to pray and hope through the impact of his encounter with Christ (22:10). His blindness was spiritual as well as physical, and when he received the laying on of hands his sight was restored and his heart was opened to redeeming grace. His regeneration appears to have occurred at the time of his baptism, since it was then that his sins were washed away (22:16). On the Damascus road he had been touched by the Spirit, but later he came to be indwelt by and filled with the Spirit. He had been converted from being an anti-Christian to a pre-Christian and then to a born-again Christian.

* * * * * *

A similar trajectory can be detected in Acts 16:16-34, which relates the story of the conversion of the jailer by Paul and Silas. The prisoners heard Paul and Silas praying and singing; suddenly there was an earthquake, and everyone's fetters were unfastened. Supposing the prisoners had escaped, the jailer drew his sword and was about to kill himself when Paul cried out, "Do not harm yourself, for we are all here." Calling for lights, the jailer rushed in and fell down before the two missionaries saying, "Men, what must I do to be saved?" And they replied, "Believe in the Lord Jesus, and you will be saved, you and your household." They then spoke the Word of the Lord to him and that same hour he was baptized with his whole family. After washing their wounds he brought them up to his house and set food before them. We read that he and his entire family rejoiced that he had become a believer in God.

Here again we see the steps to salvation as delineated in various other New Testament passages. The jailer had been converted from the status of a non-Christian to a seeker and then to a regenerate Christian. The evidence of his regeneration was both the spirit of love that led him to bandage the wounds of his prisoners and bring them food and his readiness to be baptized with all his family.

* * * * * *

Pentecostals commonly refer to Galatians 4:6-7 to support their view that the baptism of the Spirit comes after faith: "As you are sons, God has sent into our hearts the Spirit of his Son crying, 'Abba, Father'; and so you are no longer a slave, but a son; and if a son, then an heir, by God's own act" (NJB). What Paul is asserting is that our adoption as sons and daughters of God is inseparably tied to the gift of the Spirit, who confirms and ratifies our inclusion in the family of God. By virtue of our adoption and election as children of God we are given the Holy Spirit to seal within us the benefits of Christ's redemption. The Holy Spirit is both the means by which we realize our kinship with God and the evidential corroboration of the status conferred on us by God. The gift of the Spirit is not a gift higher than faith or in addition to faith but the means by which we come to faith in Christ. It is also the transformative power that enables us to act in faith. We need to read our text in relation to Galatians 3:26-27: "In Christ Jesus you are all sons of God, through faith. For as many of you as were baptized into Christ have put on Christ." We should also note the parallel passage in Romans:

All who are guided by the Spirit of God are sons of God; for what you received was not the spirit of slavery to bring you back into fear; you received the spirit of adoption, enabling us to cry out, "Abba, Father!" The Spirit himself joins with our spirit to bear witness that we are children of God (8:14-16 NJB).

I here find myself in substantial agreement with James Boice: "The gift of God's Spirit is not something the child of God is to strive after as if, having been given his salvation, he must now work to realize it or achieve it on a higher level. The Spirit is the gift of God to every believer because he is a son."[124]

Paul is adamant that "one cannot belong to Christ unless one has the Spirit of Christ" (Rom 8:9 GNC). We become children of God as the Spirit communicates to us the life-giving energy of the risen Christ through the preaching of the gospel. According to James Dunn:

The gift of the Spirit is for Paul the same as justification by faith; it is that which brings the individual into the covenant of promise, that which begins his Christian life (Gal. 3:3, 14). . . . Paul gives no indication that he is thinking in 4:6 of a different coming of the Spirit than that referred to in ch. 3.[125]

In comparing Galatians 4:6-7 and Romans 8:15, Herman Ridderbos concludes that there is no contradiction between these passages but instead an affirmation of the reciprocity of the gift of the Spirit and sonship. Our adoption into the family of God through the atoning work of Christ on the cross is the basis of our being engrafted into Christ by the renewing work of the Spirit. At the same time, we do not become aware of our divinely given status as sons and daughters of God until the Holy Spirit opens our inward eyes to the glorious fact of Christ's redemption.[126]

It is possible to argue on the basis of Galatians 3:2-5 that the gift of the Spirit is contingent on hearing the gospel with faith. Paul says: "Does he who supplies the Spirit to you and works miracles among you do so by works of the law, or by hearing with faith?" (Gal 3:5). Faith is indeed necessary for the Spirit to manifest his miraculous works in our lives, but Paul also insists that faith itself is a work of the Spirit. He declares that "through the Spirit, by faith, we wait for the hope of righteousness" (Gal 5:5). Ridderbos comments that *through the Spirit* refers to the Holy Spirit in His life-giving power, establishing the bond between Christ and His own." "The words *by faith*" indicate that "what the Spirit gives and works is known and received by faith." For Paul the "working of faith" has its source in "the life-giving power of the Spirit."[127] At the same time, faith is the catalyst for the continuing manifestation of the Spirit in a person's life.[128]

* * * * * *

Sacramentalists often appeal to 1 John 5:6-8 to bolster their thesis that the gift of the Spirit and the rites of the church are inseparable: "This is the one who came by water and blood—Jesus Christ. He did not come by water only, but by water and blood. And it is the Spirit who testifies, because the Spirit is the truth. For there are three that testify: the Spirit, the water and the blood; and the three are in agreement" (NIV). While the church fathers generally sought to give these verses a sacramental interpretation, most biblical scholars today entertain other possibilities.[129] The commanding scholarly consensus is that the writer of 1 John sought to counter an early Gnostic heresy that accepted the baptism of Jesus but denied the reality of his death. John makes clear that Jesus' ministry included both the baptism of water and the baptism of his passion (cf. Lk 12:49-50). According to Amos Wilder the water represents Jesus' own baptism in which he was endowed with the Spirit and the blood his historical death on the cross commemorated in the Lord's Supper.[130] Georg Strecker also sees a sacramental reference in these verses but is adamant that the Johannine author is not teaching sacramentalism, "even though he emphasizes the paradoxical fusion of the eschaton with history not only in the earthly existence of Jesus Christ but also in the sacraments."[131] Yet in John's understanding "the sacraments do not work *ex opere operato*, and have nothing in common with magic. Rather, they are characterized by their connection with the *pneuma*, to whom the function of [witness] is expressly attributed."[132]

James Dunn is particularly insistent that water and blood pertain to historical rather than sacramental realities. In his view "the water and the blood refer no more to the sacraments in 5:8 than they did in 5:6. Rather they designate the key events in the incarnate ministry of Jesus."[133] Yet Dunn seems to go too far by denying any sacramental dimension in these verses, for quite frequently in the New Testament and in the Johannine literature in particular, verses may have secondary as well as primary meanings.

Liberal and existential theologies tend to see 1 John as embracing an experiential norm, since it seems that with verse 7 the focus changes from past history to present Christian experience. Paul Hoon draws the debatable conclusion that "religion does not err when it appeals to personal experience, despite all the risks in doing so."[134] To be sure John affirms that those who believe in the Son of God have the testimony in themselves (1 Jn 5:10), and this testimony is greater than mere human testimony (1 Jn 5:9). John, however, only questions the sufficiency of human testimony that remains outward or external. The apostolic testimony, which mirrors the living Christ and is animated by his Spirit, is irrevocably binding on us.

I believe that the final authority for the Johannine writer is the paradoxical unity of Word and Spirit, since he appeals both to the witness of objective history that is mediated by church tradition and to the interior witness of the Spirit. The continuing witness and developing tradition of the apostolic church needs to be illumined by the Spirit if it is to have final or ultimate authority for faith. At the same time, John is not espousing subjectivism, for the spirits must be tested (1 Jn 4:1-2). Inward commitment must be united with external allegiance: "Anyone who does not stand by the teaching about Christ, but goes beyond it, does not possess God; he who stands by it possesses both the Father and the Son" (2 Jn 9 REB).

Immersion in the water of baptism and communion with the blood of Christ in the Lord's Supper bear witness to the redeeming events in the life, ministry and death of Jesus. Yet water is irrefragably a symbol that points beyond itself to the water of life, the living water that alone cleanses from sin. Similarly, the breaking of the bread and drinking from the cup in the Lord's Supper direct us beyond outward rites to the historical reality of Christ's death and resurrection. Sacraments or rituals may very well aid us in our grasp of the faith and strengthen us as we seek to live out our faith, but they do not in and of themselves redeem from sin. The New Testament here presents a unified and consistent witness. God is free in his bestowal of grace, but he does make use of visible means, the chief of which are the words and acts of Jesus Christ himself. Jesus is the one mediator between God and humanity, and the sacramental rites do not supplement his mediation but bear witness to it and thereby put us in contact with this life-giving reality.

·ELEVEN·

THE HIGHWAY OF HOLINESS

And a highway will be there;
it will be called the Way of Holiness.
The unclean will not journey on it;
it will be for those who walk in that Way.
ISAIAH 35:8 NIV

The Spirit and the Bride say, "Come!"
Let everyone who listens answer, "Come!"
Then let all who are thirsty come:
all who want it may have the water of life, and have it free.
REVELATION 22:17 NJB

Where zeal for integrity and holiness is not in force,
there neither the Spirit of Christ nor Christ himself are present.
JOHN CALVIN

If I am left with my experiences,
my experiences have not been produced by Redemption.
The proof that they are produced by Redemption
is that I have been led out of myself all the time.
OSWALD CHAMBERS

We talk of *having* faith, of *having* the Holy Spirit,
not of living in and by faith, of receiving and being sent forth by the Holy Spirit.
JACQUES ELLUL

A spirituality centered in the prophetic tradition of biblical faith will be markedly different from the mystical heritage of the church, which is shaped to a considerable degree by Neo-platonism.[1] The former focuses on the pilgrim road, the latter on the mystic way. Those who adhere to the biblical worldview will seek not to forget or disparage created things but to bring all creation into submission to the high and holy God.[2] Their attention is directed to the highway of holiness rather than the mountain of purgation or the stairway to a wholly transcendent perfection. God does not call us into the desert in order to escape the follies of the world. Instead, he creates a highway in the wilderness to lead us to a new city that will arise out of the ashes of the old.[3] By means of this highway the holiness and truth of God will find access to all areas of human life. The building of this highway will involve the flattening out of the valleys of ignorance and the mountains of prejudice. The glory of the Lord shall be revealed, and all flesh shall see it together. In evangelical perspective the highway of holiness describes both the eschatological inbreaking of the kingdom and the pilgrimage of faith in which we prepare the way for the coming of God's rule. It signals both God's generous dispensation of grace and the arena in which we demonstrate our gratitude for his grace.[4]

While the literature in Christian mysticism is replete with methods of ascent to the highest, the biblical prophetic worldview focuses on the descent of the highest into the midst of the travail and affliction of this world. True religion celebrates not the *ascent* of the spiritual master to the all-sufficient Absolute but the *descent* of the loving and redeeming God to the sinner in need. Biblical faith speaks of ascent as well as descent, but this is primarily the ascent of Jesus Christ to the right hand of God in heaven. He brings with him many captives (Eph 4:7-10); in him we also are risen and we also ascend. By ourselves, by our own works of holiness, we cannot secure a place in heaven. It is the king of glory who gains entrance into the heavenly city (Ps 24:7-10), and if we but cling to him in faith we will be assured of being included in his triumphal procession.[5]

In the perspective of biblical faith, holiness is not a quality we can measure but a pathway we can walk. It is not an experience of heavenly rapture (though it may include heavenly experiences) but a journey we embark upon. Our goal is not to extricate ourselves from our mortal flesh and attain to the realm of pure spirit (as in gnosticism) but to allow "the life of Jesus" to "be manifested in our mortal flesh" (2 Cor 4:11). Our task as Christians is not to make ourselves worthy in God's sight but to make ourselves available for service to God's glory. Our mandate is to be pleasing to God in all our actions; yet the aim should never be to make ourselves acceptable to God but simply to give glory to God in gratitude for his grace to undeserving sinners.

Biblical faith upholds a this-worldly holiness that is lived out in the midst of the pain and conflict of the world. Among mystics the aim is frequently to rise above the afflictions of life into an eternal repose that makes life bearable. Both types of spirituality speak of taking up the cross and following Christ, but the biblical Christian goes further and holds out the promise of sharing in the rule of Christ. We do not simply endure but we overcome through the anointing and empowering of the Holy Spirit. Oppression, pain, sickness and destitution are not to be sublimely accepted in the hope that they will be made to serve vicarious redemption. Instead they belong inescapably to the old order of existence that serves sin and death. The forces that maim and enslave are to be counteracted and dispelled through the redeeming power of the Spirit of Jesus Christ manifested in his cross and resurrection and poured out on his followers at Pentecost.

Biblical, evangelical spirituality also sounds the call to social holiness. We look forward not to individual mansions in heaven but to a redeemed community that begins here on earth. We do not climb upward to the kingdom of heaven, but we spearhead the advance of this kingdom in the world. We do not sound the call to flight from the world but entertain the hope of transforming the world through the power of the Spirit. Our asceticism is geared not to separate the higher self within us from our bodily passions (as in Platonism) but to equip us for a life of service and conquest as warriors of the king of glory.[6] The vision of Calvin and the Puritans was the formation of a holy commonwealth or holy community in which every area of life would be permeated by the love and forbearance that characterize the lives of the saints.[7]

A Life of Battle

The metaphor that most clearly describes the living out of a Christian life is "battle," a motif that pervades the New Testament. Faith does not lead us beyond conflict but right into conflict, for the devil fights for our souls as we try to remain steadfast in our determination to give glory to Christ. This is a spiritual warfare, to be sure, since we conquer not with worldly weapons but with the sword of the Spirit, which is the Word of God (Eph 6:17). "Our struggle is not against enemies of blood and flesh, but against the rulers, against the authorities, against the cosmic powers of this present darkness, against the spiritual forces of evil in the heavenly places" (Eph 6:12 NRSV). Because the demonic forces have already been dethroned through Christ's cross and resurrection victory, they derive their power from the lie that they still have real power. The way to overcome the principalities and powers is to expose them to the light of truth, and this means through the preaching of the gospel.

The idea of the Christian engaged in spiritual warfare was pervasive among the Puritans, but it is also found in the mainstream of the Reformation, even in the mystical tradition of Christian faith.[8] While the mystics focused their attention on the need to subdue our lower nature, the Puritans and evangelicals also waged war against the entrenched forces of wickedness in society. They were intent on altering the structures of society in order to make them more malleable to the rule of God. Though persuaded that true faith can never be the product of legal coercion, they did believe that every area of life could be made to serve and reflect the law of God. Laws cannot make people moral, but they can restrain immoralities and thereby make society safe as well as just.

In biblical, evangelical spirituality we do not simply "let go and let God," but we fight with God against the powers of unrighteousness.

God does not need our help, but he chooses to make us his instruments, and we must make sure that we are prepared for this task. When we pray "Thy will be done" our prayer is one of subversion and conversion, not just of submission.[9] The Christian goal is not servile resignation but fervent expectation that the crumbling foundations of society presage a new order where peace and justice shall reign.

Salvation is comprised not of two levels but of two moments: conversion to Christ and conversion to the world. We not only turn to Christ in faith and repentance, but we also turn to the world with the message of Christ, empowered by his Spirit to witness to his victory over evil. In faith we are baptized into the passion of Christ and rise with him to battle the powers of evil. The baptism of the Spirit does not transport us out of the world but sends us into the midst of the world's affliction and tribulation with a message that can heal and redeem.

The accent in biblical, evangelical faith is on the perseverance of the saints, not flight from the world but remaining steadfast to Christ while living out our vocation in the world. The Christian is one who perseveres and overcomes rather than one who retreats from the challenges of life to a spiritual oasis in order to cultivate the garden of the soul. Evangelical Christianity makes a place for periods of withdrawal from the storms of life but only for the purpose of returning to the battle lines inwardly strengthened and spiritually refreshed. Those Christians standing in the mystical tradition of faith tend to envisage the Christian life in terms of divinization, rising above the merely human, rather than of humanization, making the world more just and humane.[10] The mystics indeed powerfully remind us that we need to draw near to God before we can bring others to Christ. But we who adhere to the Reformation rediscovery of the gospel of justification are constrained to remind our brothers and sisters in Christ in the Catholic and Orthodox communions that the goal of the spiritual life must always be the great commission, the sharing of the good news of reconciliation and redemption through the vicarious atonement of Jesus Christ and teaching people to observe all that Christ commanded.

Evangelicals do not disclaim the salutary role of spiritual disciplines, which equip the Christian for battle in the name of Christ. Faith by itself is sufficient for laying hold of justification, but disciplines of devotion are necessary to help us to live out the implications of our faith in the world. Faithful attendance at worship services, where we hear the Word of God proclaimed; frequent participation in the Lord's Supper, where we receive both pardoning and strengthening grace; the practice of fervent prayer, which involves adoration, petition and intercession; the daily study of God's Word, which gives nourishment to the soul; moderation in eating and drinking, which clears the mind for service; the careful avoidance of entertainment that numbs moral sensitivity; periodic meditation on the law of God—all of these are important in enabling us to remain true to the vows that we made, either at our baptism or at our confirmation, to uphold the faith once delivered to the saints. Spiritual disciplines do not make reparation for sin, nor do they merit grace, which is always undeserved. What they do is to strengthen faith and enhance our witness as we are guided by the Spirit into the needs of our neighbor. The Holy Spirit alone makes our witness spiritually fruitful, but he does not witness for us. He speaks with us and through us as we speak and pray in obedience to the divine imperative of being a disciple and herald of the Lord Jesus Christ.

Holiness and Justification

While evangelical theology is adamant that the ground of our righteousness before God is the atoning sacrifice of Christ on our behalf, it is equally insistent that the Spirit of God motivates us to demonstrate our gratitude to God through holy living. Our salvation is based on the extrinsic righteousness of Christ that is imputed to us in faith, but our salvation is manifest in our striving for personal holiness. We are justified by grace alone *(sola gratia)* received through faith alone *(sola fide)* (cf. Rom 3:21-22; Eph 2:8-9). But we are sanctified through works of love in the power of grace. We are justified *by* grace, but we are justified *for* holiness. As the apostle explains, "Now by Christ's death in his body of flesh and blood God has reconciled you to himself, so that he may bring you into his own presence, holy and without blame or blemish" (Col 1:22 REB). God's work of reconciliation both confers on us a new status and implants within us the beginnings of a new character.

The Reformers were convinced that even though our justification is complete, our sanctification has only begun, and the whole Christian life is an expression of our commitment to personal holiness. God's justifying work is not the same as his sanctifying work. Yet the two works are inseparable, for no one is truly justified without also being sanctified. These works of God cannot be merged into one another, but they are also not to be separated.[11] We are not justified unless we are also on the way to being sanctified. We do not receive the righteousness of Christ without at the same time being engrafted into this righteousness. Our obedience is not salvific, but our disobedience threatens our salvific status. Our salvation is a free gift of God, but our salvation can be imperiled through arrogance and sloth. We have eternal security through faith in Christ, yet we must take care not to presume on God's kindness. Calvin trenchantly observed that our salvation once begun can nevertheless wither away.[12]

John Wesley inveighed against what he called "solifidianism" on the grounds that too much emphasis on grace and faith can undermine the call to holiness, which is incumbent on every Christian. Like Calvin before him, Wesley sounded the call to Christian perfection, but for Wesley this perfection could be realized in this life. Yet we must not be too hasty in accusing Wesley of perfectionism.[13] For him perfection does not mean *perfectus* in the sense of moral faultlessness, but *teleios*—completeness and fulfillment.[14] He taught that in our Christian sojourn we can always advance toward a greater perfection, and we must constantly battle against sin and temptation. We can never be free of sins of omission, but we can gain victory over any particular sin. Wesley can be faulted for failing to make sufficiently clear that the more progress we make in holiness the more cognizant we will be of our own depravity and iniquity. He held that in the experience of entire sanctification the very root of bitterness is taken out of us, thereby making us inwardly pure and holy. From my perspective we can never in this life be free from the proclivity to sin, but we can be victorious over every temptation and sin that confront us.

While the righteousness that redeems lies outside us in Jesus Christ, this righteousness does not remain outside us but is reflected in our thoughts and actions. By faith we are engrafted into this righteousness, and by love we move toward this righteousness. Paul declared, "May the Lord make you increase and abound in love for one another and for all, just as we abound in love for you. And may he so strengthen your hearts in holiness that you may be blameless before our God and Father at the coming of our Lord Jesus with all his saints" (1 Thess 3:12, 13 NRSV). If we are engrafted into the righteousness of Christ, and if we manifest this righteousness in our daily lives, we will most certainly be welcomed by God the Father and acknowledged as his sons and daughters. In this life we will never be morally impeccable, but we can be perfected in holiness through steadfast faith in the living Christ (cf. 2 Cor 7:1).

In Isaiah 35:9-10 the people of God are not now accounted either "clean" or "unclean," but they are called "redeemed" or "ransomed of the Lord." Even in their condition of moral vulnerability and fallibility they are justified and redeemed by God's free grace. One commentator observes, "It is not mankind's faith and careful observance of the law which is considered to be decisive, but it is the grace of the Lord who has redeemed and ransomed his people."[15]

The holy life is a life of faith in the mercy of God shown forth in Jesus Christ. Our focus should always be on what God has done for us in Christ, not on what we can do for God to allow Christ to come to us. We should set our hope on the grace that Jesus Christ will bring us when he is revealed (1 Pet 1:13). We are never to compare our own holiness with the unholiness of others, for this presumes that we are morally superior to them. Our progress in holiness is due to the sanctifying work of the Spirit within us, but the way in which we live our lives testifies to the authenticity of our faith in Christ. For J. Hudson Taylor the hallmark of Christian living is "not a striving to have faith, or to increase our faith." Instead "a looking at the faithful one seems all we need. A resting in the loved one entirely, for time, for eternity."[16]

This position does not preclude self-examination in the light of God's holy Word. We should on occasion take stock of ourselves, even gaze into ourselves, but we must not remain in ourselves. We may look into ourselves only in order to be reminded of our own sinfulness. Then we will all the more appreciate God's grace and mercy toward us. Self-examination and self-mortification do not gain us access to the Spirit of God, but they proceed from the Spirit's first grasping us and turning us toward Jesus Christ. The knowledge of God's love in Christ is prior to the knowledge of our sin. The outpouring of the Spirit precedes mortification and confession. The gospel has priority over the law, for only when we have been confronted by the gospel of God's incomparable love and forgiveness can we really hear the harsh condemnation of the law. Human repentance does not gain divine forgiveness, but it proceeds out of a recognition of this forgiveness. Both Catholic mysticism and Protestant pietism have for the most part lost sight of the biblical truth that God's undeserved grace precedes the striving for faith and that the preaching and hearing of the gospel is the only adequate preparation for the dispensing of God's grace and love.

Confession of sin does not simply lie at the beginning of the Christian life; it is the hallmark of the entire Christian life. In Luther's words, "the whole life of the Christian is to be one of repentance."[17] It is the person of faith who prays: "Rescue me from my rebellion, for even fools mock me when I rebel" (Ps 39:8 NLT; cf. Rom 7:7-25). Yet evangelical spirituality is not exclusively penitential (as in some strands of mysticism). It is also eucharistic in the sense of proceeding out of a deep gratefulness for all that Christ has done for us. We do not remain in sorrow for our sins, but cast our burdens on the Lord in the confident expectation that he will sustain us. After repentance we who believe then take up our own cross and follow Christ in the assurance that God's grace is greater than all our sin, that God's Spirit will pull us through every difficulty and empower us to give a sound and steadfast witness to the truth as we live out our vocation under the cross of Golgotha.

Stages on Life's Pilgrimage

Although we are saved wholly by grace, we can make progress toward righteousness in the power of grace. The apostle Paul testified that "we are being transformed into his likeness with ever-increasing glory, through the power of the Lord who is the Spirit" (2 Cor 3:18 REB). Calvin held out this hope: "Since he has partly enlightened us already by his Holy Spirit, it may please him to increase his grace in us more and more, until he has communicated it wholly to us."[18]

On the basis of Scripture one may draw the conclusion that there are four stages on life's pilgrimage: the pre-Christian, the carnal Christian, the mature or perfected Christian and the transfigured person. The pre-Christian is seeking for the truth of God but has not yet found it. The disciples of Jesus prior to Pentecost, the God-fearers in Acts 10 and the Old Testament prophets all fit into this category. The carnal Christian or the babe in Christ (1 Cor 3:1-3) believes but is not yet sanctified in daily life, though sanctification as a process has indeed begun with the awakening to faith. The mature or sanctified Christian, what Paul calls the spiritual person (1 Cor 2:15-16), labors to make his or her holiness perfect through self-giving love and obedience. This person is not only indwelt by the Spirit but empowered by the Spirit to bear public witness to the faith.[19] The perfected Christian not only believes in the cross but takes up the cross in order to follow Christ. Finally there is the fourth stage: transfiguration or deification, in which we are totally transformed into the likeness of God (Rom 8:29). This occurs beyond death when we see Christ face to face (1 Cor 13:12).

It is always necessary to be reminded that God's grace is at work throughout this salvific process, even before it. Even before we begin to seek, the Spirit of God stirs our conscience and awakens within us a hunger for the truth. Luther declared, "Before thou callest upon God or seekest Him, God must have come to thee and found thee."[20] God's election precedes our decision; indeed, we can decide and obey only through the power of God's redeeming grace.

Against decisionism I contend that the decision of faith does not procure our salvation but ratifies and confirms it. It does not make us acceptable before God but certifies that God has accepted us in Jesus Christ. The decision of faith is both an instrument by which the Spirit seals the love of Christ within us and a confirmation of God's undeserved mercy extended to us in Christ. It is also an evidence that the Spirit is at work in our lives. It does not induce God to grant us his salvation, but it carries salvation forward in our lives. Our decision and our subsequent obedience contribute to the efficacy of Christ's saving work in our faith pilgrimage.

I espouse on the one hand a *springtime* theology over a *wintry* theology that we see in orthodox Calvinism and Lutheranism, and on the other, a *summery* theology, evident in the Holiness movement and Pentecostalism. We participate in the fellowship of Christ's sufferings but also in the glory of his resurrection. We not only bear the cross in faith but also experience the comfort that the cross of Christ brings through the Holy Spirit. We die daily as we battle against the powers of sin and death, but we also experience victory over these powers, even though it is only partial. Paul spoke much about the tribulations that Christians must undergo, but he also gave thanks that God "always leads us in triumph in Christ, and through us diffuses the fragrance of His knowledge in every place" (2 Cor 2:14 NKJ). He urged us to "exult in the hope of the divine splendour that is to be ours" (Rom 5:2 NEB). A springtime theology holds out the possibility of ever new beginnings. Even though we may experience shame and defeat at one point in our lives, we can rise again and continue the battle through a new dispensation of grace. A theology of the cross needs to be held together with a theology of glory. If we have only the former we will be tempted to despair. If we have only the latter we will be ensnared in self-deception.

Conversion is both an event and a continuous process. It begins in the baptism of the Spirit, who engrafts us into the mystical body of Christ through faith and repentance. It continues as the Spirit fills us and directs us in the arduous task of living out our faith. If we fall away from the faith we need to be engrafted once more into the body of Christ and experience a new baptism of the Spirit. It is possible to believe and yet quench and grieve the Spirit by not committing ourselves unreservedly to Christ. We must then pray that the Spirit's baptizing work might be made complete in our lives through the obedience of faith and works of love.

Our submission to the sacramental rite of baptism both confirms God's electing grace in our lives and prepares the way for the demonstration of this grace as we embark on the pathway of faith and repentance. If we grow cold in our faith and fall backward in our walk with Christ we must not seek a new baptism, for there is only "one Lord, one faith, one baptism" (Eph 4:5). We must return to the promises of God's mercy, which the sacrament testifies to and communicates. If we renege completely on our commitment to Christ, we then stand in need of a new baptizing work of the Spirit; but the sacrament itself should never be repeated, for the reality that it signifies—Christ's baptism into death—is always sufficient to cover our sins and present us as righteous before a holy God.

The Paradox of Sanctity

All Christians, indeed all mortals, are called to be saints (cf. Rom 1:7; 1 Cor 1:2), but this mandate cannot be fulfilled without the outpouring of the Holy Spirit. The Holy Spirit himself is indeed the sanctifier, the one who works sanctity within us. But we too have a role—not in the creation of sanctity but in its manifestation and proclamation. Theologians often err by overemphasizing divine sovereignty and minimizing human responsibility in salvation. Calvin for the most part held on to the paradox of divine grace and human accomplishment. He was not only a theologian of the Word but also a theologian of the Holy Spirit, and this means that he sedulously endeavored to relate objective redemption and subjective appropriation. Yet on occasion he lapsed into divine determinism, thereby denying the open situation of preaching and hearing. He could declare, "Our salvation is not only helped forward by God, but also . . . it is begun, continued and perfected by him, without any contribution of our own."[21] This is a sound observation so long as we are speaking about the procuring of God's mercy and grace, but it loses sight of the truth that we are called to be coworkers with God in making known the good news of Christ's redemption (Rom 16:3, 9; 1 Cor 3:9; 16:16; 2 Cor 8:23; Col 4:11; 3 Jn 8). Salvation is not only a gift to be received but also a task to be performed. It is not only a privilege to be conferred but also a race to be won, a crown to be gained (1 Cor 9:24; Heb 12:1; 2 Tim 4:8). Lutherans are often better than Calvinists in affirming the paradox of divine agency in the procuring of salvation and human responsibility for the loss of salvation.

As Christians we are not to try to make ourselves pious in the sense of spiritually superior, but true piety will be seen in our lives by others if we strive to obey God's commandments. Our task is not to become self-consciously holy, for then our focus is on our own supposed holiness rather than on Jesus Christ. We are summoned to make a determined effort to obey the divine imperative and follow Christ wherever he might lead us, but all the while our attention should be focused on what he commands, not on our own progress toward perfection. In our good works we do not crave divine or human recognition; we are content simply to serve in self-giving love. Reinhold Niebuhr put it succinctly: "The service of God is to be performed not only without hope of any concrete or obvious reward, but at the price of sacrifice, abnegation and loss."[22]

The paradox of sanctity is also evident in the biblical principle that it is through the loss of self that we find ourselves (Mt 10:39; Lk 17:33). It is through giving up our worldly security that we find eternal security. It is by letting go of our desire to make something of ourselves that we realize our vocation of being ambassadors and heralds of the Lord Jesus Christ. We are not even to find our security in the rites and rituals of the church, but our hope and confidence should be in Jesus Christ alone, whom these rites acclaim and celebrate.

Again Scripture teaches that it is by proceeding downward that we ascend upward. It is by declaring our solidarity with those in need that we find the peace that only Christ can give. It is in the dispossessed and outcasts of society that we discern the face of God. Our mission is to take the gospel not to the righteous but to sinners (Mk 9:13; Mt 9:13; Lk 5:32). It is not those who are well that need a physician but those who are ill and seek a remedy for their condition (Mt 9:12). General William Booth, founder of the Salvation Army, gave this command to his officers: "Go for souls and go for the worst!"

Christ also taught that it is through humility that we are exalted (Mt 18:4; 20:26; 23:11-12). The vocation to sainthood is not the embracing of the heroism that wins worldly acclaim but the willingness to live and serve in obscurity if this is God's will. It is not the heroic way of our choosing but the little way of his choosing that more often than not characterizes the life of the Christian. Deeds of self-giving love cannot be kept hidden, however, and those who are made instruments of the Holy Spirit in his work of manifesting the glory of God will eventually become known to the wider community of faith, sometimes even to the wider world. Those who make progress in being the light of the world and the salt of the earth (Mt 5:13-14) will be sought out by those who are intent on escaping the darkness that engulfs them.

I have already alluded to the paradox of divine grace and human freedom. It is through God's grace that we become truly free—free not to do what we please but free for obedience. We find our true destiny in submission to Jesus Christ, not in the exaltation of self. To be truly free means to be liberated from the power of sin and death. In this liberation wrought by the Spirit of God within us we are enabled to live out our vocation of being servants and heralds of the king. Paul declares, "It is God, for his own loving purpose, who puts both the will and the action into you" (Phil 2:13 JB). When God's grace confronts us we are then set free to work out our salvation "with fear and trembling" (Phil 2:12).

A final paradox of sanctity is the recognition that it is through death that we find life. The prophet Hosea exclaimed, "Come, let us return to the Lord; for it is he who has torn, and he will heal us; he has struck down, and he will bind us up" (6:1 NRSV; cf. Heb 12:3-11). It is only when we experience the disciplining rod of God's judgment that we come to sense and appreciate the depth of his mercy. Paul wrote that we should exult in our sufferings because suffering produces hope (Rom 5:3-4). "Such hope is no fantasy" (Rom 5:5 REB) because "God's love has been poured into our hearts through the Holy Spirit that has been given to us" (Rom 5:5 NRSV). Too often today, especially in New Age and New Thought circles, the Christian life is reduced to realizing human potential through cultivating self-esteem. A more solid biblical perspective is given by Wilhelm Herrmann, who here echoes Luther: "God takes our self-esteem and creates for us an unbreakable spirit; he destroys our joy in life and makes us blessed; he kills and makes us alive."[23]

Yet it is possible to err in the other direction by viewing the glorifying of God as the reduction of humanity to nothingness. The human person is not a zero but one who has been created for sainthood. We are called to be not merely servants of God but his sons and daughters. Through the mediation and resurrection of Christ we are assured of a glorious destiny so long as we have faith in Christ and practice love. *Soli Deo Gloria* in Christian tradition means that our focus should be on giving glory only to God, but if we do so we will certainly be made to share in this glory. Christianity is not exclusively theocentric but theoanthropocentric. It seeks not only the exaltation of God but also the restoration and transfiguration of humanity. Irenaeus put it well: "The glory of God is humanity fully alive."

It is fashionable in ultra-Reformation circles to downplay the importance of good works in the effort to give all the credit for our emancipation to God's grace. Ragnar Bring's comment is typical: "The Christian ethic is characterized not by the good deeds of the converted, the holy people and saints but by God's judgment and grace over one and all."[24] What is missing here is the imperative laid on Christians to be rich in good works (1 Tim 6:18) and to be a holy people. It is not enough simply to believe, but we must "go on toward perfection" (Heb 6:1 NRSV). If we strive to make our holiness perfect in the fear of God we will be proving the genuineness of our faith and thereby giving glory to Jesus Christ, who is the author and finisher of our faith (Heb 12:2).

As I see it there are two dangers in the Christian walk: perfectionism and moral defeatism. The first denies our continuing frailty and vulnerability to sin and temptation. The second downplays the power of redeeming grace that enables us to overcome every sin and resist every temptation. The Pentecostal healer T. L. Osborn commits the first error when he says, "Confess that your redemption is complete—from sin and sickness!"[25] To be sure, the work of redemption is complete in Jesus Christ, but the subjective appropriation of his redemption will always be woefully incomplete so long as we are in mortal flesh. We are not yet redeemed in the sense of being purified from sin, but we are on the road to redemption. We need to imbibe Luther's words of wisdom: "Everyone who believes in Christ is righteous, not yet fully in fact but in hope. For he has begun to be justified and healed, like the man who was half-dead (Lk. 10:30)."[26] Yet it is possible to so underplay the depth of our renewal by the Holy Spirit that the heights of sanctity are hidden from us. We are to be not only seekers after righteousness but conquerors of unrighteousness—both in ourselves and in the world (Rom 8:37).

True sanctity entails not the cultivation of self-righteousness but the increasing longing for perfect righteousness (cf. Rom 8:18-25; 2 Cor 4:16-18; Col 3:4; 1 Pet 1:13; 4:13; 5:4). This perfect righteousness is, of course, Jesus Christ himself; yet we look forward not only to meeting Christ face to face but also to being taken up into Christ. The Orthodox theologian Alexander Schmemann shares these pertinent reflections:

The one true sadness is "that of not being a saint," and how often the "moral" Christians are those precisely who never feel, never experience this sadness, because their own "experience of salvation," the feeling of "being saved" fills them with self-satisfaction; and whoever has been "satisfied," has received already his reward and cannot thirst and hunger for that total transformation and transfiguration of life which alone makes "Saints."[27]

The new birth stands at the beginning of the Christian life, and the earmark of holiness is to press on toward the grand culmination in which the glory of God will flood the world. Holiness is not a necessary preparation for faith but its fruit and evidence.[28] Faith is decisive for a life of victory over the powers of sin and death, but this victory will not be complete until the parousia—the eschatological day of redemption. We look forward to seeing the shining of Christ both in our lives and in the whole world in the confidence that nothing can sever us from his love. This confidence is apparent in the chorale "In Thee Is Gladness"— the theme song of the Confessing Church in Germany in the 1930s:

Our hearts are pining to see thy shining,

dying or living,

to thee are cleaving

   naught can us sever.[29]

Finally, it is incumbent on us to explore the enigmatic relation between God's sovereign freedom and human instrumentality. Our Puritan and Reformation forebears were convinced that God ordinarily works through outward means not only in effecting salvation but also in implanting and nurturing holiness. Samuel Hopkins was adamant that "the use of means is absolutely necessary" for any "exercise of the new heart or of Christian holiness at any time."[30] This does not preclude the Holy Spirit's working immediately on the human soul in conferring justifying and sanctifying grace, but it means that he generally chooses to work in conjunction with outward means, such as the preaching of the gospel, the reading of Scripture, the observance of the sacraments and fervent, persistent prayer.[31] God is sovereignly free not only in imparting grace but in using means to prepare us for grace and confirm us in grace. Faith comes by hearing, and hearing comes by preaching (Rom 10:17), but it is the Holy Spirit who converts the words of the preacher into the Word of life and who renders the sacrament of baptism efficacious as the vehicle of the water of life. The hope for redemption rests finally on God, on his work of reconciliation in Jesus Christ, on the sending forth of his Spirit at Pentecost. Our task is to celebrate and proclaim the good news that Christ has overcome the powers of sin and death and that he continues to overcome through the Holy Spirit who works within us and upon us as we go forward in the life of faith.

Appendix D: A Theology of the Cross

In his provocative *In the Face of God,* Michael Horton offers a significant critique of secularizing trends in both liberal and evangelical Christianity.[32] This book speaks powerfully to the disintegration of doctrinal allegiances and the rise of an experiential religion that reduces Christian faith to interior states of consciousness. Horton scores the "scandalous familiarity with God" that characterizes evangelical services of worship and the tacit dismissal of the sacraments of baptism and the Lord's Supper as veritable means of grace. Like a latter-day prophet he warns the church of heretical movements that are sapping its vitality, thereby rendering it impotent to challenge the forces of evil in society. He locates the source of the enervation and confusion in Protestantism today in what he calls "gnostic mysticism," which teaches salvation from the bonds of the flesh and de-emphasizes the sacraments. The gnostic revival, he rightly perceives, is more interested in the Spirit than in the Son, "for the Spirit is the symbol of freedom, experience and disembodied existence. The Son is rooted in human history, incarnate in human flesh, and saves us by a bloody death that is applied to us through material means."[33] Horton deplores the tendency to separate the action of the Spirit from the atoning and redeeming work of Christ. He criticizes prominent theologians in the evangelical movement like Lewis Sperry Chafer for distinguishing between one who is merely a Christian and one who is "spiritual" and regarding only the latter as "rightly related to the Spirit, in addition to his relation to Christ in salvation."[34] His critique of Pentecostalism is especially devastating, since he believes that this movement signifies a wholesale defection from historical evangelical Christianity. "Those who seek to hear, see, and touch God in their own inner experience find themselves chasing shadows, chimeras, and mirages that dazzle for a moment, only to disappoint. But those who take God up on his promise to give us Christ's body and blood through the Word, baptism, and bread and wine will never be disappointed."[35]

In place of a theology of religious experience Horton champions a theology of the cross—centered not in signs and wonders that confound the imagination but in historical events that remain true even when the message they carry is rejected. In a theology of the cross the Christian is both a sinner and righteous at the same time. The life of the Christian is not one of ever deepening experiences of God's presence but is "a mixture of faith and doubt, obedience and disobedience, health and sickness, ease and distress."[36] God is to be found not in visions and raptures but in the fellowship of Christ's sufferings. The voice of God is never heard directly but always indirectly through outward means: the preaching of the gospel and Holy Scripture.

Horton gives a particularly incisive critique of the profanization of Christian music today, especially in evangelical circles. He laments hymns that celebrate Jesus coming into one's heart as opposed to Christ coming into the world to save sinners. He expresses doubts about the theological validity of hymns like "In the Garden," "Blessed Assurance," and "Heaven Came Down." He calls for a reappropriation of the hymns of an earlier period that uphold God's majesty and holiness, that acclaim the incarnation of the Son of God in human flesh, his atoning work on the cross and his glorious resurrection from the grave. We need hymns, he argues, that focus not on cultivating spiritual intimacy with God but on celebrating God's incomparable act of deliverance in Jesus Christ in past history.

The reader will not be surprised that I stand with Horton in his trenchant warnings against gnosticism and his impassioned call for worship that is done in spirit and in truth. At the same time the book
leaves me with a profound sense of uneasiness: in correcting one
grave imbalance he seems to create another. Horton is to be commended for his indictment of egocentric piety, but does he see the danger on the other side: a religion that disparages the biblical call to
holiness, the cheap grace that subverts human responsibility in working out the implications of salvation in fear and trembling? He defines
the gospel as "the announcement of our free justification in Christ."[37]
While the declaration of justification belongs to the essence of the gospel, it is not the whole of the gospel, for the gospel includes not only
the good news of God's free grace but also the power unto salvation
that enables us to live lives of victory over sin (cf. Rom 1:16; 1 Cor
1:18). In Horton's view the reborn Christian must settle for a "partial
victory" over sin, and while it is true that sin continues in every Christian, surely the gospel holds out the possibility of total victory over any
particular sin, even though this possibility is not always realized in
daily life. Horton would very likely withhold his endorsement of popular gospel songs like "Victory in Jesus" and "Higher Ground" because
they either tend toward perfectionism or assign too great a role to the
human will in realizing salvation. Yet it is indisputable that many of
these songs have instilled hope in countless tormented souls struggling for interior peace and freedom.[38]

Horton describes Christianity as "an objective religion with subjective application."[39] The truth of the gospel, he says, is anchored "not in
what happens inside a person, but in what happened in the ancient
land of Israel two thousand years ago."[40] Yet does not the gospel
include Pentecost as well as Calvary, and are not we called to celebrate
both the mystery of the cross of Christ and the indwelling of Christ by
his Spirit (cf. Col 1:27)? Horton upholds a purely extrinsic and forensic
justification, contending that what is decisive for our salvation happens wholly outside the self. Yet surely we need to make contact with

God's justifying act or this act has no tangible bearing on human life and experience. The answer to subjectivism is not objectivism but a theology of divine-human encounter in which truth is both declared from the outside and appropriated from the inside. The answer to experientialism is not creedalism or confessionalism but a theology of Word and Spirit in which truth does not remain external and historical but becomes by the action of the Spirit internal and existential. Horton acknowledges that sanctifying grace accompanies the justifying act of God; yet he tends to depict inward spiritual purification as a byproduct of redemption rather than an integral element in redemption itself.

The author appeals to the Reformers in his defense of a wholly extrinsic justification and a wholly objective revelation. In so doing, however, he fails to do justice to the mystical dimension in the theologies of both Calvin and Luther to which the Pietists appealed in their struggle against Protestant orthodoxy. For Calvin "it is not enough to know Christ as crucified and raised up from the dead, unless you experience, also, the fruit of this. . . . Christ therefore is rightly known, when we feel how powerful his death and resurrection are, and how efficacious they are in us."[41] And in Luther's words: "It is one thing to preach, sing and say that God is all these things. It is quite another to feel the gracious, merciful, and righteous God in the heart. The pious and upright have this not only on their tongue but also in their heart."[42] Indeed, "since Christ comes into our heart through the gospel, he must also be accepted by the heart. As I now believe that he is in the gospel, so I receive him and have him already. So Paul says: I carry Christ in my heart, for he is mine."[43] As the Reformation moved forward, Luther became alarmed at the antinomian distortion of his teachings and insisted that Calvary be supplemented by Pentecost in our preaching, for otherwise we presume on God's goodness.[44]

Horton rightly upholds the polarity of law and gospel, which was indeed significant in the preaching and ministry of the Reformers and their followers. Yet he tends to make this polarity too stringent and fails to recognize with the Reformers that there is an underlying unity between law and gospel, though it is not immediately perceptible. Calvin referred to the gospel as "the soul of the law." For both Reformers the law is always God's gracious law (though this is more apparent in Calvin than in Luther) and is not to be associated exclusively with God's judgment and wrath. In a later work Horton contends that we *believe* the gospel and *obey* the law. He objects to the exhortation "to live the gospel."[45] Horton could learn from Karl Barth that law and gospel belong together in a paradoxical unity and that we are summoned to obedience only in the context of having already been accepted by God's grace, though we are basically unacceptable in the light of his inviolable standard of holiness.

I fully concur with Horton's critique of contemporary music that makes the praise of God serve the satisfaction of the human heart, thereby transforming worship into therapy. But we must not be too hasty in excising from our hymnals gospel songs and chorales that celebrate Christ *in* us, for we are then emptying faith of its mystical content, and a faith without a small dose of mysticism can only grow cold and formalistic. It is surely not our goal to become God's frozen chosen.

Horton is especially displeased with the legacy of John Wesley, which he believes sacrifices the gospel of justification to a gospel of religious experience. Yet he is on shaky ground when he contends that "it was John Wesley who made Law's perfectionism part of mainstream teaching."[46] Various scholars have shown that Wesley sharply challenged Law's eros spirituality and decisively rejected Law's contention that holiness is the cause of salvation.[47] Wesley sought to bring together the Catholic concern for holiness and the evangelical emphasis on free grace, and this is a legitimate goal for all Christians who seek both the unity and the renewal of the church in our time. While Wesley and Whitefield could not agree on the exact relationship of grace and human decision, they remained fellow workers in the cause of revival and made their pulpits open to each other. Today's Calvinists need to learn from the Arminian protest against divine determinism, and Arminians need to become more alert to the perils of Pelagianism and semi-Pelagianism, which subvert the Reformation call to give glory to God alone *(soli Deo Gloria)*. Wesley can help Calvinist evangelicals recognize that the search for perfection does not have to be self-defeating, that Christians can make real progress against sin through the power of the indwelling Holy Spirit.

Finally, I detect in Horton the remnants of an evangelical rationalism that account for his describing truth in exclusively propositional terms. He faults Pentecostals for finding truth in the "Rhema" Word "that is spoken directly to the human spirit by God's Spirit," whereas the "Word that truly saves" is "the written text of Scripture."[48] Yet it would be closer to Reformation theology to aver that the truth that really saves is the living Word of God—Jesus Christ—who speaks to us in the Scriptures by his Spirit. The Cambridge Declaration, with which Horton identifies, denies "that personal spiritual experience can ever be a vehicle of revelation."[49] But if revelation excludes religious experience it is then reduced to propositions that are communicated exclusively from one intellect to another. The evangelical experience of an awakened heart (P. T. Forsyth) is surely an integral element in divine revelation. Revelation entails the experience of God's living presence as well as the conveyance of information about God. If we deny the former we become trapped in the confines of a barren orthodoxy. Horton lists Calvin, Luther and Barth as among his mentors, but he confounds their more existential understanding of truth with the scholastic understanding of later Reformed orthodoxy. Evangelical rationalism is also evident in Horton's tendency to tie the Spirit too narrowly to the sermon.[50] Here again we can learn from Wesley that God speaks not only through Scripture and the sermon but also through holy lives and deeds. The means of grace in biblical religion are more comprehensive than Horton seems to allow.

Horton has rendered the wider church a signal service by calling for a rediscovery of Luther's theology of the cross *(theologia crucis)*. But if we are to do justice to the total witness of the Reformation we will make a place for a theology of glory *(theologia gloriae)* as well. Indeed, the cross without the resurrection becomes a pretext for despair just as the resurrection without the cross becomes a fantasy that deceives. Our mandate is to herald both the reconciling work of Christ on the cross and the redeeming power of the Spirit of Christ who seals the truth of the gospel within us through the experience of faith. We are to preach both the justification of the ungodly to be received by faith and the sanctification of the righteous as we seek to live out the implications of our faith through deeds of self-giving love. Christianity includes both the descent of God's immeasurable grace and the ascent of Christians through the power of grace. The symbol of salvation is not the down escalator in which God comes to us (as Horton contends) but the elevator of free grace in which Christ descends to us and we ascend with Christ to God after we enter the elevator through a simple act of faith.[51] Horton acknowledges that "it is only by Christ's ascension that we are carried into the heavenlies, where we are seated with Christ (Eph 2:6). This is not something to be achieved, but to be received."[52] Yet is not our ascension with Christ also a task, since our inclusion in his kingdom is dependent on our response to his grace in faith and obedience? We are here again confronted with the paradox that God's redeeming grace includes rather than excludes human seeking, willing and obeying.

Horton rightly warns against placing our trust in signs; yet signs and wonders will surely follow the proclamation of the gospel—signs of the healing of broken relationships; the dawning of faith through the power of the Spirit; deliverance from the powers of sickness and death; mystical communion with the living Christ; liberation from bondage to fear and despair; and upwelling joy in Christ's salvation. Can we bear the cross with joy and steadfast faith without some intimation of the glory that is yet to be revealed? At the same time can we have a foretaste of the glory of being redeemed from sin and the power of evil without taking up the cross and following Christ in costly discipleship? The way to glory is through the cross, but the cross itself brings assurance of glory, for the Spirit surprises us with joy even in our descent into the darkness of sacrificial service in the name of Christ.

Notes

Chapter One

[1]George A. Lindbeck, *The Nature of Doctrine: Religion and Theology in a Postliberal Age* (Philadelphia: Westminster Press, 1984), pp. 15-45. For my earlier discussion of Lindbeck in this Christian Foundations series see Bloesch, *A Theology of Word & Spirit* (Downers Grove, Ill.: InterVarsity Press, 1992), pp. 23, 25, 28, 30, 118, 132, 271, 276-78; and *Holy Scripture* (Downers Grove, Ill.: InterVarsity Press, 1994), pp. 209-10, 216, 218, 343-44, 346.

[2]Trevor Hart, *Faith Thinking* (Downers Grove, Ill.: InterVarsity Press, 1996), p. 88.

[3]For an astute critique of Lindbeck's position see ibid., pp. 81-89, 92-95. According to Hart, Lindbeck espouses a religious pluralism that is agnostic concerning claims to final truth. Also see Brad J. Kallenberg, "Unstuck from Yale: Theological Method After Lindbeck," *Scottish Journal of Theology* 50, no. 2 (1997): 191-218.

[4]See George Lindbeck, "Atonement & the Hermeneutics of Intratextual Social Embodiment," in *The Nature of Confession: Evangelicals & Postliberals in Conversation,* ed. Timothy R. Phillips and Dennis L. Okholm (Downers Grove, Ill.: InterVarsity Press, 1996), pp. 221-40.

[5]Nancey Murphy, *Beyond Liberalism and Fundamentalism: How Modern and Postmodern Philosophy Set the Theological Agenda* (Valley Forge, Penn.: Trinity Press International, 1996).

[6]Ibid., p. 45. She rightly discerns in my work a struggle to maintain both the propositional element in theology and the mythopoetic or narrational element.

[7]*Luther's Works*, ed. Jaroslav Pelikan, trans. J. Pelikan and A. T. W. Steinhaeuser (St. Louis: Concordia, 1956), 21:299.

[8]Clark H. Pinnock, *Flame of Love: A Theology of the Holy Spirit* (Downers Grove, Ill.: InterVarsity Press, 1996).

[9]Ibid., p. 61.

[10]Ibid., p. 201.

[11]Cornelius was numbered among the so-called God-fearers—Gentiles who had accepted the truth of the Jewish religion and had become loose adherents of the synagogue. See the discussion by G. H. C. MacGregor in "Acts," *Interpreter's Bible,* ed. G. A. Buttrick (Nashville: Abingdon-Cokesbury, 1954), 9:131-41. For my more extensive assessment of Pinnock in this volume see pp. 247-51.

[12]See Arthur C. Danto, *Nietzsche as Philosopher* (New York: Columbia University Press, 1965), pp. 68-99.

[13]For a careful analysis and critique of Rorty, Derrida and other philosophers of postmodernism see Stanley J. Grenz, *A Primer on Postmodernism* (Grand Rapids: Eerdmans, 1996). Grenz wishes to learn positively from postmodernity while remaining in continuity with historic Christianity.

[14]On the Cambridge Declaration see James M. Boice and Benjamin E. Sasse, eds., *Here We Stand! A Call from Confessing Evangelicals* (Grand Rapids: Baker, 1996). I do not deny that the Cambridge Declaration has some of the earmarks of a vital confession of faith, but regrettably it sees the adversary to faith only in the guise of experientialism and not also of rationalism, which often takes the form of an authoritarian dogmatism and creedalism. The Cambridge Declaration speaks to the religio-cultural climate of today, but it does not directly address the critical theological and moral issues that confront the church in our time, such as religious inclusivism and pluralism, human sexuality, abortion, environmental pollution, racism and weapons of mass extermination.

[15]It was in this Hegelian sense that Karl Barth used the word *Aufhebung* in his critique of religion in the light of the Christ revelation. See his *Die Kirchliche Dogmatik* (Zollikon-Zürich: Evangelischer Verlag, 1945), 1(2):304. Cf. Barth, *Church Dogmatics*, ed. G. W. Bromiley and T. F. Torrance, trans. G. T. Thomson and Harold Knight (Edinburgh: T. & T. Clark, 1956), 1(2):280.

[16]Even Nietzsche held to the hope of a bright future when the superman will gain ascendancy. See Julian Roberts, *German Philosophy* (Atlantic Highlands, N.J.: Humanities Press International, 1988), pp. 213, 215, 223, 228, 232.

[17]For Tillich's concept of the latent church see his *Systematic Theology* (Chicago: University of Chicago Press, 1963), 3:152-56, 162, 181-82, 246-47.

[18]See François Wendel, *Calvin*, trans. Philip Mairet (London: Collins, 1963), pp. 263-84.

[19]See Carter Lindberg, *The Third Reformation?* (Macon, Ga.: Mercer University Press, 1983), p. 140.

[20]Ibid., p. 165.

[21]Barth's final view on the Christian life is articulated in *The Christian Life*, trans. Geoffrey W. Bromiley (Grand Rapids: Eerdmans, 1981). This book represents lecture fragments designed for *Church Dogmatics* 4(4).

[22]In the fuller view one could say that the cross of Christ signifies the objective culmination of salvation and the decision of faith the subjective culmination. The latter belongs to the unfolding of redemption and is not merely a confirmatory sign of redemption. At the same time, it is not the source or essence of redemption but the flower and fruit of redemption.

[23]For my earlier discussion see Bloesch, *Jesus Christ: Savior & Lord* (Downers Grove, Ill.: InterVarsity Press, 1997), pp. 148-58.

[24]I affirm the objectivity of Christ's mystical presence in the Eucharist but no automatic saving efficacy. If we partake of the sacrament without faith and repentance we will be eating and drinking judgment on ourselves (1 Cor 11:27-32).

[25]In this study I am using the term *rationalism* in the broad sense to include an appeal to empirical validation as well as to rational demonstration. The methods of both deduction and induction presuppose confidence in human rational faculties to come to truth. John Locke, a key figure in the early Enlightenment, was an ardent defender of empiricism and a vehement critic of innate ideas. At the same time, he viewed truth as lying in the affirmation or negation of propositions "which is no more but apprehending things to be as they really are and do exist." Frederick Copleston comments: "He was a rationalist in the sense that he believed in bringing all opinions and beliefs before the tribunal of reason and disliked the substitution of expressions of emotion and feeling for rationally grounded judgements." Copleston, *A History of Philosophy* (1963; reprint, New York: Doubleday, 1985), 5:69, 108.

The term *idealism* here denotes the position that views reality as fundamentally rational in nature and thereby accessible to rational investigation. It is possible to be both idealistic and empiricist (as was George Berkeley), but generally an idealist appeals to rational demonstration and an empiricist to experiential corroboration in arriving at truth.

[26]See Roger Olson, "Postconservative Evangelicals Greet the Postmodern Age," *Christian Century* 112, no. 15 (May 3, 1995): 480-83; Olson, "Back to the Bible (Almost): Why Yale's Postliberal Theologians Deserve an Evangelical Hearing," *Christianity Today* 40, no. 6 (May 20, 1996): 31-34; Nancey Murphy, *Beyond Liberalism and Fundamentalism* (Valley Forge, Penn.: Trinity Press International, 1996); and Timothy R. Phillips and Dennis L. Okholm, eds., *The Nature of Confession: Evangelicals and Postliberals in Conversation* (Downers Grove, Ill.: InterVarsity Press, 1996). It should be noted that some of the contributors to this last work have profound misgivings about postliberal theology. For an astute critique of narrative theology by an evangelical theologian who perceives its strengths as well as its weaknesses see Alister McGrath, *A Passion for Truth* (Downers Grove, Ill.: InterVarsity Press, 1996), pp. 119-61.

[27]See James Montgomery Boice and Benjamin E. Sasse, eds., *Here We Stand!* (Grand Rapids: Baker, 1996); and Michael Horton, *In The Face of God* (Dallas: Word, 1996). It is interesting to compare Horton's book and Clark Pinnock's *Flame of Love* (Downers Grove, Ill.: InterVarsity Press, 1996). The former defends traditionalist Calvinism while the latter is clearly postconservative.

[28]See Emil Brunner, *Truth as Encounter*, trans. Amandus W. Loos, David Cairns and T. H. L. Parker, 2nd ed. (Philadelphia: Westminster Press, 1964); Jaroslav Pelikan, *From Luther to Kierkegaard* (St. Louis: Concordia, 1950), pp. 49-96; Paul Tillich, *A History of Christian Thought*, ed. Carl E. Braaten (New York: Harper & Row, 1968), pp. 276-83; and Jack B. Rogers and Donald K. McKim, *The Authority and Interpretation of the Bible* (San Francisco: Harper & Row, 1979), pp. 147-99. Not all of these authors can be classified as neo-orthodox, but they all seek a fresh appropriation of the biblical and classical heritage of faith.

[29]William C. Placher, *The Domestication of Transcendence* (Louisville: Westmin-

ster John Knox, 1996), p. 79.

[30]Ibid., p. 87.

[31]See esp. *The Philosophy of Gordon H. Clark*, ed. Ronald H. Nash (Philadelphia: Presbyterian & Reformed, 1968), pp. 149-51; and Edward John Carnell, *An Introduction to Christian Apologetics* (Grand Rapids: Eerdmans, 1948), pp. 140-51.

[32]Thomas F. Torrance, *Karl Barth, Biblical and Evangelical Theologian* (Edinburgh: T. & T. Clark, 1990), pp. 221-22.

[33]Ibid.

[34]Ibid., p. 223.

[35]Ibid., p. 226.

[36]Ibid., p. 227

[37]Carl F. H. Henry, *God, Revelation and Authority* (Waco: Word, 1979), 4:456.

[38]Ibid., 2:74.

[39]George Hunsinger, "What Can Evangelicals and Postliberals Learn from Each Other?" in *Nature of Confession*, ed. Phillips and Okholm, pp. 134-50. See esp. pp. 146-49. Also see the poignant critique of Carl Henry and evangelical rationalism by Alister McGrath in his *Passion for Truth,* pp. 166-73.

[40]"Narrational theology" here refers to any position that holds that revelation comes to us primarily in the form of story or narrative. While it is roughly equivalent to "narrative theology," the latter most often refers to a particular school of theology (as "the Yale School" or "the Chicago School").

[41]See George A. Lindbeck, *The Nature of Doctrine: Religion and Theology in a Postliberal Age* (Philadelphia: Westminster Press, 1984).

[42]See Geiko Müller-Fahrenholz, *God's Spirit: Transforming a World in Crisis* (New York: Continuum, 1995), p. 4.

[43]Ibid., pp. 4-5.

[44]Ibid., p. 6.

[45]Richard Clutterbuck, "Jürgen Moltmann as a Doctrinal Theologian," *Scottish Journal of Theology* 48, no. 4 (1995): 494. See Moltmann, *The Church in the Power of the Spirit*, trans. Margaret Kohl (New York: Harper & Row, 1977), p. 225.

[46]Clutterbuck, "Moltmann as a Doctrinal Theologian," p. 494.

[47]Jürgen Moltmann, *The Trinity and the Kingdom*, trans. Margaret Kohl (San Francisco: Harper & Row, 1981), p. 190.

[48]See Donald G. Bloesch, *Jesus Christ: Savior & Lord* (Downers Grove, Ill.: InterVarsity Press, 1997), pp. 229-49.

[49]See Max Stackhouse's cogent critique of Stanley Hauerwas in "Liberalism Dispatched vs. Liberalism Engaged," *Christian Century* 112, no. 29 (Oct. 18, 1995): 962-67.

[50]Other philosophers who could be mentioned in this connection are Benedict Spinoza, who was staunchly idealistic, and Thomas Reid, who was more realistic.

[51]In gnostic tradition God is accessible not to theoretical reason but only to flashes of insight. God is not "thought thinking thought" (as in Aristotle) but

"the eternal silence" or "ineffable mystery."

[52]Cf. these words of the psalmist:

My people, listen to my teaching,
   pay attention to what I say.
I will speak to you in poetry,
   unfold the mysteries of the past. (Ps 78:1, 2 NJB)

[53]The conventional view is that while Plato used myth as a literary device to convey abstract truths, he remained more of a rationalist than a mystic. Nygren argues, however, that scholars are coming more and more to recognize that Plato's theory of knowledge rests on a primitive religious experience, the Dionysiac vision. See Anders Nygren, *Agape and Eros*, trans. Philip S. Watson (Philadelphia: Westminster Press, 1953), pp. 171-81.

[54]"Westminster Confession of Faith" (1:10) in Philip Schaff, *The Creeds of Christendom* (1877; reprint, New York: Harper & Bros., 1919), 3:605-6.

[55]See Thomas Aquinas, *Summa Theologica* I, 1.2 and 2 in fin.

[56]Eugene F. Rogers Jr., *Thomas Aquinas and Karl Barth: Sacred Doctrine and the Natural Knowledge of God* (Notre Dame: University of Notre Dame Press, 1995), p. 103.

[57]Ibid., p. 176.

[58]Cf. Norman L. Geisler, *Thomas Aquinas: An Evangelical Appraisal* (Grand Rapids: Baker, 1991).

[59]Pannenberg has been appreciated by a significant number of evangelical theologians including Stanley Grenz, Roger Olson and Millard Erickson. The Lutheran confessional theologian Carl Braaten has also had kind words for Pannenberg. Critics of Pannenberg include Robert Blaikie, Kenneth Hamilton, Paul Molnar and Donald Bloesch. For a pungent criticism of the early Pannenberg see Robert J. Blaikie, *"Secular Christianity" and God Who Acts* (Grand Rapids: Eerdmans, 1970), pp. 155-61, 206-9.

[60]Wolfhart Pannenberg, *Systematic Theology*, trans. Geoffrey W. Bromiley, (Grand Rapids: Eerdmans, 1991), 1:53.

[61]Paul D. Molnar, "Some Problems with Pannenberg's Solution to Barth's 'Faith Subjectivism,' " *Scottish Journal of Theology* 48, no. 3 (1995): 322.

[62]Ibid., p. 329.

[63]Pannenberg, *Systematic Theology,* 1:359.

[64]Colin E. Gunton, *A Brief Theology of Revelation* (Edinburgh: T. & T. Clark, 1995). Gunton's position is somewhat suspect when he claims that propositions have the capacity to "mediate revelation" (p. 105). He is convinced that the world, the Bible and sacred tradition also have this capacity. I would argue that the finite cannot of itself apprehend or communicate the infinite, but the infinite can enter into the finite and communicate itself. I concur with Gunton when he says that "revelation does not consist in . . . the transmission of authoritative propositions. Rather, Christianity is a revealed religion in the sense that essential to its being what it is, is its articulation by means of affirmations and confessions in which are implicit certain claims about what is true of God, the world and human life" (p. 17). Interestingly, Gunton warns

against narrative theology on the grounds that it is "too tied to the old 'history of salvation' theology which tends to exclude due reference to creation" (p. 112).

[65]Thomas Aquinas, *Summa Theologica,* II–II, 1.2 ad 2. It is well to note that Benjamin Warfield, in whom rationalist tendencies were conspicuous, came to a similar conclusion: "The revelations of the Scriptures do not terminate upon the intellect. They were not given merely to enlighten the mind. They were given through the intellect to beautify the life. They terminate on the heart." Warfield nonetheless envisaged revelation as fundamentally propositional in content. *Selected Shorter Writings of Benjamin B. Warfield,* ed. John E. Meeter, (Nutley, N.J.: Presbyterian and Reformed, 1973), 2:671.

[66]Jacob Neusner, *The Ecology of Religion: From Writing to Religion in the Study of Judaism* (Nashville: Abingdon, 1989).

[67]Ibid., pp. 54-57.

[68]Ibid., p. 55.

[69]Ibid., p. 56.

[70]Ibid., p. 57.

[71]See Charles Hodge, *Systematic Theology,* (New York: Charles Scribner's Sons, 1914), 1:10. For a succinct exposition of the Princeton School of Theology (Archibald Alexander, Charles Hodge, A. A. Hodge, Benjamin Warfield) see Rogers and McKim, *Authority and Interpretation of the Bible,* pp. 265-379.

[72]The theology of crisis that I endorse is focused not on the negativities of history but on God's judgment over history that we see in Jesus Christ. The early Barth tended to envisage cultural upheavals as the medium of God's revelation, and therefore one could say that he was still working with liberal assumptions. By the time of his second edition of *Romans,* however, he viewed the crises of the time not as mediating the word of divine judgment but as directing us to the divine judgment over all humanity that occurred in the life and death of Jesus Christ. "Crisis" became for Barth in the second edition of *Romans* a basically christological rather than sociological category (as with his colleague Friedrich Gogarten). See Bruce L. McCormack, *Karl Barth's Critically Realistic Dialectical Theology: Its Genesis and Development 1909-1936* (Oxford: Clarendon, 1995), pp. 116-17, 156, 212-13, 214-16, 224-25, 284-85.

[73]Langdon Gilkey, "Nature, Religion and the Sacred." Address to American Theological Society, University of Chicago Divinity School, November 3, 1989.

[74]*Jeremy Taylor: Selected Works,* ed. Thomas K. Carroll (New York: Paulist, 1990), pp. 374, 371. For the evangelical thrust of Taylor's spirituality see H. Trevor Hughes, *The Piety of Jeremy Taylor* (London: Macmillan, 1960), pp. 153-72.

[75]See Rogers and McKim's helpful analysis of Warfield on this matter in their *Authority and Interpretation of the Bible,* pp. 323-61. For my critique of this book see Donald Bloesch, *Holy Scripture* (Downers Grove, Ill.: InterVarsity Press, 1994), pp. 131-40.

[76]Cf. Carnell, *Introduction to Christian Apologetics,* pp. 70, 365; and *Christian Commitment: An Apologetic* (1957; reprint, Grand Rapids: Baker, 1982), pp. 76-78. Note that Carnell differentiates between "generic faith" and "saving faith,"

though the second will include the first.

Chapter Two
[1]For my discussion of Joachimism in this volume see pp. 89-90.
[2]See Léon Joseph Cardinal Suenens, *A New Pentecost?* (New York: Seabury, 1975).
[3]Cited in Stanley M. Burgess, *The Spirit and the Church: Antiquity* (Peabody, Mass.: Hendrickson, 1984), p. 6.
[4]See Friedrich Schleiermacher, *The Christian Faith*, ed. H. R. Mackintosh and J. S. Stewart, (1928; reprint, New York: Harper & Row, 1963), 2:560-85.
[5]See my discussion in this volume on pp. 260-64.
[6]Amy Plantinga Pauw, "Who or What Is the Holy Spirit?" *Christian Century* 113, no. 2 (Jan. 17, 1996): 48.
[7]Ibid.
[8]See H. Shelton Smith, *Faith and Nurture* (New York: Charles Scribner's Sons, 1941).
[9]See William James, *The Varieties of Religious Experience* (1902; reprint, New York: Penguin, 1985), pp. 80ff.
[10]See Clark H. Pinnock, *Flame of Love* (Downers Grove, Ill.: InterVarsity Press, 1996), p. 68. Pinnock regards the Spirit as a divine person within a social Trinity but explores various metaphors to denote this reality.
[11]Quoted in Yves Corgar, *I Believe in the Holy Spirit,* trans. David Smith (New York: Seabury, 1983) 3:88-89. Cf. Paul Evdokimov, *The Art of the Icon: A Theology of Beauty,* trans. Steven Bigham (Redonde Beach, Calif.: Oakwood Publications, 1990), p. 254.
[12]H. Wheeler Robinson, *The Christian Experience of the Holy Spirit* (London: James Nisbet, 1928).
[13]Hendrikus Berkhof, *The Doctrine of the Holy Spirit* (1964; reprint, Richmond: John Knox Press, 1967), pp. 109-21.
[14]Philip J. Rosato, *The Spirit as Lord: The Pneumatology of Karl Barth* (Edinburgh: T. & T. Clark, 1981).
[15]J. H. E. Hull, *The Holy Spirit in the Acts of the Apostles* (London: Lutterworth, 1967), pp. 90-91.
[16]Cf. G. W. H. Lampe, *The Seal of the Spirit* (1951; reprint, New York: Longmans, Green, 1956); Frederick Dale Bruner, *A Theology of the Holy Spirit* (Grand Rapids: Eerdmans, 1970); Richard A. Jensen, *Touched by the Spirit* (Minneapolis: Augsburg, 1975); Michael Green, *I Believe in the Holy Spirit* (Grand Rapids: Eerdmans, 1975); and Pinnock, *Flame of Love.*
[17]Congar, *I Believe in the Holy Spirit*, 2:192.
[18]See Markus Barth, "Baptism and Evangelism," *Scottish Journal of Theology* 12, no. 1 (March, 1959): 32-40; *Die Taufe—ein Sakrament?* (Zollikon-Zürich: Evangelischer Verlag, 1951); and Karl Barth, *Church Dogmatics*, ed. G. W. Bromiley and T. F. Torrance, trans. G. W. Bromiley (Edinburgh: T. & T. Clark, 1969), 4(4).
[19]James D. G. Dunn, *Baptism in the Holy Spirit,* Studies in Biblical Theology 2/15 (London: SCM Press, 1970).

[20]David Pawson, *The Normal Christian Birth* (London: Hodder & Stoughton, 1989), p. 165.

[21]In Simon Tugwell, *Did You Receive the Spirit?* (New York: Paulist, 1972), p. 52.

[22]See George A. Maloney, *The Mystic of Fire and Light: St. Symeon the New Theologian* (Denville, N.J.: Dimension Books, 1975), pp. 56-58.

[23]Kevin and Dorothy Ranaghan, *Catholic Pentecostals* (New York: Paulist, 1969), p. 20.

[24]See Stanley M. Burgess, *The Holy Spirit: Eastern Christian Traditions* (Peabody, Mass.: Hendrickson, 1989), p. 99.

[25]Maloney, *Mystic of Fire and Light*, pp. 127-28.

[26]Tugwell, *Did You Receive the Spirit?* p. 106.

[27]Ibid., p. 116.

[28]Ibid., p. 106.

[29]See Bruner, *Theology of the Holy Spirit*, pp. 139-40, 314-19.

[30]See Alister E. McGrath, *Iustitia Dei: A History of the Christian Doctrine of Justification* (New York: Cambridge University Press, 1986), 1:23-36. See esp. p. 34.

[31]Congar, *I Believe in the Holy Spirit,* 3:65. See *Gregory Palamas: The Triads,* ed. John Meyendorff, trans. Nicholas Gendle (New York: Paulist, 1983).

[32]See Regin Prenter, *Spiritus Creator*, trans. John M. Jensen (Philadelphia: Fortress, 1953), pp. 228-37; and Arthur Crabtree, *The Restored Relationship* (Valley Forge, Penn.: Judson Press, 1963), pp. 165, 186.

[33]See R. C. Sproul, *Faith Alone: The Evangelical Doctrine of Justification* (Grand Rapids: Baker, 1995).

[34]The Joint Declaration on the Doctrine of Justification (Oct. 31, 1999), signed by representatives of the Roman Catholic Church and the Lutheran World Federation, might suggest the emergence of a new ecumenical consensus on this volatile issue. While both sides should welcome this statement, neither should be overly confident. It is well to recognize that Roman Catholics have not adopted the Reformation position, but they have tried to build bridges to that tradition. For the diverse reaction of evangelicals and other Christians to the declaration, see *Pro Ecclesia* 7, no. 4 (Autumn 1998); Douglas A. Sweeney, "Taming the Reformation," *Christianity Today* 44, no. 1 (Jan. 10, 2000): 63-65; and "On Earth Peace?" *World* 14, no 50 (Dec 25, 1999-Jan. 1, 2000): 16-21.

[35]For my earlier discussion see Bloesch, *Holy Scripture* (Downers Grove, Ill.: InterVarsity Press, 1994), pp. 85-92.

[36]Paul M. Quay, *The Mystery Hidden for Ages in God* (New York: Peter Lang, 1995), p. 417.

[37]Cf. Walter E. Stuermann, *A Critical Study of Calvin's Concept of Faith*, lithoprinted (Ann Arbor: Edwards Brothers, 1952); and Colin Gunton, *A Brief Theology of Revelation* (Edinburgh: T. & T. Clark, 1995), pp. 9, 83-87.

[38]Moreover, Calvin was convinced that "in heavenly mysteries the whole power of the human mind disappears and fails." Calvin, *The Gospel According to St. John*, trans. T. H. L. Parker, ed. David W. Torrance and Thomas F. Torrance (Grand Rapids: Eerdmans, 1959), 1:174.

[39]See Thomas A. Smail, *Reflected Glory* (Grand Rapids: Eerdmans, 1975). On the Toronto Blessing see Bill Randles, *Weighed and Found Wanting: Putting the Toronto Blessing in Context* (Cedar Rapids, Iowa: n.p., n.d.); Lloyd Pietersen, ed., *Mark of the Spirit? A Charismatic Critique of the "Blessing" Phenomenon* (Carlisle, Penn.: Paternoster, 1998); and B. J. Oropeza, *A Time to Laugh: The Holy Laughter Phenomenon Examined* (Peabody, Mass.: Hendrickson, 1995).

[40]Cited in Burgess, *The Spirit and the Church: Antiquity*, p. 6.

[41]Léon Joseph Cardinal Suenens, *New Pentecost?*

[42]For a cogent contemporary defense of the traditional Reformed position see Sinclair B. Ferguson, *The Holy Spirit* (Downers Grove, Ill.: InterVarsity Press, 1996), pp. 207-39. For a penetrating critique of modern Protestant cessationism—that the extraordinary gifts have ceased with the passing of the apostles—see Max Turner, *The Holy Spirit and Spiritual Gifts in the New Testament Church and Today* (1996; rev. ed., Peabody, Mass.: Hendrickson, 1998), pp. 286-302.

[43]Burgess, *The Holy Spirit: Eastern Christian Traditions*, pp. 172-75.

[44]See the discussion in Daphne Hampson, *Theology and Feminism* (Cambridge, Mass.: Basil Blackwell, 1990), pp. 92-96.

[45]Gary Steven Kinkel, *Our Dear Mother the Spirit: An Investigation of Count Zinzendorf's Theology and Praxis* (Lanham, Md.: University Press of America, 1990), p. 89.

[46]Elizabeth A. Johnson, *She Who Is* (New York: Crossroad, 1992).

[47]Jürgen Moltmann, *Spirit of Life,* trans. Margaret Kohl (Minneapolis: Fortress, 1992), p. 157.

[48]Geiko Müller-Fahrenholz, *God's Spirit: Transforming a World in Crisis* (New York: Continuum, 1995), p. 82.

[49]Edward Schillebeeckx and Catherina Halkes, *Mary: Yesterday, Today, Tomorrow,* trans. John Bowden (New York: Crossroad, 1993), p. 28.

[50]Donald L. Gelpi, *The Divine Mother: A Trinitarian Theology of the Holy Spirit* (Lanham, Md.: University Press of America, 1984).

[51]See Alvin F. Kimel Jr., ed., *Speaking the Christian God: The Holy Trinity and the Challenge of Feminism* (Grand Rapids: Eerdmans, 1992); John Cooper, *Our Father in Heaven: Christian Faith and Inclusive Language for God* (Grand Rapids: Baker, 1998); and Donald G. Bloesch, *The Battle for the Trinity* (Ann Arbor: Servant, 1985).

[52]Thomas Hopko, "Apophatic Theology and the Naming of God in Eastern Orthodox Tradition," in *Speaking the Christian God,* ed. Kimel, p. 161. Interestingly another theologian speaking out of the perspective of Orthodoxy, Emmanuel Clapsis, argues that "the very incomprehensibility of God demands a proliferation of images, and a variety of names, each of which acts as a corrective against the tendency of any particular one to become reified and literal." Emmanuel Clapsis, "Naming God: An Orthodox View" in *Constructive Christian Theology in the Worldwide Church,* ed. William R. Barr (Grand Rapids: Eerdmans, 1997), p. 126.

[53]Congar, *I Believe in the Holy Spirit,* 3:157.

⁵⁴Ibid., 2:219.

⁵⁵In Amy Plantinga Pauw, "Who or What Is the Holy Spirit?" p. 49.

⁵⁶Ibid.

⁵⁷Ibid., p. 48.

⁵⁸Yves Congar, *The Word and the Spirit*, trans. David Smith (London: Geoffrey Chapman, 1986), p. 126.

⁵⁹See Karl Barth, *Church Dogmatics,* ed. G. W. Bromiley and T. F. Torrance, trans. G. W. Bromiley (Edinburgh: T. & T. Clark, 1961), 4(3/1): 89-97, 114-15, 118, 122, 355-56, 478.

Chapter Three

¹James Dunn contends that John's baptism in the Jordan is a graphic symbol of the coming baptism in the Spirit and fire—"God's fiery *pneuma* like a great stream through which all men must pass." In *The New International Dictionary of New Testament Theology,* ed. Colin Brown (Grand Rapids: Zondervan, 1975-1978), 3:695. See Dunn's helpful discussion on the integral relation of fire and Spirit in this same section. For pertinent biblical passages see Is 4:4-5; Mt 3:7-12; Lk 3:15-17; 12:49-50.

²See Rudolf Bultmann, *Theology of the New Testament*, trans. Kendrick Grobel (New York: Charles Scribner's Sons, 1951-1955), 1:155-63. Also see Hans Küng, *The Church*, trans. Ray and Rosaleen Ockenden (New York: Sheed & Ward, 1967), pp. 163-64.

³One scholar sees in the quasi-personal agencies operating on humans a survival from Israel's animistic past. R. Birch Hoyle, "Spirit (Holy), Spirit of God," in *Encyclopaedia of Religion and Ethics,* ed. James Hastings (New York: Charles Scribner's Sons, 1920), 11:784-803. See esp. p. 785. Hoyle refers to Stade, *Biblische Theologie des Alten Testaments* (Tübingen: Mohr, 1905), p. 99.

⁴See Alasdair I. C. Heron, *The Holy Spirit* (Philadelphia: Westminster Press, 1983), pp. 17-20.

⁵Ibid., p. 9.

⁶It should be recognized that these two views often blend into one another in early Israel. The energy or power that confronts us from without is most often a psychic or spiritual power. "The wind of heaven in its mighty, mysterious, quasi-personal activity is very similar to the action of 'spirits', and both suggest the miraculous, supersensible power which streams through nature and into human life with such startling effects." R. Birch Hoyle, *Encyclopaedia of Religion and Ethics*, ed. Hastings, 11:786. In primitive religion there is no cleavage between the animate and the inanimate.

⁷For an insightful discussion of animism, animatism, totemism, fetishism and demonology see Leslie Spier, "Primitive Religion," in *Collier's Encyclopaedia*, ed. Lauren S. Bahr and Bernard Johnston (New York: P. F. Collier, 1994), 19:355-60.

⁸Hans Küng maintains with some plausibility that both animism and dynamism are superseded in the New Testament. Küng, *On Being a Christian*, trans. Edward Quinn (New York: Doubleday, 1976), pp. 469-72.

⁹Bultmann, *The Gospel of John: A Commentary*, trans. G. R. Beasley-Murray, ed. R. W. N. Hoare and J. K. Riches (Philadelphia: Westminster Press, 1971), p. 191.

¹⁰Joseph E. Fison, *Fire Upon the Earth* (London: Edinburgh House Press, 1958), p. 1.

¹¹See Cuthbert A. Simpson, "Exegesis of Genesis," in *Interpreter's Bible*, ed. G. A. Buttrick (New York: Abingdon-Cokesbury, 1952), 1:466-67.

¹²New Testament texts that associate wisdom and the Spirit include Acts 6:3, 10; 1 Cor 12:8; Eph 1:17.

¹³John 3:5 is sometimes taken to imply a feminine activity of the Spirit. Raymond Brown has this astute comment: "The passive of the verb *gennan* can mean either 'to be born,' as of a feminine principle, or 'to be begotten,' as of a masculine principle; the same two meanings are possible for the Hebrew root *yld*. The early versions took *gennan* here in the sense 'to be born,' and, more precisely, in the OL, 'to be reborn.' . . . Despite the fact that the Spirit, mentioned in vs. 5 as the agent of this birth or begetting, is feminine in Hebrew (neuter in Greek), the primary meaning seems to be 'begotten.' In the Gospels there is no attribution of feminine characteristics to the Spirit; and there are Johannine parallels that clearly refer to being begotten rather than being born (i 12; I John iii 9)." Brown, *The Gospel According to John,* Anchor Bible (Garden City, N.Y.: Doubleday, 1966-1970), 1:130.

¹⁴For my earlier discussion of gender in God see Bloesch, *God the Almighty* (Downers Grove, Ill.: InterVarsity Press, 1995), pp. 25-27; and *Jesus Christ: Savior & Lord* (Downers Grove, Ill.: InterVarsity Press, 1997), pp. 75-79. Also see my *Battle for the Trinity* (Ann Arbor: Servant, 1985).

¹⁵*Interpreter's Bible,* 1:722-28.

¹⁶See my discussion on pp. 310-11 of this book.

¹⁷Albert Schweitzer, *The Mysticism of Paul the Apostle*, trans. William Montgomery (1931; reprint, New York: Macmillan, 1956), p. 360.

¹⁸Lampe suggests that Apollos received "a direct commission from the Lord" which "conferred upon him the Spirit, for he ranked very high among the apostles, being regarded by the Corinthians as standing approximately upon the same level as St. Peter or St. Paul." G. W. H. Lampe, *The Seal of the Spirit* (London: Longmans, Green, 1951), p. 66.

¹⁹F. F. Bruce, *Commentary on the Epistle to the Hebrews,* New International Commentary on the New Testament (Grand Rapids: Eerdmans, 1964), p. 20.

²⁰See Lampe, *Seal of the Spirit*, pp. 120-21.

²¹G. R. Beasley-Murray, *Baptism in the New Testament* (London: Macmillan, 1962), p. 265.

²²Not all charismatic or ecstatic prophets were condemned by the leading prophets of Israel, for some were truly messengers of the Lord. See Joseph Mihelic, "The Function of *Ruach Yahweh* in the Old Testament" (unpublished paper, Dubuque Theological Seminary archives, n.d.). Mihelic includes in the category of ecstatic prophets Deborah, Samuel, Gad, Nathan, Ahijah, Jehu ben Hanani, Elijah, Elisha and Micaiah ben Imlah.

²³See R. P. C. Hanson, *The Attractiveness of God: Essays in Christian Doctrine*

(Richmond: John Knox Press, 1973), p. 120.

[24]Ibid., p. 121

[25]Hendrikus Berkhof, *The Doctrine of the Holy Spirit* (Richmond: John Knox Press, 1964), pp. 13-29.

[26]See Jürgen Moltmann, *The Church in the Power of the Spirit*, trans. Margaret Kohl (New York: Harper & Row, 1977), pp. 236-38.

[27]See my earlier discussion on pp. 34-47.

Chapter Four

[1]Rudolf Sohm, noted jurist and Protestant church historian, presents a credible case that the charisma of the New Testament church was eclipsed by growing ritualism and legalism in the postapostolic church. See his *Outlines of Church History*, trans. May Sinclair (Boston: Beacon, 1958), esp. James Luther Adams's introduction, pp. ix-xv. In Sohm's view the sacred power was first identified with charisma, then with office and finally with sacrament. His judgment that the church in apostolic times was wholly lacking in structure and hierarchy is open to question.

[2]See A. W. Argyle, "Baptism in the Early Christian Centuries," in *Christian Baptism,* ed. A. Gilmore (London: Lutterworth, 1959), p. 197.

[3]Irenaeus *Adversus haereses* 4.20.1. See discussion in Alasdair I. C. Heron, *The Holy Spirit* (Philadelphia: Westminster Press, 1983), pp. 64-67.

[4]Tertullian *On Baptism* 6, cited in Michael Harper, *As at the Beginning* (London: Hodder & Stoughton, 1969), p. 100.

[5]Tertullian *On Baptism* 20. See Simon Tugwell, *Did You Receive the Spirit?* (New York: Paulist, 1972), p. 76.

[6]G. W. H. Lampe, *The Seal of the Spirit* (London: Longmans, Green, 1951), pp. 156-57.

[7]Cited in Father Farrell, *The Parish Catechism* (Chicago: United Book Service, 1954), p. 69. See the discussion in Lampe, *Seal of the Spirit*, pp. 170-78.

[8]Cyprian. *Ep.* 74. 5. See Jaroslav Pelikan, *The Christian Tradition* (Chicago: University of Chicago Press, 1971), 1:166.

[9]Cyril of Jerusalem *Catechetical Lectures* 3.14, in *The Works of Saint Cyril of Jerusalem*, trans. Leo P. McCauley and Anthony A. Stephenson (Washington, D.C.: Catholic University of America Press, 1969), 1:116.

[10]Cyril of Jerusalem *Catechetical Lectures* 5.11, in McCauley and Stephenson, *Works of Saint Cyril,* 1:145.

[11]St. Basil the Great, *On the Holy Spirit* (Crestwood, N.Y.: St. Vladimir's Seminary Press, 1980), 12.28 (p. 50).

[12]Quoted in Lampe, *Seal of the Spirit*, p. 237.

[13]See Hans Küng's discussion in *Why Priests?* trans. Robert C. Collins (New York: Doubleday, 1972), pp. 63-66.

[14]Augustine *De bapt.* 4.22, 29. Cited in Burkhard Neunheuser, *Baptism and Confirmation*, trans. John Jay Hughes (New York: Herder & Herder, 1964), p. 122.

[15]See Neunheuser, *Baptism and Confirmation*, pp. 116-34.

[16]Lampe, *Seal of the Spirit*, p. 248.

[17]Cited in J. Gilchrist Lawson, *Deeper Experiences of Famous Christians* (Anderson, Ind.: Warner, 1911), p. 63. Cf. Neunheuser, *Baptism and Confirmation*, p. 133.

[18]Tugwell, *Did You Receive the Spirit?* p. 86. See Thomas Aquinas *Summa Theologica* 3a q. 66. a.11.

[19]*Veni, Creator Spiritus* in *Service Book and Hymnal* (1958; reprint, Minneapolis: Augsburg, 1961), no. 117.

[20]*The Book of Catholic Worship* (Washington, D.C.: Liturgical Conference, 1966), p. 734.

[21]Ibid., p. 735.

[22]See Joseph Martos, *Doors to the Sacred: A Historical Introduction to Sacraments in the Catholic Church* (1981; rev. ed., Liguori, Mo.: Triumph Books, 1991), p. 198; *Catechism of the Catholic Church* (United States Catholic Conference, 1994), p. 333.

[23]Tugwell, *Did You Receive the Spirit?* p. 96.

[24]*The Works of Bernard of Clairvaux* (Spencer, Mass.: Cistercian Publications, 1970), 1:144.

[25]Quoted in H. B. Swete, *The Holy Spirit in the Ancient Church* (1912; reprint, Grand Rapids: Baker, 1966), p. 262.

[26]See Ronald A. Knox, *Enthusiasm* (New York: Oxford University Press, 1951).

[27]See Walter Schmithals, *Paul and the Gnostics*, trans. John E. Steely (Nashville: Abingdon, 1972), p. 97.

[28]See Elaine Pagels, *The Gnostic Gospels* (New York: Random House, 1979); Kurt Rudolph, *Gnosis*, trans. Robert McLachlan Wilson (San Francisco: Harper & Row, 1983); and Alastair H. B. Logan, *Gnostic Truth and Christian Heresy* (Peabody, Mass.: Hendrickson, 1996).

[29]Hippolytus *Refutationis Omnium Haeresium* 8.15.1-2. Cited in Pagels, *Gnostic Gospels*, p. xix.

[30]Pagels, *Gnostic Gospels,* p. 134.

[31]See *The Confessions of St. Augustine*, trans. and ed. John K. Ryan (New York: Doubleday Image, 1960), pp. 20-21.

[32]*Encyclopaedia Britannica*, ed. Robert McHenry (Chicago: University of Chicago Press, 1993), 14:784.

[33]Hans Jonas, *The Gnostic Religion* (Boston: Beacon, 1963), pp. 207-8.

[34]See Jaroslav Pelikan, *The Finality of Jesus Christ in an Age of Universal History: A Dilemma of the Third Century* (Richmond: John Knox Press, 1966), pp. 38-47; and Christine Trevett, *Montanism: Gender, Authority & the New Prophecy* (Cambridge: Cambridge University Press, 1996).

[35]Knox, *Enthusiasm*, p. 52.

[36]See Paul Tillich, *A History of Christian Thought* (New York: Harper & Row, 1968), pp. 131-33.

[37]See *Encyclopaedia Britannica,* 2:324-25; and Robert I. Moore, *The Origins of European Dissent* (New York: St. Martin's Press, 1977), pp. 151-67.

[38]See Tillich, *History of Christian Thought*, pp. 175-80, 205-6; and Philip Schaff, *History of the Christian Church* (Grand Rapids: Eerdmans, 1949-

1957), 5:373-78.

[39]The Joachim vision of a new age of the Spirit is also reflected in Marxism, National Socialism (which heralded the "Third Reich") and the New Age movement, with its "Third Wave."

[40]See Stanley M. Burgess, *The Holy Spirit: Medieval Roman Catholic and Reformation Traditions* (Peabody, Mass.: Hendrickson, 1997), pp. 134-40.

[41]Closely related groups were the Brethren of the Common Life and the Brethren of the Free Spirit. For all of these movements see Philip Schaff, *History of the Christian Church*, 6:269-84, 499-500.

[42]The Flemish mystic John of Ruysbroeck (b. 1273) echoed the mystical vision when he declared that the way to know God is to enter into ourselves in a simple manner where we meet God "without intermediary." *Adornment of the Spiritual Marriage*, trans. C. A. Wynschenk Dom, ed. Evelyn Underhill (London: J. M. Dent & Sons, 1916), p. 150.

[43]Even those mystics who teach the deification of the human person through faith are quick to emphasize that in this process our humanity is not cancelled but instead transfigured. At the same time, the lines between mysticism and enthusiasm are not always distinct, and some mystics can also justly be categorized as enthusiasts.

[44]*Meister Eckhart*, ed. Raymond Blakney (New York: Harper, 1941), p. 127. Note that not all the sermons in Blakney's collection are really from Eckhart, but they may be from his disciples. For a more authentic rendition of Eckhart see Edmund Colledge and Bernard McGinn, eds., *Meister Eckhart* (New York: Paulist, 1981); James M. Clark and John V. Skinner, *Treatises and Sermons of Meister Eckhart* (New York: Harper, 1958); and Matthew Fox, ed., *Breakthrough: Meister Eckhart's Creation Spirituality in New Translation* (New York: Doubleday Image, 1980).

[45]*Meister Eckhart*, ed. Blakney, p. 198.

[46]Note that in Symeon's view if genuine conversion is lacking, one undergoes a baptism only with water. What makes one a Christian is the "second baptism," that "of the Spirit," which is manifest in tears. Others who referred to a baptism of tears are John Climacus, Isaac the Syrian, Margery Kempe, John Cassian, Gregory the Great and Peter Damian.

[47]Anders Nygren, *Agape and Eros*, trans. Philip S. Watson (Philadelphia: Westminster Press, 1953), p. 596.

[48]St. Bernard, *Sermons for the Seasons and Principal Festivals of the Year* (Westminster, Md.: Carroll Press, 1950), 2:315.

[49]*Meister Eckhart*, ed. Blakney, pp. 14, 16. See Bernard McGinn's comments on Eckhart's spirituality in *Meister Eckhart*, ed. and trans. Colledge and McGinn, pp. 60-61.

[50]John of the Cross, *Ascent of Mount Carmel*, trans. and ed. E. Allison Peers (New York: Doubleday Image, 1958), prologue, p. 13.

[51]Brother Lawrence, *The Practice of the Presence of God* (Old Tappan, N.J.: Revell, 1958), pp. 62-63.

[52]Ibid., pp. 42-43.

[53]The leading Quietists in the seventeenth century were Madame Guyon, M. de Molinos and François Fénelon. Quietism was condemned by the Roman Catholic Church in 1687.

[54]François Fénelon, *Talking with God*, trans. Hal M. Helms (Brewster, Mass.: Paraclete Press, 1997), p. 91.

[55]Ibid., p. 90.

[56]See n. 46 above.

[57]See Schaff, *History of the Christian Church,* 5:370-73.

[58]See Walter Nigg, *Great Saints*, trans. William Stirling (Hinsdale, Ill.: Henry Regnery, 1948), pp. 91-116.

[59]Even so, Teresa remained adamant that "the highest perfection does not consist in feelings of spiritual bliss nor in great ecstasies or visions nor yet in the spirit of prophecy, but in bringing your will into conformity with that of God." Stephen Clissold, *The Wisdom of the Spanish Mystics* (New York: New Directions, 1977), p. 76.

[60]See Eddie Ensley, *Sounds of Wonder* (New York: Paulist, 1977).

[61]*The Cloud of Unknowing and the Book of Privy Counseling*, ed. William Johnston (New York: Doubleday Image, 1973), p. 91.

[62]See *Meister Eckhart*, ed. Blakney, p. 139.

[63]*The Art of Prayer: An Orthodox Anthology,* comp. Igumen Chariton of Valamo, trans. E. Kadloubovsky and E. M. Palmer, ed. Timothy Ware (London: Faber & Faber, 1966), p. 174.

[64]The more perspicacious theologians would say we are co-redeemers *in* Christ.

[65]Lev Gillet, *Orthodox Spirituality: An Outline of the Orthodox Ascetical and Mystical Tradition* (London: SPCK, 1961), p. 63.

[66]Ibid., p. 62.

[67]John of Ruysbroeck, *Adornment of the Spiritual Marriage*, p. 171; *The Book of Supreme Truth,* in *The Adornment of the Spiritual Marriage,* trans. C. A. Wynschenk Dom, ed. Evelyn Underhill (London: J. M. Dent & Sons, 1916), p. 241.

[68]See *Breakthrough*, ed. Fox, pp. 55–74.

Chapter Five

[1]*Luther's Works*, ed. Jaroslav Pelikan, trans. Martin H. Bertram (St. Louis: Concordia, 1957), 22:287.

[2]Hugh Thomson Kerr Jr., ed., *A Compend of Luther's Theology* (Philadelphia: Westminster Press, 1943), p. 165.

[3]On Calvin's position on the preparation of the heart see Norman Pettit, *The Heart Prepared: Grace and Conversion in Puritan Spiritual Life* (New Haven: Yale University Press, 1966), pp. 42-44.

[4]John Calvin, *Institutes of the Christian Religion*, ed. John T. McNeill, trans. Ford Lewis Battles, 2 vols. (Philadelphia: Westminster Press, 1960), 3.1.1 (1:538).

[5]Ibid., p. 542.

[6]John Calvin, *Sermons on the Saving Work of Christ*, trans. Leroy Nixon (1950; reprint, Grand Rapids: Baker, 1980), p. 263.

[7]John Calvin, *Commentary upon the Acts of the Apostles*, ed. Henry Beveridge

(Edinburgh: Calvin Translation Society, 1844), 1:121.

[8]See my further discussion on pp. 294-97.

[9]Calvin, *Commentary upon Acts*, 1:121. Calvin is clear that the gift of the Spirit brings salvation and entrance into the kingdom of God as well as charisms for service (see p. 85).

[10]Calvin, *Sermons on the Saving Work of Christ*, p. 263. For an interesting discussion on how some of Calvin's insights on the gift of the Spirit can be appropriated by Pentecostals see J. Rodman Williams, *Renewal Theology* (Grand Rapids: Zondervan, 1990), 2:205-6.

[11]Cited in Geoffrey W. Bromiley, *Historical Theology: An Introduction* (Grand Rapids: Eerdmans, 1978), p. 277.

[12]Ibid., p. 278.

[13]On Melanchthon's intellectualizing of faith see Jaroslav Pelikan, *From Luther to Kierkegaard* (St. Louis: Concordia, 1950), pp. 24-43.

[14]For Pannenberg's perceptive critique of Melanchthon in this area of theology see Wolfhart Pannenberg, *Systematic Theology*, trans. Geoffrey W. Bromiley (Grand Rapids: Eerdmans, 1998), 3:225-27, 233-34. Pannenberg notes that Melanchthon failed to give proper recognition to the integral relation between justification and water baptism.

[15]Philip Melanchthon, *Apology of the Augsburg Confession* (article 4) in *The Book of Concord*, trans. and ed. Theodore G. Tappert (Philadelphia: Fortress, 1959), p. 152.

[16]See R. T. Kendall, *Calvin and English Calvinism to 1649* (London: Oxford University Press, 1979), p. 35.

[17]See Hans Küng's discussion in *The Church*, trans. Ray and Rosaleen Ockenden (New York: Sheed & Ward, 1967), pp. 194-95.

[18]See Carter Lindberg, *The Third Reformation? Charismatic Movements and the Lutheran Tradition* (Macon, Ga.: Mercer University Press, 1983), pp. 57-74.

[19]*Westminster Dictionary of Church History*, ed. Jerald C. Brauer (Philadelphia: Westminster Press, 1971), p. 160.

[20]On Luther's repudiation of Karlstadt see Walter Sundberg, "A Primer on the Devil," *First Things* 29 (Jan. 1993): 16-17. Sundberg maintains that in Karlstadt the individual conscience becomes the sole criterion of faith.

[21]Some of these men could also be categorized as Spiritualists, since they elevated the Spirit over the Bible.

[22]See Kenneth Ronald Davis, *Anabaptism and Asceticism* (Scottdale, Penn.: Herald, 1974), p. 164.

[23]See George H. Williams, *The Radical Reformation* (Philadelphia: Westminster Press, 1962), pp. 51, 382-83, 858-59.

[24]*Luther's Works*, ed. Abdel Ross Wentz (Philadelphia: Muhlenberg, 1959), 36:91.

[25]*Luther's Works*, ed. Eric W. Gritsch, trans. Charles M. Jacobs (Philadelphia: Fortress, 1966), 41:114.

[26]Calvin, *Institutes*, trans. Battles, 4.19.8 (2:1457).

[27]See Calvin, *The Gospel According to St. John*, trans. T. H. L. Parker, ed. David W. Torrance and Thomas F. Torrance (Grand Rapids: Eerdmans, 1959), 1:30,

64-67.

[28]See Max Thurian, *Consecration of the Layman*, trans. W. J. Kerrigan (Baltimore: Helicon, 1963), pp. 1-9, 65-68.

[29]See Lindberg, *Third Reformation?* p. 273.

[30]Luther, WA 22:182, 38-183, 10. Cf. also WA 41:655, 5ff. See Lindberg, *Third Reformation?* p. 275.

[31]Calvin, "The Catechism of the Church of Geneva," in *Calvin: Theological Treatises,* ed. J. K. S. Reid (Philadelphia: Westminster Press, 1954), p. 133.

[32]Calvin, *Sermons on the Saving Work of Christ*, p. 257.

[33]John Calvin, *Sermons on the Epistle to the Ephesians* (Edinburgh: Banner of Truth Trust, 1973), p. 550.

[34]Sometimes Calvin had in mind the so-called seven gifts of the Spirit in Is 11:1-2, which are promised to every believer.

[35]Calvin, *Sermons on Ephesians*, p. 364.

[36]Calvin, *Institutes*, trans. Battles, 4.19.19 (2:1467).

[37]Calvin, *Commentary on a Harmony of the Evangelists, Matthew, Mark, and Luke,* trans. William Pringle (Edinburgh: Calvin Translation Society, 1846), 3:389.

[38]See Williams, *Radical Reformation*, p. 443; and Franklin H. Littell, *The Origins of Sectarian Protestantism* (New York : Macmillan, 1964), p. 19.

[39]J. Heinrich Arnold, *Discipleship* (Farmington, Penn.: Plough, 1994), pp. 119-20, 252.

[40]Martin Luther, *Sermons on the Passion of Christ*, trans. E. Smid and J. T. Isensee (Rock Island, Ill.: Augustana, 1956), p. 187.

[41]*Luther: Lectures on Romans*, trans. and ed. Wilhelm Pauck (Philadelphia: Westminster Press, 1961), p. 144.

[42]See Regin Prenter, *Spiritus Creator*, trans. John M. Jensen (Philadelphia: Fortress, 1953), pp. 80, 87, 97-98, 245.

[43]Calvin, *Institutes*, trans. Battles, 3.16.2 (2:800).

[44]Calvin, *Sermons on Ephesians*, p. 103.

[45]See Robert Friedmann, *The Theology of Anabaptism* (Scottdale, Penn.: Herald, 1973), pp. 96-97.

[46]*Luther's Works*, ed. and trans. Jaroslav Pelikan (Saint Louis: Concordia, 1963), 26:387.

[47]This dimension of Luther's theology is brought out by Bengt R. Hoffman in *Luther and the Mystics* (Minneapolis: Augsburg, 1976).

[48]*Luther's Works*, ed. Jaroslav Pelikan, trans. A. T. W. Steinhaeuser (Saint Louis: Concordia, 1956), 21:299; WA 7:546.

[49]*Luther's Works,* 26:129-30.

[50]Calvin, *Institutes*, trans. Battles, 4.17.1 (2:1360).

[51]Calvin, *Commentaries on the Book of the Prophet Jeremiah and the Lamentations*, trans. John Owen (Edinburgh: Calvin Translation Society, 1850), 1:508.

[52]Calvin, *Commentary on Philippians*, trans. John Pringle (Edinburgh: Calvin Translation Society, 1851), p. 98.

[53]David S. Yeago, "The Promise of God and the Desires of Our Hearts," *Lutheran Forum* 30, no. 2 (May 1996): 23.
[54]Ibid., p. 27.

Chapter Six
[1]See Iain H. Murray, *The Puritan Hope* (London: Banner of Truth Trust, 1971); Leland Ryken, *Worldly Saints* (Grand Rapids: Zondervan, 1986); John Marlowe, *The Puritan Tradition in English Life* (London: Cresset, 1956); I. Morgan, *Puritan Spirituality* (London: Epworth, 1973); James I. Packer, *A Quest for Godliness: The Puritan Vision of the Christian Life* (Wheaton, Ill.: Crossway, 1990); and D. M. Lloyd-Jones, *The Puritans: Their Origins and Successors* (Edinburgh: Banner of Truth Trust, 1987).
[2]Lewis Bayly, *The Practice of Piety* (1842; reprint, Morgan, Penn.: Soli Deo Gloria, 1994), pp. 233-34.
[3]In Norman Pettit, *The Heart Prepared* (New Haven: Yale University Press, 1966), p. 82. See William Ames, *The Marrow of Sacred Divinity* (London, 1642), p. 182. For a new translation from the third Latin edition (1629) see *The Marrow of Theology,* trans. John Dykstra Eusden (Boston: Pilgrim, 1968), p. 211.
[4]See Pettit, *Heart Prepared.*
[5]*The Complete Works of Richard Sibbes*, ed. Alexander B. Grosart (Edinburgh: James Nichol, 1862-1864), 3:462; 5:432-33; 6:377-78. He sometimes portrayed the inner sealing of the Spirit as following faith.
[6]Sibbes, *Works,* 5:439.
[7]Ibid., 1:287.
[8]Ibid., 1:340.
[9]Ibid., 3:331.
[10]John Owen, *The Holy Spirit: His Gifts and Power* (Grand Rapids: Kregel, 1954), p. 132.
[11]Thomas Goodwin, *The Works of Thomas Goodwin* (Edinburgh: James Nichol, 1861), 1:233, 236.
[12]Ibid., p. 247.
[13]Michael R. Watts, *The Dissenters* (Oxford: Clarendon, 1978), p. 205.
[14]John Bunyan, *Grace Abounding to the Chief of Sinners* (Chicago: Moody Press, 1959), p. 104.
[15]Ibid., pp. 104-5.
[16]See Ernest W. Bacon, *Spurgeon: Heir of the Puritans* (Grand Rapids: Eerdmans, 1968). Other self-acknowledged heirs to the Puritans include D. Martyn Lloyd-Jones and James I. Packer.
[17]Charles H. Spurgeon, *Spurgeon's Expository Encyclopedia* (Grand Rapids: Baker, 1951), 9:49.
[18]Ibid., p. 51.
[19]*The Treasury of Charles H. Spurgeon*, ed. Wilbur M. Smith (Westwood, N.J.: Revell, 1955), p. 143.
[20]Bayly, *Practice of Piety*, p. 156.
[21]See Dale W. Brown, *Understanding Pietism* (Grand Rapids: Eerdmans, 1978);

Peter C. Erb, ed., *Pietists: Selected Writings* (New York: Paulist, 1983); F. Ernest Stoeffler, *The Rise of Evangelical Pietism* (Leiden: Brill, 1965); and Stoeffler, *German Pietism During the Eighteenth Century* (Leiden: Brill, 1973).

[22]See Carter Lindberg, *The Third Reformation?* (Macon, Ga.: Mercer University Press, 1983), p. 174.

[23]*Johann Arndt: True Christianity*, ed. Peter Erb (New York: Paulist, 1979), p. 265.

[24]Ibid., p. 174.

[25]Ibid., p. 235.

[26]See K. James Stein, *Philipp Jakob Spener: Pietist Patriarch* (Chicago: Covenant Press, 1986).

[27]Erb, *Pietists: Selected Writings*, p. 48. From Spener's *Pia Desideria*.

[28]See Dale Brown, *Understanding Pietism*, pp. 64-82.

[29]See Gary R. Sattler, *God's Glory, Neighbor's Good: A Brief Introduction to the Life and Writings of August Hermann Francke* (Chicago: Covenant Press, 1982), p. 241. From Francke's "Confession of a Christian."

[30]Quoted by Gary R. Sattler, "August Hermann Francke and Mysticism," *Covenant Quarterly* 38, no. 4 (1980): 5.

[31]See ibid.

[32]Ibid., p. 10.

[33]Sattler, *God's Glory, Neighbor's Good*, p. 248.

[34]Gary R. Sattler, *Nobler Than the Angels, Lower Than a Worm: The Pietist View of the Individual in the Writings of Heinrich Müller and August Hermann Francke* (Lanham, Md.: University Press of America, 1989), p. 109.

[35]*Nicholaus Ludwig Count von Zinzendorf: Nine Public Lectures on Important Subjects in Religion*, trans. and ed. George W. Forell (Iowa City: University of Iowa Press, 1973), p. 34.

[36]Ibid., p. 44.

[37]Quoted in John R. Weinlick, *Count Zinzendorf* (Nashville: Abingdon, 1956), p. 79.

[38]Ibid.

[39]Quoted in Louis Bouyer, *Orthodox Spirituality and Protestant and Anglican Spirituality*, trans. Barbara Wall (London: Burns & Oates, 1969), p. 202.

[40]Ibid., p. 201.

[41]See the discussion by John Joseph Stoudt in *Jacob Boehme's The Way to Christ*, ed. Stoudt (New York: Harper, 1947), pp. xiii-xxxix.

[42]See Paul Tillich, *Perspectives on 19th and 20th Century Protestant Theology* (New York: Harper & Row, 1967), pp. xxi-xxix, 194-95; and *Oxford Dictionary of the Christian Church*, ed. F. L. Cross and E. A. Livingstone, rev. ed. (Oxford: Oxford University Press, 1983), pp. 182-83.

[43]Donald Gelpi, *Pentecostalism: A Theological Viewpoint* (New York: Paulist, 1971), pp. 14-15. Cf. Ronald A. Knox, *Enthusiasm* (New York: Oxford University Press, 1951), pp. 176-230.

[44]See Gelpi, *Pentecostalism,* pp. 19-20.

[45]See Karl Barth, *Protestant Theology in the Nineteenth Century* (Valley Forge, Penn.: Judson Press, 1973), pp. 643-53. Also see Robert Lejeune, *Christoph*

Blumhardt and His Message (Rifton, N.Y.: Plough, 1963).

⁴⁶See Lejeune, *Christoph Blumhardt*, p. 28. Note these are the words of Johann Christoph Blumhardt.

⁴⁷In *Inner Words*, ed. Emmy Arnold (Rifton, N.Y.: Plough, 1975), pp. 29-30.

⁴⁸Ibid., pp. 77, 83.

⁴⁹See Tormod Engelsviken, *The Gift of the Spirit: An Analysis and Evaluation of the Charismatic Movement from a Lutheran Theological Perspective* (Wartburg Seminary, Dubuque, Iowa: A Doctoral Dissertation from Aquinas Institute of Theology, 1981), pp. 161-205.

⁵⁰See Donald G. Bloesch, "Evangelicalism," in *A New Handbook of Christian Theology,* ed. Donald W. Musser and Joseph L. Price (Nashville: Abingdon, 1992), pp. 168-73.

⁵¹There are, of course, other strands in evangelicalism including Lutheran, Anabaptist and Barthian. Yet the polarity seems to fall between Reformation monergism (esp. Calvinist) and Anabaptist and Wesleyan synergism. Theologians in all these traditions have sought to reconcile the gift of divine grace and the necessary human response to this grace. At their best they have grasped to at least some degree the mystery that salvation is both God's act *for* us and *in* us, but we too are involved in the salvific process as we respond and believe through the power of the Spirit. What Calvinists, Lutherans and Barthians have affirmed is that we of ourselves do not contribute to the procuring of our salvation, but we do contribute to its demonstration and manifestation as we are acted upon and moved by the Spirit.

⁵²See *John Wesley*, ed. Albert C. Outler (New York: Oxford University Press, 1964); Colin W. Williams, *John Wesley's Theology Today* (Nashville: Abingdon, 1960); Vinson Synan, ed., *Aspects of Pentecostal-Charismatic Origins* (Plainfield, N.J.: Logos International, 1975); and Donald W. Dayton, *Theological Roots of Pentecostalism* (Grand Rapids: Zondervan, 1987).

⁵³John Wesley, *A Plain Account of Christian Perfection* (London: Epworth, 1952), pp. 47, 52-53. Cf. Harald Lindström, *Wesley and Sanctification* (Wilmore, Ky.: Francis Asbury Press, n.d.), pp. 118, 142.

⁵⁴John Wesley, *Sermons on Several Occasions* (London: Epworth, 1944), p. 523.

⁵⁵See W. E. Sangster, *The Path to Perfection* (Nashville: Abingdon-Cokesbury, 1943), p. 84.

⁵⁶*Sermons*, 1:71-72. See Colin Williams, *John Wesley's Theology Today*, p. 117.

⁵⁷Mack B. Stokes, *The Holy Spirit and Christian Experience* (Nashville: Graded Press, 1975), p. 166.

⁵⁸Wesley, *Works* (3rd ed., 1872; reprint, Grand Rapids: Baker, 1986), 10:55.

⁵⁹Cited in Michael Harper, *Walk in the Spirit* (Plainfield, N.J.: Logos International, 1968), p. 79.

⁶⁰See Donald W. Dayton, *Theological Roots of Pentecostalism*, p. 50.

⁶¹Charles Wesley, "I Want the Spirit of Power Within," in *Wesley's Hymns* (London: 1874), no. 376.

⁶²Cited in Steve Durasoff, *Bright Wind of the Spirit* (Englewood Cliffs, N.J.: Prentice-Hall, 1972), p. 39.

⁶³In Vinson Synan, *The Holiness-Pentecostal Movement in the United States* (Grand Rapids: Eerdmans, 1971), pp. 19-20.

⁶⁴Jonathan Edwards, *Religious Affections* (Grand Rapids: Sovereign Grace, 1971), p. 58.

⁶⁵Edwards held that the grace that makes seeking for God possible is common, not saving grace. The seeker is still a "natural man" until that person is sealed by the Spirit in conversion. See Conrad Cherry, *The Theology of Jonathan Edwards* (New York: Doubleday Anchor, 1966), pp. 56-70.

⁶⁶Edwards, *Religious Affections,* p. 190.

⁶⁷*The Works of Jonathan Edwards* (1834, reprint; Edinburgh: Banner of Truth Trust, 1974), 2:275.

⁶⁸Cited in Hugh Evan Hopkins, *Charles Simeon of Cambridge* (London: Hodder & Stoughton, 1977), p. 185.

⁶⁹James D. Bratt, "Abraham Kuyper," in *Encyclopedia of the Reformed Faith,* ed. Donald K. McKim (Louisville: Westminster John Knox, 1992), pp. 212-13. See also James D. Bratt, "Raging Tumults of Soul: The Private Life of Abraham Kuyper," *Reformed Journal* 37, no. 11 (Nov. 1987): 9-13.

⁷⁰Abraham Kuyper, *The Work of the Holy Spirit,* trans. Henri De Vries (1900; reprint, Grand Rapids: Eerdmans, 1941), pp. 522-37.

⁷¹See James F. Findlay Jr., *Dwight L. Moody: American Evangelist 1837-1899* (Grand Rapids: Baker, 1973), pp. 132-33, 236-40.

⁷²R. A. Torrey, *The Baptism with the Holy Spirit* (London: James Nisbet & Co., 1904), pp. 18-20. Also see Dayton, *Theological Roots of Pentecostalism,* pp. 102-4.

⁷³See John Nelson Hyde, *Life and Letters of Praying Hyde,* ed. Gratia Hyde Bone and Mary Hyde Hall (Springfield, Ill.: Williamson Press, n.d.); E.G. Carré, ed., *Praying Hyde: A Challenge to Prayer* (London: Pickering & Inglis, n.d.); and Basil Miller, *Praying Hyde: A Man of Prayer,* 6th ed. (Grand Rapids: Zondervan, 1943).

⁷⁴For my further discussion of the Plymouth Brethren see pp. 172-73, 371.

⁷⁵Sangster, *Path to Perfection,* p. 125.

⁷⁶See Melvin E. Dieter, *The Holiness Revival of the Nineteenth Century,* 2nd ed. (Lanham, Md.: Scarecrow, 1996).

⁷⁷See Vinson Synan, *Holiness-Pentecostal Movement,* p. 29; and Melvin E. Dieter, "Wesleyan-Holiness Aspects of Pentecostal Origins," in *Aspects of Pentecostal-Charismatic Origins,* ed. Synan, pp. 62-66.

⁷⁸See "The Church of the Nazarene," *Ecumenical Review* 23, no. 3 (July 1971): 304.

⁷⁹See J. Kenneth Grider's discussion in his *A Wesleyan-Holiness Theology* (Kansas City, Mo.: Beacon Hill, 1994), pp. 295-96. Grider holds that Wesley basically affirmed sinless perfection but was reluctant to use the term because it is so easily misunderstood.

⁸⁰See Dale T. Irvin, "'Holiness Unto the Lord': Toward a Holiness Christian Dialogue with Judaism," *Journal of Ecumenical Studies* 34, no. 1 (Winter 1997): 13-37.

⁸¹See Synan, ed., *Aspects of Pentecostal-Charismatic Origins,* pp. 55-98.

⁸²It should be noted that most of these churches did not remain separatist, and

some were ecumenical from the beginning.

[83]Camps Farthest Out has featured such speakers as Agnes Sanford, Hannah Hurnard and Tommy Tyson, all of whom teach the experience of the baptism of the Holy Spirit beyond conversion. The Disciplined Order of Christ was founded in 1945 by a Methodist clergyman, Albert Edward Day, who had a definite conversion experience and later an experience of what he called "the Baptism of the Holy Spirit." He described it as "like refining fire swiftly coursing through the whole physical being, cleansing but not consuming. It was an ecstasy that had no resemblance to the ordinary expansive emotions of adolescence, but was an inner gladness so intense as to be almost unendurable yet requiring no outer expression save one thrilling 'Alleluia.' " Albert E. Day, *An Autobiography of Prayer* (New York: Harper, 1952), pp. 23-24. Day drew on not only the Wesleys but also Christian mystics like William Law, Brother Lawrence, Teresa of Ávila, Meister Eckhart and Evelyn Underhill, and post-Christian mystics like Gerald Heard and Aldous Huxley. The Disciplined Order of Christ should be described as a fellowship of seekers after holiness rather than a Holiness organization.

[84]William Booth, *The Founder Speaks Again*, ed. Cyril J. Barnes (London: Salvationist Publishing, 1960), p. 26. Booth also referred to this experience as "the baptism of fire" and "the baptism of love" (pp. 41-42, 85).

[85]See Geddes MacGregor, "Holiness in the Reformed Tradition," in *Man's Concern with Holiness,* ed. Marina Chavchavadze (London: Hodder & Stoughton, 1970), p. 85.

[86]Samuel Brengle, *When the Holy Ghost Is Come* (1909; rev. ed., London: Salvationist Publishing, 1955), p. 22.

[87]Ibid., p. 60.

[88]In Ernest Gordon, *A Book of Protestant Saints* (1946; reprint, Three Hills, Alberta: Prairie Bible Institute, 1968), p. 122.

[89]Ibid.

[90]See Charles E. Hambrick-Stowe, *Charles G. Finney and the Spirit of American Evangelicalism* (Grand Rapids: Eerdmans, 1996). The author tries to establish points of continuity between Finney and the older Calvinist tradition.

[91]Charles G. Finney, *Lectures on Revivals of Religion* (Cambridge: Belknap, 1960), p. 197.

[92]See William G. McLoughlin Jr., *Modern Revivalism* (New York: Ronald Press, 1959), pp. 16, 66-94. John Gresham argues that the original experience of the baptism of the Holy Spirit in Finney's life was separate from his conversion. He also contends that Finney allowed for fresh baptisms of the Spirit after the initial one. See John L. Gresham Jr., *Charles G. Finney's Doctrine of the Baptism of the Holy Spirit* (Peabody, Mass.: Hendrickson, 1987), pp. iv, 11-12, 24-57, 86-91.

[93]See John Opie, "Finney's Failure of Nerve: The Untimely Demise of Evangelical Theology," *Journal of Presbyterian History* 51, no. 2 (Summer 1973): 155-73. See esp. p. 170.

[94]See Delbert R. Rose, *A Theology of Christian Experience* (Minneapolis: Bethany

Fellowship, 1965).

⁹⁵See Hannah Whitall Smith, *The Christian's Secret of a Happy Life* (Old Tappan, N.J.: Revell, 1966).

⁹⁶Ibid., pp. 25-26.

⁹⁷Ibid., p. 167.

⁹⁸Ibid., p. 92.

⁹⁹Ibid., p. 156.

¹⁰⁰Andrew Murray, *Abide in Christ* (New York: Grosset & Dunlap, n.d.), p. 200.

¹⁰¹Cited in *Message of the Cross* 41, no. 4 (July-August 1977): 27.

¹⁰²See Arthur Carl Piepkorn, *Profiles in Belief* (San Francisco: Harper & Row, 1979), 3:20-22; and Andrew L. Byers, *Birth of a Reformation: The Life and Labors of Daniel S. Warner* (Guthrie, Okla.: Faith Publishing House, 1966).

¹⁰³Oswald Chambers, *My Utmost for His Highest* (1935; reprint, Uhrichsville, Ohio: Barbour, 1963), p. 148.

¹⁰⁴Oswald Chambers, *The Shadow of an Agony* (1934; reprint, London: Marshall, Morgan & Scott, 1965), p. 93.

¹⁰⁵Oswald Chambers, *He Shall Glorify Me* (London: Marshall, Morgan & Scott, 1965), p. 15.

¹⁰⁶Frank S. Mead, *Handbook of Denominations in the United States,* 6th ed. (Nashville: Abingdon, 1979), p. 77.

¹⁰⁷In Michael Griffiths, *Three Men Filled with the Spirit* (London: Overseas Missionary Fellowship, 1970), p. 45.

¹⁰⁸A. W. Tozer, *The Divine Conquest* (Harrisburg, Penn.: Christian Publications, n.d.), p. 127.

¹⁰⁹A. W. Tozer, *That Incredible Christian* (Harrisburg, Penn.: Christian Publications, 1964), p. 25.

¹¹⁰Ibid., p. 37.

¹¹¹In David J. Fant Jr., *A. W. Tozer: A Twentieth Century Prophet* (Harrisburg, Penn.: Christian Publications, 1964), p. 107.

¹¹²Tozer, *Born After Midnight* (Harrisburg, Penn.: Christian Publications, 1959), p. 141.

¹¹³Theodore Hegre, *The Will of God Your . . . Sanctification* (Minneapolis: Bethany Fellowship, 1961), p. 55.

¹¹⁴*Message of the Cross* 23 (March-April 1970): 5.

¹¹⁵J. Sidlow Baxter, *A New Call to Holiness* (Grand Rapids: Zondervan, 1967), p. 155.

¹¹⁶See Garth Lean, *On the Tail of a Comet: The Life of Frank Buchman* (1985; reprint, Colorado Springs: Helmers & Howard, 1988); and Peter Howard, *Frank Buchman's Secret* (London: Heinemann, 1961).

¹¹⁷Buchman confessed that he came to know the Holy Spirit as his "light, guide, teacher and power. What I am able to do, I do through the power that comes in the early hours of morning quiet." Lean, *Frank Buchman,* p. 171.

¹¹⁸Carl F. H. Henry, *Confessions of a Theologian* (Waco, Tex.: Word, 1986), pp. 39-59.

¹¹⁹Lean, *On the Tail,* p. 318.

¹²⁰William McDonald, a Holiness writer, declared: "In regeneration sin does not *reign;* in sanctification it does not *exist.*" Quoted in A. M. Hills, *Holiness and*

Power for the Church and the Ministry (Salem, Ohio: Schmul, 1988), p. 77.

[121]Some Holiness churches stress that spiritual baptism alone has merit and have discontinued the rite of water baptism.

[122]On Wesley's social message see Howard A. Snyder, *The Radical Wesley* (Downers Grove, Ill.: InterVarsity Press, 1980).

[123]See Donald W. Dayton, *Discovering an Evangelical Heritage* (New York: Harper & Row, 1976). Note that for Dayton the evangelical heritage is wider than Wesleyanism.

[124]John Calvin, *Commentaries on the Epistle of Paul the Apostle to the Romans*, trans. and ed. John Owen (Edinburgh: Calvin Translation Society, 1849), p. 276.

Chapter Seven

[1]In the broad sense *heresy* and *heterodoxy* are practically equivalent, but I am here using these terms in a technical sense. While heterodoxy connotes a definite though sometimes slight deviation from the faith, heresy is an attack on the vitals of the faith. This distinction is helpful because it allows us to discriminate between something that is out of kilter and something that is clearly ruinous and subversive.

[2]The sect mentality is invariably schismatic. Augustine drew a helpful distinction between schismatics and heretics: the first cut the bond of love, the second the bond of faith. Peter Beyerhaus builds on this distinction in his critique of the Zionists (Pentecostals) in South Africa whom he views as heretics. See Walter J. Hollenweger, *The Pentecostals* trans. R. A. Wilson (Minneapolis: Augsburg, 1972), pp. 161-62.

[3]Cults tend to be syncretistic whereas sects are prone to be insular and separatistic.

[4]Arianism can be classified as both sectarian and cultic in that it signifies both an unwarranted emphasis on some tenet of the faith to the exclusion of others and an outright denial of tenets that belong to the substance of faith.

[5]The term *cultic movement* can be distinguished from *cult* in that the former may indicate only a cultic thrust rather than outright heresy. In this book the two designations are virtually synonymous, though there are a few exceptions. I agree with Dan McConnell that the Faith movement within Pentecostalism is cultic, but it is not a cult as such. See Daniel McConnell, *A Different Gospel*, 2nd ed. (Peabody, Mass.: Hendrickson, 1995), pp. 15-28.

[6]See Dean Freiday, ed., *Barclay's Apology in Modern English* (privately published, 1967), p. 301.

[7]See George Fox, *Journal*, ed. John L. Nickalls (1694; rev. ed., Cambridge: Cambridge University Press, 1952), p. 35.

[8]The original Quakers are properly classified as an evangelical sect rather than a cult or cultic movement because of their intense fidelity to Jesus Christ. The Ranters and Shakers, whom I will discuss presently, constitute a more serious theological aberration.

[9]See James Black, *New Forms of the Old Faith* (London: Thomas Nelson, 1948), pp. 111-12.

[10]Norman Cohn, *The Pursuit of the Millennium* (1957; rev. and expanded edition

New York: Oxford University Press, 1970), p. 290.

[11]In Thomas Molnar, *God and the Knowledge of Reality* (New York: Basic Books, 1973), pp. 158-59.

[12]See Donald L. Gelpi, *Pentecostalism: A Theological Viewpoint* (New York: Paulist, 1971), pp. 19-20.

[13]See "Quietism," in *The Oxford Dictionary of the Christian Church*, ed. F. L. Cross and E. A. Livingstone, 2nd ed. (New York: Oxford University Press, 1983), p. 1152; P. N. Hillyer, "Quietism," in *New Dictionary of Theology*, ed. Sinclair B. Ferguson and David F. Wright (Downers Grove, Ill.: InterVarsity Press, 1988), pp. 554-55; and Ronald A. Knox, *Enthusiasm* (Oxford: Clarendon, 1950), pp. 231-355.

[14]See Charles A. Nordhoff, *The Communistic Societies of the United States* (New York: Harper & Bros., 1875), pp. 115-256; Anna White and Leila S. Taylor, *Shakerism, Its Meaning and Message* (Columbus, Ohio: Fred J. Heer, 1904); Marguerite Fellows Melcher, *The Shaker Adventure* (Old Chatham, N.Y.: Shaker Museum, 1941); Stephen J. Stein, *The Shaker Experience in America: A History of the United Society of Believers* (New Haven: Yale University Press, 1992); Robley Edward Whitson, ed., *The Shakers: Two Centuries of Spiritual Reflection* (New York: Paulist, 1983); Robert S. Ellwood Jr., *Alternative Altars* (Chicago: University of Chicago Press, 1979), pp. 65-83; Charles W. Ferguson, *The New Books of Revelations* (1928; reprint, New York: Doubleday, 1931), pp. 321-39; and Marcus Bach, *Strange Sects and Curious Cults* (New York: Dodd, Mead & Co., 1961), pp. 202-16.

[15]See Cyriel O. Sigstedt, *The Swedenborg Epic* (New York: Twayne, 1952); John Howard Spalding, *Introduction to Swedenborg's Religious Thought* (New York: Swedenborg Publications, 1956); Signe Toksvig, *Emanuel Swedenborg: Scientist and Mystic* (New Haven, Conn.: Yale University Press, 1948); Wilson Van Dusen, *The Presence of Other Worlds: The Psychological/Spiritual Findings of Emanuel Swedenborg* (New York: Harper & Row, 1974); Ferguson, *New Books of Revelations*, pp. 340-64; and Ellwood, *Alternative Altars*, pp. 84-91.

[16]Quoted in Sigstedt, *Swedenborg Epic*, p. 211.

[17]Van Dusen, *Presence of Other Worlds*, p. 228.

[18]See Walter R. Martin, *The Kingdom of the Cults* (Grand Rapids: Zondervan, 1965), p. 251.

[19]See Ellwood, *Alternative Altars*, pp. 95-103; G. W. Butterworth, *Spiritualism and Religion* (London: SPCK, 1944); Charles Braden, *These Also Believe* (New York: Macmillan, 1949), pp. 319-57; Ferguson, *New Books of Revelations*, pp. 15-48; Arthur Ford and Margueritte Harmon Bro, *Nothing So Strange* (New York: Harper & Row, 1958); Jane T. Stoddart, *The Case Against Spiritualism* (New York: George H. Doran, n.d.); and Ruth Brandon, *The Spiritualists* (New York: Alfred A. Knopf, 1983).

[20]Van Dusen, *Presence of Other Worlds*, p. 140.

[21]See J. F. C. Wright, *Slava Bohu: The Story of the Dukhobors* (New York: Farrar & Rinehart, 1940); Ferguson, *New Books of Revelations*, pp. 110-32; and Bach, *Strange Sects and Curious Cults*, pp. 182-201.

[22]Ferguson, *New Books of Revelations*, p. 114.

[23]See Arthur C. Piepkorn, *Profiles in Belief* (San Francisco: Harper & Row, 1978), 2:511-17.

[24]Ibid., pp. 515-16.

[25]See Everett Webber, *Escape to Utopia: The Communal Movement in America* (New York: Hastings House, 1959). Also see Nordhoff, *Communistic Societies of the United States.*

[26]See Webber, *Escape,* pp. 274-97; Nordhoff, *Communistic Societies,* pp. 25-59; Barbara S. Yambura and Eunice W. Bodine, *A Change and a Parting* (Ames: Iowa State University Press, 1960).

[27]Bertha M. H. Shambaugh, *Amana That Was and Amana That Is* (1932; reprint, New York: Arno Press, 1976), p. 263.

[28]See *Hymns: Church of Jesus Christ of Latter-day Saints* (Salt Lake City: Corporation of the Church of Jesus Christ of Latter-day Saints, 1985), no. 2.

[29]See Martin, *Kingdom of the Cults*, pp. 147-98. For a more appreciative treatment of Mormonism see Jan Shipps, *Mormonism: The Story of a New Religious Tradition* (Urbana: University of Illinois Press, 1987); Mary Farrell Bedndarowski, *New Religions and the Theological Imagination in America* (Bloomington, Ind.: Indiana University Press, 1989); and Richard N. Ostling and Joan K. Ostling, *Mormon America: The Power and the Promise* (San Francisco: HarperCollins, 1999).

[30]Charles Penrose, *Mormon Doctrine* (Salt Lake City, 1888). Quoted in Martin, *Kingdom of the Cults*, p. 185.

[31]*Teachings of the Prophet Joseph Smith* (Salt Lake City: Confirm Book, 1977), p. 243.

[32]See P. E. Shaw, *The Catholic Apostolic Church* (New York: King's Crown Press, 1946).

[33]Piepkorn, *Profiles in Belief,* 4:169.

[34]Ibid., pp. 56-58. See Philip L. Cook, *Zion City, Illinois: Twentieth Century Utopia* (Syracuse: Syracuse University Press,1996). Also see E. L. Blumhofer, "Dowie, John Alexander," in *Dictionary of Pentecostal and Charismatic Movements*, ed. Stanley M. Burgess and Gary B. McGee (Grand Rapids: Zondervan, 1988), pp. 248-49.

[35]On the cultic flavor of the last see Danny Aguirre, "The Proliferation of a Movement: The International Churches of Christ," *SCP Journal* 23:2-23:3 (1999): 30-35.

[36]See Piepkorn, *Profiles in Belief,* 2:629-50; Richard T. Hughes, "Are Restorationists Evangelicals?" in *The Variety of American Evangelicalism,* ed. Donald W. Dayton and Robert K. Johnston (Downers Grove, Ill.: InterVarsity Press, 1991), pp. 109-34; and J. B. North, "Restoration Movement," in *Dictionary of Christianity in America,* ed. Daniel G. Reid et al. (Downers Grove, Ill.: InterVarsity Press, 1990), pp. 1005-8 (see also pp. 253-55, 277-78).

[37]See P. Gerard Damsteegt, *Foundations of the Seventh-day Adventist Message and Mission* (Grand Rapids: Eerdmans, 1977); and Martin, *Kingdom of the Cults*, pp. 359-422. Note that Martin contends that Seventh-day Adventists are

not cultists but an evangelical sect with a peculiar emphasis.

[38]*Seventh-day Adventists Believe* . . . (Washington, D.C.: General Conference of Seventh-day Adventists, 1988), p. 219.

[39]Cited in Anthony Hoekema, *The Four Major Cults* (Grand Rapids: Eerdmans, 1963), p. 107.

[40]See the discussion in Geoffrey J. Paxton, *The Shaking of Adventism* (Wilmington, Del.: Zenith, 1977); and Laura L. Vance, *Seventh-day Adventism in Crisis: Gender and Sectarian Change in an Emerging Religion* (Champaign, Ill.: University of Illinois Press, 1999).

[41]See " 'Deliverance Ministry' Increases Among Adventists," *Eternity* 35, no. 3 (March 1984): 9.

[42]Richard Hammill, "Spiritual Gifts in the Church Today," *Ministry* 55, no. 7 (July 1982): 16.

[43]I here agree with the assessment of Walter Martin over Anthony Hoekema, who regards Seventh-day Adventism as a cult.

[44]Ellen G. White, *Revival—and Beyond* (Washington, D.C.: Review & Herald, 1972), p. 50.

[45]See Braden, *These Also Believe*, pp. 358-84; Marley Cole, *Jehovah's Witnesses* (London: George Allen & Unwin, 1956); Walter Martin and Norman Klann, *Jehovah of the Watchtower* (1953; rev. ed. Chicago: Moody Press, 1974); and Barbara Grizzuti Harrison, *Visions of Glory: A History and a Memory of Jehovah's Witnesses* (New York: Simon & Schuster, 1978).

[46]See Hoekema, *Four Major Cults*, pp. 290-92.

[47]Martin, *Kingdom of the Cults*, p. 46.

[48]See Mose Durst, *To Bigotry, No Sanction: Reverend Sun Myung Moon and the Unification Church* (Chicago: Regnery Gateway, 1984); Young Oon Kim, *Unification Theology and Christian Thought,* rev. ed. (New York: Golden Gate, 1976); and Bednarowski, *New Religions.*

[49]Bednarowski, *New Religions*, p. 80.

[50]See the discussion in Kim, *Unification Theology*; and Ruth Tucker, *Another Gospel* (Grand Rapids: Zondervan, 1989), pp. 252-53.

[51]*The Divine Principle* (Washington, D.C.: Holy Spirit Association for the Unification of World Christianity, 1973), p. 10.

[52]Bob Larson, *Larson's Book of Cults* (Wheaton, Ill.: Tyndale House, 1982), pp. 224-33.

[53]See Matthew Fox, *The Coming of the Cosmic Christ* (San Francisco: Harper & Row, 1988), pp. 3-6, 106-7.

[54]Note that Fox calls this the dawning of a new Pentecost.

[55]See Duncan Ferguson, ed., *New Age Spirituality* (Louisville: Westminster John Knox, 1993); and Paul Heelas, *The New Age Movement: Celebrating the Self and the Sacralization of Modernity* (Oxford: Blackwell, 1996).

[56]These are not necessarily contradictions. Some New Agers, particularly those who lean toward gnosticism, are also inclined to see the world as a crucible.

[57]In her *New Religions* Bednarowski associates New Age with Theosophy and Mormonism with the Unification Church. But the goal of being gods is evident

in both New Age and Mormonism.

[58]See Hannah Hurnard, *The School of Earth Experiences* (London: C. W. Davies, n.d.). For a penetrating review of this book see Ron Kangas, "Spiritual Deviations," *Affirmation and Critique* 1, no. 3 (July 1996): 58-59.

[59]Albert Edward Day, *An Autobiography of Prayer* (New York: Harper & Bros., 1952), p. 205.

[60]Reformed theology generally holds that the Spirit always acts *"with* the Word" but *"immediately with* the Word" in the human heart. The power of the new life in Christ comes directly from God and not from the visible signs or means of grace, yet always in conjunction with these signs and means. See the discussion in Conrad Cherry, *The Theology of Jonathan Edwards* (New York: Doubleday Anchor, 1966), pp. 47-48.

[61]Cf. Lewis Sperry Chafer, *Dispensationalism* (Dallas: Dallas Theological Seminary Press, 1936); Clarence B. Bass, *Backgrounds to Dispensationalism* (Grand Rapids: Eerdmans, 1960); C. Norman Kraus, *Dispensationalism in America* (Richmond: John Knox Press, 1958); Charles C. Ryrie, *Dispensationalism* (1966; new ed., Chicago: Moody Press, 1995); John H. Gerstner, *A Primer on Dispensationalism* (Phillipsburg, N.J.: Presbyterian & Reformed, 1982); John H. Gerstner, *Wrongly Dividing the Word of Truth: A Critique of Dispensationalism* (Brentwood, Tenn.: Wolgemuth & Hyatt, 1991); Anthony Hoekema, *The Bible and the Future* (Grand Rapids: Eerdmans, 1979), pp. 194-222; Millard Erickson, *Contemporary Options in Eschatology* (Grand Rapids: Baker, 1977), pp. 109-81; Daniel P. Fuller, *Gospel and Law: Contrast or Continuum? The Hermeneutics of Dispensationalism and Covenant Theology* (Grand Rapids: Eerdmans, 1980); Vern S. Poythress, *Understanding Dispensationalists* (Grand Rapids: Zondervan, 1987); and Hans. K. LaRondelle, *The Israel of God in Prophecy* (Berrien Springs, Mich.: Andrews University Press, 1983).

[62]See D. H. Kromminga, *The Millennium in the Church* (Grand Rapids: Eerdmans, 1945), pp. 22, 81-88, 194-214.

[63]On Fletcher's dispensationalism see Donald W. Dayton, *Theological Roots of Pentecostalism* (Grand Rapids: Zondervan, 1987), pp. 51-53.

[64]*Scofield Reference Bible* (1909; reprint, New York: Oxford University Press, 1917), p. 5.

[65]See Millard Erickson, *Contemporary Options in Eschatology,* pp. 117-22.

[66]In some dispensational groups Communion is no longer practiced. See Piepkorn, *Profiles in Belief,* 4:44-45.

[67]See F. L. Arrington, "Dispensationalism," in *Dictionary of Pentecostal and Charismatic Movements,* ed. Burgess and McGee, pp. 247-48.

[68]Plymouth Brethren scholar Rex A. Koivisto seeks to do justice to the catholicity of the church in his welcome book *One Lord, One Faith* (Wheaton, Ill.: Victor, 1993). All denominations can benefit from his devastating and much-needed critique of sectarianism and restorationism.

[69]Plymouth Brethren have also been active in New Tribes Mission, Youth with a Mission and many other evangelical mission agencies. A sectarian bent is sometimes apparent among Brethren missionaries in their attitude toward

Roman Catholics and Eastern Orthodox, whom they refuse to recognize as Christians. See the missions report of John Spyralatos, "A Small Light is Starting to Shine" in *Christian Missions in Many Lands Inc.* 26, no. 11 (Dec. 1997): 11-14. At the same time most Brethren missionaries fully accept evangelicals from other Protestant denominations. Open Brethren can be described as a group with a sectarian background that is on the way to becoming a church, theologically speaking. Closed Brethren by contrast bear almost all the marks of a sect and in their attempt to control the lives of their members sometimes exhibit cultic manifestations. See Nigel Scotland, "Encountering the Exclusive Brethren: A Late Twentieth-Century Cult," *European Journal of Theology* 6, no. 2 (1997): 157-67.

[70]The Brethren movement on the whole is a cross between Reformed Pietism and dispensationalism, and it is its Calvinistic base that enables this movement to be assimilated into the wider evangelical family. For a helpful though somewhat critical appraisal of the Brethren by a respected Reformed theologian and churchman see James Black, *New Forms of the Old Faith* (London: Thomas Nelson & Sons, 1948), pp. 138-58. Also see Elmer T. Clark, *The Small Sects in America* (1937; rev. ed. Nashville: Abingdon-Cokesbury, 1949), pp. 181-84. For a fair and balanced treatment of the Plymouth Brethren see Harold H. Rowdon, "Plymouth Brethren," in *New 20th Century Encyclopedia of Religious Knowledge*, ed. J. D. Douglas (1955; rev. ed. Grand Rapids: Baker, 1991), pp. 655-56.

[71]For the new climate in some dispensational circles today see Craig A. Blaising and Darrell L. Bock, *Progressive Dispensationalism* (Wheaton, Ill.: Victor, 1993); and Robert L. Saucy, *The Case for Progressive Dispensationalism* (Grand Rapids: Zondervan, 1993).

[72]See *Larson's Book of Cults*, pp. 123-29.

[73]See J. K. Van Baalen, *The Chaos of Cults*, 2nd ed. (Grand Rapids: Eerdmans, 1956), p. 14.

[74]Coming back to the fold of the holy catholic church does not necessarily imply changing denominational affiliations. One can discover the catholicity of the church even while remaining in a sect—here understood as either a nonconformist body or a mainline denomination that has drifted from its moorings. As I have already indicated, my recommendation for biblical Christians is to work for renewal within their own churches as a leaven. But when sectarianism of either the left or right begins to extinguish the flame of the gospel of salvation by free grace, the time may be fast approaching when God's commandment is for separation. For my earlier discussion in this chapter see pp. 144-46.

[75]By contrast, a mystical society is more likely to blur the lines between Christ and culture, and this accounts for the ease with which mystical and occultic groups penetrate the upper echelons of society.

Chapter Eight
[1]See Edith Blumhofer, Russell Spittler and Grant Wacker, eds., *Pentecostal Cur-*

rents in American Protestantism (Champaign, Ill.: University of Illinois Press, 1999); Walter J. Hollenweger, *The Pentecostals: The Charismatic Movement in the Churches*, trans. R. A. Wilson (Minneapolis: Augsburg, 1972); Hollenweger, *Pentecostalism: Origins and Developments Worldwide* (Peabody, Mass.: Hendrickson, 1997); and John Thomas Nichol, *Pentecostalism* (New York: Harper & Row, 1966). For the unabridged version of Hollenweger's first book see his *Enthusiastisches Christentum: Die Pfingstbewegung in Geschichte und Gegenwart* (Zürich und Wuppertal: Theologischer Verlag Rolf Brockhaus und Zwingli Verlag, 1969).

[2]See Patricia Lefevere, "Ecumenism is Slow but Steady, Cardinal Says," *National Catholic Reporter* 32, no. 39 (Sept. 13, 1996): 5. Note that Cardinal Cassidy's estimate of the Pentecostal constituency is slightly lower than mine.

[3]See Harvey Cox, *Fire from Heaven* (Reading, Mass.: Addison-Wesley, 1995), p. 168.

[4]Quoted in John L. Sherrill, *They Speak with Other Tongues* (New York: McGraw-Hill, 1964), p. 27.

[5]See Laurence W. Wood, *Pentecostal Grace* (Wilmore, Ky.: Francis Asbury, 1980).

[6]Stanley Frodsham, *Smith Wigglesworth: Apostle of Faith* (Springfield, Mo.: Gospel Publishing House, 1948), p. 15.

[7]R. A. Torrey, *What the Bible Teaches* (London: James Nisbet, 1898), p. 271.

[8]James H. McConkey, *The Three-fold Secret of the Holy Spirit* (Chicago: Moody Press, 1897), pp. 33, 39.

[9]See Alma White, *Demons and Tongues* (1936; reprint, Zarephath, N.J.: Pillar of Fire, 1949).

[10]Reformed theology defines holiness as separation from the world rather than sinless perfection and therefore would question this part of sacred tradition.

[11]C. X. J. M. Friethoff, *A Complete Mariology* (Westminster, Md.: Newman Press, 1958), p. 90.

[12]See Nichol, *Pentecostalism*, p. 18; and Charles W. Conn, *Like A Mighty Army* (Cleveland, Tenn.: Church of God Publishing House, 1955), pp. 18-27.

[13]Bob Larson, *Larson's Book of Cults* (Wheaton, Ill.: Tyndale House, 1982), pp. 176-80.

[14]David J. du Plessis, *The Spirit Bade Me Go* (Plainfield, N.J.: Logos International, 1970), pp. 70-73, 79, 99-106.

[15]Note that this church is part of the Oneness movement in Pentecostalism.

[16]See D. J. Wilson, "William Marrion Branham," in *Dictionary of Pentecostal and Charismatic Movements*, ed. Stanley M. Burgess and Gary B. McGee (Grand Rapids: Zondervan, 1988), pp. 95-97; and Michael G. Moriarty, *The New Charismatics* (Grand Rapids: Zondervan, 1992), pp. 47-56.

[17]See L. Christenson, "Dennis and Rita Bennett," in *Dictionary of Pentecostal and Charismatic Movements*, pp. 53-54.

[18]See Larry Christenson, *Speaking in Tongues* (Minneapolis: Bethany Fellowship, 1968).

[19]See Francis MacNutt, *Healing* (Notre Dame, Ind.: Ave Maria Press, 1974).

[20]Basilea Schlink, *When God Calls* (Minneapolis: Bethany Fellowship, 1968).

[21]See Larson, *Larson's Book of Cults*, pp. 136-39.

[22]See D. R. McConnell, *A Different Gospel*, rev. ed. (Peabody, Mass.: Hendrickson, 1995); L. Lovett, "Positive Confession Theology," in *Dictionary of Pentecostal and Charismatic Movements*, pp. 718-20; and John D. Fickett, *Confess It, Possess It: Faith's Formula?* (Oklahoma City: Presbyterian & Reformed Renewal Ministries International, 1984).

[23]This college is named after Charles Wesley Emerson, who embraced various philosophies, including Transcendentalism and Unitarianism.

[24]See McConnell, *Different Gospel*, pp. 38-54.

[25]Fickett, *Confess It*, p. 13.

[26]See McConnell, *Different Gospel*, p. 94.

[27]Fickett, *Confess It*, p. 12.

[28]Ibid., p. 23.

[29]Some Faith teachers are critical of Paul for accepting poverty and suffering. Dan McConnell offers this pungent rebuttal: "What they fail to recognize is what Paul knew so well: *to believe in the crucified Messiah is to submit to the claim of his cross.*" *Different Gospel*, p. 177.

[30]See Hollenweger, *Pentecostals*, pp. 231-43; and J. Rodman Williams, *The Pentecostal Reality* (Plainfield, N.J.: Logos International, 1972), p. 64.

[31]A personal letter from Bernie L. Gillespie dated January 27, 1997.

[32]C. E. Jones, "Church of the Living God," in *Dictionary of Pentecostal and Charismatic Movements*, p. 211.

[33]Alan Walker, "Where Pentecostalism Is Mushrooming," *Christian Century* 85, no. 3 (Jan. 17, 1968): 81-82.

[34]Among many Pentecostals the healing power is attributed to the strength of one's faith and not simply to the free decision of God. They are then often led to the absurd conclusion that those who are not healed lack faith.

[35]See P. T. Forsyth, *The Soul of Prayer* (1916; reprint, Grand Rapids: Eerdmans, n.d.), p. 42.

[36]For his overall appraisal of the gifts of the Spirit see J. Oswald Sanders, *The Holy Spirit and His Gifts* (London: Marshall, Morgan & Scott, 1940).

[37]For my critical appraisal of the Pentecostal doctrine of demons see pp. 213-15.

[38]See R. P. Spittler, "Glossolalia," *Dictionary of Pentecostal and Charismatic Movements*, p. 335.

[39]Charles W. Conn, *Pillars of Pentecost* (Cleveland, Tenn.: Pathway Press, 1956), p. 57.

[40]William J. Samarin gives a helpful treatment of this point of view in his *Tongues of Men and Angels* (New York: Macmillan, 1972), pp. 22-26. Besides James and Myers, Samarin includes in his discussion Albert Coe, George B. Cutten and William Sargant.

[41]Ira Jay Martin III, *Glossolalia in the Apostolic Church* (Berea, Ky.: Berea College Press, 1960), pp. 55, 100.

[42]Morton T. Kelsey, *Tongue Speaking* (New York: Doubleday, 1964), p. 212.

[43]Samarin, *Tongues of Men and Angels*, p. 235.

[44]Ibid., p. 33.

[45]Frank Stagg, E. Glenn Hinson and Wayne E. Oates, *Glossolalia: Tongue Speaking in Biblical, Historical, and Psychological Perspective* (Nashville: Abingdon, 1967), pp. 76-99, esp. p. 90.

[46]George Barton Cutten, *Speaking with Tongues* (New Haven: Yale University Press, 1927), pp. 4-7, 169-70.

[47]James N. Lapsley and J. H. Simpson, "Speaking in Tongues," *Princeton Seminary Bulletin* 58, no. 2 (Feb. 1965): 3-18.

[48]Kelsey, *Tongue Speaking*, p. 199. Cf. Martin, *Glossolalia in the Apostolic Church*, p. 100.

[49]Virginia Hine, "Pentecostal Glossolalia: Toward a Functional Interpretation," in *Speaking in Tongues: A Guide to Research on Glossolalia,* ed. Watson E. Mills (Grand Rapids: Eerdmans, 1986), p. 442.

[50]Merlin R. Carothers, *Power in Praise* (Plainfield, N.J.: Logos International, 1972), p. 53.

[51]Donald Gelpi, *Pentecostalism: A Theological Viewpoint* (New York: Paulist, 1971), p. 185.

[52]Edward D. O'Connor, *The Pentecostal Movement in the Catholic Church* (Notre Dame, Ind.: Ave Maria Press, 1971), p. 87.

[53]Ibid., p. 199.

[54]"An Interview with Cardinal Suenens," *New Covenant* 2, no. 12 (June 1973): 1-5.

[55]Cited in Kelsey, *Tongue Speaking*, p. 197.

[56]Dietrich Bonhoeffer, *Life Together,* trans. John W. Doberstein (New York: Harper & Row, 1954), p. 79.

[57]Frederick Dale Bruner, *A Theology of the Holy Spirit* (Grand Rapids: Eerdmans, 1970), p. 95.

[58]Ibid., p. 111.

[59]Prudencio Damboriena, *Tongues As of Fire: Pentecostalism in Contemporary Christianity* (Washington, D.C.: Corpus Books, 1969), p. 90.

[60]James Kallas (citing Vincent Taylor, *Forgiveness and Reconciliation*) argues that Luther lacked a doctrine of sanctification: "This lack of a program of sanctification, a call to personal endeavor, is thus accounted for in a dual fashion. First, and positively, there *is no* need for man to do anything because the Spirit does all. Secondly and negatively, man *must not* do anything, for in trying to do so, he is rejecting God as insufficient." *The Satanward View: A Study in Pauline Theology* (Philadelphia: Westminster Press, 1966), p. 109. Lutheran Pietists would take exception to this interpretation of Luther, but that there is this strand in Luther is unassailable. It seems to me that Pentecostals and Pietists are closer to Scripture in maintaining that believers are actively involved in their sanctification. Yet I would say that they are involved not in the procuring of sanctification but in its manifestation and demonstration.

[61]In Hollenweger, *Pentecostals*, p. 473.

[62]See Walter Martin, *The New Cults* (Santa Ana, Calif.: Vision House, 1980), pp.

269-96.

[63]William R. Read, *New Patterns of Church Growth in Brazil* (Grand Rapids: Eerdmans, 1965), p. 39.

[64]Du Plessis, *The Spirit Bade Me Go*, p. 106.

[65]O'Connor, *Pentecostal Movement*, p. 227.

[66]J. Sidlow Baxter, *Divine Healing of the Body* (Grand Rapids: Zondervan, 1979), p. 287.

[67]See David F. Wells, *No Place for Truth* (Grand Rapids: Eerdmans, 1993).

[68]Among scholars of significant repute who are associated with Pentecostalism are Gordon Fee of Regent College, J. Rodman Williams of Regent University, Larry D. Hart of Oral Roberts University, and Walter J. Hollenweger, formerly of the University of Birmingham, England.

[69]Cited by Karl Barth in *The Epistle to the Romans,* trans. from 6th ed. by Edwyn C. Hoskyns (1933; reprint, London: Oxford University Press, 1975), p. 39. Cf. Luther: "The richness by which we are justified and saved is not visible: it must be believed . . . even though I sense sin, death, and contrary feelings." *Luther's Works*, ed. and trans. Jaroslav Pelikan (St. Louis: Concordia, 1968), 29:86.

[70]In Barth, *Romans*, p. 143.

[71]Ibid., p. 38.

[72]Nils Bloch-Hoell, *The Pentecostal Movement: Its Origin, Development, and Distinctive Character* (London: Allen & Unwin, 1964), p. 101.

[73]Cf. Luther: "Since these divine blessings are invisible, incomprehensible, and deeply hidden, nature cannot attain or love them unless it is lifted up through the grace of God." *Luther's Works*, 29:216.

[74]Forsyth, *Soul of Prayer*, p. 82.

[75]Jeremy Taylor was representative of orthodox Anglicanism in the seventeenth century and was suspected of Catholic sympathies by his Calvinist opponents. See *Jeremy Taylor: Selected Works*, ed. Thomas K. Carroll (New York: Paulist, 1990).

[76]Du Plessis, *The Spirit Bade Me Go*, p. 93.

[77]See Vinson Synan, ed., *Aspects of Pentecostal-Charismatic Origins* (Plainfield, N.J.: Logos International, 1975) p. 10.

[78]Nichol, *Pentecostalism*, p. 80.

[79]Vinson Synan, *The Holiness-Pentecostal Movement in the United States* (Grand Rapids: Eerdmans, 1971), p. 196.

[80]*Dictionary of Pentecostal and Charismatic Movements*, pp. 95-97.

[81]See Bruner, *Theology of the Holy Spirit*, p. 250.

[82]Hans Küng, *The Church,* trans. Ray and Rosaleen Ockenden (New York: Sheed and Ward, 1967), p. 163.

[83]For a devastating appraisal of Benny Hinn's novel reconception of the Holy Spirit in his *Good Morning, Holy Spirit* (Nashville: Thomas Nelson, 1990), see Gary Evans, "Taking the 'Une' out of 'Triune,' " *Affirmation & Critique* 1, no. 3 (July 1996): 53-56. Also see Ron Kangas's critique of Hinn's *Welcome Holy Spirit (*Nashville: Thomas Nelson, 1995) in "A Defective Pneumatology," *Affir-*

mation & Critique 1, no. 4 (Oct. 1996): 55-56.

[84]See O'Connor, *Pentecostal Movement*, pp. 228-31.

[85]Barth, *Romans*, p. 323.

[86]Du Plessis, *The Spirit Bade Me Go*, p. 106.

[87]" 'Mr. Pentecost' Talks to the Episcopal (Anglican) Community," *Acts 29: Newsletter of the Episcopal Renewal Ministries* 1, no. 2 (1983): 5.

[88]Michael Harper, *Walk in the Spirit* (Plainfield, N.J.: Logos International, 1968), p. 39. Note that Michael Harper has recently converted to the Orthodox Church.

[89]Don Basham, *True and False Prophets* (Greensburg, Penn.: Manna Books, 1973), p. 105.

[90]In Russell P. Spittler, ed., *Perspectives on the New Pentecostalism* (Grand Rapids: Baker, 1976), p. 115.

[91]Larry Christenson, *A Message to the Charismatic Movement* (Minneapolis: Bethany Fellowship, 1972), p. 106.

[92]Cited in DeVern Fromke, *Unto Full Stature* (Cloverdale, Ind.: Sure Foundation Publishers, 1965), p. 208.

[93]Bernie L. Gillespie, *"How God Helped Me Understand the Gospel": A Personal Testimony and Confession of Faith* (Findlay, Ohio: In Christ Alone Ministries! 1996), pp. 24-25. Gillespie shares his personal struggle that led him out of the United Pentecostal Church to form an independent evangelical congregation. He still regards himself as a Pentecostal, since he strongly affirms the important role of the gifts of the Spirit in the church's ministry, but his message is now focused on justification by faith alone. See also Gillespie, *"I Am Not Ashamed of the Gospel of Christ": Assurance Through the Gospel of Jesus Christ Alone* (1996).

[94]Shamanism and animism are also evident in the new interest in Native American spirituality and in such cults as Wicca, the Unification Church and Theosophy.

[95]See Heiko A. Oberman, *Luther: Man Between God and the Devil*, trans. Eileen Walliser-Schwarzbart (1990; reprint, New York: Doubleday, 1992).

[96]See Walter Sundberg, "A Primer on the Devil," *First Things* 29 (Jan. 1993): 16.

[97]Ibid., p. 18.

[98]Rudolf Otto, *The Kingdom of God and the Son of Man*, trans. Floyd V. Filson and Bertram Lee Woolf (Grand Rapids: Zondervan, n.d.), pp. 346-50, 355-56. Also see Otto, *The Idea of the Holy*, trans. John W. Harvey (1923; reprint, New York: Oxford University Press, 1958).

[99]Paul Tillich, *The Interpretation of History*, trans. N. A. Rasetzki and Elsa L. Talmey (New York: Charles Scribner's Sons, 1936), p. 85; *Systematic Theology* (Chicago: University of Chicago Press, 1963), 3:102-6.

[100]Tillich, *Systematic Theology*, 3:102.

[101]Ibid., 3:103.

[102]In Paul Tillich, *The Protestant Era*, trans. and ed. James Luther Adams (Chicago: University of Chicago Press, 1948), p. 304.

[103]Tillich, *Interpretation of History*, p. 86.

[104]See Karl Barth, *Church Dogmatics*, ed. G. W. Bromiley and T. F. Torrance, trans. G. W. Bromiley and R. J. Ehrlich (Edinburgh: T. & T. Clark, 1960), 3 (3):289-531. As with Tillich it is questionable whether Barth does justice to the personal character of demons.

[105]Sundberg, "Primer on the Devil," p. 16.

[106]James S. Stewart, "On a Neglected Emphasis in New Testament Theology," *Scottish Journal of Theology* 4, no. 3 (Sept. 1951): 294.

[107]William Manson, "Principalities and Powers," *Studiorum Novi Testamenti Societas Bulletin* 3 (1952): 15. Cited in James Kallas, *The Significance of the Synoptic Miracles* (London: SPCK, 1961), p. 108.

[108]allas, *Significance of the Synoptic Miracles*, p. 79.

[109]Not all illnesses fomented by demonic attack are physical or even emotional in nature. Some take the form of an inner deformation of the soul. Some degree of deformation is presupposed in all cases of demonic entrapment.

[110]Walter Wink, *Unmasking the Powers: The Invisible Forces That Determine Human Existence* (Philadelphia: Fortress, 1986), p. 63.

[111]For a perceptive critique of Wink from an evangelical perspective see Stephen F. Noll, *Angels of Light, Powers of Darkness* (Downers Grove, Ill.: InterVarsity Press, 1998), pp. 24-26.

[112]S. Vernon McCasland, *By the Finger of God* (New York: Macmillan, 1951), pp. 11426-45.

[113]See Michael Welker, *God the Spirit*, trans. John F. Hoffmeyer (Minneapolis: Fortress, 1994), pp. 197-203; and Ernst Käsemann, "Die Heilung der Besessenen," in *Kirchliche Konflikte* (Göttingen: Vandenhoeck & Ruprecht, 1982), p. 189.

[114]Anton Fridrichsen, "The Conflict of Jesus with Unclean Spirits," trans. Hugo Odeberg, *Theology* 22, no. 129 (March 1931): 126-27. In comparing the witness of biblical revelation to primitive religion in Africa, Keith Ferdinando sees the latter as holding to "an anarchy of spirits and occult forces, over which God may in principle be supreme, but in which he rarely if ever intervenes. This in turn explains the fear and uncertainty often experienced in traditional Africa; the individual is conscious of being at the mercy of a variety of unpredictable spiritual forces, whose activities are in practice largely unrestrained." The author can be faulted for not perceiving the presence of the primitive worldview in the culture of ancient Palestine as well. See Keith Ferdinando, "Screwtape Revisited: Demonology Western, African, and Biblical," in *The Unseen World*, ed. Anthony N. S. Lane (Grand Rapids: Baker, 1996), p. 124.

[115]Henri Daniel-Rops, *Daily Life in the Time of Jesus*, trans. Patrick O'Brian (New York: Hawthorn, 1962), p. 353.

[116]Ibid.

[117]Kallas, *Significance of the Synoptic Miracles*, p. 67.

[118]Madeleine S. Miller and J. Lane Miller, *Harper's Bible Dictionary* (New York: Harper & Bros., 1952), p. 136.

[119]See Don Basham, *Deliver Us from Evil* (Lincoln, Va.: Chosen Books, 1972), pp. 219-20. Also see T. L. Osborn, who portrays demons as wandering, discarnate spirits "seeking a body in which they can enter and find expression to carry out their mission of evil." Osborn, *Healing the Sick* (1951; reprint, Tulsa: Harrison House, 1992), p. 144.

[120]According to Osborn "our spirits are from God. Demon spirits are from Satan." *Healing the Sick*, p. 143. One can discern a strain of gnostic dualism in Osborn.

[121]See Derek Prince, *Expelling Demons* (Fort Lauderdale: Derek Prince, n.d.), pp. 1–2.

[122]Thomas A. Boogaart, "Satan Is a Son of God," *Perspectives* 12, no. 8 (Oct. 1997): 19. Boogaart betrays an Origenistic bent when he looks forward to the restoration of the devil and his cohorts to God's kingdom. Origen taught the universal restoration of all things (apocatastasis). Boogaart discerns correctly that the demons were originally children of light and that we as Christians are called to resist them but not torment them (cf. 2 Pet 2:10-11). Yet Boogaart can be questioned when he entertains the hope of a return of the devil to the kingdom of light. See also Peter C. Boogaart and Thomas A. Boogaart, "A Critical Review of *This Present Darkness,*" *Reformed Review* 47, no. 1 (Autumn 1993): 5-16.

From my theological perspective, our mission is not to plot the demise of the demons but to rejoice in Christ's victory over them and then to carry this victory forward in our lives. In our engagement with the demons we rely not on our own strategies but on God's promise to be present with all who call on his name.

[123]Quoted in Alan Richardson, *The Miracle-Stories of the Gospels* (1941; reprint, London: SCM Press, 1956), p. 68.

[124]I cannot go along with Pentecostal evangelist T. L. Osborn, who flatly declares that "demons are the cause of disease." Osborne, *Healing the Sick*, p. 153.

[125]Some illnesses may indeed be attributed to demonic influences, but even in these cases humans share some of the blame, since they allow themselves to be beguiled by the Tempter.

[126]On my earlier discussion of human responsibility in evil see the fourth volume of my Christian Foundations series, *Jesus Christ: Savior & Lord* (Downers Grove, Ill.: InterVarsity Press, 1997), pp. 40-52.

[127]There are anticipations of this notion in the Old Testament. See Is 14:12-15; Gen 6:1-4.

[128]Fridrichsen, "Conflict of Jesus," p. 127.

[129]Ibid.

[130]T. H. Gaster, "Demon, Demonology," in *Interpreter's Dictionary of the Bible*, ed. G. A. Buttrick (New York: Abingdon, 1962), 1:818.

[131]Louis Monden, *Signs and Wonders* (New York: Desclee, 1966), p. 159. Monden does not consider that on occasion Jesus did engage in conversation with the demonic spirits that held the afflicted person in bondage and that at least in one instance he did heed their requests for mercy (cf. Mt 8:28-32; Mk 5:1-13; Lk 8: 26-33). On the other hand, Jesus often rebuked the demons and would not

allow them to speak (cf. Mk 1:23-26; 9:25-26; Lk 4:41; 9:42). One should also note in this discussion that in his direct confrontation with the devil in the wilderness, Jesus entered into dialogue with his angelic adversary (cf. Mt 4:1-11; Mk 1:12-13; Lk 4:1-13).

[132]Bernard Ramm, *Offense to Reason* (San Francisco: Harper & Row, 1985), p. 105.

[133]For a helpful guide on ministering to those under the spell of the demonic see John Richards, *But Deliver Us from Evil: An Introduction to the Demonic Dimension in Pastoral Care* (New York: Seabury, 1974).

[134]Michael Welker speaks of the suspension of "the free formation of the will" of the possessed individual. "Without the free contribution of the affected person, he is controlled to his own harm and to his own endangerment. . . . To the detriment of the stricken persons, the demons unforeseeably incapacitate their will, bring them into a domain between death and life, and hold them in this domain." Welker, *God the Spirit*, pp. 198-99. He points to Mk 9:21-22 as illustrative of the self-destruction that demonic possession precipitates.

[135]Cf. Fridrichsen: "The advent of the Divine Kingdom first and foremost signified that the prince of this world would be dethroned, fettered, and imprisoned. Therefore in each act of exorcism Jesus saw a defeat of Satan, a presage of the final triumph that was soon to come to pass." "Conflict of Jesus," p. 127.

[136]Kallas, *Significance of the Synoptic Miracles*, p. 102.

[137]Richardson, *Miracle-Stories of the Gospels*, pp. 68-69.

[138]See Kallas, *Significance of the Synoptic Miracles*, p. 73.

[139]My main difficulty with this best-selling novel is that it implies that the demons are nearly as powerful as the divine forces of righteousness. Frank E. Peretti, *This Present Darkness* (Wheaton, Ill.: Crossway, 1986). Peretti portrays the world as demon infested rather than demon exorcized (as in Barth). He also supports the mythological concept of territorial spirits who stake out a claim on certain localities.

[140]See Kallas, *Significance of the Synoptic Miracles*; and *The Satanward View.*

[141]The local church itself should be a center of Christian renewal, but because this is so often not the case, Christendom stands in need of special forms of witness and service that make the message of the gospel concrete. See Bloesch, *Centers of Christian Renewal* (Philadelphia: United Church Press, 1964); and *Wellsprings of Renewal* (Grand Rapids: Eerdmans, 1974).

[142]See Kallas, *Satanward View*, pp. 81-82.

[143]Walter Lüthi, *The Lord's Prayer*, trans. Kurt Schoenenberger (Richmond, Va.: John Knox Press, 1961), p. 22.

[144]For my extensive critique of Bultmann and his program of demythologizing see Bloesch, *Holy Scripture* (Downers Grove, Ill.: InterVarsity Press, 1994), pp. 223-54.

Chapter Nine

[1]See H. Wheeler Robinson, *The Christian Experience of the Holy Spirit* (London:

James Nisbet, 1928).

[2]Ibid., p. 231; cf. p. 280.

[3]Ibid., p. 231.

[4]Ibid., p. 271.

[5]Ibid., p. 40.

[6]Ibid., p. 26.

[7]Ibid., p. 40.

[8]Ibid., p. 41.

[9]Ibid., p. 242.

[10]Alasdair I. C. Heron, *The Holy Spirit* (Philadelphia: Westminster Press, 1983), p. 176.

[11]Karl Barth, *Church Dogmatics*, ed. G. W. Bromiley and T. F. Torrance, trans. G. W. Bromiley (Edinburgh: T. & T. Clark, 1956), 4(1):312.

[12]Barth, *Church Dogmatics,* trans. G. W. Bromiley (Edinburgh: T. & T. Clark, 1969), 4(4):31.

[13]Ibid., p. 90.

[14]Ibid.

[15]Ibid., p. 115.

[16]*Church Dogmatics,* trans. G. T. Thomson (Edinburgh: T. & T. Clark, 1936), 1(1):521.

[17]*Church Dogmatics,* trans. G. W. Bromiley (Edinburgh: T. & T. Clark, 1958), 4(2):828.

[18]Ibid., p. 829.

[19]Ibid., pp. 829-30.

[20]Ibid., p. 836.

[21]Karl Barth, *The Epistle to the Romans*, trans. Edwyn Hoskyns (1933; reprint, London: Oxford University Press, 1975), p. 298.

[22]John Thompson, *The Holy Spirit in the Theology of Karl Barth* (Allison Park, Penn.: Pickwick, 1991), pp. 98-99. Cf. Karl Barth, *The Faith of the Church: A Commentary on the Apostles' Creed According to Calvin's Catechism*, trans. Gabriel Vahanian (London: Fontana, 1958), pp. 132-33.

[23]Thompson, *Holy Spirit in the Theology of Karl Barth,* pp. 205-6.

[24]On Karl Barth's Pietist lineage see Eberhard Busch, *Karl Barth und die Pietisten* (Munich: Chr. Kaiser, 1978).

[25]See Dawn DeVries, *Jesus Christ in the Preaching of Calvin and Schleiermacher* (Louisville: Westminster John Knox, 1996), p. 101. Barth sometimes contradicts himself, especially when he sees preaching as sacramental.

[26]On Tillich's appreciation of Hegel and Schelling see Tillich, *Perspectives on 19th and 20th Century Protestant Theology*, ed. Carl E. Braaten (New York: Harper & Row, 1967), pp. 114-52.

[27]On Tillich's doctrine of the Spirit see Tillich, *Systematic Theology* (Chicago: University of Chicago Press, 1963), 3:111-282.

[28]See ibid., 1:239.

[29]Ibid., p. 249.

[30]Ibid., 3:148; cf. p. 285.

[31]Ibid., pp. 117-18.

[32]Ibid., p. 117.

[33]Paul Tillich, *The Future of Religions,* ed. Jerald C. Brauer (New York: Harper & Row, 1966), pp. 87-88.

[34]See Friedrich Schleiermacher, *On Religion: Speeches to Its Cultured Despisers,* trans. John Oman (New York: Harper & Row, 1958), pp. 242-53. See esp. p. 252.

[35]Tillich, *Systematic Theology,* 3:148.

[36]Ibid., p. 112.

[37]Ibid., p. 275.

[38]Ibid., p. 115.

[39]Ibid.

[40]See my discussion of Bultmann in Bloesch, *Holy Scripture* (Downers Grove, Ill.: InterVarsity Press, 1994), pp. 223-54.

[41]See Rudolf Bultmann, "New Testament and Mythology," in *Kerygma and Myth,* ed. Hans Werner Bartsch, trans. Reginald H. Fuller (1953; reprint, London: SPCK, 1960), pp. 1-44, 191-211.

[42]See Rudolf Bultmann, *Theology of the New Testament,* trans. Kendrick Grobel (New York: Charles Scribner's Sons, 1951), 1:155-57.

[43]See Bultmann's discussion of miracles in the New Testament in ibid., 1:8, 32, 41, 48, 61, 83, 86, 127, 130–31, 135, 154, 161, 325, 337. See also 2:44-45.

[44]Ibid., 1:163.

[45]bid., 1:144.

[46]See the discussion in James Luther Adams's introduction to Rudolf Sohm, *Outlines of Church History,* trans. May Sinclair (Boston: Beacon, 1958), pp. ix-xv.

[47]Jürgen Moltmann, *The Spirit of Life,* trans. Margaret Kohl (Minneapolis: Fortress, 1992), pp. 228-29.

[48]Jürgen Moltmann, *God in Creation,* trans. Margaret Kohl (San Francisco: Harper & Row, 1985), p. 279.

[49]Ibid., pp. 98, 103.

[50]Moltmann, *Spirit of Life,* p. 295.

[51]Cf. Moltmann, *God in Creation,* pp. 258-59; and his *Trinity and the Kingdom,* trans. Margaret Kohl (San Francisco: Harper & Row, 1981), p. 221.

[52]Moltmann, *God in Creation,* p. 258.

[53]Moltmann, *Spirit of Life,* p. 212.

[54]Moltmann, *God in Creation,* p. 100.

[55]Jürgen Moltmann, *The Coming of God,* trans. Margaret Kohl (Minneapolis: Fortress, 1996), p. 336.

[56]Ibid., pp. 326-30.

[57]Ibid., p. 332.

[58]Jürgen Moltmann, *The Church in the Power of the Spirit,* trans. Margaret Kohl (New York: Harper & Row, 1977), p. 163.

[59]Jürgen Moltmann, "Christianity in the Third Millennium," *Theology Today* 51, no. 1 (April 1994): 88.

[60]Ibid.

[61]Moltmann, *God in Creation*, p. 97.

[62]The first is much more acceptable than the second from the viewpoint of rthodox theology.

[63]Moltmann, *Coming of God*, p. 305.

[64]Moltmann, *Spirit of Life*, pp. 187, 259-62. For an able delineation of these two types of love see Anders Nygren, *Agape and Eros,* trans. Philip S. Watson (Philadelphia: Westminster Press, 1953).

[65]For Moltmann's discussion of these two types of love see *Spirit of Life*, pp. 248-63.

[66]Ibid., p. 250.

[67]Ibid., p. 187. Cf. Jürgen Moltmann, *The Source of Life: The Holy Spirit and the Theology of Life,* trans. Margaret Kohl (Minneapolis: Fortress, 1997), pp. 63-64.

[68]On the typology of mystical and prophetic spirituality see Bloesch, *The Struggle of Prayer,* 2nd ed. (Colorado Springs: Helmers & Howard, 1988); and Friedrich Heiler, *Prayer,* trans. Samuel McComb and J. Edgar Park (New York: Oxford University Press, 1958).

[69]Moltmann, *God in Creation*, p. 312.

[70]Moltmann, *Spirit of Life*, p. 36.

[71]Moltmann, *Coming of God*, pp. 272-75.

[72]Ibid., p. 272.

[73]*Church in the Power of the Spirit*, pp. 358-59.

[74]Yves M. J. Congar, *I Believe in the Holy Spirit*, trans. David Smith (New York: Seabury, 1983), 1:160-61.

[75]Ibid., 2:41.

[76]Ibid., 1:106

[77]Ibid.

[78]Ibid., 2:17.

[79]Congar, *The Word and the Spirit*, trans. David Smith (London: Geoffrey Chapman, 1986), p. 126.

[80]Congar, *I Believe,* 1:163-64.

[81]Ibid., 2:100.

[82]Regin Prenter, *Spiritus Creator*, trans. John M. Jensen (Philadelphia: Fortress, 1953).

[83]Ibid., pp. 69, 96.

[84]Ibid., p. 254.

[85]Ibid., p. 245; cf. pp. 87-88.

[86]Ibid., p. 69.

[87]Ibid., p. 128.

[88]Ibid., p. 166.

[89]Ibid., pp. 131-34. While Prenter is not altogether happy with "a spiritual understanding of the divine" when applied to Luther, he acknowledges that many Luther scholars regard it as true to Luther's basic intention.

[90]Regin Prenter, "Holiness in the Lutheran Tradition," in *Man's Concern with Holiness,* ed. Marina Chavchavadze (London: Hodder & Stoughton, 1970), pp. 121-44.

[91]Ibid., p. 125.

[92]Clark H. Pinnock, *Flame of Love: A Theology of the Holy Spirit* (Downers Grove, Ill.: InterVarsity Press, 1996), p. 80.

[93]Ibid., p. 82.

[94]For my earlier discussion of Pinnock in this book see pp. 25-26.

[95]Pinnock, *Flame of Love*, p. 124.

[96]Ibid., p. 173.

[97]Ibid., p. 29.

[98]Ibid., pp. 161, 179.

[99]See Clark H. Pinnock, *A Wideness in God's Mercy: The Finality of Jesus Christ in a World of Religions* (Grand Rapids: Zondervan, 1992), pp. 157-80.

[100]On the divergence between prophetic and mystical religion with regard to the goal of the Christian life see H. Richard Niebuhr, *The Kingdom of God in America* (1937; reprint, Hamden, Conn.: Shoe String Press, 1956), pp. 17-44.

[101]Pinnock, *Flame of Love*, p. 233.

[102]Luther too did not see grace inherent in the Word or the sacraments. See Prenter, *Spiritus Creator*, pp. 166-67.

[103]See Pinnock, *Flame of Love*, p. 159-62.

[104]See Paul Evdokimov, *The Art of the Icon: A Theology of Beauty,* trans. Steven Bigham (Redondo Beach, Calif.: Oakwood Publications, 1990); *The Struggle with God*, trans. Sister Gertrude (Glen Rock, N.J.: Paulist, 1966); *Présence de L'Esprit Saint dans la tradition orthodoxe* (Paris: Cerf, 1969; reprint, 1977); *Woman and the Salvation of the World*, trans. Anthony P. Gythiel (Crestwood, N.Y.: St. Vladimir's Seminary Press, 1994); *La Nouveauté de l'Esprit* (Bégrolles en Mauges: Abbaye de Bellefontaine, 1977); *The Sacrament of Love*, trans. Anthony P. Gythiel and Victoria Steadman (Crestwood, N.Y.: St. Vladimir's Seminary Press, 1985); "Holiness in the Orthodox Tradition" (trans. Constance Babington Smith), in *Man's Concern for Holiness*, ed. Chavchavadze, pp. 145-84; H. Cazelles, P. Evdokimov and A. Greiner, *Le Mystère de l'Esprit-Saint* (Tours: Maison Mame, 1968).

[105]Cazelles et al. *Mystère de l'Esprit-Saint*, p. 79.

[106]Ibid., pp. 97-98.

[107]Evdokimov, *Art of the Icon*, p. 119.

[108]Cazelles et al. *Mystère de l'Esprit-Saint*, p. 98.

[109]Evdokimov, *Struggle with God*, p. 148.

[110]Evdokimov, *Nouveauté de l'Esprit*, p. 57.

[111]Evdokimov, "Holiness in the Orthodox Tradition," p. 167.

[112]Evdokimov, *Woman and the Salvation of the World*, p. 221.

[113]See the critical review of Evdokimov's *Woman and the Salvation of the World* by Leon Podles in *Touchstone* 8, no. 4 (Autumn 1995): 35-36.

[114]Evdokimov, *Art of the Icon*, p. 196.

[115]Evdokimov, *Woman and the Salvation of the World*, p. 230.

[116]Evdokimov, *Art of the Icon*, pp. 15, 39; *Woman and the Salvation of the World*, pp. 57, 61. Evdokimov rejects Anders Nygren's dichotomy between eros and

agape, viewing these as "two correlative expressions of God's love." *Sacra-ment of Love*, p. 82.

[117]Evdokimov, *Struggle with God*, p. 205.

[118]Evdokimov, *Nouveauté de l'Esprit*, p. 100.

[119]Ibid., p. 98.

[120]Evdokimov, *Struggle with God*, p. 139.

[121]Evdokimov, *Woman and the Salvation of the World*, pp. 68-69, 124-25, 198-99.

[122]Hendrikus Berkhof, *The Doctrine of the Holy Spirit* (Richmond: John Knox Press, 1964).

[123]Ibid., p. 116.

[124]Ibid., p. 117.

[125]See Berkhof, *Christian Faith*, trans. Sierd Woudstra (Grand Rapids: Eerdmans, 1979), pp. 330-37. See the criticism of Berkhof in Heron, *Holy Spirit*, pp. 126-27, 200.

[126]Berkhof, *Christian Faith*, p. 332.

[127]Berkhof, *Doctrine of the Holy Spirit*, p. 115.

[128]Wolfhart Pannenberg, *Systematic Theology*, trans. Geoffrey W. Bromiley (Grand Rapids: Eerdmans, 1991), 1:383-84.

[129]Pannenberg, *Christian Spirituality* (Philadelphia: Westminster Press, 1983), p. 47.

[130]Pannenberg, *Theology and the Kingdom of God* (Philadelphia: Westminster Press, 1969), p. 98.

[131]I agree with the position associated with Lutheranism that if we are under the mark of baptism we are already on the road to faith. Yet I must insist that we do not come to faith apart from a conscious decision of trust and commit-ment that signifies a break with the old way of living.

For Pannenberg we are in continuity with the Spirit of God even if we belong to another religion or to no religion. The freedom of the Spirit can break into human existence even outside the parameters of faith, thereby giv-ing life a new integrity. Pannenberg, *Theology and the Kingdom of God*, pp. 74-81.

[132]Peter C. Hodgson, *Winds of the Spirit: A Constructive Christian Theology* (Louis-ville: Westminster John Knox, 1994), p. 283.

[133]Ibid., p. 153.

[134]Paul Lakeland, "Peter C. Hodgson," in *A New Handbook of Christian Theolo-gians,* ed. Donald W. Musser and Joseph L. Price (Nashville: Abingdon, 1996), pp. 229-35.

[135]Hodgson, *Winds of the Spirit*, p. 192.

[136]Ibid., p. 208.

[137]Ibid., p. 289.

[138]Ibid., p. 155.

[139]See Michael Welker, *God the Spirit*, trans. John F. Hoffmeyer (Minneapolis: Fortress, 1994).

[140]His theology is constructed from the "bottom-up" data of the creaturely experience of the Spirit. See Duane H. Larson's review in *Dialog* 36, no. 1 (Winter 1996): 70.

[141]Welker, *God the Spirit*, p. 262. Also see pp. 116-17, 226ff.

[142]See ibid., p. 275.

[143]Ibid., p. 278.

[144]Ibid., p. 312.

[145]Ibid., p. 213.

[146]Ibid., p. 243.

[147]Ibid., p. 271,

[148]See Michael Welker, "The Holy Spirit," in *Constructive Christian Theology in the Worldwide Church,* ed. William R. Barr (Grand Rapids: Eerdmans, 1997), pp. 169, 182.

[149]Philip J. Rosato, *The Spirit as Lord: The Pneumatology of Karl Barth* (Edinburgh: T. & T. Clark, 1981), p. 178.

[150]Ibid., p. 148.

[151]Ibid., p. 133.

[152]Ibid., p. 164.

[153]Thompson, *Holy Spirit,* p. 199.

[154]Rosato, *Spirit as Lord*, p. 147.

[155]Thompson, *Holy Spirit*, p. 199.

[156]Ibid.

[157]Rosato, *Spirit as Lord*, p. 171.

[158]Ibid., p. 183.

[159]Thompson, *Holy Spirit*, p. 207.

[160]J. Rodman Williams, *Renewal Theology* (Grand Rapids: Zondervan, 1990); *The Era of the Spirit* (Plainfield, N.J.: Logos International, 1971); and *The Pentecostal Reality* (Plainfield, N.J.: Logos International, 1972).

[161]Williams, *Era of the Spirit*, pp. 51-52, 65-66.

[162]Ibid., p. 57.

[163]Williams, *Renewal Theology*, 2:215.

[164]Ibid., 2: 235.

[165]Ibid., 2:285.

[166]Ibid., 2:207.

[167]Heron, *Holy Spirit*, p. 176.

[168]Welker, *God the Spirit*, pp. 43-44.

[169]Granted that most if not all theologians would affirm that the Spirit works through preaching as well as sacraments, the question is whether the focus of attention is on sacramental rites as the unique medium of the Spirit or on the freedom of the Spirit to manifest himself directly apart from sacramental rites or even to withhold his presence from such rites.

Chapter Ten

[1]In Christian history there has always been a dichotomy between academic theology and popular religion. It is the latter that veers toward tritheism.

[2]The collapse into tritheism occurs only when the subjects in the Godhead are conceived of individualistically.

[3]I believe we should not discard traditional formulations but instead supplement them in language that is more meaningful for our situation in human history. No formulation is sacrosanct in the sense of being beyond criticism, but some formulations can be normative and authoritative for the church in every age. The church must always confess "one God in three persons," but it needs to amplify and clarify its confession with new metaphors and concepts. For a contemporary poignant defense of the use of "person" to describe the members of the Trinity see Alan J. Torrance, *Persons in Communion* (Edinburgh: T. & T. Clark, 1996). Torrance is critical of Barth's substitution of "modes of being" for persons, since "modes" do not love each other. He argues that Barth is inconsistent in his restatement of the Trinity in light of the fact that he wishes to make a place for communion between the members of the Trinity. From my perspective, one difficulty with the Barthian reconception of the Trinity is that one cannot pray to modes of being but only to persons. At the same time, we need to bear in mind that we pray not to separate persons but to the one divine being who exists in modes of relationship. We may, of course, address God by any of his trinitarian names, but these names do not connote separate wills but different expressions of the one will. For a penetrating critique of Torrance's book from a Barthian perspective see Paul D. Molnar's review in *Karl Barth Society Newsletter* no. 16 (spring 1997): 9-10.

[4]See Donald P. Richmond, "Towards Reshaping the Theological Enterprise" (unpublished essay, 1997), p. 1. I fully concur with the author that God is a relational being.

[5]See the discussion in Verna E. F. Harrison, "Word as Icon in Greek Patristic Theology," in *Constructive Christian Theology in the Worldwide Church,* ed. William R. Barr (Grand Rapids: Eerdmans, 1997), p. 67.

[6]See Jaroslav Pelikan, *The Light of the World* (New York: Harper & Brothers, 1962).

[7]Personal phone conversation, April 1997.

[8]Karl Barth, *Göttingen Dogmatics*, trans. Geoffrey Bromiley, ed. Hannelotte Reiffen (Grand Rapids: Eerdmans, 1991), 1:129-30.

[9]See John Thompson, *The Holy Spirit in the Theology of Karl Barth* (Allison Park, Penn.: Pickwick, 1991), p. 30.

[10]To use a more graphic image, we could argue that the essence of the Godhead is the inexhaustible and unquenchable fire of holy love.

[11]This contention is not self-contradictory, though it appears to be so, but is based on the varying definitions of *person*. It is theologically permissible to describe the Trinity as both one inclusive person in three modalities of being and one diversified being in three states of personal interaction.

[12]See Irenaeus *Adversus haereses* 5.1.3. See also *A History of Christian Doctrine*, ed. Hubert Cunliffe-Jones and Benjamin Drewery (Philadelphia: Fortress, 1978), p. 45. In Calvin and Luther the Spirit-Word polarity is basically that between Spirit and Scripture.

[13]*The Table Talk of Martin Luther*, ed. Thomas S. Kepler (New York and Cleveland: World, 1952), p. 143.

[14]Calvin, *Institutes of the Christian Religion*, ed. John T. McNeill, trans. Ford Lewis Battles (Philadelphia: Westminster Press, 1960), 1.9.3 (1:96).

[15]See Wilhelm Niesel, *The Theology of Calvin*, trans. Harold Knight (Philadelphia: Westminster Press, 1956), p. 36; *Corpus Reformatorum* 54:285; and *Institutes*, trans. Battles, 1.9.3 (1:95).

[16]Dorner declares that for Calvin Scripture is "not the mere sign of something absent, but has the divine content, the divine breath, within itself, which makes itself felt." I. A. Dorner, *Geschichte der protestantischen Theologie* (Munich: Gotta'schen Buchhandlung, 1867), p. 380. See Edward A. Dowey Jr., *The Knowledge of God in Calvin's Theology* (New York: Columbia University Press, 1952), pp. 107-8.

[17]Calvin, *Commentaries on the Epistle of Paul the Apostle to the Romans*, trans. and ed. John Owen (Edinburgh: Calvin Translation Society, 1849), pp. 400-401.

[18]See J. K. S. Reid, *The Authority of Scripture* (New York: Harper & Bros., 1957), pp. 72-102. See esp. pp. 82-83.

[19]François Wendel, *Calvin*, trans. Philip Mairet (London: Collins, 1963), p. 157.

[20]Ronald S. Wallace, *Calvin's Doctrine of the Word and Sacrament* (Grand Rapids: Eerdmans, 1957), p. 79.

[21]See Ragnar Bring's helpful discussion of Luther's position in Bring, *How God Speaks to Us* (Philadelphia: Muhlenberg, 1962), pp. 20-33.

[22]*Luther's Works*, trans. and ed. Jaroslav Pelikan (St. Louis: Concordia, 1968), 29:172.

[23]Some orthodox Lutheran theologians would interpret Luther differently, particularly on the relation between the Word of God and Scripture.

[24]In his so-called middle period Barth's theology took the form of a neo-Calvinism which made an important place for "means of grace." But as his *Church Dogmatics* progressed he veered in the direction of a christomonism, which depicted Jesus Christ as the only sacrament in the sense of an efficacious sign of invisible grace.

[25]See Wallace, *Calvin's Doctrine*, p. 90. Also see John Calvin, *Commentary on the Epistles of Paul the Apostle to the Corinthians,* trans. John Pringle (Edinburgh: Calvin Translation Society, 1849), 2:170-75.

[26]Barth, *Göttingen Dogmatics*, 1:216.

[27]Michael Horton, *In the Face of God* (Dallas: Word, 1996), p. 30.

[28]This is why my theology can be deemed sacramental rather than propositional. But it is not sacramentalist in the sense that the sign contains the grace it signifies (the position of the Council of Trent).

[29]Richard A. Jensen, *Touched by the Spirit* (Minneapolis: Augsburg Press, 1975), p. 123.

[30]See my discussion on pp. 303-5.

[31]Philip Edgcumbe Hughes, *A Commentary on the Epistle to the Hebrews* (Grand Rapids: Eerdmans, 1977), p. 412.

[32]Donald A. Hagner, *Hebrews* (Peabody, Mass.: Hendrickson, 1990), p. 165.

[33]Fred D. Gealy, "Titus," in *Interpreter's Bible,* ed. G. A. Buttrick (Nashville: Abingdon-Cokesbury, 1955), 11:545.

[34]See Friedrich Heiler, *Prayer*, ed. and trans. Samuel McComb and J. Edgar Park (New York: Oxford University Press, 1958), pp. 65-73.

[35]Markus Barth, *Ephesians 1-3,* Anchor Bible (Garden City, N.Y.: Doubleday, 1974), p. 143.

[36]*Calvin's New Testament Commentaries*, trans. T. H. L. Parker, ed. David W. Torrance and Thomas F. Torrance (Grand Rapids: Eerdmans, 1965), 11:130-33.

[37]F. F. Bruce, *The Epistle to the Ephesians* (Westwood, N.J.: Revell, 1961), p. 36. Bruce is clear that the sealing in Ephesians (Eph 1:13-14; 4:30) refers primarily to the gift of the Spirit, but he allows that this gift may be accompanied or confirmed by the external sign of baptism.

[38]G. W. H. Lampe, *The Seal of the Spirit* (London: Longmans, Green, 1951), p. 5.

[39]James D. G. Dunn, *Baptism in the Holy Spirit,* Studies in Biblical Theology 2/15 (London: SCM Press, 1970), p. 189.

[40]Ibid., p. 191.

[41]On the salvific status of Apollos see F. F. Bruce, *Commentary on the Book of Acts* (1954; reprint, Grand Rapids: Eerdmans, 1968), pp. 380-83. Also see note 18, chapter 3 of this volume (p. 353).

[42]Dunn, *Baptism in the Holy Spirit,* p. 101.

[43]Frederick Dale Bruner, *A Theology of the Holy Spirit* (Grand Rapids: Eerdmans, 1970), p. 168.

[44]Ibid., p. 170.

[45]Augustine *De bapt.* 4.22, 29. Quoted in Burkhard Neunheuser, *Baptism and Confirmation*, trans. John Jay Hughes (New York: Herder & Herder, 1964), p. 122.

[46]Neunheuser, *Baptism and Confirmation*, p. 127.

[47]Ibid., pp. 126-27.

[48]For Luther what saves is not the water of baptism but its action and use when joined with the Word of God.

[49]*Luther's Works,* 29:82.

[50]Quoted in Neunheuser, *Baptism and Confirmation*, p. 147. See Basil *De Spiritu Sanctu* 12.28.

[51]The Reformers steadfastly held that there is no sacrament without faith (*nullum sacramentum sine fide*), though they interpreted this in various ways. See *Luther's Works,* 29:172.

[52]See Paul Tillich, *A History of Christian Thought*, ed. Carl. E. Braaten (New York: Harper & Row, 1968), pp. 34-36.

[53]This note is captured by the seventeenth-century Anglican theologian Jeremy Taylor: "The holy Spirit which descends upon the waters of baptism does not instantly produce its effects in the soul of the baptized; and when He does, it is irregularly, and as He pleases." In Taylor's view "the church may administer rightly, even before God gives the real grace of the sacrament." *Whole Works*, ed. Reginald Heber (new edition, London: Longmans, Green, 1864), 2:253-54.

[54]I cannot subscribe to the radical monergism of R. C. Sproul, who sees regeneration clearly before the advent of faith or even the beginnings of seeking for

faith. In the biblical personalist view that I uphold regeneration is always correlative with either faith or seeking. Regeneration does not first occur and then seeking, but regeneration is realized through seeking and then finally through faith. God, to be sure, takes the initiative and in this sense grace always comes first. But grace finds its completion and goal in human response, though this response is itself contingent on grace. We are not fully or truly regenerate apart from the experience and decision of faith. See R. C. Sproul, *The Mystery of the Holy Spirit* (Wheaton, Ill.: Tyndale House, 1990), pp. 103-11.

[55]Even at infant baptism I affirm a beginning on the road to salvation. The Spirit is operative even then, but Spirit baptism does not occur until the dawning of faith.

[56]Among Finnish Lutherans there is presently an attempt to show that "deification" is not foreign to Luther's theology and indeed is integral to it. See Carl E. Braaten and Robert W. Jenson, eds., *Union with Christ: The New Finnish Interpretation of Luther* (Grand Rapids: Eerdmans, 1998). For my earlier discussion of deification see Bloesch, *God the Almighty* (Downers Grove, Ill.: InterVarsity Press, 1995), pp. 234-36; and *Jesus Christ: Savior & Lord* (Downers Grove, Ill.: InterVarsity Press, 1997), pp. 176, 284.

[57]Paul is here speaking metaphorically referring to both the fading splendor of the old legal order and the emergence of the new order in which the Spirit's work is permanent. See Floyd V. Filson, "2 Corinthians," *Interpreter's Bible* (1953), 10:308-9.

[58]Some Orthodox theologians (e.g., Theodore Stylianopoulos) hold that in the strict sense deification is best applied to the parousia when we see God face to face.

[59]See Antonio Royo and Jordan Aumann, *The Theology of Christian Perfection* (Dubuque, Iowa: Priory Press, 1962), pp. 615-75.

[60]Cited in Kevin and Dorothy Ranaghan, *Catholic Pentecostals* (New York: Paulist, 1969), p. 199.

[61]David du Plessis, *The Spirit Bade Me Go* (Plainfield, N.J.: Logos International, 1970), pp. 81-91, 103-6.

[62]Forsyth also says: "We cannot truly pray even for ourselves without passing beyond ourselves and our individual experience." P. T. Forsyth, *The Soul of Prayer* (1916; reprint, Grand Rapids: Eerdmans, n.d.), pp. 11, 36.

[63]James D. G. Dunn, *Jesus and the Spirit* (Philadelphia: Westminster Press, 1975), pp. 84ff.

[64]Ibid., p. 255.

[65]Simon Tugwell, *Did You Receive the Spirit?* (New York: Paulist, 1972), p. 104.

[66]D. S. Cairns, *The Faith That Rebels: A Re-Examination of the Miracles of Jesus* (New York: Richard R. Smith, 1930), p. 76.

[67]Ibid., p. 78.

[68]See Frank Hudson Hallock, *The Gifts of the Holy Ghost* (London: SPCK, 1936), pp. 91-102.

[69]Harold R. Fray Jr., *Conflict and Change in the Church* (Boston: Pilgrim, 1969), p. 5.

[70]Hans Küng, *The Church,* trans. Ray and Rosaleen Ockenden (New York: Sheed & Ward, 1967), p. 182.

[71]Ibid., p. 187.

[72]With Calvin I hold that the enduring basis of our assurance lies in the mercy of God revealed in Jesus Christ and apprehended by faith, but this assurance needs to be renewed and confirmed in daily obedience under the cross. Faith itself brings assurance of salvation, but works of love deepen this assurance. See Randall C. Zachman, *The Assurance of Faith: Conscience in the Theology of Martin Luther and John Calvin* (Minneapolis: Fortress, 1993), pp. 11, 188-223.

[73]Jonathan Edwards, *Religious Affections* (Grand Rapids: Sovereign Grace, 1971), p. 67.

[74]*The Confessions of St. Augustine*, ed. and trans. John K. Ryan (New York: Doubleday Image, 1960), 10.35 (p. 265).

[75]See Fyodor Dostoyevsky, *The Brothers Karamazov*, trans. Constance Garnett (1957; reprint, New York: New American Library, 1980), pp. 227-43.

[76]Cited in James S. Torrens, "Admiring Cardinal Suenens," *America* 174, no. 20 (June 22-29, 1996): 4.

[77]Many Pentecostals disclaim the term *second blessing* because they associate it with entire sanctification, but they nonetheless adhere to the baptism of the Spirit as a blessing subsequent to conversion.

[78]We also read that after his resurrection Jesus upbraided his disciples for "their unbelief and hardness of heart, because they had not believed those who saw him after he had risen" (Mk 16:14).

[79]See my discussion of this biblical text on pp. 307-9.

[80]Luther, Erlangen edition, 11:347. Quoted in Wilhelm Herrmann, *The Communion of the Christian with God*, ed. Robert T. Voelkel, trans. J. Sandys Stanyon and R. W. Stewart (Philadelphia: Fortress, 1971), p. 192.

[81]*The Works of John Wesley,* 3rd ed. (reprint, Grand Rapids: Baker, 1986), 8:49.

[82]Calvin, "Reply to Sadolet," in *Calvin: Theological Treatises*, trans. and ed. J. K. S. Reid (Philadelphia: Westminster Press, 1954), p. 236.

[83]Karl Adam, *Christ Our Brother* (London: Sheed & Ward, 1931), p. 165.

[84]Cited in Bruner, *Theology of the Holy Spirit*, p. 97.

[85]Charles Hodge, *A Commentary on the First Epistle to the Corinthians* (London: Banner of Truth, 1964), p. 254.

[86]Evelyn Underhill, *The Mystics of the Church* (1926; reprint, New York: Shocken, 1964), p. 163.

[87]See D. Elton Trueblood, *The People Called Quakers* (New York: Harper & Row, 1966), p. 178.

[88]See Thérèse of Lisieux, *Autobiography of Saint Thérèse of Lisieux: The Story of a Soul,* trans. John Beevers (New York: Doubleday, 1989), chap. 4, p. 54.

[89]Barth, *Church Dogmatics,* ed. G. W. Bromiley and T. F. Torrance, trans. G. W. Bromiley (Edinburgh: T. & T. Clark, 1969), 4(4):39.

[90]Jonathan Edwards, *Religious Affections* (Grand Rapids: Sovereign Grace, 1971), p. 142.

[91]Samuel Rutherford, *Selected Letters of Samuel Rutherford* (London: SCM Press,

1957), p. 89.

[92]Herrmann, *Communion of the Christian with God*, p. 351.

[93]For my previous discussion see pp. 279-81.

[94]See Leon Morris, *Commentary on the Gospel of John,* New International Commentary on the New Testament (Grand Rapids: Eerdmans, 1971), p. 217.

[95]*Luther's Works*, ed. and trans. Jaroslav Pelikan (St. Louis: Concordia, 1957), 22:283.

[96]R. V. G. Tasker, *The Gospel According to St. John,* Tyndale New Testament Commentary (1960; reprint, Grand Rapids: Eerdmans, 1992), p. 71.

[97]F. F. Bruce, *The Gospel of John* (Grand Rapids: Eerdmans, 1983), pp. 84-85.

[98]Rudolf Bultmann, *The Gospel of John*, ed. R. W. N. Hoare and J. K. Riches, trans. G. R. Beasley-Murray (Philadelphia: Westminster Press, 1971), pp. 138-39.

[99]Raymond E. Brown, *The Gospel According to John,* Anchor Bible (New York: Doubleday, 1966), 1:144.

[100]Ben Witherington III, *John's Wisdom: A Commentary on the Fourth Gospel* (Louisville: Westminster John Knox, 1995), p. 97.

[101]Ibid.

[102]See esp. Brown's discussion in *Gospel According to John*, 1:144-46.

[103]Ibid., 2:1038.

[104]Pierre Benoit, *Jesus and the Gospel*, trans. Benet Weatherhead (New York: Herder & Herder, 1973), 1:250.

[105]Brown, *Gospel According to John*, 2:1039.

[106]Norval Geldenhuys, *Commentary on the Gospel of Luke,* New International Commentary on the New Testament (1951; reprint, Grand Rapids: Eerdmans, 1966), pp. 643-44.

[107]R. A. Torrey, *The Holy Spirit* (Old Tappan, N.J.: Revell, 1927), pp. 112-15.

[108]Brown, *Gospel According to John*, 2:677.

[109]Frederick Dale Bruner makes this astute observation: "The text [Acts 5:32] does *not* say either that the Holy Spirit *will* be given to those who shall obey him, or that the Holy Spirit *was* given to those who previously obeyed him, but . . . that the Holy Spirit was given in the past to those who are *now* obeying him. The text reads literally: 'and so is the Holy Spirit whom God gave to those who are obeying him.' One meaning of the text is at least this: obedience is the present *result* of the *prior* gift of the Spirit." *A Theology of the Holy Spirit* (Grand Rapids: Eerdmans, 1970), p. 172.

[110]Ibid., p. 168.

[111]While I affirm that the baptism of the Holy Spirit generally happens just once in a believer's life, since I regard it as the rite of initiation into the Christian community, it is possible on the premises of my theology to hold that those who fall away from the faith after having once espoused it need a new infusion of grace to reestablish them in the body of Christ. And this new infusion may legitimately also be called a baptism of the Spirit.

[112]G. W. H. Lampe, *The Seal of the Spirit* (1951; reprint, London: Longmans, Green, 1956), p. 70.

[113]Michael Green, *I Believe in the Holy Spirit* (Grand Rapids: Eerdmans, 1975), pp. 136-39.

[114]Richard J. Dillon, "Acts of the Apostles," in *New Jerome Biblical Commentary*, ed. Raymond E. Brown, Joseph A. Fitzmyer and Roland E. Murphy (Englewood Cliffs, N.J.: Prentice Hall, 1990), p. 743.

[115]John Calvin, *Commentary upon the Acts of the Apostles,* trans. Henry Beveridge (Edinburgh: Calvin Translation Society, 1844), 1:329-48.

[116]James D. G. Dunn, *Baptism in the Holy Spirit,* Studies in Biblical Theology 2/15 (London: SCM Press, 1970), pp. 55-72; George T. Montague, *The Holy Spirit: Growth of a Biblical Tradition* (New York: Paulist, 1976), pp. 293-95.

[117]Dunn, *Baptism in the Holy Spirit*, p. 66.

[118]Montague, *Holy Spirit*, p. 294.

[119]Dillon, "Acts," p. 743.

[120]J. H. E. Hull, *The Holy Spirit in the Acts of the Apostles* (London: Lutterworth, 1967), pp. 90-91.

[121]Biblical and historical scholars are divided on whether laying on of hands signified an element within baptism or a rite separate from baptism. See Lampe's discussion in *Seal of the Spirit*, pp. 46-94, 223-31.

[122]I concur on this question with Bruner and Dunn, among many others. For another position on the Ephesians in Acts 19 see Johannes Munck, *The Acts of the Apostles,* rev. William F. Albright and C. S. Mann (Garden City, N.Y.: Doubleday, 1967), pp. 187-88. Munck contends that the word *disciples* in Acts 19:1 indicates Christians rather than followers of John the Baptist, but Christians who did not have a solid grasp of Christian doctrine.

[123]See Dunn, *Baptism in the Holy Spirit*, pp. 96-97. Dunn cites Luke 3:3, Acts 2:38 and Acts 22:16 as furnishing support for the indispensable role of repentance and faith in regeneration.

[124]James Montgomery Boice, "Galatians," in *The Expositor's Bible Commentary*, ed. Frank E. Gaebelein (Grand Rapids: Zondervan, 1976), p. 473. I would add that Christians may pray for a deeper manifestation of the Spirit in their lives.

[125]Dunn, *Baptism in the Holy Spirit*, p. 113.

[126]Herman N. Ridderbos, *The Epistle of Paul to the Churches of Galatia,* New International Commentary on the New Testament (1953; reprint, Grand Rapids: Eerdmans, 1968), pp. 157-58.

[127]Ibid., pp. 189, 191.

[128]Raymond Stamm gives this interpretation of Galatians 5:5ff.: "He [the Spirit] creates faith, hope, and love, and gives patience and strength to wait for the perfect righteousness which will come with the redemption of the body." At the same time, the Spirit comes " 'out of' the realm of faith . . . 'into' the hearts of believers in Christ in response to their faith." For Paul "the initiative of God's grace creates the faith by which man responds to this love. . . . In union with Christ as a member of his body the church, man's faith is activated by God's love to invest in the lives of others and reproduce itself in them." Raymond T. Stamm, "The Epistle to the Galatians," *Interpreter's Bible*, ed. G. A. Buttrick (Nashville: Abingdon-Cokesbury, 1953), 10:549-50.

[129]T. W. Manson and W. Nauck argue that "the three terms, spirit, water, and blood, refer to a single rite of initiation, preserved in the Syriac church, that began with anointing and continued with baptism and eucharist." Kenneth Grayston, *The Johannine Epistles*, New Century Bible Commentary (Grand Rapids: Eerdmans, 1984), p. 139.

[130]Amos Wilder, "1 John," in *Interpreter's Bible* (1957), 12:292-93.

[131]Georg Strecker, *The Johannine Letters*, trans. Linda M. Maloney, ed. Harold Attridge (Minneapolis: Fortress, 1996), p. 185.

[132]Ibid.

[133]Dunn, *Baptism in the Holy Spirit*, p. 204.

[134]Paul W. Hoon, "1 John," *Interpreter's Bible*, 12:296.

Chapter Eleven

[1]I am here indebted to Friedrich Heiler's *Prayer*, ed. and trans. Samuel McComb (New York: Oxford University Press, 1958).

[2]See H. Richard Niebuhr, *The Kingdom of God in America* (New York: Harper & Bros., 1935), pp. 45-87.

[3]"This is the highway followed by pilgrims on their way to Zion" (Is 35:10), in S. H. Widyapranawa, *The Lord Is Savior: Faith in National Crisis—A Commentary on the Book of Isaiah 1—39*, International Theological Commentary (Grand Rapids: Eerdmans, 1990), p. 223.

[4]In Isaiah and Jeremiah the highway to holiness is depicted as the road through the wilderness by which the exiles return to Zion (cf. Is 11:16; 35:8-10; 40:3-4; 57:14; 62:10; Jer 31:21). In New Testament spirituality this comes to symbolize the pathway to the heavenly Zion that is traveled by faith (cf. Mt 3:3; Lk 3:4-6; Mk 1:2-3). Note that in the New Testament *Zion* becomes a symbolic term with apocalyptic implications (cf. Heb 12:22; 1 Pet 2:6; Rev 14:1). See Madeleine S. Miller and J. Lane Miller, *Harper's Bible Dictionary*, 7th ed. (New York: Harper & Row, 1961), pp. 841-42.

[5]Ps 24:7-10 depicts the triumphal entry of a conquering king who comes to take his kingdom. He bids the gates not simply to open but to lift up their heads, "for they must extend beyond the skies to admit the one whom 'heaven itself cannot contain.' " J. W. Rogerson and J. W. McKay, *Psalms 1-50*, Cambridge Commentary on the NEB (Cambridge: Cambridge University Press, 1977), pp. 107-11. Cf. A. F. Kirkpatrick, *The Book of Psalms*, Cambridge Bible for Schools and Colleges (Cambridge: Cambridge University Press, 1957), pp. 127-31. See Michael Horton's penetrating exposition of Psalm 24, *In the Face of God* (Dallas: Word, 1996), pp. 87-100.

[6]Max Weber referred to a "worldly asceticism" as an apt description of Reformation spirituality. See Max Weber, *The Protestant Ethic and the Spirit of Capitalism*, trans. Talcott Parsons (New York: Charles Scribner's Sons, 1958), pp. 95-183.

[7]I do not wish to make the lines of demarcation between biblical faith and mysticism too stringent, for the great majority of Christian mystics also drew on Scripture, and many of them sounded the call to service and mission in

the world. Yet for the most part their spirituality was oriented much more about eros (the drive for self-realization) than agape (the sacrifice of self for the welfare of others). Even a more evangelical mystic like Bernard of Clairvaux, who was appreciated by the Reformers, depicted the highest kind of love as the love of self for the sake of God. (See his *Love of God*, ed. James M. Houston [Portland: Multnomah Press, 1983], pp. 158-61.) Here we see a synthesis of self-love and love of God and neighbor, a synthesis that is foreign to evangelical and Reformation spirituality, though this compromise reappeared in Pietism and in Protestant liberalism. The biblical-classical synthesis is also apparent in Augustine, who regarded the highest kind of love as the love of God for God's sake, but this was nevertheless seen as meeting the need for the self's aspiration to spiritual fulfillment.

[8]In classical Christian mysticism the emphasis is on the struggle between the higher self and the lower self rather than on the battle for Christ's kingdom and his righteousness. In Puritanism as opposed to the mystical tradition the battle is waged in the assurance that the victory is already ours and that God's grace is invincible. For the tensions between the mystical tradition, particularly as exemplified in John Cassian, and the New Testament understanding see Owen Chadwick, *John Cassian* (Cambridge: Cambridge University Press, 1950), pp. 77-108. Also see Chadwick's introduction in *John Cassian: Conferences*, trans. Colm Luibheid (New York: Paulist, 1985), pp. 25-27.

[9]See Donald G. Bloesch, *The Struggle of Prayer* (1980; reprint, Colorado Springs: Helmers & Howard, 1988), pp. 131-70.

[10]I have acknowledged that there is a dimension of the Spirit's activity in the life of the Christian that can be denominated as "deification," but this metaphor most properly applies to our transfiguration beyond death when we see God face to face. See my previous discussion on pp. 288-89.

[11]Barth aptly says: "Justification is not sanctification and does not merge into it. Sanctification is not justification and does not merge into it. Thus, although the two belong indissolubly together, the one cannot be explained by the other." *Church Dogmatics,* ed. G. W. Bromiley and T. F. Torrance, trans. G. W. Bromiley (Edinburgh: T. & T. Clark, 1958), 4(2):503. Yet I must caution that the lines between the two must not be made too stringent. Justification can encompass sanctification, and sanctification can serve justification.

[12]John Calvin, *Institutes of the Christian Religion*, ed. John T. McNeill, trans. Ford Lewis Battles (Philadelphia: Westminster Press, 1960), 3.16.1 (1:503).

[13]Michael Horton conveniently overlooks the qualifications that Wesley assigns to Christian perfection. See Horton, *In the Face of God*, pp. 161-63.

[14]See Outler's helpful discussion in Albert C. Outler, ed., *John Wesley* (New York: Oxford University Press, 1964), pp. 30-33.

[15]Widyapranawa, *Lord Is Savior,* p. 224.

[16]J. C. Pollock, *Hudson Taylor and Maria: Pioneers in China* (Eastbourne: Kingsway, 1962), p. 205. These words, taken from a letter from John McCarthy, greatly helped Taylor.

[17]Luther, *Ninety-five Theses*, no. 1.

[18]John Calvin, *Sermons on the Epistle to the Ephesians,* trans. William Pringle (Edinburgh: Banner of Truth, 1973), p. 168.

[19]The babe in Christ has this power by virtue of being indwelt by the Holy Spirit but has yet to discover it in the practice of the faith in daily life.

[20]*Luther's Works*, Erlangen ed., 10:11. See Wilhelm Herrmann, *The Communion of the Christian with God*, ed. Robert T. Voelkel (Philadelphia: Fortress, 1971), p. 203.

[21]Calvin, *Sermons on Ephesians*, p. 156.

[22]Reinhold Niebuhr, *An Interpretation of Christian Ethics* (New York: Harper & Bros., 1935), p. 52.

[23]Cited in Hendrikus Berkhof, *Two Hundred Years of Theology*, trans. John Vriend (Grand Rapids: Eerdmans, 1989), p. 149. For the not inconsiderable impact of Herrmann's theology on Barth see Bruce L. McCormack, *Karl Barth's Critically Realistic Dialectical Theology: Its Genesis and Development 1909-1936* (Oxford: Clarendon, 1995), pp. 49-77, 91, 93, 98.

[24]Ragnar Bring, *How God Speaks to Us* (Philadelphia: Muhlenberg, 1962), p. 111.

[25]T. L. Osborn, *Healing the Sick* (1951; reprint, Tulsa, Okla.: Harrison House, 1992), p. 106.

[26]*Luther's Works*, ed. and trans. Jaroslav Pelikan (St. Louis: Concordia, 1964), 27:227.

[27]Alexander Schmemann, *For the Life of the World* (New York: National Student Christian Federation, 1963), p. 57. Schmemann is here criticizing the kind of decisionism characteristic of later Protestant revivalism, which results, in his opinion, in a premature assurance of salvation. We need to take his critique seriously, since it is obvious that many decisions for Christ that take place in the context of mass revival meetings do not penetrate the human heart and result only in superficial change. Yet he overlooks the fact that in not a few of these meetings the work of the Holy Spirit is in evidence, resulting not only in genuine conversion but also in a budding passion for social righteousness and a lively hope in the coming again of Jesus Christ in power and glory bringing in the new heaven and the new earth.

Schmemann quotes Georges Bernanos on the sadness of not being a saint, and Protestants in the Reformation tradition need to recognize the biblical thrust of this observation. When evangelical Christians use the word *saints* they generally apply this to the whole Christian community, and indeed this is in accord with the New Testament. Yet evangelical tradition has nevertheless made a place for holy persons, those in whom the holiness of Christ is transparent to others. This note is especially prominent in evangelical Pietism and Puritanism.

[28]For the conflict between John Wesley and the mystical writer William Law on the relation of justification and sanctification, faith and works see Robert G. Tuttle Jr., *Mysticism in the Wesleyan Tradition* (Grand Rapids: Zondervan, 1989), esp. pp. 114-19.

[29]*United Methodist Hymnal* (1989; reprint, Nashville: United Methodist Publishing

House, 1992), no. 169.

[30]See Edward Hindson, ed., *Introduction to Puritan Theology* (Grand Rapids: Baker, 1976), p. 188.

[31]See pp. 96-97, 128-29, 362, 388-89 in this book.

[32]Michael Horton, *In the Face of God* (Dallas: Word, 1996).

[33]Ibid., p. 161.

[34]Ibid.

[35]Ibid., p. 228.

[36]Ibid., p. 185.

[37]Ibid., p. 100.

[38]He might also have difficulty with some of the German chorales, especially those associated with the Pietist awakening such as "One Thing Needful" (*Eins Ist Not*); J. Franck's "Jesus Priceless Treasure" (*Jesu Meine Freude*); and Gerhard Tersteegen's "God Himself Is with Us" (*Wunderbarer König*), which speaks of the temple of God as being within the self.

[39]Horton, *In the Face of God*, p. 112.

[40]Ibid.

[41]John Calvin, *Commentary on Philippians,* trans. John Pringle (Edinburgh: Calvin Translation Society, 1851), p. 98 on 3:10.

[42]Barbara Owen, ed., *Daily Readings from Luther's Writings* (Minneapolis: Augsburg, 1993), p. 252.

[43]Ibid., p. 250.

[44]See *Luther's Works*, ed. and trans. Conrad Bergendoff (Philadelphia: Fortress, 1958), 40:269-320. The controversy with the antinomians erupted in 1525-1527, 1537-1538 and 1540-1545. From Professor Ralph Quere, Wartburg Seminary, Dubuque, Feb. 11, 1998.

[45]Michael S. Horton, "The *Sola's* of the Reformation," in *Here We Stand! A Call from Confessing Evangelicals,* ed. James Montgomery Boice and Benjamin E. Sasse (Grand Rapids: Baker, 1996), p. 111.

[46]Horton, *In the Face of God*, p. 161.

[47]For the sharp divergence between William Law and the mature Wesley see Robert G. Tuttle Jr., *Mysticism in the Wesleyan Tradition* (Grand Rapids: Zondervan, 1989); and Harald Lindström, *Wesley and Sanctification* (Wilmore, Ky.: Francis Asbury Publishing, 1980), pp. 56-75, 161-84.

[48]Horton, *In the Face of God*, p. 30.

[49]Boice and Sasse, eds., *Here We Stand*, p. 16.

[50]Horton, *In the Face of God*, pp. 133-36.

[51]Interestingly this insight is shared by the Roman Catholic nun Thérèse of Lisieux, who was recently made a doctor of the church. See *The Autobiography of Saint Thérèse of Lisieux: The Story of a Soul*, trans. John Beevers (New York: Doubleday, 1989), p. 114.

[52]Horton, *In the Face of God*, p. 94.

Name Index

Adam, Karl, 390
Adams, James Luther, 210, 354
Aguirre, Danny, 368
Albright, William F., 392
Alexander, Archibald, 348
Ambrosiaster, 62
Ames, William, 360
Ammonas of Egypt, 55, 59
Anselm, 43
Anthony of Padua, 95
Aquinas, Thomas, 40, 41, 42, 43, 44, 60, 83, 84-85, 347
Aristotle, 36, 40, 346
Arnauld, Antoine, 123
Arndt, Johann, 119, 120, 361
Arnold, Eberhard, 1, 21, 64
Arnold, Emmy, 362
Arnold, J. Heinrich, 108, 359
Arrington, F. L., 370
Asbury, Francis, 125
Augustine, 42, 51, 54, 56, 59, 82, 89, 92, 144, 150, 230, 242, 273, 283, 296, 354, 355, 366
Aulén, Gustav, 32
Aumann, Jordan, 389
Bach, Marcus, 367
Bacon, Ernest W., 360
Barclay, Robert, 148
Barratt, T. B., 186, 190, 201
Barth, Karl, 23, 24, 32, 41, 51, 52, 75, 124, 203, 211, 220, 223, 226-30, 239, 255, 262, 267, 269, 272, 277, 278, 301, 339, 344, 348, 349, 352, 361, 375, 377, 380, 387, 394
Barth, Markus, 53, 63, 267, 388
Basham, Don, 207, 376, 378
Basil of Caesarea, 81, 283, 354
Basilides, 86

Bavinck, Herman, 38
Baxter, J. Sidlow, 140, 199, 365, 375
Baxter, Richard, 115, 149
Bayly, Lewis, 115, 360
Beasley-Murray, G. R., 72, 267, 353, 391
Bednarowski, Mary Farrell, 368-69
Benedict of Nursia, 90
Benezet, Anthony, 148
Bengel, Johann Albrecht, 305
Bennett, Dennis, 186, 372
Benoit, Pierre, 305, 391
Bergson, Henri, 167, 236
Berkhof, Hendrikus, 76, 256, 257, 349, 354, 384, 395
Bernanos, Georges, 395
Bernard of Clairvaux, 84, 92, 93, 94, 355, 356, 394
Beza, Theodore, 102
Bittlinger, Arnold, 190
Black, James, 366, 370
Blaikie, Robert, 347
Blaising, Craig A., 371
Blake, William, 151
Bloch-Hoell, Nils, 375
Blumhardt, Christoph, 123, 362
Blumhardt, Johann Christoph, 123
Boehme, Jakob, 92, 122, 154, 230
Boice, James M., 344, 392, 396
Bonaventure, 92
Bonhoeffer, Dietrich, 247, 374
Bonnke, Reinhard, 186
Boogaart, Thomas A., 214, 378
Booth, Catherine, 133
Booth, William, 133, 331, 364
Bouyer, Louis, 361
Braaten, Carl E., 389
Braden, Charles, 369
Branham, William, 186, 202, 372
Bratt, James D., 363

Subject Index

Albigenses. *See* Cathari.
Anabaptists, 103-5, 110, 111, 180, 359
angels, 211, 215, 221
Anglicanism, 106, 116, 175, 375, 388
Anglo-Catholicism, 307
animism, 65, 66, 67, 192, 209, 211,
  212, 213, 221, 293, 352, 376
apologetics, 46, 348
apostasy, 145
Arianism, 163, 366
Arminianism, 125, 339
asceticism, 358, 393
Assemblies of God, 184, 185
baptism
  of blood, 77, 80, 103-4, 226-27, 282,
    306, 315, 316, 317, 322
  of the Holy Spirit, 14, 16, 52, 58, 70,
    76, 81, 84, 97, 99, 105, 113, 125,
    127, 128, 133, 134, 135, 137, 190,
    191, 223, 227, 228, 264, 281, 282,
    288, 299, 300, 309, 352, 363, 391
  of tears, 92, 94, 300
  water, 14, 52 58, 70, 75, 76, 81, 84,
    97, 99-105, 120, 125, 163, 182, 223,
    241, 252, 258, 276, 280, 282, 298,
    302, 304, 313, 329, 335, 358, 392
Basel Mission, 123
Bethany Fellowship, 139
biblical personalism, 46, 283, 289
Bogomils, 89
Calvinism, 17, 31, 33, 125, 328, 339,
  340, 364
Cambridge Declaration, 340, 344
Camps Farthest Out, 168, 364
Cathari, 90
Catholic Apostolic Church, 157-58,
  368
charismatic movement, 50, 54, 56, 60,
  161, 186-87, 199, 202, 243, 373, 375
Children of God, 175
Christian and Missionary Alliance,
  133, 137, 138, 182
Christian Catholic Church, 158-59
Christian Science, 188
Church of God (Anderson, IN), 136
Church of God (Cleveland, TN), 185
Church of God in Christ, 185
Church of God of Prophecy, 185
Church of the Nazarene, 133, 182
Churches of Christ, 159
clericalism, 235
confirmation, 54, 82, 83, 105-6, 241,
  242, 245, 252, 311
conversion, 50, 80, 97, 120, 130, 134,
  142, 198, 204, 226, 300, 301, 311,
  312, 322, 329, 356, 364
cults, 146, 173, 174, 176
decisionism, 328
deification, 57, 240, 249, 253, 288,
  289, 327, 394
demonic powers, 192, 209-21, 234,
  310, 321, 372, 377-79
Disciplined Order of Christ, 168, 364
dispensationalism, 169-73, 370
dualism, 87, 91, 248
Dukhobors, 152, 367
ecumenism, 18, 243, 251, 284, 364,
  372
election, 26, 100, 112, 129, 300, 329
Enlightenment, 27, 46, 114, 209
eschatology, 74-76, 233, 238, 284,
  319, 334
evangelism, 130, 204, 295, 349
evolution, 238, 259
existentialism, 59, 236, 264
feminist theology, 60-62, 69, 351
foundationalism, 27, 28
Friends of God, 91